The BASICS *of* AMERICAN GOVERNMENT

Fifth Edition

Carl D. Cavalli

Editor

Contributors

Ross C. Alexander

Jaimie Edwards-Kelly

Craig B. Greathouse

Brian M. Murphy

Glen Smith

Carl D. Cavalli

Joseph Gershtenson

Jonathan S. Miner

K. Michael Reese

Charles H. "Trey" Wilson III

Student Contributor: Hayden Lathren

UNG
UNIVERSITY *of* NORTH GEORGIA™
UNIVERSITY PRESS
Blue Ridge | Cumming | Dahlonega | Gainesville | Oconee

Published by:
University of North Georgia Press
Dahlonega, Georgia

Book design by Corey Parson.
Cover design by Natalie Montpas and Corey Parson.

ISBN: 978-1-959203-11-7

For more information, please visit: http://ung.edu/university-press
or e-mail: ungpress@ung.edu

If you need this textbook in another format, please contact corey.parson@ung.edu.

Table of Contents

Online Companion

Additional learning materials are available online thanks to the dedicated staff at eCore. To access the Online Companion for *The Basics of American Government*, please visit:

go.ung.edu/bag

Digital Version

You can access a digital version (PDF) of the textbook at the site of the University of North Georgia Press.:

https://ung.edu/university-press/books/the-basics-of-american-government-fifth-edition.php

This digital version is courtesy of Affordable Learning Georgia.

The Basics of American Government on Social Media

Stay up to date on info regarding our textbook, our authors, and the latest issues in American politics!

Facebook: https://www.facebook.com/basicsofamericangovernment/

Instagram: https://www.instagram.com/americangovernment_basics/

Preface to the Fifth Edition

Change is in the air! In the four years since the publication of our previous edition we have seen partisan shifts in both houses of Congress; a new Supreme Court justice along with significant Court decisions involving abortion rights, affirmative action, and presidential immunity; ongoing controversies involving the 2020 presidential election, voting rights, religion, gender, and other social issues. We also saw the fall and rise of Donald Trump, who, on January 20th, 2025 became only the second person to take the oath of office as president for a second non-consecutive term. We touch on many of these issues and put them in political context throughout our textbook.

This edition is the most significant update since our original publication back in 2011. We say farewell to two of our founding contributors, Marie Goodall[1] and Barry Friedman. We also say farewell to our student contributor, Mary Catherine Beutel, as well as our special guest contributor for the previous edition, former Georgia governor Nathan Deal.

We welcome new contributors Jaimie Edwards-Kelly, Joseph Gershtenson, and Glen Smith, along with a new student contributor, Hayden Lathren. Hayden is not wholly new to our textbook. She was credited as a researcher for the presidency case study in the previous edition. In this update, her contributions to an updated presidency case study now rise to the level of co-author. Drs Edwards-Kelly, Gershtenson, and Smith provide us with completely rewritten chapters on bureaucracy, public policy, and political socialization and the media, respectively. Other chapters by our veteran contributors have been thoroughly updated as well. It is also worth noting that our team has grown in prestige. We now boast a department head (Craig B. Greathouse) and a university president (Ross C. Alexander)!

As with previous versions, this edition examines the rise of new political figures and the exit of others, the shifts in policy and political focus at both the

---

1   As a contributor to this textbook, she was known as Maria J. Albo.

state and federal levels, changes in the public, increasing partisan polarization, and shifting views of government in everyday life.

Of course, we also continue to correct and clarify our content. While we bring you many changes and updates, we have not lost sight of our original mission to provide direct, no-frills information on the basics of American government.

Carl D. Cavalli, editor
December 2024

Preface to the First Edition

This book is a collaborative effort among seven current and three former[2] University of North Georgia faculty members in the Political Science and Criminal Justice departments, all of whom have extensive experience teaching and conducting academic research in the field of American politics. All of these professors were concerned with both the rising cost and lack of academic rigor among American government texts on the market. So, they decided to write their own.

The purpose of this book is twofold. First, it provides a thorough, no-frills overview and analysis of the American political system. Second, most chapters include a work of original academic scholarship that demonstrates or highlights the chapter content. In addition, all chapters provide questions for discussion and several feature a "civic engagement exercise" designed to spur students to become more involved in the political system. Ultimately, this book combines the best aspects of both a traditional textbook and a reader, presented in a concise, low-cost format. The reader will see that the "basics" of the American political system are all addressed. However, in addition, this text devotes entire chapters to topics not found in most texts on the market, i.e. state and local government and civic engagement. Unlike other textbooks, but consistent with political science research, this book is presented utilizing the APA format, with in-text citations. A secondary goal of the authors is to familiarize the reader with scholarship in the field, making it easier to locate the sources used to craft the chapters.

The authors hope you enjoy the book and are inspired to learn more about the American political system.

Ross C. Alexander and Carl D. Cavalli, editors
June 2011

---

2   Updated as of 2024.

Acknowledgments

We would like to thank all the peer reviewers who diligently reviewed each chapter in both initial and later editions of this textbook. We are also grateful for the feedback from our discussion panel at the 2010 Georgia Political Science Association annual meeting. Lastly, we are grateful to the people at the University of North Georgia Press including the director, Bonnie Robinson, and editors, both past and present—Corey Parson, Ariana Adams, Elizabeth Odom, Jillian Murphy, Amy Beard, April Loebick, and Matt Pardue—for taking a chance on an unusual idea, turning it into a reality, and maintaining that reality for the past decade. The corrections, edits, and suggestions of all the aforementioned made *The Basics of American Government* a better finished product. We would also like to thank Affordable Learning Georgia (https://www.affordablelearninggeorgia.org/) for making a digital version of this textbook freely available to students.

Thanks also to Maria Albo's summer 2011 American government class for their feedback on a draft copy of the original edition, along with the numerous critiques and suggestions we have received from students and faculty over the years. Any remaining errors are, of course, our own.

Ross C. Alexander and Carl D. Cavalli
June 2011 (updated December 2024)

Theories of Democracy and Types of Government

Ross C. Alexander

Learning Objectives

After covering the topic of theories of democracy, students should understand:

1. How democracy has evolved in the historical and contemporary sense.
2. How democracy in America functions, comparing and contrasting it with other systems around the world.
3. How foundational pieces in political philosophy influenced the establishment of our republic, most notably the contributions of John Locke.

Abstract

What is democracy? How does it differ from other political structures and systems that existed over the past two millennia? In this chapter, we address these foundational questions, in addition to others, to provide a solid framework for the remainder of the book. By examining those thinkers, philosophers, and scholars who have had an impact on the American political system, we can define democracy in the American sense and contrast it with other systems today and throughout time. To accomplish this end, this chapter offers an in-depth examination of Locke's Second Treatise of Government to determine its effect on the American brand of democracy.

Introduction—Toward a Definition of Democracy

Most texts addressing the American political system invariably begin with an attempt to define democracy, which is vaguely understood as "rule by the people." But what, exactly, does that mean? How does democracy differ from other systems of government? Philosophers, thinkers, politicians, and students have been trying to address and answer these questions for hundreds, if not thousands, of years with little consensus. Over 2,500 years ago, Aristotle, the godfather of western political thought, in *The Politics*, offered a discourse on different systems of government, and outlined six possible forms—three positive or "good" and three negative or "bad"—each linked with another. For example, with regard to rule by one individual, **kingship** was the positive form, **tyranny,** the negative. Regarding rule by few in society, **aristocracy** was desirable, while **oligarchy** was undesirable. Finally, concerning rule by many in society, **polity** was the positive outcome, and **democracy** the negative. To fully understand Aristotle's distinctions, his terminology must be defined. His view of kingship was one of an enlightened, benevolent monarch ruling in the best interests of the people. Conversely, if kingship would erode into tyranny, the tyrant would function as a self-interested despot who would do anything to stay in power. For Aristotle, aristocracy was not rule by the rich, but rather rule by the most capable in society, whether it be the most educated, most experienced, or most enlightened. Conversely, as aristocracy devolved into oligarchy, power would fall into the hands of the power-hungry few. Finally, Aristotle viewed a polity as a representative democracy, where citizens would elect qualified leaders to carry out their wishes in government. As polity devolved into democracy, Aristotle envisioned rule by the mob which is different than the modern view of democracy. For Aristotle, this constitutional cycle was inevitable. Every enduring society would experience all these systems of government as it progressed and evolved (Aristotle, 1984).

So, if democracy is not simply "rule by the people," what is it? For Aristotle, democracy had a negative connotation and was marked by mob rule, chaos, and disorder. From a modern perspective, many political scientists and theorists have attempted to define the notion of democracy. E.E. Schattschneider defined democracy thusly: "Democracy is a competitive political system in which competing leaders and organizations define the alternatives of public policy in such a way that the public can participate in the decision-making process" (Schattschneider, 1960, p. 141). Schmitter and Karl viewed the concept as the following: "Modern political democracy is a system of governance in which rulers are held accountable for their actions in the public realm by citizens, acting indirectly through the competition and cooperation of their elected representatives" (Schmitter and Karl, 1991, p. 76). Vanhannen contended that "Democracy is a political system in which different groups are legally entitled to compete for power and in which institutional power holders are elected by the people and are responsible to the people" (Vanhannen, 1997, p. 31). Perhaps the CIA World Fact Book defines the concept of **democracy** best, with the following: "a form of government in which the supreme power is retained by the people, but which is usually exercised indirectly through a system of representation and delegated authority periodically renewed" (Central Intelligence Agency, 2024). So, while it is impossible to offer an authoritative, singular definition of democracy, the common components of these various definitions seem to be concepts such as competition, accountability to the public, election of representatives, respect for the law, equal opportunity, encouragement and respect for debate, and involving the people in political decisions.

Since the 19th century, most "democracies" are better described as republics. A **republic** is an indirect democracy, a representative democracy whereby eligible voters (the electorate) choose representatives to carry out their wishes in the government. Most republics throughout the world function as **constitutional democracies**, meaning that the government draws its legitimacy from some authoritative document (a **constitution**) that defines the nation's system of government, its laws, and usually the rights of citizens (Central Intelligence Agency, 2024). The United States is, of course, a constitutional democracy or **constitutional republic**. In most republics and democracies today, the basic functions of government could include the following: 1) protecting citizens, 2) providing public goods such as education, parks, roads, sanitation, and health care, and 3) ensuring some degree of equality among its citizens. With regard to the American style of constitutional democracy, the relative degree of "success" is due in large part to many factors, including the relatively high level of affluence in the U.S. which contributes to governmental and societal stability, a high level of education among the populace which encourages participation, and plentiful resources with which to create jobs. To better understand the American political system and its governmental structure, it is helpful to compare and contrast it with other systems throughout history and today.

Other Systems of Government

When the U.S. Constitution was written in 1787 and ratified in 1789, most forms of government throughout the world were either **monarchies**—whereby a single sovereign (a king or a queen) exercised rule over a given populace and territory with power transfer based upon heredity, but in which laws and rights were established—or **absolute monarchies**—whereby the sovereign ruled with absolute power and authority with no defined laws or rights. Throughout the 19th century, during the Industrial Revolution, communism and socialism took root as a backlash against oppressive economic and social conditions in society created largely by industrialization. **Marxism**, based upon the writings of Karl Marx, espoused the inevitability that the working classes in society (who were the overwhelming majority) would shrug off the oppressive yoke of the capitalist industrialists who were exploiting them, and set up a classless society in which goods would be shared by all people with the guidance of an authoritarian ruling party, which is what came to be known as **communism** (Marx, 1848). In most cases, including the Soviet Union, China, Cuba, and North Korea, communism devolved into **totalitarianism**, where the state controlled all aspects of life, including the economic, political, social, and cultural spheres, and where any dissent was quickly punished by the ruling party elite. This system functioned very much like a **dictatorship**, in which a single person or small group exercises absolute power, like North Korea under Kim Jong Un. In **theocracies**, or states with a strong religious influence, there is no separation of church and state, and the church, in effect, constitutes or controls the government, such as is the case in several Islamic republics in the Middle East today.

In the 19th century, **socialism** was often conflated, rightly or wrongly, with Marxism or communism. In the 20th century and today, socialism functions differently. In those nations that utilize modern or quasi-socialist systems, most notably the Scandinavian nations of Sweden, Norway, and Denmark, the state provides many public goods such as universal health care and public education and also places controls on some aspects of the economy. Yet, citizens enjoy many of the same rights and liberties as those living in democratic republics, including freedom of speech and expression, freedom of the press, and freedom of religion, to name a few. One primary distinction between socialist nations and capitalist nations is the level of taxation. Obviously, taxes are much higher in socialist nations where the state places controls on economy and provides more public goods to its citizens. Finally, **anarchy** is the unfortunate situation in which no government authority exists whatsoever with total chaos ensuing.

Democracy in the United States—Separating Myth from Reality

Are there certain characteristics and experiences that are unique to Americans or the American political experience? Do Americans have a unique political culture or common set of values shared by all? In his famous examination of Americans and the American political system in the early 19th century, French author Alexis de Tocqueville contended that Americans were individualistic, pragmatic, hard-working, freedom-loving, and industrious among other qualities. In his treatise, *Democracy in America*, he argued that these common American qualities allowed its people to form a government that reflected these values which, at the time, were unique in his estimation (Tocqueville, 1945). So, was Tocqueville correct? Are these qualities uniquely and exclusively American? Do they apply to all Americans, or just some? Do they *still* apply to twenty-first century America? Can they be applied to other cultures in other nations as well? These questions are difficult, if not impossible, to answer. So, what is myth, and what is reality? What constitutes *American* democracy?

Political culture influences the political system. Individuals voting in elections determine the nature of government, or so most are taught. This notion of **political equality**, or one person, one vote, is often cited as a cornerstone of the American political system. The notion that everyone's vote counts equally regardless of race, gender, sexual orientation, socioeconomic status, or religious affiliation is something taught to students in schools beginning at a very young age. Is political equality myth or reality? Do all citizens have an equal ability to impact the political system? Some would argue yes, others no. Both would be correct. In a practical sense, citizens can only cast one vote per election, seemingly resulting in political equality. However, some have more ability to impact the political system than others, largely through money, influence, power, or connections to policymakers, which would shatter the notion of political equality. The previous exercise sheds light on the nature of the American political system and its unique brand of democracy. There are many questions and few simple answers. If political equality does not exist, the myth does endure. How about **equality of opportunity**?—does it exist? The "work hard and you'll get ahead" myth has been ingrained in the American experience for generations[1], but is it accurate? Do we all have equal opportunity to succeed? Again, some would argue yes, others no. Those arguing "yes" would be quick to point out that we have relatively equal access to public goods such as a free education, as well as equal freedoms of speech, association, and expression. Those arguing "no" would contend that some in society are inherently better off than others, having access to better schools, business connections, nicer neighborhoods, and even more stable families. Who is correct? Both sides. Again, there are no easy answers.

Ultimately, these opposing forces have shaped and forged the American republic. The common perception of the American political system that students learn in elementary, middle, and high school is that the majority of citizens, voting in elections, determine the nature of government. Is that accurate? Is the United States a system governed by individuals exercising **majority-rule democracy**, or does this model exist only in a textbook? Can the *individual* shape the American political system? Perhaps. Does the individual, exercising his or her political rights, have the ability to cause change at the national level? Probably not. Does

---

1   See for example, Horatio Alger's *Ragged Dick* series. It is available online from the Project Gutenberg site: http://www.gutenberg.org/ebooks/20689

this same individual have the ability to cause change in his or her community by becoming involved in political matters at the local level? Probably.

If individuals do not substantively shape or influence the political system at the national level, what forces do? In our system, in the modern sense, groups exercise a tremendous amount of power and exert significant influence over the political system, largely through money. This notion of groups having a profound impact on the political system is referred to as **pluralism**. Groups donate significant amounts of money to finance the campaigns of politicians, including members of Congress, the Senate, and the president. These "special interests" lobby policymakers to enact laws and regulations that benefit their interests and are discussed in much greater detail in Chapter 5. Groups are able to exert this level of influence for many reasons, most notably because they possess constitutional protection that allows them to lobby government. The First Amendment to the U.S. Constitution reads, "Congress shall make no law respecting an establishment of religion, or prohibiting the free exercise thereof; or abridging the freedom of speech, or of the press; or the right of the people peaceably to assemble, *and to petition the Government for a redress of grievances*" (italics added). While the shifting of power towards interest groups has surely had negative consequences, including an over-emphasis on the interests of groups with the most money, there have been positive outcomes as well, such as those groups advocating for social and educational policy influencing lawmakers to pass bills in those arenas. While the functioning of government in the United States is pluralistic in nature, it is by no means exceptional compared to democracies and republics throughout the world, where special interests also have tremendous degrees of power.

In sum, the myths of the development and functioning of the American political system can be separated from the realities in some cases, but not others. While much of what students learn about the system in grade levels is over-simplified and inaccurate, some is not. The founding and development of the American political system is a complex and fascinating case, but it can be compared to other nations' development as well. Furthermore, it is difficult to offer an authoritative set of political values that all Americans share or treasure, which is why American politics are so fascinating.

Case Study: The Influence of John Locke on The Declaration of Independence

To gain a better understanding of the American political process and the nature of American democracy, we need to examine the influences on the founders during the colonial and Revolutionary War eras. When Thomas

Jefferson authored the *Declaration of Independence* in 1776 under the guidance of Benjamin Franklin and John Adams, he demonstrated the degree to which he had been influenced by other great minds. Jefferson, like most of the delegates present in Philadelphia in 1776, was an educated, well-read man who had studied the classics (the writings of Greek and Roman historians and philosophers), as well as the works of the **Enlightenment Period** of the previous century. Arguably, the author who influenced Jefferson most was John Locke. Locke's ideas are woven throughout the *Declaration*. What follows is an in-depth examination of Locke's most famous writing and the impact that it had on Jefferson and the *Declaration of Independence* in particular.

John Locke (1632–1704) was an English political philosopher, commentator, and thinker who wrote during a time of great political change and upheaval when the monarchy was being challenged in England before the "Glorious Revolution" in 1688 and during the Enlightenment Period. Locke was considered one of the greatest minds of the Enlightenment era along with such luminaries as Voltaire, Rosseau, and Hobbes. Locke proposed and discussed many radical political beliefs during this period of upheaval and political change which dealt with the responsibilities of government, the rights of common people, and the philosophical basis of government in general (Locke, 1988, pp. 16–20). Unlike previous generations, and contrary to the very nature of monarchy, Locke believed that humans were born free (in a state of nature) and possessed inherent, inalienable rights that could not be arbitrarily removed by the government (the king). Locke assumed that the rights of people were bestowed not by the monarch, but by their creator (God), which was a radical idea at the time (Locke, 1988).

Locke's most famous work, *The Second Treatise of Government*, contains the passages and ideas that were most influential to Jefferson and are easiest to identify in the *Declaration of Independence*. As Jefferson advocated the *Declaration*, Locke believed in limited government. For Locke (and Jefferson), human freedom was the greatest right, bestowed not by government, but by God (an inalienable right). For Locke, people are born natural, reasonable, and free, beholden to no one, possessing inherent civil liberties and natural rights, including freedom and self-determination (Locke, 1988). Furthermore, people are able to acquire wealth from their labor, which is best evidenced through the accumulation of **private property**. For Locke, then, the primary duty of government is to preserve one's property, noting, " . . . whereas Government has no other end but the preservation of Property" (Locke, 1988, p. 94). For Locke, government exists to preserve life, liberty (freedom), and property, a theme paraphrased by Jefferson in the *Declaration* as, "That all men are created equal; that they are endowed by their

Creator with certain unalienable rights; that among these are life, liberty, and the pursuit of happiness . . . " (Jefferson, 1776).

Another Lockean theme that influenced Jefferson was the notion that citizens consent to be governed—that the people create, craft, and mold the government because they allow it to exist—which was an extremely radical supposition at the time. The idea that government exists to serve the people and only exercises power over them because the people allow it to was contrary to the very ideals of monarchy. The impact this idea had on Jefferson is observable in the *Declaration*: " . . . governments are instituted among men, deriving their just powers from the consent of the governed; that whenever any form of government becomes destructive of these ends, it is the right of the people to alter or abolish it, and to institute a new government . . . " (Jefferson, 1776). Ultimately, according to Locke and Jefferson, people and government enter into a **contract** of sorts, each with duties, responsibilities, and obligations. Government's obligation to its citizens is to exercise power in a limited fashion securing the life, liberty, and property of the people. The obligations of the people involve following the laws set forth by the government (which the people create) and respecting the rights and property of others. If government violates this contract, according to Locke, the people have the right to: 1) change the government, 2) leave society (keeping their property and wealth), and 3) revolt, an idea which especially appealed to Jefferson (Locke, 1988).

Locke's influence on Jefferson and the *Declaration of Independence* is profound and easily observable. Locke's radical teachings from the century before the founding period had far-reaching effects on the establishment of our republic (and others, such as France). Lockean teachings and principles are found in the *Constitution* as well, even if they are a bit harder to find at first glance. For example, Locke strongly advocated for separation of powers, which is a hallmark of our constitutional system. Locke wrote, "Therefore, 'tis necessary there should be a *Power always in being,* which should see to the *Execution* of the Laws that are made, and remain in force. And thus the *Legislative* and *Executive Power* come often to be separated" (p. 365, italics in original). Ultimately, Locke believed that people were inherently good. Furthermore, because of their inherent "goodness," they should not be constrained by government. Therefore, the responsibilities and duties of government were the following:

1. to provide a universal application of the laws to everyone, regardless of class,
2. making laws that are designed for the common good of the people,
3. ensuring low taxes, with tax increases being approved by the people or their representatives, and

4. ensuring that the power of government, especially with regard to lawmaking, resides in the legislature, because they are representatives of the people (Locke, 1988).

As can be plainly seen, Locke's ideals have impacted our republic since its founding, and still do so today.

Discussion Questions

1. Which definition of democracy do you prefer? Craft your own definition and compare it to the one you chose.
2. Which form of government is most similar to democracy? The most different? What positives and negatives do you see in each?
3. With its emphasis on pluralism, has the United States moved too far away from the ideal form of democracy? Do interest groups have too much power in our system?
4. In your opinion, how would Locke view our democracy today? Which of his ideals do we see reflected in our political system?

References

Aristotle. (1984). *The politics.* (C. Lord, Trans.). University of Chicago Press. (Original work published 350 B.C.E.).

Central Intelligence Agency. (2024). Field listing: Government type. *The World Fact Book.* Retrieved September 12, 2024 from https://www.cia.gov/the-world-factbook/field/government-type/

Jefferson, T. (1776). *Declaration of Independence.* https://avalon.law.yale.edu/18th_century/declare.asp

Locke, J. (1988). *Two treatises of government.* P. Laslett, (ed.). Cambridge University Press. (Original work published 1690).

Marx, K. & Engel, F. (1848). *The communist manifesto.* Progress Publishers.

Schattschneider, E. E. (1960). *The semisovereign people.* Holt, Rinehart and Winston.

Schmitter, P. C., & Karl, T. L. (1991). What democracy is . . . and is not. *Journal of Democracy, 2*(3), 75–88.

Tocqueville, A. (1945). *Democracy in America.* Alfred A. Knopf, Inc. (Original work published 1835).

Vanhannen, T. (1997). *Prospects of democracy: A study of 172 countries.* Routledge.

The U.S. Constitution

Ross C. Alexander

Learning Objectives

After covering the topic of the U.S. Constitution, students should understand:

1. How forces during the Revolutionary War era led to the writing and ratification of the Constitution.
2. The basic structure and functioning of the U.S. government as laid out in the Constitution.
3. How the flexibility of the Constitution has allowed it to endure, but also resulted in debate and controversy.
4. How the framers of the Constitution stated their case to the American people in *The Federalist*.

Abstract

The Constitution is a revered, enduring document that provides the framework for our democratic republic, but it is not without controversy. It is brief, flexible, and open to interpretation, just as the framers intended. As a result, the document has been able to remain largely intact in its original form for over 230 years. The Constitution provides both the theoretical and practical framework for our government, providing insight into the intentions of the framers during the Revolutionary and Founding periods. In a practical sense, the document provides a framework for our branches of government, means by which they check and balance each other, and the scope and limits of the power of the national government. The Constitution was a product of events and forces culminating throughout the Colonial and Revolutionary War eras, not something that was produced in a vacuum in 1787. This chapter not only describes and analyzes the Constitution itself, but also the historical events leading up to it. It also examines the legacy of the document and the reasons for the controversy it has caused.

The Events Leading to the Constitution
The Revolution

The **American Revolution** raged from 1775, when shots were first fired at Lexington and Concord, until 1783 when the Treaty of Paris formally ended the war (even though the final battle was fought at Yorktown in 1781). Students learn in school that the Revolution was brought about by freedom-loving patriots who desired self-governance, shedding off the oppressive yoke of British rule. This story is partly true. The causes of the Revolution are varied and complex, and by no means did the entirety of the population of the colonies support the uprising. Many were fighting for the right to self-rule and determination while others were fighting for largely economic reasons (they were sick of paying high taxes to fund the various wars of the British Empire or they did not want to pay off their British creditors) while others yet were fighting for adventure. Some, especially along the western frontier of the colonies, paid little attention to the war in the east as it did not directly affect them. Finally, many colonists remained loyal to the crown and even fought side by side with their British cousins against the rebels. Regardless of their politics, loyalties, and motivations, most would have agreed that the chances of a rag-tag, loosely-associated, underfunded, diverse group of colonies defeating the strongest military empire in the world would have been slim at best.

Discontent with British rule had been culminating for at least ten years before the skirmishes at Lexington and Concord. The British viewed the resource-rich colonies as a commodity that could be exploited and taxed to fund their extensive wars and campaigns around the globe. These increasing taxes on goods such as stamps and tea resulted in the beginnings of organized dissent, like the Boston Tea Party in 1773. Coupled with these high taxes was the reality that the planter classes in the middle Atlantic and southern colonies owed more and more to their British creditors for goods bought on credit—something that George Washington and Thomas Jefferson understood and experienced firsthand. A small, influential group of citizens believed that the colonies would be better as a sovereign, self-governing entity, divorced from British rule and control. These influential few echoed the sentiments of many who saw themselves as British citizens but did not have the rights and privileges of those living in Britain. That is, they paid taxes to the British crown yet had no representative voice in Parliament. This notion of "taxation without representation" was a rallying cry for many itching for rebellion.

The Declaration of Independence

On July 4, 1776, 56 delegates to the **Second Continental Congress** signed the **Declaration of Independence** (including Lyman Hall and Button Gwinnett from

Georgia). The treatise was penned by Thomas Jefferson, one of the youngest and brightest delegates to the Congress, under the tutelage of the more experienced John Adams and Benjamin Franklin. The document is one of rebellion, not reconciliation. It is written almost as a personal letter to King George III of England and explains in detail the reasons for rebellion against the crown. Jefferson borrowed liberally from many contemporary and historical sources, most notably John Locke's *Second Treatise of Government*, where Locke's "life, liberty, and property" became Jefferson's "life, liberty, and the pursuit of happiness" (Locke, 1988). In the document, Jefferson argues for a limited government that exists at the consent of the governed: the people, who possess these "inalienable" rights (see: https://guides.loc.gov/declaration-of-independence). Those who signed the Declaration were literally putting their lives on the line. Had the Revolution been lost, they would have been tried (and probably executed) for treason. The Declaration is one of our sacred founding documents largely because it articulates the philosophical basis for our political system.

The Articles of Confederation

After the former colonies had formally declared independence from Great Britain, one of the first orders of business was setting up some sort of government, largely in order to effectively wage war. The 13 former British colonies did not necessarily view themselves as one nation. Rather, they viewed themselves as 13 independent, sovereign countries, loosely affiliated, but working together (somewhat ineffectively) to fight the Revolution. The idea of one "United States of America" had not yet taken hold. However, some sort of government had to be created to coordinate the activities of all the former colonies. In November 1777, the **Articles of Confederation**, written by John Dickinson, was established. The hallmark of this new government was that the national government possessed very little real power. Rather, the true power remained with the states. A confederation is a loose association of independent or quasi-independent states. The national government under the Articles was so weak that it could not levy taxes, wage war, regulate commerce, or issue a uniform currency among all the states. It contained no executive branch, which resulted in relatively poor leadership. Rather, the power that did exist was concentrated in the legislature, or Congress. However, passing legislation or amending the Articles was onerous and difficult, requiring a unanimous vote of all 13 members (Kammen, 1986, pp. 10–18). It quickly became apparent that the Articles was an inefficient, ineffective system of government and was created in a haphazard fashion. It was not even formally ratified by the states until 1781. The result was that funding the Revolution was uncoordinated and ineffective, making the American victory even more impressive. Nevertheless, the Articles was our first system of uniquely American government and existed until the late 1780s. It should also be noted that it is within the Articles that the words "United States of America" are mentioned for the first time, which is a rather odd coincidence considering the weak nature of the national government provided by the document.

The Great Compromise

By 1787, many in the new nation realized the inherent inefficiencies of the Articles of Confederation. They argued that such a weak national government could leave the new nation exposed to financial ruin or ripe for future foreign invasion by Great Britain, France, or Spain, all of whom still laid claim to vast stretches of the North American continent. However, others argued that there was no need for more government beyond what the states and the weak national government provided. Both sides tended to agree that the Articles could or should be amended to function better. That was the charge of those delegates who met in Philadelphia in the summer of 1787—to amend the Articles, not create a new system of government. That is, however, exactly what they did. Twelve states sent delegates to the **Constitutional Convention**, everyone except Rhode Island. The meetings occurred in secret; the windows were nailed shut, and sentries were posted at the doors and entrances. The framers very quickly understood that they would be proposing a brand new government, one which looked radically different from what existed under the Articles. They also understood that such a development would not be without controversy.

Two Plans of Government

Many delegates from the various states made speeches and proposals as to what the new government should look like. However, the proposals of two factions soon became the most popular and seriously considered. The Virginia delegates proposed the **Virginia Plan** or Randolph Plan, which was written by James Madison, who had come to the Convention with the proposal already written for the most part. The Virginia Plan proposed a radical new form of government, one in which the national government was significantly more powerful than that found under the Articles. If accepted, the states would be ceding a great deal of power to the national government. The plan proposed a bicameral or two-house legislature with representation in both houses based on population, which favored the large population states such as Virginia, Pennsylvania, and Massachusetts. The people would choose members of the lower house, while state legislatures would choose members of the upper house (https://www.ourdocuments.gov). The plan proposed a fusion-of-power or parliamentary system, whereby the legislature would choose the chief executive (this is the type of arrangement present in Britain, and with which the framers were familiar) (Kammen, 1986, pp. 22–25). With regard to the judicial system, the Virginia Plan proposed a type of "supreme court" chosen by the upper house of the legislature (https://www.ourdocuments.gov). In a philosophical sense, the Virginia Plan viewed governmental power as being derived from one, unified American "people," rather than from the states; much different than the Articles, which was state-based in terms of power.

In contrast, the New Jersey delegates proposed the **New Jersey Plan**, or Paterson Plan. This plan looked very similar to the Articles, because it proposed a unicameral or one-house legislature with equal representation regardless of state population and favored the small population states such as New Jersey and New Hampshire. It proposed a multi-person chief executive chosen by the legislature (Kammen, 1986, pp. 25–30). In a philosophical sense, the New Jersey plan assumed that national government power would be derived from the states, not the American people as a whole. In our Constitution, there are elements of each proposal with more weight given to the Virginia Plan. After much debate, a compromise was reached by the framers, which came to be called the **Great Compromise** or **Connecticut Compromise**, because it was largely brokered by the Connecticut delegation. The proposal that resulted from the Constitutional Convention represented a radical departure from the government under the Articles.

The Document

The United States Constitution possesses seven articles, the first three of which detail the various branches of government. Article I outlines the powers of Congress (who would pass the laws); Article II the powers of the president (who would execute the laws); and Article III the powers of the judiciary (who would interpret the laws). The framers chose this sequence deliberately, believing that Congress, the legislature, is the strongest branch of government. They were familiar with how a strong legislature functioned (British parliament) and were wary that the president (which had never before existed) would become tyrannical or king-like, and they had just had a bad experience with a king leading up to the Revolution. Some among the framers (like Alexander Hamilton) even advocated that the president *should* possess powers similar to a king, serving a life term and functioning as the strongest entity in the government, yet they were overruled. Rather, they reasoned, a bicameral (two-house) legislature possessing the most power would best articulate the wishes of the people. Therefore, Article I is long and detailed. Conversely, Article II, which deals with the presidency, and Article III, which addresses the Courts, are brief and less detailed. Neither a president nor an independent judiciary had ever existed, and the framers were not exactly sure how either would function.

The document provides for a bicameral legislature. The lower house, the **House of Representatives**, is directly elected by the people. Representation in the House is based upon state population; the more people in a state, the more representatives it has in the House. However, representation in the upper house, the **Senate**, is equal with each state possessing two, regardless of population. According to the Constitution, *state* legislatures choose each state's senators, a provision in place until the passage of the **17th Amendment** in 1913, which resulted in the direct election of senators by the people. House members serve two-year terms, must be 25 years old, and must be U.S. citizens for a minimum of seven years. Senators serve six-year terms, must be 30 years old, and have been U.S. residents for at least nine years. Both House members and senators must reside in the state they represent. Today, there are 435 members of the House of Representatives (14 from Georgia) and 100 members of the Senate (two per state).

According to the Constitution, the president must be 35 years of age, a natural-born U.S. citizen, and a resident of the U.S. for the previous 14 years. The president serves a four-year term of office and is not limited to any specific number of terms. Presidents for nearly 150 years served a maximum of two terms not because of any constitutional regulation, but rather because it was the precedent set by George Washington. Franklin D. Roosevelt was the only president to break with tradition having been elected to four terms of office—1932, 1936, 1940, and 1944—during the Great Depression and World War II. In 1951, the **Twenty-Second Amendment** was ratified, which now limits the president to two terms of office.

The framers were not common men. Rather, they were the elite, the powerful, the educated, the aristocrats of the new nation. As such, they were a bit wary of giving too much power to the common people, and they structured the presidential election procedure uniquely. We do not directly elect the president as we directly elect members of Congress. Rather, when we vote for president, we are technically voting for a "slate of electors" who, in turn, several weeks after the general election, vote for the president. Therefore, the true mechanism for choosing the president is this Electoral College. Electors are chosen by their respective political parties to serve this role. Representation in the **Electoral College** is based largely upon population. A state's total number of electors is the sum of its representatives plus its senators (Kimberling, 1992). For example, in Georgia, this number is 16.

Therefore, states with more people have more electors. Today, the total number of electors is 538—which is the total number of representatives (435) plus the total number of senators (100) plus three representing the District of Columbia. In all states except Maine and Nebraska, the candidate who wins the majority of the popular vote receives all that state's electors. For example, if candidate A receives 60% of the popular vote in a state and candidate B receives 40%, candidate A would receive 100% of the electors. To win the presidential election, a candidate must receive a majority (270) of the votes (Kimberling, 1992). Therefore, candidates for the presidency are wise to gear their campaigns toward competitive states with high numbers of electoral votes (currently states like Georgia, Michigan, North Carolina, and Pennsylvania). Because of the Electoral College, the person receiving the majority of electoral votes (not popular votes in the general election) becomes the president. In fact, five times, most recently in 2016, the "victor" actually received fewer popular votes than the "loser," but received more votes where it counted—the Electoral College.

While no federal rule requires electors to choose the winner of their state's popular vote, most states have such rules. Until recently though, no so-called "faithless elector" was ever punished. There have been a few such electors, but none were decisive. They were always isolated protest votes. After the 2016 election, the states of Washington and Colorado attempted to punish such electors by fining or replacing them. The Washington state Supreme Court and a federal court in Colorado issued conflicting decisions on whether electors had the right to vote their conscience. The Supreme Court accepted the Colorado case, and unanimously decided that states *could* punish electors: "[A] State may enforce its pledge law against an elector" (*Chiafalo v. Washington*, 591 U.S. 578, 2020).

Impeachment is the formal means of removing the president from office. It is a two-step process involving both houses of Congress. First, the House of Representatives conducts an investigation to determine if the president has committed some sort of crime. If so, "Articles of Impeachment" can be voted against the president, requiring a simple majority vote. The "Articles" then go to the Senate for the formal trial of the president. Here, the senators serve as the jury, and the Chief Justice of the Supreme Court oversees the proceedings. For presidents to be convicted and forced to leave office, they must be found guilty of "High Crimes and Misdemeanors," requiring a super-majority (two-thirds) vote. Three presidents, Andrew Johnson, Bill Clinton, and Donald Trump, have had Articles of Impeachment voted against them, but none was convicted of High Crimes and Misdemeanors. In the modern era especially, the process of impeachment has devolved into an increasingly political tactic or ploy.

Article III established the **Judicial Branch** of government, or the courts. An independent judiciary had never existed, so Article III is very vague. In it, the framers described the parameters of the highest court in the land—the Supreme Court. Today, the Court has nine members. However, the Constitution does not require a specific number of justices. The most controversial aspect of this Article is the notion that federal judges receive life appointments, serving as long as they are deemed to be in good standing.

Article V of the Constitution describes the formal **amendment** process. The U.S. Constitution is amended infrequently, only 27 times in total. The first 10 amendments serve as the Bill of Rights (adopted in 1791). The process of both proposing and ratifying an amendment is onerous and requires more than a majority vote. There are two methods of proposing an amendment to the Constitution. The more common method is by a two-thirds vote in both houses of the U.S. Congress. The less common method is at the request of two-thirds of the state legislatures. With regard to ratifying a proposed amendment, the more common method is by a three-quarters vote of all state legislatures. The less common method of ratification is by three-quarters of the states in a special convention. With respect to both the proposal and ratification process, a relatively small minority can block the will of the majority, which has resulted in only 17 amendments being ratified since 1791.

Slavery

The words "slave" or "slavery" do not appear in the Constitution, yet the framers were very aware of the controversial nature of the institution. Slavery is addressed indirectly, most notably by the **Three-Fifths Compromise.** Article I, Section Two, Paragraph Three of the Constitution describes how slaves would be counted as three-fifths of a person in terms of representation, when determining the total number of persons in a state. The slave-holding states of the South argued that slaves should be counted in terms of representation, resulting in more representatives in the House for those states. The non-slave-holding states contended that they should not count as "persons" because they were considered property. The resulting compromise was that slaves would be counted as three-fifths of a person.

Many framers were slaveholders, including Washington and Jefferson. Others were abolitionists who abhorred the practice and desired to see it ended immediately. Most, however, understood that ending slavery would be difficult, as the many Southern states depended upon it economically. Had slavery been outlawed in the Constitution, it would probably not have been ratified, because many Southern states would have withdrawn their support. Valid arguments can be made saying that the framers should have outlawed slavery at the founding. The counterargument that ending slavery at that time would have resulted in the Constitution not being ratified is also valid. There are no simple or authoritative answers on this subject.

Controversy
Enumerated v. Implied Powers

The framers understood that they could not possibly predict the challenges that the Constitution would have to face, yet they wanted to create a document that would endure and be applicable for future generations. To that end, they crafted a purposefully ambiguous product that could be molded, changed, and applied somewhat differently by future policymakers. One mechanism they included to allow for this constitutional evolution is found in Article I. Article I, Section Eight of the U.S. Constitution is referred to as the **Necessary and Proper Clause.** This clause, sometimes referred to as the "Elastic Clause," allows for the future expansion and evolution of the power of the federal government. It says Congress has the power "To make all Laws which shall be necessary and proper for carrying into the Execution the foregoing Powers, and all other Powers vested by this Constitution in the Government of the United States, or in any Department or Officer thereof." This relatively simple provision, which leaves open-ended the power of the federal government, has sparked a great deal of controversy about the limits of its authority.

At the time of the founding, and even today, many argued that the powers of the federal government should be limited to those specifically listed, or enumerated, in the Constitution—no more, no less—and that the powers of the federal government are not open-ended. Rather, they argued, the states should possess those powers not listed in the Constitution. These states' rights advocates also looked to the Constitution and the Bill of Rights to substantiate their case. The 10th Amendment to the Constitution is referred to as the **Reserved Powers Clause**, which simply states: "The Powers not delegated to the United States by the Constitution, nor prohibited by it to the states, are reserved to the states respectively, or to the people."

These two clauses, one found in the Constitution and one found in the Bill of Rights, are contradictory in nature. The Necessary and Proper Clause assumes that the federal government possesses **implied powers** beyond what are listed in the Constitution. Conversely, the Reserved Powers Clause assumes that the federal government possesses **enumerated powers,** or those listed in the Constitution, with all others being given or reserved to the states. This ambiguity has caused a great deal of debate, confusion, conflict, and even rebellion over the past 200 years, resulting in events leading to the Civil War and conflicts between the states and the federal government ever since. What did the framers actually intend? It is impossible to know exactly. They purposely crafted and envisioned a flexible document that is open to interpretation by future generations. However, they also understood the need for strong state governments.

Federalists v. Anti-Federalists

The ratification of the Constitution was not a foregone conclusion. Many were opposed to its passage. Mostly, they were fearful of a tyrannical national government that would take all power away from the states, causing them to wither away. These anti-Constitution forces were largely fearful of what was referred to at the time as consolidation of power, or the notion that all governmental power would be concentrated in one level of government (the national level in this case). Rather, they contended, power should be decentralized across two levels of government—the national and the state—leaving the states with considerable power and authority. The forces in favor of the Constitution were dubbed **Federalists**, while those opposed to it were called **Anti-Federalists**.

The Federalists included such dignitaries as James Madison, John Adams, Alexander Hamilton, and George Washington—those who had attended the Constitutional Convention and played a large part in the crafting of the document. The Federalists saw the need for a strong, energetic, and efficient national government that would unify the new republic as one nation. They assumed that power would be somewhat consolidated under the national government but realized that states would play a major role in this power-sharing arrangement. The Federalist base of support was much stronger in New England and the Middle Atlantic States, in the cities, and among intellectuals, merchants, and scholars. Conversely, the Anti-Federalists believed that the states should remain strong, that they be at least co-equal players with the national government, and that power should be dispersed among these levels of government. The Anti-Federalist base of support was stronger in rural areas, the South, and among farmers, frontier settlers, and individualists.

Case Study: Marketing the Constitution: *The Federalist*

Once the Constitution was written, it needed to be ratified by the states. To become the law of the land, nine of the thirteen states had to support it. To ensure passage, the framers needed to explain to the states, and more importantly, to the people, why the Constitution was in their best interests. The primary method they chose to sell the Constitution to the people was through a series of periodic essays published in newspapers throughout the states, laying out in simple terms, the basic provisions of the Constitution. These 85 essays, collectively called *The Federalist,* appeared in newspapers and were widely circulated in 1787–88. Not only did they explain how the Constitution was structured and how it would function, the essays provided insight into the framers' philosophical and theoretical reasoning when crafting the document. Three men wrote the 85 essays, James Madison, Alexander Hamilton, and John Jay. Madison and Hamilton penned the vast majority. Overall, Madison's essays are probably the most famous, because he laid out a common sense, nuanced, and balanced argument, which respectfully addressed the concerns of the Anti-Federalists. Hamilton, on the other hand, was more direct and less conciliatory towards the Anti-Federalists.

The framers reasoned that if people could read these essays and understand their reasoning, they would ultimately support the new Constitution. The Anti-Federalists wrote a number of rebuttal essays that in many cases provide excellent arguments against the Constitution. However, because the Constitution ultimately is ratified and the Federalists "won," the Anti-Federalists' essays have been largely marginalized or forgotten. Throughout this year and a half, Madison and Hamilton would publish periodic essays under the pen name "Publius" and various Anti-Federalist writers, many of whom would also use a pen name, would respond with a counter-essay. What follows is an analysis of some of the most famous essays of *The Federalist*—those that lay out the argument of the Federalists best. Collectively, the 85 papers that comprise *The Federalist* are probably the third-most important set of documents of the founding era, behind only The Declaration of Independence and the Constitution. These three pieces comprise the basis of American political philosophy.

Federalist #10, written by James Madison, is probably the most famous and influential of all the essays. It best summarizes the Federalists' collective argument in favor of the Constitution. In this essay, Madison primarily addresses the issue of factions, what we would call special interests or interest groups, or even political parties today. With incredible foresight into the development of the modern American political system, Madison explained that if a strong, energetic government was not established, factions would dominate the system, alienating the people and negatively influencing the crafting of legislation and public policy (which, many today would argue, is exactly what occurred). Madison defined factions as ". . . a number of citizens, whether amounting to a majority or minority of the whole, who are united and actuated by some common impulse of passion, or of interest, adverse to the rights of other citizens, or to the permanent and aggregate interest of the community" (Hamilton, Jay, & Madison, 2001, p. 92). Madison explained that factions would always exist, but government should ensure that their effects are tempered or diminished. To accomplish this end, he reasoned, a strong national government, a republic, must be established to safeguard the liberties and will of the people. He further argued that too much freedom and liberty can result in too much faction: "Liberty is to faction what air is to fire" (Hamilton, et al., 2001, p. 92). Madison further explained that the best system of government to limit the power and influence of factions is a republic, a representative democracy. Echoing Rousseau and others, Madison understood that democracy was predisposed to breeding faction. However, he reasoned, the United States, with its large territory and population, was uniquely situated and comprised to limit factions. Factions were inevitable, but could be marginalized in a large, vast republic. Madison envisioned a system whereby the people would choose the best, brightest, and most capable members of society to represent them in government. He, in fact, advocated for a "natural" aristocracy that would represent the people in government. Like the rest of the framers, he was a well-educated aristocrat who felt that some were better fit to lead than others. Throughout *#10*, and in other essays, the authors refer to "men of fit character" who would govern in the best interests of the people.

Federalist #39, also penned by Madison, addresses the primary concern of the Anti-Federalists—that the proposed Constitution would result in a consolidated government whereby all power would be concentrated in the national government, and the states would lose all or significant power, causing them to wither away. Madison does concede that the states would lose some power, but would remain very important partners in this unique power-sharing arrangement that the Constitution proposes, where there are multiple levels of sovereign government existing at the same time, which is the definition of **federalism**. Today, we use the terms "federal" and "national" almost interchangeably. To Madison, they were different. In explaining how the states would retain power under the Constitution, he made a detailed distinction between "federal" and "national." Madison explained that the government would function simultaneously as federal and national in nature. When governmental authority flowed from the states, it was federal in nature. However, when governmental authority flowed directly from the people, it was national in nature. Therefore, the proposed Constitution viewed its power as derived from sovereign states individually as well as from the American people collectively. For one of the first times, the nation was beginning to view itself as one, unified entity.

Most of the essays written by Hamilton are not nearly as delicate as Madison's. In fact, at times, they tend to even contradict Madison. In *Federalist #15*, Hamilton also addresses the issue of consolidation of power and is not nearly as conciliatory to states' rights advocates, explaining that a powerful national government is the best guarantee of national progress and health as a nation. He even refers to the Articles (which guaranteed the strength and power of the states) as a "national humiliation." In this essay, Hamilton argues that the fledgling nation needs to be grounded on firm financial footing and possess an ability to defend itself, something that can only occur through the establishment and leadership of a strong national government. He argues that the states had proven to be ineffective in either of these areas. Hamilton also argues strongly for consolidation, even at the expense of state power: "...we must resolve to incorporate into our plan those ingredients which may be considered as forming the characteristic difference between a league and a government; we must extend the authority of the Union to the persons of the citizens—the only proper objects of government" (Hamilton, Jay, & Madison, 2001, p. 111). Here, Hamilton is advocating that the government rightly serves all Americans as individual citizens of one nation, not the interests of the states. Until then, he reasoned, the new nation would remain financially insolvent, fractured, and ripe for foreign invasion.

A Civic Engagement Challenge: Draft a Constitution

Are there aspects to the Constitution that do not seem just or fair? Did the framers err when drafting certain articles that left the document open to interpretation and speculation that did not mirror their intent? Would you like to see certain amendments made to the Constitution? Here's your chance. Break into groups of five or so students and draft your own Constitution for a nation you have created. Be sure to include the following: a brief description of your society or nation, a Preamble or "mission statement," and 10–12 realistic, detailed, specific changes and/or provisions your group would like to seen enacted. Your document can be focused at a national, state, community, or even campus level. After you have finished, trade papers with another group to see what they have crafted. Be serious, but have fun!

Discussion Questions

1. Are the Declaration of Independence and the Constitution compatible documents? How are they similar? How are they different?
2. How do you think the framers would react to the evolution of the power of the president over the past 200 years? Has the office become too powerful? Was that their intent?
3. Should the federal government be more limited to the enumerated powers found in the Constitution or is it inevitable that it assumes implied powers over time? What are the consequences or implications? What did the framers intend?
4. Should the framers have ended the institution of slavery in the Constitution? Why or why not?
5. If you were alive in 1787, would you have been a Federalist or Anti-Federalist? Why? What were their basic differences?

References

Hamilton, A., Jay, J., & Madison, J. (2001). *The Federalist.* G. W. Carey & J. McClellan (eds.). Liberty Fund. (Original work published 1788).

Kammen, M. (ed.). (1986). *The origins of the American constitution: A documentary history.* Penguin.

Kimberling, W. C. (1992). *The electoral college.* https://www.fec.gov/pdf/eleccoll.pdf

Locke, J. (1988). *Two treatises of government.* Peter Laslett, (ed.). Cambridge University Press. (Original work published 1690).

United States Constitution. (n.d.). https://topics.law.cornell.edu/constitution. (Original work published 1878).

Court Cases

Chiafalo v. Washington, 591 U.S. 578 (2020).

Federalism

Charles H. "Trey" Wilson III

Learning Objectives

After covering the topic of federalism, students should understand:

1. What federalism is and how the U.S. Constitution allocates powers to both the national and state governments to create a federalist system in the United States.
2. The evolution of American federalism from inception to its modern manifestations. The concepts of "dual federalism," "cooperative federalism," "New Federalism," and "New Age Federalism."
3. The future of federalism in light of recent Supreme Court decisions affecting the distribution of power between the national and state governments.

Abstract

Federalism in the United States refers to a governmental system outlined in the Constitution in which power is distributed between the national government and the state governments. The U.S. Constitution allocates power to the national government chiefly through the enumerated powers, the implied powers, the power to tax, and the Supremacy Clause, and to the state governments through the "Reserved Powers Clause." The nuances of federalism have evolved and changed in the U.S. as views altered over time about how power should be shared between the federal government and state governments. Political scientists routinely use labels such as "dual federalism," "cooperative federalism," "New Federalism," and "New Age Federalism" to describe the various incarnations of federalism. The future of federalism may be dynamic depending upon how the U.S. Supreme Court chooses to adjudicate cases in which the distribution of power in government is at issue.

Introduction

Federalism may be defined as a political system in which power is divided between a central government and multiple constituent, provincial, or state governments. While the U.S. Constitution never expressly states anything like "the United States will have a federal system," various provisions in the document confer or deny powers to the national government while others reserve or withhold powers for the fifty state governments. In this way, a federal system was created for America. This system has evolved and changed over time and continues to do so today, as a kind of tension has grown to exist between the central and the state governments over which will exercise power. Understanding this system and its nuances is requisite to fully grasping American government, since federalism is at the heart of how government is organized in the United States.

Why Federalism?

For the framers, federalism was a kind of middle ground between two other systems of government that had proven to be unsatisfactory for Americans. In one such system (called a **unitary** system by political scientists), a centralized, national government retained virtually all governmental power, as in the case of the British monarchy. Many colonists believed they had been subjected to tyrannical oppression at the hands of the king, and so were wary of conferring too much power on what they feared would become a distant and unfamiliar national government. However, the opposite extreme of government was equally undesirable. While the **confederal** system created by the Articles of Confederation did create a national government, the Articles gave relatively little power to that central government and instead reserved most governing power for the several states. While this provided for a great deal of local autonomy, the result was a puny national government. Indeed, this national government was too weak and ill-equipped to respond to even internal crises such as Shays' Rebellion (a minor uprising of Massachusetts farmers angered over an ailing economy), let alone external threats from powerful neighbors. A **federal** system empowered to some extent both the state and national governments, thereby combining the benefits of both.

Creating a Federal System

Empowering a National Government

Four items contained in the U.S. Constitution serve to confer the lion's share of power on the national government: the "enumerated powers," the "implied powers," the "Supremacy Clause," and the power to tax.

To enumerate something simply means to count it off, one by one, as in a list. Hence, the **enumerated powers** are essentially contained in list form in the U.S. Constitution, specifically in Article I, Section 8. This text gives "Congress," which should be taken to mean the national government, the power to do many specific things, including coining money, establishing post offices, and maintaining a navy, among others.

While the enumerated powers specify many things that the federal government can do, the framers knew that they could never create an exhaustive list of powers for the Congress. After all, times change, and much would doubtlessly occur in the future that they could not even anticipate, let alone write about. Consequently, the framers included language in Article I, Section 8 which has come to be known as the **Elastic Clause**, so-called because it lets the federal government expand and stretch its power under certain circumstances. The Elastic Clause provides that Congress shall have the power to make all laws which are "necessary and proper" for executing any of its enumerated powers (The Elastic Clause is sometimes referred to as the "Necessary and Proper Clause" because of this language). The result is that, provided Congress can demonstrate that a law it likes is both necessary and proper, it may be able to do something that might, at first glance, seem beyond the scope of its enumerated powers. Of course, determining exactly how "necessary" and "proper" should be defined in any given circumstance is often a matter of fierce debate in government, and anyone who does not like the law in question will certainly argue that it is unnecessary and improper. Political scientists refer to powers the national government derives from the Elastic Clause and the enumerated powers as **implied powers** since, while they are not overtly stated, such powers may be fairly construed to exist.

Article VI of the U.S. Constitution contains what is referred to as the **Supremacy Clause**. Occasionally, both the federal government and one or more state governments might each claim some power to do something—for example, the power to regulate the issuance of monopolies on steamboat ferry transportation across the Hudson Bay (see the Supreme Court case of *Gibbons v. Ogden* later in the chapter). The Supremacy Clause states that in these conflicts, the federal government shall be presumed to win out over the state government(s). Chief Justice John Marshall put it more eloquently in the judicial opinion he wrote in 1819 for the U.S. Supreme Court case of *McCulloch v. Maryland*. Marshall declared, "the Constitution and the laws made in pursuance thereof are supreme . . . they control the constitution and laws of the respective States, and cannot be controlled by them." The framers included this provision because they had seen firsthand under the Articles of Confederation how the nation could suffer under an impotent national government.

Finally, the national government derives much of its power from the ability to tax. To avoid the myriad problems of inadequate revenue that surfaced under the Articles of Confederation, the framers empowered the federal government with the ability to levy charges against such things as activities, products, and, with the Sixteenth Amendment, income. The power to tax can be a powerful tool to shape public policy. Consider, for example, consumption or "sin" taxes imposed by government on everything from alcohol to tobacco products to "gas guzzling" vehicles. Proponents of such taxes hope tacking on additional expenses to the cost of taxed products will discourage people from acquiring them and, eventually, make the products so unattractive to consumers that they disappear from the market.

Empowering State Governments

Like the federal government, state governments derive power from the U.S. Constitution. Regarding state power, Supreme Court Justice Hugo Black once wrote that federalism meant, "a proper respect for state functions, a recognition of the fact that the entire country is made up of a Union of separate State governments, and a continuance of the belief that the National Government will fare best if the States and their institutions are left free to perform their separate functions in their separate ways" (*Younger v. Harris*, 44). Indeed, having lived for a decade with the Articles of Confederation under which states maintained virtually all governmental power, it would have gone without saying for many of the framers that states would retain power under the U.S. Constitution. Consequently, relatively little is stated outright regarding state power in the Constitution's articles. However, Anti-Federalist concerns over the national government usurping too much power eventually led to the inclusion of the Tenth Amendment in the U.S. Constitution. It states, "The powers not delegated to the United States by the Constitution, nor prohibited by it to the States, are reserved to the States respectively, or to the people." Political scientists refer to this bit of text as the **Reserved Powers Clause** and these powers as "reserved powers" or, alternatively, "police powers." While the latter term might conjure up images of men and women in blue brandishing pistols and handcuffs, think of it more broadly. Besides being a noun, "police" can also be a verb. To "police" something essentially means to keep something maintained in good order. In the context of federalism, a state's "police powers" let it exclusively regulate within its borders things like law and order, health, safety, and morality as it sees fit and prohibits the federal government from interfering with state interests in these areas. This explains why some states may permit some practices (such as same-sex marriage or capital punishment), while others do not. Each state is exercising its reserved powers autonomously.

Powers Shared Between (and Denied to) the Federal and State Governments

We have seen how the U.S. Constitution confers power onto the national government and onto state governments to create America's federal system. However, to completely grasp how federalism functions, we must also understand the concepts of concurrent powers (or shared powers) and prohibited powers (or denied powers). **Concurrent powers** are powers that are held by both the federal and the state governments. For example, both the federal government and the several state governments have the power to establish a court system. This is why the United States has a federal Supreme Court, just as each state has its own state supreme court of last resort for cases moving through the state judicial system. Another example of a shared power would be the power to tax. If you have not already begun doing so, every year around mid-April, you will submit your Federal Income Tax Return, probably the (in)famous I.R.S. Form 1040. In most states, such as Georgia, you will also submit an income tax return to the state you live in around this time as well. Some states, such as Florida, Nevada, and New Hampshire, do not have a state income tax. As the name implies, concurrent powers may be exercised by the states and the national government simultaneously. However, note that states may exercise these shared powers only up to the point that they do not violate or conflict with national law. For example, while the state of Georgia does have the power to tax, the state could not begin taxing goods slated to be exported to other countries through its shipping ports. This is because the U.S. Constitution contains a clause that prohibits export taxes from being used (note that Georgia and other states can tax *imported* goods—providing they obtain approval from Congress to do so).

The prohibition on export taxes is a good example of a "prohibited power." As the name implies, a **prohibited power** is one that is denied to either the federal government, the state governments, or, at times, denied to both governments. For example, the Constitution contains a clause that reads, "No Title of Nobility shall be granted by the United States." Hence, as nifty as they might sound, there will never be a "John Jones, Duke of Dahlonega" or "Susan Smith, Duchess of Dawsonville"—at least not officially, anyway. Another example of a prohibited power relates to what are called *ex post facto* laws. "*Ex post facto*" is Latin for "after the fact." An *ex post facto* **law** is one that would criminalize some action for the purpose of prosecuting it *after* someone had already performed the action at a time when it was legal to do so. Vengeful politicians in neither the federal government nor any state government can enact such laws. Examples of powers prohibited to only state governments would include the power to make treaties or to coin money. Examples of powers prohibited to only the federal government could include things like establishing a drinking age or setting the age of consent for marriage, since these would be considered state police powers protected from federal government intrusion thanks to the Tenth Amendment.

"Horizontal Federalism" and Relations between the States

The foregoing material describes how the U.S. Constitution allocates (or does not allocate) powers to the national and state governments. Some political scientists qualify this as **vertical federalism** since it describes a dynamic occurring between government on two different levels, federal and state. Just as important, however, is how power is shared *between* the several different governments that all inhabit the state level.

To many people, part of what makes the United States a remarkable country is the heterogeneity of its fifty states. The size, population, resources, natural environment, and political culture of no two states are exactly alike. What is it that keeps big California with its population of around 40 million people and vast resources from trying to throw its weight around against other, smaller states? In fact, several provisions of the Constitution serve to put all the states on one level (i.e., horizontal) playing field. Four of the most significant of these provisions of **horizontal federalism** are the Full Faith and Credit Clause, the Privileges and Immunities Clause, and the Interstate Rendition (a.k.a. Extradition) Clause, which are all contained in Article IV, and interstate compacts.

The **Full Faith and Credit Clause** requires each state to respect "the public Acts, Records, and judicial Proceedings of every other State." Practically speaking, this statement means that contracts and judicial orders arising out of one state will continue to be binding in other states, mostly because it better facilitates national commerce. It is the reason a couple can drive cross-country all night, get married at a 24-hour wedding chapel in Las Vegas, and then return home, still married, even though their ceremony occurred several states away. Assuming the marriage contract was valid in Nevada, the Full Faith and Credit Clause requires that other states recognize it as well.

But what if something permitted by a minority of states happens to be a thing that a majority of other states would rather *prohibit*? Could the Full Faith and Credit clause compel that majority of states to kowtow to the policy of the minority? A scenario rather along these lines emerged in the U.S. beginning around the 1990s. A handful of states (including Hawaii, Vermont, and Massachusetts) began legalizing either civil unions for same-sex couples or same-sex marriage. For a variety of reasons, many other states and many lawmakers in the Federal government bristled at this. In 1996, the federal congress passed and President Clinton signed into law the "Defense of Marriage Act" (DOMA) which, among other things, essentially defined marriage as being a union between one man and one woman. As well, by around 2006, more than a dozen states had amended their own constitutions to deny recognition and acknowledgment within their borders of what became popularly termed "gay marriages" that had been performed in other jurisdictions.

The next decade saw much litigation over the constitutionality of DOMA and state-authored gay marriage bans. Court battles culminated in June of 2015, when a closely-divided U.S. Supreme Court ruled in the case of *Obergefell v. Hodges* (2015) that same-sex marriage bans were unconstitutional. Interestingly, though, the Court did not rely at all upon the Constitution's Full Faith and Credit clause to inform its ruling that essentially legalized gay marriage in the U.S. Rather, the Court struck down the bans because, in its view, they violated Fourteenth Amendment guarantees of equal protection under the law to all citizens, including homosexuals.

Does this leave unanswered the question of whether or not the Full Faith and Credit Clause can subordinate a majority of states to the will of a minority of states? Not entirely. In another case decided in 1988, the Supreme Court noted that the Full Faith and Credit clause "does not compel a State to substitute the statutes of other States for its own statues dealing with a subject matter concerning which it is competent to legislate" (*Franchise Tax Bd. of Cal. v. Hyatt*, 2003, citing *Sun Oil Co. v. Wortman*, 1988). Language such as this has been interpreted by some legal observers as giving states the prerogative to claim what is termed a "public policy exception" to the Full Faith and Credit clause. Though there is not a great deal of case law providing much nuance about the exception, states can presumably invoke it in at least some instances to avoid having to embrace some unwanted policy adopted by a sister state. Whether it would be the public policy exception or the rule (i.e., the Full Faith and Credit clause) that would control in any given situation is, of course, something that the judiciary would determine. Like the Full Faith and Credit Clause, the **Privileges and Immunities Clause** also serves to equalize power distribution between states. This clause guarantees that citizens of one state shall be deemed to possess the same fundamental rights as citizens of all other states. It is occasionally referred to as the "Comity Clause" because it prevents any state from discriminating against visiting citizens from another state in certain respects, which would tend to preserve harmony as people travel between states ("comity" means a friendly social atmosphere, which probably would better come about if everyone thought they were on equal footing with everyone else). Note that this clause applies only to basic constitutional rights such as those discussed in Chapter 11. So, for example, a state might legally charge residents one price to enter a state museum but charge non-state-residents a higher price since museum-going is not a fundamental right protected by the U.S. Constitution.

Interstate Rendition (or perhaps more commonly, if not entirely correctly, referred to as "extradition") occurs when a fugitive apprehended in one state is handed over to the authorities of another state for prosecution for crimes committed in that latter state. To preserve interstate comity, when rendition occurs, it typically does so without much incident. However, occasions have arisen when one state may not want to turn over a fugitive to another state. Perhaps the most celebrated instance of this in recent years came in the legal case of *Puerto Rico v. Branstad*. In this case, an Iowa governor declined to extradite a man charged with homicide in Puerto Rico who had fled to Iowa while released on bail. The man (who was white) stood accused of killing a Hispanic woman, and the governor did not believe he could get a fair trial owing to racial circumstances. The case eventually reached the U.S. Supreme Court, which ruled that federal courts have the power to force states to hand over fugitives thanks to the Extradition Clause in Article IV, Section 2, Clause 2. (See *Puerto Rico v. Branstad*, 1987).

Interstate compacts are discussed in Article 1, Section 10 of the U.S. Constitution and also serve to harmonize relationships between states. These compacts are legally binding agreements between two or more states to do something that must be approved by Congress before taking effect. They can be on any subject, but often revolve around natural resources (such as lakes and rivers) that touch or flow through multiple states. Signatories to these compacts agree to share power and resources to maintain the common natural resource and prevent any one state from polluting or overusing the resource.

Ultimately, these several provisions of the U.S. Constitution do much to help the fifty states get along. Except for one unfortunate period from 1861 to 1865, horizontal federalism has worked for over two hundred years. This track record should argue powerfully that horizontal federalism is just as important as federalism in the vertical sense when it comes to American government.

The Evolution of Federalism
Early Years: The "Supremacy" Period

Our present understanding of federalism and the manner in which power is allocated between the state governments and the national government did not spring into being overnight. Rather, this understanding has changed over the last two hundred-plus years. This process began with the writing of the U.S. Constitution. The framers meant for that text to communicate much about how power would be distributed; hence, we have the enumerated powers, the implied powers, the reserved powers, etc., discussed earlier. At the same time, the framers meant for their words to be interpreted by future generations. They understood that times would change and that phrases such as "necessary and proper" and words like "supremacy" would have to be qualified in the future to be meaningful in light of those changes. The job of qualifying this constitutional language typically falls to the United States Supreme Court. How that language has been qualified over time by the Court in response to changing times is the evolutionary process of federalism.

This evolution of federalism really commenced in the early 1800s when Chief Justice John Marshall, a very talented jurist, headed the U.S. Supreme Court. In 1819, the Marshall Court heard a case called *McCulloch v. Maryland*, which is often referred to as "the bank case" for reasons soon to become apparent. In a simplified version, things began when Congress chartered a national bank and located a branch office of this bank in Baltimore. Maryland's state legislature, which doubtlessly disliked the idea of added competition for state-owned banks within its borders, responded by levying a steep tax on all banks operating in the state that had not been chartered by Maryland. When James McCulloch, the head of the Baltimore branch of the federal bank, received the tax notice, he refused to pay. The state of Maryland sued McCulloch in state court and, unsurprisingly perhaps, won. McCulloch appealed to the U.S. Supreme Court.

There were two central issues in the case that the Supreme Court was asked to decide, and both related to federalism. The first was, "Did Congress have the authority to charter a bank?" Maryland pointed out that the U.S. Constitution never mentioned such a power; indeed, the word "bank" never even appeared in the document. However, the Supreme Court sided with the federal government's argument on this issue. That argument asserted that it was reasonable to *imply* that Congress should have the power to charter a bank thanks to the Elastic Clause. After all, the Constitution did expressly give Congress the power to issue currency, collect taxes, and to borrow money in the enumerated powers. A bank could assist with doing these things—indeed, the U.S. government claimed it was *necessary* to have a bank to do them efficiently. Also, a national bank was not some arcane, complicated contraption that Congress conjured up out of nowhere. Many countries had national banks of one form or another even back then. Hence, one could say that having a national bank was *proper* as well as necessary for a nation like the United States to thrive. The Supreme Court decided that the federal government had made its case that the national bank was "necessary and proper" to the exercise of Congress's enumerated powers involving revenue and currency. And, according to the Elastic Clause, if something Congress wants to do can be deemed "necessary and proper," then that something is a constitutionally permissible exercise of federal government power.

The second question presented for resolution in *McCulloch v. Maryland* related to taxation. Maryland argued that, assuming the national bank could exist, nothing should stop the state from taxing it. After all, the bank was on Maryland soil and so was potentially a burden to the state, albeit a minor one. The tax would compensate the state for its trouble. The Supreme Court did not buy it. Chief Justice Marshall, who wrote the majority opinion in the case, invoked the Constitution's Supremacy Clause and held that a state law taxing the bank must be trumped by a federal law permitting the bank to operate freely.

McCulloch v. Maryland is an important case in the evolution of federalism because of how the Supreme Court interpreted the Elastic Clause and the Supremacy Clause. In both instances, the Court read the U.S. Constitution in such a way that opened the door for the expansion of the federal government's power. Consider that the Court *could have* qualified "necessary and proper" in such a way that would have made it very difficult for the federal government to characterize anything as either necessary and/or proper. It did not. Rather, the Court put the entire country on notice that satisfying the parameters of the Elastic Clause was something doable. Likewise, the Court could have adopted a more limited definition of "supremacy." Again, it chose not to, sending in the process a clear signal to states that their laws would fare poorly in competition with federal statutes (see *McCulloch v. Maryland*, 17 U.S. 316 [1819]).

Another landmark case affecting federalism came before the Marshall Court only a few years after *McCulloch*. In 1824, the Court heard *Gibbons v. Ogden*, which has come to be known as the "steamboat case"—again for reasons that will soon become apparent. Though the case eventually turned out to be somewhat complicated on several levels, the main issues in dispute were actually fairly simple. Aaron Ogden, who had ties to Robert Fulton, the inventor of the steamboat, had secured exclusive rights from the New York State legislature to operate a steamboat passenger ferry service on the Hudson River between New

York and New Jersey. About the same time, Thomas Gibbons, a former business partner of Ogden's, also secured exclusive rights to do roughly the same thing—but his license came from Congress, not a state legislature. Ogden sued to protect his monopoly.

Before the Court, the case turned chiefly on how the **Interstate Commerce Clause** of the Constitution would be interpreted. This clause states that Congress, not the states, shall have the power "To regulate Commerce with foreign Nations, and among the several States, and with the Indian Tribes." No one much disputed that the two steamboat services were operating "among" states. However, the parties to the lawsuit differed over how the word "commerce" in the clause should be defined. Ogden argued that commerce should amount to what people probably typically think of when they think of commerce—namely, exchanging money for goods. Since Ogden's steamboat ferry provided a service, not goods, in exchange for money, he argued that what he did fell outside of the definition of commerce. And, if what he did was not commerce, then the Interstate Commerce Clause could not apply to give Congress the power to issue anything.

The Supreme Court demurred. Justice Marshall wrote that commerce should be broadly defined to include "intercourse, all its branches." So, you would be engaging in commerce if you swapped money for goods, money for services, services for goods, goods for goods, etc. Hence, the Congressional license granted to Gibbons was the valid one since the national government and not the state of New York was constitutionally empowered to regulate commercial activities that involved more than one state, which the steamboat ferry service did. This broad interpretation of what constituted commerce would let Congress use the Interstate Commerce Clause as a rationale to regulate many things over the next two centuries, much to the chagrin of many states. While during this time period the Court would occasionally reformulate its ruling on the matter (sometimes contracting when the clause could apply only to re-expand it at a later time), the clause has still always remained a powerful resource for the federal government (see *Gibbons v. Ogden*, 1824).

The final truly significant Supreme Court case that qualified federalism during its age of supremacy was that of *John Barron v. The Mayor and City Council of Baltimore*, which was decided in 1833. Barron owned part of a lucrative wharf in the Baltimore harbor. He sued Baltimore for damages, claiming that when the city had diverted the flow of several streams to facilitate road work, the diversion caused sand and silt to collect around his wharf. Barron asserted that this hurt his business by making the water around the wharf too shallow to accommodate many big vessels that sought to dock and unload their cargos there. Barron won the suit in the lower court, but Baltimore appealed the ruling, eventually all the way up to the Supreme Court.

The key issue in the case was whether or not state government takings of private property for public use (known in the law as "eminent domain," which, essentially, this was) required just compensation to individuals deprived of property. The Court held that while the Fifth Amendment of the U.S. Constitution did require this, the requirement only applied to the *federal* government and not the several state governments. Importantly, the Court essentially ruled that the freedoms guaranteed by the Bill of Rights did not restrict the state governments but, rather, applied only to the federal government. This qualifier was important in the development of federalism because it furthered a divide between federal and state governments (see *Barron v. Mayor of Baltimore*, 1833).

The Era of "Dual Federalism"

While the Supreme Court's rulings in both *McCulloch* and *Gibbons* interpreted constitutional language in such a way that favored the federal government over the states, this would not always be the outcome. Over the next several decades following these decisions, the Court would be asked many times to decide just how far federal government power extended. The justices occasionally ruled against the federal government, thereby firming up the power of state governments.

Perhaps the most (in)famous instance of this occurred in the 1857 case of *Dred Scott v. Sandford*. In this dispute, an African American slave sued for his freedom after moving with his owners from the slave-holding South to a free state in the North, believing his residence on free soil had ended his slave status. In an extremely controversial opinion, the Court held that Scott and other slaves should be "regarded as beings of an inferior order" not considered citizens of the United States, and so prohibited from filing suit in federal court. From a federalism standpoint, the case is significant because the Court declared that Congress lacked the power to ban slavery in the western territories such as Kansas and Nebraska, something it had attempted to do with the Missouri Compromise of 1820. States, then, and their citizens, would determine the fate of the "peculiar institution" (as slavery was sometimes euphemistically called) within their borders, not the federal government (see *Dred Scott v. Sandford*, 1856).

Supreme Court rulings like that in *Dred Scott* that conferred power on state governments or rulings like those in *McCulloch* and *Gibbons* that conferred power on the national government collectively created what political scientists refer to as **dual federalism**. Under this scheme, the federal government and the state governments are viewed as each having their own "sphere of influence" in which each exercises power and into which the other may not encroach. The national government derives its power to control everything in its sphere largely from the expressed and implied powers of the U.S. Constitution. The state governments control their spheres and keep the federal government out of their business largely thanks to the Reserved Powers Clause in the Tenth Amendment.

A time-honored model used by American government students to visualize the arrangement of dual federalism is a two-layer cake. Think of the federal government as being the top layer and the state governments as being the bottom layer. Each otherwise identical layer of cake is analogous to a sphere of influence, and each is separated from the other by a thick layer of gooey icing, an insulating confection whipped together by the U.S. Constitution.

The basic belief in dual federalism controlled American constitutional jurisprudence until the 1930s. Despite the notion of duality, the federal government's overall power as compared to the states arguably, if gradually, increased during this interval. Perhaps the biggest factor for this increase was the Civil War. Ironically, this conflict that started out to increase the power of state governments ended up augmenting the national government's power in many ways. For example, the federal income tax came into being. This taxation gave the national government a revenue source it had not possessed before. The tax would eventually become a permanent fixture in American life with the ratification of the Sixteenth Amendment and provide the federal government with vast capital resources (see U.S. Department of the Treasury, 2010).

Also out of the Civil War came the Thirteenth, Fourteenth, and Fifteenth Amendments to the U.S. Constitution. These so-called "Civil War Amendments" all dealt with race and sought to uplift free-blacks in whatever state they lived. However, judicial rulings like *Plessy v. Ferguson* (discussed in detail in Chapter 11) often thwarted this aim by returning power to states to make their own civil rights laws.

Some years after the war, another kind of fight would increase the federal government's power. Congress enacted the Sherman Antitrust Act in 1890 to combat the growth of corporate monopolies in America. This act permitted the federal government, not the states, to regulate many aspects of business and commerce in the name of protecting consumers from anti-competitive practices.

While the Civil War Amendments and the Sherman Act empowered the federal government, not everything during the era of dual federalism was a loss for state governments. Supreme Court rulings in some cases, like *Plessy*, empowered states. For example, states enjoyed relative autonomy to legislate in the areas of voting and civil rights within their own separate spheres.

The Era of "Cooperative Federalism"

Dual federalism became old news in 1933 with the advent of the New Deal. "New Deal" was the name given to a collection of radical government programs championed by President Franklin Roosevelt to get the United States out of the economic quagmire that was the Great Depression. Almost any problem one could think of (unemployment, crime, etc.) loomed large in America during this age. About the only entity anyone believed was sizable enough to even stand a chance at combating these ills was the federal government. Congress enacted law after law, creating new federal agencies geared toward promoting some aspect of economic recovery. These agencies had names like the Civilian Conservation Corps or the Tennessee Valley Authority, but were more often known by their initials. Collectively, history knows the CCC, the TVA, and others somewhat jokingly as the "Alphabet Soup Agencies." The laws that created them demanded cooperation from multiple levels of government.

The laws associated with the New Deal demanded that multiple levels of government (federal, state, and, now for the first time, often municipal governments) work together on implementation. For example, the federal government might do something like provide funds to a state that would then hire some of its unemployed citizens to, in turn, complete a roadwork project for a city. Because of the governmental interconnectedness inherent in this arrangement, political scientists refer to this as **cooperative federalism**. Recall that under dual federalism, the different levels of government operated autonomously within their separate spheres of influence—little cooperation there, to be sure. With the advent of this new kind of federalism, the lines between governmental spheres blurred and became more fluid.

Of course, this changing federalism requires a change of metaphor as well since a slice of layer cake will always reveal two distinct parts separated from each other by frosting. Think of cooperative federalism as being illustrated by a piece of marble cake instead. A slice of that confection—when viewed from the side—reveals a swirling, intermixing of light and dark cake. Just as it is difficult to discern precisely where one cake starts and the other stops in a marble cake, cooperative federalism accepts that the boundaries of power for federal, state, and local governments are no longer fixed and distinct.

You will probably have surmised that the shift from dual federalism to cooperative federalism was a radical one. Many people feared this unprecedented growth of the federal bureaucracy, and some filed legal challenges to New Deal legislation that made it all the way to the Supreme Court. Initially, the Court overturned much of the legislation. The justices often agreed with challengers that aspects of the New Deal conferred too much power on the national government.

President Roosevelt fumed. In private, he derisively referred to the justices as the "nine old men." Publicly, he proposed a plan that would essentially have given him and a sympathetic Congress the power to expand the Supreme Court from nine to fifteen justices. Of course, the additional jurists he would install would be New Deal supporters.

Roosevelt's **court-packing plan**, as it came to be known, proved to be largely unpopular with the American people, who resented his effort to tamper with the judiciary. However, merely proffering the plan may have had the effect FDR desired. Perhaps a bit spooked by the court-packing threat, the high court began ruling in favor of much New Deal legislation starting around 1935. These rulings cleared the way for Congress to increase its sway over states (see Leuchtenburg, 1969).

Since the New Deal era, the primary tool employed by the federal government to induce states and municipalities to do their share of the cooperating in cooperative federalism was something called a **categorical grant**. A grant is simply an assignment of funds—usually a lot of funds when it is a federal program in question. The federal government had provided a few grant programs to states over the years prior to the Great Depression (such as the Morrill Land Grant Act of 1862, which gave states federal land to establish public colleges), but these were nothing compared to New Deal grant programs in either size or scope. The term "categorical" is meant to describe how Congress doles out federal dollars to states to accomplish distinct things in some particular area—as opposed to giving states money to spend however they might wish.

Using categorical grants, Congress can, for all intents and purposes, regulate just about anything. Indeed, even though the Tenth Amendment reserves some powers to states, Congress can often tempt states with grants to induce them to police something in a way desired by the federal government. For example, there was a period of time during the 1970s where many oil-rich Arab countries instituted an oil embargo against the United States, mostly to punish Americans for historical support of Israel. Gasoline prices spiked, hours-long lines at pumps were common, and many places ran out of gas entirely as refinery oil supplies dwindled. The federal government wanted the nation to drive slower to conserve fuel. However, setting speed limits is a classic police power, and lowering them is something only individual states could do thanks to the Tenth Amendment. Still, the federal government would get its way. It offered states large grants of highway improvement money if they would only lower their interstate speed limits to 55 mph. Hungry for those highway funds, virtually all did so in a relatively short time. Hence, the national government accomplished its goal almost just as if it had regulated things directly (see Weiner, 1997).

Beginning in the 1960s, the tone of cooperation between the states and the federal government began to change. Prior to that decade, most states had been generally content to work with the federal government under the terms of categorical grants, believing as they did that the two levels of government shared common aims. However, as the federal government advanced programs to combat poverty and discrimination under the Kennedy and Johnson administrations, many states—particularly in the South—abandoned this view. This occurred largely because the national government found ways to bypass state legislatures en route to achieving national objectives. Local governments and even community organizations received much federal funding, since Congress believed they would be more likely than several staunchly conservative states to spend money in ways benefitting African Americans and other marginalized groups. From many states' points of view, the cooperation in federalism had disappeared.

Equally vexing for states was the fact that many of the federal government programs that did emerge in the 1960s and 1970s contained what are known as **unfunded federal mandates**. Put simply, this term means that the federal government enacted some regulation that states were required to abide by but gave no money to states to spend for this purpose. For example, in 1974, Congress passed the Safe Drinking Water Act. Essentially, this act stated that public water sources had to meet Environmental Protection Agency standards of purity within a given time frame. While everyone will agree that clean drinking water is a good thing, Congress left to the states and local governments the responsibility and expense of getting water supplies tested and of removing pollutants and impurities if any were found. Governments that did not comply with the act faced stiff federal penalties and, in extreme circumstances, could be forced to find some other water supply—however inconvenient or expensive doing so might be. State and local governments, already short of time and money, bristled at what they saw as unreasonable burdens imposed by SDWA. This and other unfunded federal mandates would eventually be amended or repealed so as to lessen the burden on state and local governments; however, while they were in effect, relations between these governments and the federal government strained.

"New Federalism" and Beyond

Ronald Reagan assumed the presidency in 1981 with an eye toward vastly curbing federal government power that had increased thanks to the growth of unfunded mandates and the deterioration of cooperative federalism. Reagan, a conservative political thinker dubious of big government, served as governor of the state of California from 1967 to 1975. He had experienced firsthand the frustration visited upon states by the federal government and unfunded mandates. Reagan sought to shrink federal government power and return more autonomy to the states by greatly reducing unfunded mandates and by changing how federal grants operated. In doing so, he built upon the groundwork laid by another Republican president, Richard Nixon, who had initiated a practice of *revenue sharing* in 1972 in an effort to shift some power and responsibility back to state and local government through a federal assistance program.

Political scientists refer to what Reagan ushered in as **New Federalism** because of its novelty. It had several key features. Soon after assuming office, President Reagan rallied public opinion to urge Congress to make drastic cuts in both federal domestic programs and income tax rates. This action created an environment in which the federal government took in less revenue and had fewer programs to disburse back to the states the revenue it *did* collect. Consequently, state and local governments had to become more self-sufficient, which lessened the power the federal government had over them.

But things did not stop there. Another key feature of New Federalism was a heavy reliance on **block grants**. Recall that in cooperative federalism, the federal government offered states and municipalities categorical grants. These grants came with many strings attached and required states to spend any federal dollars they received doing very specific things. Block grants are very unlike categorical grants because states and local governments receive sums of money along with better flexibility in determining how the funding can be spent. Additionally, federal government oversight or monitoring of block grant funds is relatively light. All of these actions had the effect of reducing the influence of the federal government over state and local governments since the power of the purse is effectively transferred to the latter. While block grants had been around in one form or another since the 1960s or so, New Federalism employed them with a gusto not yet seen in the United States to give states increased agency in governing areas ranging from healthcare to education to transportation, etc.

The trends of New Federalism and the downsizing of the federal government generally continued to some extent for many years after President Reagan left office in 1989. For example, in the 1990s, the Clinton administration encouraged states to explore new ideas and options for policymaking. However, they had no trouble imposing federal solutions on problems that states failed to solve. Republicans gained a majority in Congress in the 1994 elections by promoting their "Contract with America." Much of this "contract" was devoted to decreasing the size of the federal government. Some provisions became law; many did not. While it may be debated as to just how much the Contract succeeded in curtailing the size and power of the federal government, that was certainly its aim.

While President George W. Bush campaigned on a platform of continuing to return power to state and local governments in 2000, the events of September 11, 2001, made doing so largely infeasible. Rather, the federal bureaucracy and the power wielded by it swelled as America fought enemies foreign and domestic and, later, grappled with natural disasters and economic crises.

The direction federalism took under the administration of President Barack Obama is not entirely settled. Obama championed a major expansion of federal policy, including an historic health care bill, a huge overhaul of financial regulation, a bail-out of America's automotive industry, the "race to the top" educational grants, sweeping immigration and gun control reforms, and heavy investment in "green" technologies. While critics asserted that these could only lead to bigger national government, states may not be out of the picture. Political scientist Caroline Cournoyer (2011) observed that Obama pursued a "unique mixture of collaborative and coercive strategies in dealing with states and localities, making it hard to define just what kind of federalism we're seeing." Cournoyer and others see a "nuanced federalism" combining both incentive grants and mandates (carrots and sticks, if you will) to gain state compliance with presidential designs.

The Trump administration's view of federalism is difficult to pin down. Since President Trump identities as a conservative, many thought he would favor curtailing federal power. Trump administration officials initially *did* express interest in curbing federal power in some areas, such as education policy. However, Trump also seemed to spurn state authority at times. For instance, he publicly criticized states supportive of "Sanctuary Cities" (cities electing not to aggressively enforce federal immigration policy) and encouraged more federal anti-narcotics policing in states moving to legalize recreational use of marijuana. Even the COVID-19 pandemic saw mixed messages from Trump regarding federal and state power. With states issuing shelter-at-home orders to combat the virus in the spring of 2020, Trump tweeted that it is "the decision of the President" as to when states would reopen (Forgey & Gerstein, 2020). Yet when states asked the federal government for medical supplies, Trump said that this is a task "for the local governments, governors and people in the state" (Forgey, 2020). Yet that summer, Trump dispatched federal law enforcement agents to Portland, Oregon, to quell protests. Given these examples, President Trump's views on federalism remained somewhat indeterminate throughout his term.

The precise state of federalism under the administration of Democratic President Joe Biden has been perhaps similarly inconclusive. Without doubt, Biden at times vigorously asserted federal government power over that of states. For instance, beginning around 2021, Republican Governor Greg Abbott of Texas sought to halt illegal immigration into his state from Mexico. Along the Texas-Mexico border at the Rio Grande River, he deployed Texas National Guardsmen. He also ordered buoys afloat in the river to prevent swimmers from crossing and had concertina razor wire fencing strung along its banks. President Biden, asserting that immigration matters are exclusively within federal, not state, purview, directed federal border patrol agents to cut or remove the fencing. Biden has also irked states with what one author described as policies to "liberate localities from the overweening power of state governments." Biden-championed legislation such as the American Rescue Plan and the Bipartisan Infrastructure Law directed much federal funding directly to American cities—bypassing state governments—to improve infrastructure, pay for social programs, and to shrink budget deficits. Yet, these same programs gave much money to states as well, mainly for highway and bridge construction or improvement. Biden's views on federalism may be informed by his past officeholding. He is one of about ten presidents—and the only one since Harry S. Truman—to have ever served in local government; Biden was a member of the County Council of New Castle County, Delaware, for two years prior to being elected to the U.S. Senate in 1972.

Federalism and the Modern Supreme Court: A (Slow) Return to States' Rights?

For most of the twentieth century, the U.S. Supreme Court generally sided with the federal government when adjudicating legal questions of federalism. Consequently, the power of the national government expanded just as that of the various states contracted. This judicial trend would shift somewhat beginning in the 1980s. As part and parcel of New Federalism, President Reagan appointed jurists who attempted to return some power to states through their legal opinions. On topics ranging from gun control to abortion to gambling on Indian reservations to physician assisted suicide, the Supreme Court handed down decisions that restricted Congress's power and rendered the states somewhat more sovereign.

The Court's recent shift toward favoring state governments has not been absolute, however. For example, in a pair of cases decided in 2004 and 2006, the justices ruled that under the Americans with Disabilities Act, Congress could require states to make their courthouses and prison facilities reasonably accessible to handicapped individuals. Also, in 2012 in the case of *Arizona v. U.S.*, the Court struck down parts of a state law that essentially would have given local law enforcement officers the authority to enforce immigration law on the grounds that federal law preempted state involvement in such matters. That same year, the Court upheld Congress' power to enact most provisions of the Patient Protection and Affordable Care Act (ACA), commonly called Obamacare, which riled some state governments. Whether these holdings herald a return for the Court to old habits or are merely aberrations along a path toward recognizing greater state sovereignty remains to be seen.

Civic Engagement and Federalism

The sheer size and scope of the United States government has doubtlessly prompted more than one person to ask, "What difference can a single individual possibly make in governing?" Indeed, unless that one person happens to be the president of the United States, a Supreme Court justice, or the like, it will probably be difficult to directly influence national policy to any great degree. However, thanks to federalism, other opportunities for civic engagement actually exist for just about anyone. Federalism encourages democratic participation by dividing government powers and responsibilities between different levels of government— and some of those levels are very accessible. The trick is to know what level of government to approach about any given issue. Given the overlapping complexity of government, discerning the layers can oftentimes be difficult. However, with diligence and an understanding of how federalism operates, one can tease out the correct federal, state, or local entity to approach about virtually any problem. The Internet can be a citizen's best friend in accomplishing this task. While the mechanics of federalism are still fresh in your mind, make it a point to visit the websites of your local, state, and federal governments. As you browse those pages, you will begin to get a sense of what agencies and departments deal with what and, just as importantly, how you can contact them. Do this and you will be doing some good, since, as Thomas Jefferson observed, "Whenever the people are well-informed, they can be trusted with their own government."

Discussion Questions

1. What is federalism? What powers does the U.S. Constitution confer on the national government? What powers does the U.S. Constitution confer on the several state governments? What powers are shared by and denied to both the federal and the state governments?

2. What is "horizontal federalism" and what are the parts of the U.S. Constitution that function to place all states on a level playing field?

3. How were the Supreme Court rulings in the cases of *McCulloch v. Maryland* and *Gibbons v. Ogden* important for federalism?
4. Compare and contrast "dual federalism," "cooperative federalism," "New Federalism," and "New Age Federalism."
5. What is the current state of U.S. Supreme Court jurisprudence on the topic of federalism?

References

Cournoyer, C. (2011). What brand of Federalism is next? *Potomac Chronicle.* https://www.governing.com/archive/gov-col-what-brand-of-federalism-is-next.html

Forgey, Q. (2020, March 19). *'We're not a shipping clerk': Trump tells governors to step up efforts to get medical supplies.* Politico. https://www.politico.com/news/2020/03/19/trump-governors-coronavirus-medical-supplies-137658

Forgey, Q., and Gerstein, J. (2020, April 13). *Trump: It's my decision, not governors', to reopen country.* Politico. https://www.politico.com/news/2020/04/13/trump-governors-decision-reopen-183405

Leuchtenburg, W. E. (1969). Franklin D. Roosevelt's Supreme Court 'packing' plan. In H. M. Hollingsworth & W. F. Holmes (Eds.), *Essays on the New Deal* (69–115). University of Texas Press.

Norris, W. (2023, April 4). How Biden is using federal power to liberate localities. *Washington Monthly.* https://washingtonmonthly.com/2023/04/04/how-biden-is-using-federal-power-to-liberate-localities/

Safe Drinking Water Act (SDWA). (P.L. 93-523), *United States statutes at large.* 88 Stat. 1660.

United States Department of the Treasury. (2010, December 5). *History of the U.S. tax system.* Retrieved September 12, 2024 from https://web.archive.org/web/20111028144429/http://www.treasury.gov/resource-center/faqs/Taxes/Pages/historyrooseveltmessage.aspx

Weiner, E. (1997). *Urban transportation planning in the United States—An historical overview, September 1997.* United States Department of Transportation. https://rosap.ntl.bts.gov/view/dot/42349

Court Cases

Arizona v United States, 567 U.S. (2012).

Barron v. Mayor of Baltimore, 32 U.S. 243 (1833).

Dred Scott v. Sandford, 60 U.S. 393 (1856).

Franchise Tax Bd. of Cal. v. Hyatt, 538 U.S. 488 (2003).

Gibbons v. Ogden, 22 U.S. 1 (1824).

McCulloch v. Maryland, 17 U.S. 316 (1819).

Obergefell v. Hodges, 576 U.S. (2015).

Puerto Rico v. Branstad, 483 U.S. 219 (1987).

Sun Oil Co. v. Wortman, 486 U.S. 717, 722 (1988).

Tennessee v. Lane, 541 U.S. 509 (2004).

United States v. Georgia, 546 U.S. 151 (2006).

Younger v. Harris, 401 U.S. 37 (1971).

Political Socialization and the News Media

Glen Smith

Learning Objectives

After covering the topics of political socialization and the communications media, students should understand:

1. How the most important agents of political socialization affect ideology, tolerance, and participation.
2. What political tolerance is and why some people are more tolerant than others.
3. The most important factors affecting political activity.
4. How the news media affects political attitudes, hostility, and participation.

Abstract

This chapter provides an introduction to political socialization and the news media. The first part of the chapter explains how political norms, values, and modes of behavior are transmitted through social institutions. The most important agents of political socialization are families, schools, peer groups, and the media. Each agent has distinct effects on political ideology, tolerance, and participation. The remainder of the chapter provides a brief history of the news media, and explains how different types of media have distinct effects on political beliefs, hostility toward political leaders, and activity in the political system. Case studies explain the gender gap among elected officials and the basics of public opinion polling.

Introduction

Where do Americans get their political beliefs? Why do blacks and atheists tend to vote for Democrats while most whites and Mormons vote for Republicans? Why does politics make some people angry while others enjoy discussing the issues of the day? Why do some people vote in every election, and attend town hall meetings, while others largely ignore politics altogether? The answers to these questions begin with political socialization, which the American Psychological Association (n.d.) defines as "the transmission of political norms through social agents, such as schools, parents, peers, or the mass media." As this definition neatly suggests, the four principal agents of political socialization are families, schools, peer groups, and the media.

Each agent of political socialization affects how people develop their political ideology, tolerance, and desire to participate in the political system. First, **political ideology** is a "set of interconnected beliefs, held by a group of individuals, which explains their preferences on individual political issues that vary along a single liberal–conservative dimension" (Carmines and D'Amico, 2015, p. 207). As the definition suggests, ideology is a broad term encompassing what people want the government to do in terms of taxing, spending, crime, foreign policy, public participation, and so on. For the most part, **conservatives** support traditional values, individualism, low taxes, economic freedom, a strong national defense, and strict adherence to law and order. In contrast, **liberals** typically believe in evolving morals, a strong social safety net, progressive taxation, rehabilitation for criminals, and using the military to promote peace and human rights. While liberals are more likely to believe that people are products of their environments, conservatives tend to believe people are ultimately responsible for their own outcomes. Conservatives believe that social safety net programs, although well intentioned, create dependence rather than hard work and self-reliance. Liberals believe that people do not succeed or fail on their own, but instead rely on a social system to succeed and that those benefiting from that system the most (the wealthy) owe a debt to the social system that allowed their success to flourish.

Ideology is also complex when it comes to the role of government in society. For the most part, conservatives desire limited government intervention into economic matters, such as economic and environment regulations, because they strongly believe that competition in the free market will bring about the best outcomes for society. Conversely, liberals believe that the unrestrained free market creates excesses such as income inequality, environmental pollution, worker abuse, among other things. Although it is tempting to say that liberals want more government and conservatives want less, that is not the case for social policy regarding personal freedom. Conservatives tend to support laws that use the legal code to outlaw (what they deem as) immoral behavior such as abortion, drug use, gambling, gay marriage, and prostitution. Meanwhile, liberals are more likely to oppose government restrictions on personal behavior and to support forgiving punishments for criminal offenses. In short, political ideology in the

United States is multifaceted and complex, involving a mix of social and economic views regarding the proper role of government in society.

Americans differ in their **tolerance** toward people who disagree with their political views. Gibson and Bingham (1982) define political tolerance as "a willingness to extend the rights of citizenship to all members of the polity—that is, to allow political freedoms to those who are politically different" (p. 604). Indeed, it is easy to tolerate those who are exactly like us, and espouse beliefs we agree with, but true tolerance includes the willingness to extend the same rights and freedoms we desire to people whose beliefs we find highly objectionable. Finally, people vary in their opportunity and willingness to **participate** in the political system to bring about desired outcomes. Political activity can come in several forms such as: voting, donating, volunteering, slapping a bumper sticker on your car, or trying to persuade a friend to vote in the next election.[1] All things equal, people engage in the political system to the extent that they 1) care about a political outcome, 2) believe they can bring about the outcome—called **political efficacy**—and 3) have the resources to engage in politics effectively. In this chapter, we will examine how each agent of socialization—family, schools, peers, and media—influences each political outcome of interest in American politics: ideology, tolerance, and participation. Although neither of these lists are exhaustive, they provide a good starting point for an introduction to the role of political socialization in American politics.

Family

Family is the first and most influential agent of political socialization (Jennings et al., 2009). For better or worse, parents and caregivers pass down political ideology, participation habits, and tolerance of other racial, ethnic, and religious groups to their children. This does not mean that children always grow up to match their caregivers' political beliefs and behavior. Some children rebel against their upbringing or live in politically apathetic households that pass down few political values. Nonetheless, it is difficult to understate the role of families in helping children formulate their political orientation at an early age. For example, a 2019 survey from the Pew Research Center found that "eight-in-ten parents who were Republican or leaned toward the Republican Party (81%) had teens who also identified as Republicans or leaned that way. And about nine-in-ten parents

---

1   Of course, some people have more opportunity to affect political outcomes given their social or economic situation. I may want to donate $1 million to a political cause I support, but that's simply not possible given my financial situation. Meanwhile others have the resources to write checks beyond that amount to support the political cause they believe in.

who were Democratic or leaned Democratic (89%) had teens who described themselves the same way" (Cooperman, 2023). Clearly, parents are very likely to pass their party identification down to their children.

How do parents shape their children's political beliefs and behavior? Biological parents influence children's political beliefs through a combination of nature and nurture, while non-biological parents only influence the nurture side of the equation. Research suggests that biological parents pass down political ideology, tolerance, and participation through genetic transmission (Alford et al., 2005; Fowler et al., 2008). Genetics influence political beliefs by way of cognitive traits (Dawes et al., 2014). People have different personalities, and their brains function in different ways. For example, some people have more negative emotional reactions to disorder in their lives, while others are more comfortable in those situations. Think of the difference between Bert and Ernie from *Sesame Street*, where Bert liked an ordered, neat environment, while Ernie was comfortable with disorder and less rigid boundaries. A desire for order in one's personal life often translates to the social world, and in doing so affects political beliefs. Those favoring social order (Bert) would be more supportive of the death penalty, militaristic foreign policy, laws enforcing traditional values, and prohibitions on drug use, than those more comfortable with disorder (Ernie).

One important study helps illustrate the power of genetics to influence political ideology. Alfred, Hibbing, and Funk (2005) compared the ideological similarities of identical and fraternal twins. Both types of twins are exposed to the same environment. Or rather, there is no systematic difference between the childhoods of identical twins compared to fraternal twins, thus controlling for *nurture* and isolating *nature* (genetics) as a treatment condition.[2] Identical twins share 100 percent of their DNA, while fraternal twins share only 50 percent of their genetic makeup. If genetics do not influence political ideology, identical twins would be no more similar in their ideology than fraternal twins. Conversely, if identical twins are more likely than fraternal twins to share ideology with their twin, it is likely because their genetics are more similar, and not because they shared a similar environment. The study found that when compared to fraternal twins, *identical twins are more similar in both their political ideology and tendency to engage in political activity* (Alford et al., 2005; Fowler et al., 2008). Furthermore, even identical twins who were separated at birth, and raised by different families, grew up to be more similar in their political ideology than fraternal twins who were also separated at birth. The authors

---

2 In social science, this is called a natural experiment, i.e. when reality creates a control and treatment group.

estimate that *roughly 50 percent* of societal differences in political ideology are caused by genetics rather than social upbringing.

To be clear, genetics does not predetermine someone to be liberal or conservative. Instead, parents genetically pass down mental processes and personality traits that predispose their child—all things being equal—to interpret the world in such a way that they will develop a similar political ideology. For example, if a liberal and conservative have the same experiences, their unique brain chemistry and cognitive functioning—that was largely passed down from their parents—will predispose them to interpret those experiences in distinct ways that fit the conservative or liberal ideologies, respectively. Parents pass down personality traits and cognitive processes that affect how people interpret their experiences. Those interpretations result in policy preferences and motivations to engage in political activity.

Religion is another important way families pass down political ideology to their children. Taking children to religious services, and discussing religion at home, socializes children into particular ways of looking at the world that have widespread effects on political beliefs. For many Americans, religious beliefs influence a variety of policy preferences surrounding abortion, drug use, the death penalty, gay marriage, free speech, public education, foreign affairs, etc. According to the Pew Research Center, over 80 percent of parents had the same religious affiliation as their teenage children (Cooperman, 2023). Although a good portion of children may stray from their parents' religion during adulthood, most children maintain the same religion all the way through their twenties. For example, a 2015 Pew survey (ibid) found that among American *adults* "eight in ten of those raised Protestant (79%) were still Protestant. About six-in-ten of those raised Catholic were still Catholic (62%), and an identical proportion of those raised with no religious affiliation were still unaffiliated (62%)." In short, parents are very effective at passing down their political and religious identities to their children, and more often than not, those affiliations last a lifetime.

In addition to passing down group identifications, parents also transmit tolerance towards people who belong to other social and political groups. Families affect political tolerance by subtle and overt comments made about other political and social groups, but also the diversity of their social interactions. Children overhear comments about other races, ethnicities, religions, sexual orientations, and political groups. How parents talk about dissimilar social groups is very influential in the formative years of childhood. One study found that even preschool-aged children already understood group dynamics and mimicked parental attitudes toward other social groups (Reifen-Tagar and Cimpian, 2022). The study also argued that parents pass down authoritarian and social dominance orientation to children, which has substantial effects on political attitudes, tolerance, and support for democratic norms throughout life. Moreover, parents teach their children to distrust and dislike political leaders, and everyday Americans, who belong to the opposing political party (Lay et al., 2022; Tyler and Iyengar, 2023). Some parents teach their children (intentionally or not) to distrust, dislike, and even hate Democrats or Republicans from a young age, which often results in discrimination, intolerance, and poor decision-making throughout the rest of their lives (Iyengar and Westwood, 2015). In short, be careful how you talk about other political and social groups in front of your children. They are little sponges for love or hate. You need to decide which they soak up.

Another way parents influence tolerance is the diversity of groups they associate with. Even when unintentional, sending children to diverse schools increases the chances that they will get to know and accept people of different races. Conversely, a child attending an all-white (or black, Hispanic, Asian, etc.) school will be more likely to internalize negative stereotypes about other races. The same is true for childhood contact with dissimilar religions, ethnicities, and sexual and political orientations. When parents rarely expose their children to actual people who belong to dissimilar social groups, members of those groups will seem foreign and untrustworthy. When children are isolated from diversity, they are also likely to adopt common negative stereotypes of dissimilar social groups, which become the basis for prejudice and bigotry.

Finally, families influence their children's political participation habits. Once again, biological parents pass down personality traits that predispose their children to become more (or less) likely to be politically active in their adult lives. Gerber and colleagues (2011) found that personality traits, which are largely passed down from parents through genetics, predispose people to engage in political activity later in life. Specifically, those scoring higher in extroversion, and openness to different experiences, were more likely to participate. Meanwhile, higher levels of neuroticism—also genetically transmitted—make people less active in the political system. Just as parents socialize their children into religions, they also socialize children into political activity by setting an example of appropriate behavior. Families socialize children to participate in politics by participating in or ignoring politics themselves (Krupnikov and Ryan, 2022). When parents bring their kids along when they vote, place yard signs before elections, attend town hall meetings, or volunteer for political campaigns, they establish norms of behavior that children are likely to emulate. Even something as simple as talking about politics, or ignoring it entirely, can have important long-term effects on political participation.

As McIntosh and colleagues (2007) show, "Adolescents who discuss politics and current events with their parents, peers, or teachers tend to score higher than other youth on measures of civic behaviors, attitudes, and skills. They develop higher levels of political knowledge, show greater intention to vote in the future, and do better on a range of civic outcomes from petitioning and boycotting to raising money for charities and participating in community meetings" (p. 495). By simply talking about politics with their children, parents are helping them become more active, informed, and engaged citizens for the rest of their lives.

Case Study: Why Do Men Dominate Politics? One Reason Is Political Socialization.

A little over a century ago, women gained the right to vote nationwide with the passage of the 19th Amendment. Unfortunately, gaining the right to participate in elections did not result in equal representation among the sexes. Despite being a majority of the U.S. population, women hold a relatively small percentage of seats in local, state, and federal offices. Indeed, women currently hold less than 30 percent of the seats in the U.S. House of Representatives and only a quarter (25%) of the seats in the Senate (Leppert and Desilver, 2023). At the state level, women currently hold roughly one-third (32%) of state legislative seats across the country. And these numbers mark all-time highs! At the turn of the new millennium, for example, women made up only 15 percent of both the U.S. House and Senate. Although female representation in Congress has increased in the last quarter century, it still has a long way to go to match representation in the population.

Why are women underrepresented in Congress? One part of the answer may come from political socialization. An interesting study found that social cues give young girls the impression that politics is a male-dominated profession where women don't belong (Bos et al., 2022). This results in girls growing up to seek more "female professions" like teaching and nursing. Furthermore, women who were taught that they don't belong in politics end up having less interest in politics overall. This is an important consequence because political interest is a key motivator for participation in the political system. This false belief that politics is a man's game becomes self-fulfilling. If women grow up thinking they don't belong in politics, they have less interest and participate less frequently. That behavior models political apathy for their daughters. Meanwhile, fewer women running for office results in most prominent elected officials being males, which furthers the false impression that politics is a man's game.

The good news is that as women take on more prominent roles in state and local government, it changes public perceptions. Over just the last 20 years, America has seen the first female Speaker of the House, Nancy Pelosi, the first female nominee for one of the major political parties (Hillary Clinton), and the first female vice president of the United States in Kamala Harris. The Republican Party has also elevated women to prominent roles such as Supreme Court Justices Sandra Day O'Connor and Amy Coney Barrett, Secretary of State Condoleezza Rice, vice presidential nominee Sarah Palin, and 2024's runner-up for the party's presidential nomination, Nikki Haley. There is also a larger share of female governors among both political parties. Regardless of how you feel about the specific women mentioned above, they all show young girls of all partisan leanings that women can be just as successful as men in the political arena. When young girls see women holding positions of political power, it becomes the norm rather than the exception.

Schools

Schools are another important agent of political socialization. In a normal week, students will spend close to 30 hours in school. Given their prominent role in children's lives, schools have an important role to play in political socialization by promoting national identity, shared culture, and a basic understanding of American history, civics, and government. Each of these things prepares future generations to be effective citizens. Democracy benefits from an informed, engaged, and patriotic citizenry. When people feel a stronger national identity, also called nationalism, they are more politically informed, engaged in current events, and likely to consistently vote in elections (Huddy and Khatib, 2007). Americans are also better citizens when they understand how the government works and recognize the most effective ways to influence the political system (Carpini and Keeter, 1996).

Of course, political socialization does not stop once someone turns 18 years old and enters adulthood. The next step in political socialization occurs when students enter higher education or opt out of that environment. There has been a great deal of research on the effects of higher education on political attitudes, tolerance, and political participation. The more formal education someone has, the more tolerant they become towards different races, religions, and sexual orientations (Bobo and Licari, 1989). Higher education also increases political tolerance as those attending college are more likely to extend civil rights and liberties to political groups that they dislike.

Research also shows that higher education increases political participation. Compared to Americans who never attended college, those attaining a four-year degree are more likely to vote and participate in politics. As Verba and colleagues state, "Educational attainment is, in fact, the single most potent predictor of an adult's political activity" (2003, p. 13). Higher education improves cognitive ability, facilitates knowledge acquisition, enhances civic skills, and provides political information. For example, Americans with a four-year college degree are more likely to vote in national elections than those without one. Highly educated voters also tend to vote more consistently across elections. The Pew Research Center examined voting across three national elections in 2018, 2020, and 2022 (Hartig et al., 2023). About half of college-educated Americans voted in all three of those elections, and 82 percent voted in at least one. Meanwhile, only 29 percent of voters without a college degree voted in all three elections, and 69 percent voted in at least one election. In other words, over one in three (36%) Americans without a college degree sat out all three national elections from 2018–2022, compared to only 18 percent of Americans with a college degree. In short, higher education increases political participation.

Peer Groups

When young people are not at home or in school, they're usually hanging out with their friends. Research in political socialization shows that peer groups have only minimal effects on ideology, largely because young people tend to hang out with politically like-minded friends (Campbell, 1980). Peer groups can increase tolerance, however, as long as they are socially diverse in their membership. If children grow up associating with members of dissimilar racial, ethnic, and religious groups, they are less likely to adopt negative stereotypes about members of those groups. When it comes to political participation, some research suggests that high schoolers are more knowledgeable and interested in politics when their peer groups are politically active (Dostie-Goulet, 2009). The evidence is correlational, however, making it difficult to determine whether peer groups increase political activity, or political interest affects one's choice of peer group. Although peer groups are an important agent of socialization, they have little effect on political attitudes early in life.

Peer groups play a more important function during adulthood because they serve as political discussion groups. Talking about politics with friends, family, and coworkers has important implications for ideology, tolerance, and political activity. Discussion groups can facilitate the learning of diverse viewpoints, lower animosity toward opposing political groups, and motivate people to participate in politics. Precisely how political discussion groups influence political attitudes and activity depends a great deal on the ideological and partisan diversity of their members. Research examining political discussion uses the terms homogeneous and heterogeneous to describe the partisan composition of group members. On a sliding scale, discussion groups composed of all Democrats or all Republicans are considered completely *homogeneous*, while groups with an equal number of both Parties are perfectly *heterogeneous*. Of course, the same person will find themselves in more homogeneous or heterogeneous discussion groups at different points in time. For example, your family might be homogeneous, but your workplace is more heterogeneous. The first thing to note is that people are more likely to talk about politics when they find themselves in a homogeneous discussion group. Mutz (2006) shows that most people avoid discussion in heterogeneous groups because they fear losing valuable social connections. In other words, they worry that disagreement will make their friends and family mad, resulting in lost friendships and family estrangement.

From the standpoint of what promotes a healthy democracy, and improves decision-making, it is fairly clear that heterogeneous discussion groups are preferred. People are likely to have more complete information when they talk about politics in heterogeneous rather than homogeneous discussion groups (Mutz, 2002). Homogeneous discussion groups only provide one side of a political debate, while heterogeneous discussion partners provide a more complete picture of the trade-offs involved in public policies and political controversies (Mutz, 2001). Research shows that discussing politics in *heterogeneous* groups increases tolerance, decreases extreme opinions, and promotes democratic values (Mutz, 2006). Conversely, talking about politics in *homogeneous* discussion groups makes people more extreme in their political opinions and hostile toward people who disagree.

In homogeneous discussion groups, **groupthink** often occurs because social pressure motivates people to find consensus and unanimity while avoiding valuable dissent and disagreement. Groupthink results from a false consensus where the group believes they are in unanimous agreement because members are afraid to speak up. Each group member privately believes they are the only one disagreeing when in reality others are similarly apprehensive about challenging the seemingly unanimous belief of the group. In extreme circumstances, this results in the "Abilene Paradox". In this paradox, a family travels to Abilene for dinner even though no one wants to go. All members of the group erroneously believe that all the others want to go to Abilene for dinner, and that they are alone in their desire to stay home. Since no one voices their true preference, all members of the group engage in an activity that no one wants. This paradox illustrates both the importance of speaking up, but also the enormous pressure that groups can impose on individual members to conform. In homogeneous discussion groups, individual members are often so worried about losing valuable friendships that it can create an unconscious motivation to adopt whatever beliefs the group holds. If most of your friends believe that the earth is flat, and the moon is made of cheese, fear of losing those friendships would motivate your unconscious mind to believe those things as well. This unconscious motivation is called **motivated reasoning** and makes you biased when evaluating evidence and arguments regarding the shape of the earth or the cheese content of the moon. In short, homogeneous discussion groups lead to one-sided information, poor decision-making, and potentially warped understandings of reality.

Homogeneous discussion groups, and the group pressure that goes along with them, are not all bad, however. The more people talk about politics in homogeneous discussion groups, the more likely they are to vote, attend rallies, and donate to political causes (Mutz, 2006). Peer groups create social pressure to act in ways consistent with group norms. Attending a political rally or school board meeting, and waiting in line to vote, seem more appealing with friends than doing those things alone. Research illustrates how shame can be an important motivator for political action within both in-person and virtual social networks (Panagopoulos, 2010). In an interesting field study, Gerber and colleagues (2010) conducted an experiment where they sent postcards to individual voters telling them that whether they voted in an upcoming election would be made public. Specifically, some subjects in the experiment received a postcard informing them that a local newspaper would publish the names of everyone *who voted* in the next election. Meanwhile, others received a similar postcard telling them that the paper would publish the names of all registered voters who did *not vote* in the election. While publishing the names of voters uses pride as an incentive, publishing the names of nonvoters uses shame to increase voter turnout. The control group in the study did not receive any postcards. Demonstrating the power of shame, the postcards that threatened to publish the names of non-voters increased turnout in the election by 6.9% over the control group who did not receive a postcard. Shame also works within peer groups when friends ask other friends if they're going to vote and perhaps offer to go along. Rosenstone and Hansen (1993) found that simply asking a friend or neighbor if they planned on voting was sufficient to increase turnout. Of course, peer groups are only likely to increase political activity if members are interested or when it is a group norm.

Social media can augment the power of peer groups to increase participation. In a social media experiment involving over 60 million participants, Bond and colleagues (2012) found that allowing people to show Facebook friends that they voted increased turnout, but the effect only worked among Facebook friends who interacted frequently. In other words, the incentive to share that one voted only motivated people to vote when they could tell close contacts. In sum, peer groups have important effects on ideology, tolerance, and participation, but the diversity and activity of the group members determine the specific effects.

History of the News Media

The final agent of political socialization that we are going to examine is the news media. People rely on the news to provide the pictures in their heads about the world outside of their direct experiences. When it comes to perceptions of the national economy, the crime rate, or even natural disasters, direct experience provides insufficient information to hold representatives accountable for their job performance. Rather than rely on subjective experiences, most people base their voting decisions on aggregate conditions at the local, state, and federal level (Mutz, 1992). For example, the unemployment rate has a larger influence on voting decisions than a person's employment situation, but nationwide unemployment only affects those who pay attention to the news on a regular basis. The point is, the news media provide people with the necessary economic, social, and political information that help them make informed voting decisions and hold politicians accountable at the ballot box.

Before examining how the news media affects public opinion, it is necessary to understand its structure, economic incentives, and audience perceptions of its credibility. As is often the case, to understand the present, we need to look to the past. That is, we need to understand the historical evolution of the American news media. Darrell West (2001) argues that we can separate the history of the American news media into five eras: *Partisan, Commercial, Objective, Interpretive,* and *Fragmented.* Each era began and ended with revolutionary technological advances that brought about fundamental changes in how Americans got their news. Additionally, each era teaches a different lesson that helps us understand the current news media industry and its place in the American political system.

Partisan Era (1770s–1840s)

In the country's early days, major newspapers were owned and funded by party leaders. Since party leaders owned most of the newspapers, they slanted the news to benefit their political purposes. During the Partisan era, the main purpose of newspapers was to advance an ideological agenda, not to present objective information about the activities of government (Sheppard, 1972; Britannica.com). In addition, most readers understood these papers had a political bias and read the papers with a degree of skepticism (West, 2000). For example, the rumor that Thomas Jefferson had an illicit affair with one of his slaves was reported at the time, but few people believed it because it came from the opposing party's newspaper (<u>National Constitution Center, 2023</u>). One other important note about the Partisan era is that access to the news media was limited to the wealthy and educated. Printing newspapers was expensive, causing papers to charge high subscription rates to cover production costs (<u>Britannica.com</u>). As a result, only wealthy Americans could afford to get the news. Limiting access to the news also limits its power to shape public opinion and facilitate democratic accountability.

During the first era of the news media, Americans witnessed one of the most brazen and appalling assaults on free speech and freedom of the press. Thus, the lesson of the Partisan era is the importance of the free speech clause of the First Amendment. In 1798, only the second president of the United States, John Adams, and his Federalist Party passed the Alien and Sedition Acts, which criminalized speech that criticized the government, including Adams and Congress. For context, the Alien and Sedition Acts were passed only seven years after the First Amendment was ratified. Many of the same people who voted to approve the First Amendment stating "Congress shall make no law . . . abridging the freedom of speech, or of the press" made a law abridging the freedom of speech and the press in the clearest terms imaginable. Below is the abbreviated text of the Alien and Sedition Acts.

That if any person shall write, print, utter or publish, or shall cause or procure to be written, printed, uttered or published, or shall knowingly and willingly assist or aid in writing, printing, uttering or publishing any false, scandalous and malicious writing or writings against the government of the United States, or either house of the Congress of the United States, or the President of the United States, with intent to defame the said government, or either house of the said Congress, or the said President, or to bring them, or either of them, into contempt or disrepute; or *to excite against them, or either or any of them, the hatred of the good people of the United States, or to stir up sedition within the United States,* or to excite any unlawful combinations therein, for opposing or resisting any law of the United States, or any act of the President of the United States, done in pursuance of any such law, or of the powers in him vested by the constitution of the United States, or to resist, oppose, or defeat any such law or act, or to aid, encourage or abet any hostile designs of any foreign nation against United States, their people or government, then such person, being thereof convicted before any court of the United States having jurisdiction thereof, *shall be punished by a fine not exceeding two thousand dollars, and by imprisonment not exceeding two years.* (National Archives, n.d., emphasis added)

Why did Adams's party pass laws violating a central tenet of the First Amendment to the U.S. Constitution? What was so important that caused them to take such a drastic measure? The simple answer is that they didn't like being criticized by opposition newspapers. John Adams and his Federalist Party used the fear of a war with France as an excuse, but they weren't really worried about protecting the country as much as preventing criticism by prominent newspapers. After all, the only people prosecuted under the Alien and Sedition Acts just happened to belong to the Federalists' main opponents, the Democratic-Republican Party—led by Thomas Jefferson and James Madison (National Archives, n.d.). The Alien and Sedition Acts were a blatant attempt to silence political dissent, but only when the dissent came from the opposing political party. John Adams's opponent during his 1800 reelection campaign was Thomas Jefferson, who made the Alien and Sedition Acts a prominent issue in his campaign. As the National Archives put it, the "Sedition Act trials, along with the Senate's use of its contempt powers to suppress dissent, set off a firestorm of criticism against the Federalists and contributed to their defeat in the election of 1800, after which the acts were repealed or allowed to expire. The controversies surrounding them, however, provided for some of the first tests of the limits of freedom of speech and press" (ibid).

The point of all this is to demonstrate the important role the press plays in criticizing and investigating those holding political power. Elected officials such as presidents, legislators, and their supporters may not like it, but the news media are supposed to play an adversarial role by bringing attention to corruption, abuse of power, poor performance, and so on. Informing the public about the performance and malfeasance of elected officials is an essential ingredient for voters to hold public officials accountable. Would you want the media to completely trust the government and simply lavish praise on whoever holds the presidency? I would certainly hope not! In sum, the lesson of the Partisan era is the importance of free speech and freedom of the press.

Commercial Era (1840s–1920s)

During the early part of the 19th century, a confluence of technological advances made it substantially cheaper to print newspapers. Everything from the advent and growth of steam power, to typesetting, the iron press, and industrialized paper production drastically reduced newspaper production costs. For example, "Paper, made by hand up to 1800, formed more than 20 percent of the cost of a book in 1740; by 1910 it had fallen to a little more than 7 percent" (Tucker and Unwin, n.d.). Publishers could mass-produce newspapers at a faster pace and cheaper rate, which provided Americans access to the news who could not afford it during the Partisan era. Newspapers also found a new source of funding called *advertising*.

The ability to mass-produce newspapers also caused a fundamental change in the economic model of news outlets. Newspapers shifted from relying on subscriptions—which were required to cover high printing costs—to advertising revenue. Publishers no longer had to rely solely on newspaper sales and subscriptions, but instead could sell advertising space to companies trying to sell their products to readers. As you probably know, the amount newspapers can charge for advertising space depends on how many readers they have. Newspaper publishers wanted to distribute their papers to as wide an audience as possible, because the greater their distribution size, the more money they could charge companies for advertising space. A shift in focus to advertising revenue had two important consequences. For one, publishers sold newspapers at a very cheap price because they made more money from advertising than selling the paper. Indeed, charging a high price for a newspaper actually *lost* publishers money because fewer people read the paper, which lowered advertising revenue. We still see this "advertising model" in use today with streaming services such as Netflix offering cheaper plans with advertisements or more expensive subscriptions to avoid commercials.

A second consequence of the Commercial era was the rise of sensationalism and tabloid journalism in political news. Competition among newspapers for market share led to a focus on controversy, shock-value headlines, and misleading (occasionally fabricated) news. Although the drive for profit led to sensationalism, it also resulted in a rise of investigative journalism, called muckraking. We can still see the consequences of the advertising model in the modern media environment. Even today, news is not driven by the importance of the topic, but instead by its entertainment value. When news is controlled by private companies, profit is the paramount concern rather than what benefits individuals or society.

News outlets have utilized modern technologies to further shape the news to meet audience preferences. In the appropriately-titled book "*All the News That's Fit to Sell*," James Hamilton (2004) showed how commercialized news production has become. Hamilton showed that local television news stations used market research to determine the exact topics and issues—such as sports, celebrity gossip, political news, etc.—that were most desired by their particular audiences. Using this information, local news outlets would devote more time to those topics in the morning and evening newscasts. For example, if people in a city like Seattle were more interested in politics and Atlanta residents preferred sports, local news in Seattle would spend more time discussing politics while sports would garner more attention in Atlanta newscasts. The residents of these cities are likely unaware that they are receiving news that is screened to their interests. Furthermore, Hamilton found that not all viewers' interests are considered equally valuable. For example, the target demographic for most advertisers is women aged 18 to 34 because they tend to make most of the shopping decisions. To appeal to women in that demographic, local news would use softer language and cover stories that appealed more to young and middle-aged women. In short, the main lesson of the Commercial era is that when profit drives the news media, *they will give the people the news they want rather than the news they need*. Whether the news media provide Americans with sufficient information to make informed decisions depends on public demand for political news.

Objective Era (1920s–1970s)

Early in the 20th century, two important changes occurred that caused the change from the Commercial to the Objective era of the news media. By the 1920s, news companies realized that they could gain a wider audience by presenting news in an objective and unbiased manner. This corresponded to the professionalization of journalism. In the past, journalists often did not have any experience or training in the field. In the Objective era, more journalists were being trained to uphold the standards of the profession. Specifically, journalists were trained to cover stories by focusing on the "who, what, when, where, and why" of the story, just the facts. This involved letting politicians speak for themselves and included more reliance on extensive direct quotes in newspapers, and sound bites on television and radio. Partly because of these practices, Americans trusted the news media more during the Objective era than at any other point in history.

Another factor increasing media trust and credibility was a shift in communication technology that made news more homogeneous across different news outlets. Specifically, the advent of radio and television decreased the number of sources, while making news content nearly identical regardless of where someone lived in the country. While local newspapers provided different versions of the news depending on where you lived, radio and television started broadcasting the same news across the country. Keep in mind that when radio and television developed, they were broadcast over the airwaves, where airspace is limited. To control the broadcast airwaves, Congress created the Federal Communications Commission (FCC), which only allowed a few television stations to broadcast nationwide to prevent signal interference between airwaves. When competition is limited and market access is controlled, each business has the incentive to reach all of the customers to dominate the market. In other words, since there were only three major networks, they all competed for all of the viewers in the country. None of the news stations wanted to offend or turn off Democrats, Republicans, conservatives, or liberals, so they developed a "balance standard" where the news would present the arguments of both the Democrats and Republicans when discussing political issues and allow the audience to decide for themselves. This allowed news media outlets to remain "neutral" without giving the appearance of political bias.

Of course, the flaw in this approach should be abundantly clear, and ultimately was the downfall of the Objective era. If one or more political parties lie, mislead, or perform poorly, simply presenting their arguments as equally valid does a disservice to viewers. As an extreme example, imagine Democrats argue that 2 and 2 is 5, while Republicans correctly counter that 2 and 2 is 4. According to the balance standard, the news would not take sides, report "down the middle," and present both arguments as equally valid. If they rightly pointed out that Democrats are wrong, they would be accused of bias in favor of Republicans. In a less extreme example, imagine if a Republican president does a poor job, or acts in a corrupt manner. How should the media report on this situation? If the media reports on the reality of the situation, they will be accused of bias against Republicans. How dare they say a president is doing a bad job, even if they are? Put simply, the balance standard wrongly assumes that (in reality) both parties are always equally good and bad, and that Democratic and Republican leaders always perform equally well in office. This is an absurd standard for the news, yet most Americans still believe the news should be reported according to the balance standard (Forman-Katz and Jurkowitz, 2022).

The confluence of journalistic routines and limited market competition, all caused a homogenization of the news. Homogeneous news creates the *illusion of objectivity,* which artificially increases the credibility of the news media. Conversely, when people are presented with different pictures of the world by different news outlets, as is the case today, they usually choose to believe whichever news source tells them what they want to believe. People come to perceive political bias in neutral news stations because they compare them to partisan news outlets. The problem is that people are terrible at identifying media bias. Perceptions of political bias in the media are often based on biases in the perceiver and attacks on the media from political elites (Smith, 2010; Vallone et al., 1985). One of the most consistent findings in political psychology is the tendency for people to perceive media coverage as biased against their side: termed the **hostile media effect** (Feldman, 2011; Hansen and Kim, 2011). People are most likely to suffer from the hostile media effect when they are interested and informed about a topic. That is why Americans with strong attachments to the political parties are more likely to think the news media are biased against their side (Reid, 2012).

The other factor affecting perceptions of media bias is accusations of bias by political leaders. When presidents and party leaders, or even other media personalities, accuse a particular news outlet of political bias, those attacks have an independent effect on people who identify with their party as well as political independents (Archer, 2023; Watts et al., 1999). Research shows that so-called *elite attacks* on the media increased perceptions of media bias independent of any actual bias in the news (Ladd, 2010; Smith, 2010). In other words, if a politician says a news outlet is biased, their supporters just believe them even if there is no evidence of bias in how they report the news (Watts et al., 1999). There is also evidence that elite attacks on the media affect where people decide to get news in the future (Archer, 2023). This allows elected leaders to potentially avoid accountability for their actions, or poor performance in office, by simply accusing the media of being biased against them (Ladd, 2012; Smith, 2010). As a result, their supporters will ignore any information from those biased sources, even when the information is accurate (Baum and Groeling, 2009). The lesson from the Objective era is that true objectivity is an impossible standard because reality is interpreted subjectively. The more journalists try to be "unbiased," the more they allow politicians to exploit their misguided "bothsidesism" to mislead voters and avoid political accountability.

Interpretive Era (1970s–2000s)

Unfortunately, Americans' positive attitude toward the news media did not last long. Following the Vietnam War and Watergate, journalists became concerned that the government had too much power to manipulate public opinion. The fear was that providing "just the facts" was facilitating government control over public opinion by spreading propaganda. As a response, journalists took it upon themselves to interpret public affairs and media events rather than simply report them. Thus, it became less important *what* a politician did, and more important *why* they did it. So-called *strategy coverage* occurs when news media frame the actions of political leaders as motivated entirely by power and electoral considerations. According to the strategy frame, elected officials pass policies to win elections and gain power, and not because they think it is the right thing to do. This interpretation resulted in declining levels of trust in the news media and increasing perceptions of political bias (Cappella and Jamieson, 1997).

The Interpretive era also saw an expansion of choice in where people got their news. During the Objective era, most Americans received their news from the three big television networks (ABC, CBS, and NBC). This allowed those networks to present homogenous public affairs-oriented news coverage. The purpose of news organizations was not to attract viewers, but to provide a public service. However, the rise of cable television forced broadcast stations to compete for viewers, which pushed them to focus more on what the public wanted rather than what they needed. Consequently, the news media provided incessant coverage of celebrities, professional sports, crime, wars, and natural disasters. When it comes to covering political news, the news media will often focus on the most controversial topics or they will create controversy where none exists. If the president gives a speech overwhelmingly devoted to policy details, news media may typically focus on the few sentences here and there that attack opponents or say something controversial.

Aside from focusing on the most controversial aspects of the news, profit considerations also shape the news through an increased focus on the *horserace coverage*, which focuses on who is winning and losing in the polls before an election. Rather than focusing on the candidates' policy prescriptions, most of the media's attention during the election season is focused on public opinion polls and which candidates are leading (Patterson, 2005). Focusing on polling numbers allows the news media to appear neutral and unbiased, whereas critiquing a candidate's policy proposal may appear biased. Horserace coverage is the most common type of coverage and proves to be the most popular among the American public (Patterson, 1994). When Americans are given a choice of which topics they would like to learn about, they usually choose horserace coverage over any other type (Iyengar et al., 2004). The problem with focusing on the horserace is that voters understand who's winning but have little knowledge of the candidates' policy positions or qualifications for office.

With the intent of making political news more interesting, news outlets started framing politics like it was a sport. Media companies concluded that talking about politics like it was a sport would increase interest in their news, thus providing them a competitive advantage in the marketplace. In other words, if politics wasn't interesting to most Americans, the news media could turn it into a sport, and in doing so increase interest in an otherwise fairly boring topic. To that end, news outlets focused their attention on who would win or lose an election, and passing legislation became about who won or lost the policy battle. Of course, they didn't mean whether Americans in general or a particular social group won or lost, but instead, media coverage only cared about which political party or presidential candidate gained a victory. By framing politics like it's a sport, viewers of both mainstream news and their cable competitors came to think about politics like it was a sporting event. The consequence of this horse race coverage is that those identifying with the political party came to look at politics like it was a sport rather than an exchange of ideas to find the best way forward for the country. Winning becomes the paramount issue and concern for many Americans, but this undermines voters' ability to hold politicians accountable (Huddy et al., 2015). When winning the game requires that your candidate does a good job, partisans are motivated to see the world in a way that benefits their party. The lesson of the Interpretive era is that the media's power to frame politics, in this case as a competitive sport, shapes people's motivations when they interpret reality.

Case Study: Public Opinion Polling

Opinion polls are not just entertainment fodder for the news media, but instead play an important role in political campaigns and elections. Public opinion polls are conducted by polling organizations, media outlets, universities, interest groups, political parties, and even individual campaigns. The results of public opinion polls influence perceptions of election competitiveness among both politicians and the public. If polls show that a race is competitive, political parties, interest groups, and large donors are more likely to pour resources into that race and avoid expending time and money in elections where there is a foregone conclusion. Likewise, citizens may be less motivated to vote when higher-level races for president or U.S. Senate are not competitive.

In order to conduct an opinion poll, a polling organization will interview a sample of individuals and ask them their opinions on political issues and who they intend to vote for. Although samples usually range from 500 to a few thousand participants, pollsters usually aim for 1,500 respondents. Perhaps you are wondering why we should care what a small group of people think. Is it wise to put so much stock in the opinions of one or two thousand people in a nation of about 260 million adults? The key is **representativeness**. That is, does the sample represent the population? If it does, then we can reasonably assume that the sample's views reflect the larger population. The margin of error for a poll is usually equal to plus or minus two standard deviations standard errors. For a poll of about 1,500 registered voters, the margin of error is (usually) +/- 3 percentage points. For example, if 50 percent of the participants in a poll said they planned to vote for a presidential candidate, there is a 95 percent chance that the actual percentage of registered voters planning to vote for that candidate is somewhere between 47 and 53 percent.

All of the above relies on an often dubious assumption that the sample (poll) adheres to the principle of **random** selection. For a poll to satisfy the principle of random selection, every member of the population must have an equal and independent chance of being selected for the sample. If a pollster wants to know who will win the election, they would have to ensure that every eventual voter has an equal and independent chance of participating in the poll. Common sense dictates that this is rarely the case, as people are excluded from polls for a variety of reasons. Not to fear, as a selection bias is only problematic if it distorts the results of the poll. As long as the bias is randomly distributed in the question of interest (e.g. voting decisions) then it is largely irrelevant.

If pollsters suspect that selection bias may affect the question of interest, they can weigh the results by known demographics of the population. Although **selection bias** always potentially threatens the accuracy of polls, some polling organizations have a better track record at predicting election results than others.

Even if poll samples are representative of the population, their results do not necessarily reflect public opinion in an accurate way. The *wording* and *ordering* of questions in a survey can cause sizable changes in the results of a poll. How a question is worded brings different considerations to mind when a respondent answers a question. Likewise, the questions that are asked right before a question will bring to mind particular considerations that then affect subsequent questions. For example, there was an interesting survey experiment a few months before the 2024 presidential election between Republican Donald Trump and Democrat Kamala Harris. This election campaign was noteworthy because Harris was trying to become the first black woman, or woman of any race for that matter, to win a presidential election. In an August 2024 poll conducted by Fairleigh Dickinson University, respondents were randomly assigned to complete slightly different surveys.

In the survey, before being asked who they were supporting in the Presidential race, respondents were given a list of five issues, and asked which ones were important to their vote. The issues included Tax Policy, Immigration Policy, Climate Change, Abortion and Foreign Policy. But not all respondents got the same list. In addition to randomizing the order of the issues, one-third of respondents were given "The Race or Ethnicity of the Candidate" as the last issue before the vote choice question, and one-third were given "Whether the Candidate is a Man or a Woman" as their last issue. The remaining one-third got all five of the issues, in no particular order. (Fairleigh Dickinson University, 2024)

When respondents were not asked about race or gender, Trump held a slim one-point lead in the race. Among respondents who were asked about the sex of the candidates, Harris (52%) took a 10-point lead over Trump (42%). Harris's lead increased to 14 points among respondents who were asked about the candidates' race. In other words, simply reminding respondents about the candidates' race and sex changed voting decisions and gave Kamala Harris a sizable lead versus a dead heat when voters were not reminded about those two considerations. Moreover, Harris's lead in the race and sex experimental groups resulted almost entirely from her gains among non-white and female voters, respectively. Priming race and gender identity increased support primarily among voters who shared Kamala Harris's race and sex. What this illustrates is the power of question ordering to change the results of public opinion polls in important ways. Now consider this: When was the last time you heard the news discuss the ordering of questions when providing the results of an opinion poll? Almost always, news media report on single questions in isolation, even when the questions were asked within a context of other questions.

Fragmented Era (2000s–Current)

As access to the internet swept across the United States, the Interpretive era gave way to the current Fragmented era of the news media. The Fragmented era is best characterized by the rapid expansion of news outlets on the internet, coupled with the aging market for traditional news. Compared to 50 years ago, Americans have a much wider selection of news choices on: television, radio, blogs, podcasts, Facebook, and Youtube, just to name a few. Gone are the days when most Americans received their news from the same news sources. Instead, in the fragmented media environment, people get different pictures of the world and live in information cocoons, where they are sheltered from undesirable facts about the world.

Even today, rapidly changing technology is fundamentally altering where young Americans get their news. Since news use is largely habitual, these changes move slowly over time. Most notable is the shift from television news to social media, especially among young Americans. To be blunt, the audience for television news is dying out, for lack of a better term. According to a 2022 YouGov study, television news is still the most popular source of political news, but its audience is predominantly senior citizens (Sanders, 2022). Roughly 40 percent of all Americans watch national television news (ABC, CBS, NBC), which is about the same as get news from cable outlets (CNN, Fox News, MSNBC). The problem for all of these television news outlets is their audiences are significantly older than the broader population. Most of those 65 and older watch television news, compared to only a quarter of Americans under 30. In contrast, over 40 percent of young people get news from social media, with roughly a third getting news from YouTube in particular. According to a different study from the Pew Research Center, roughly half of Americans get at least some political news from social media, with Facebook and YouTube cited as the most commonly used sources (Pew Research Center, 2023). In the Fragmented era, social media is becoming the preferred news source for younger Americans, who will eventually dominate the media marketplace as they get older.

The Fragmented era also ushered in the rise of selective exposure to like-minded partisan media outlets, who make money by selling fear and hatred. In a hyper-competitive media marketplace, news sources have an incentive to cater to the desires of a small and devoted audience. During the Objective era, there were only three major news outlets. Such limited competition incentivized each outlet to report the news down the middle because they wanted to appeal to everyone. In other words, all three networks competed for the entire audience and were reluctant to offend either Democrats or Republicans. Trying to capture the entire audience is unrealistic in the Fragmented era because there is too much competition, and the entry cost is extremely low. After all, anyone can start a blog or podcast for very little money and then enter the competition for audience share. Rather than appeal to everyone, each news outlet in the Fragmented era is successful to the extent they can attract an extremely devoted niche audience (Stroud, 2011). Niche news companies appeal to smaller audiences that spend a lot of time watching, reading, or listening to their news source. Attracting and maintaining such a devoted audience is the economic model of partisan media outlets.

To maintain a devoted audience, partisan media outlets shape their content to hook audiences on fear and hatred of the opposing political party. Television stations like Fox News and MSNBC, political talk radio, as well as countless news websites, have figured out that making their audiences afraid will keep them coming back more frequently and staying longer. Research shows that fear causes surveillance and a search for knowledge (Brader, 2005). The more people fear the opposing party, the more they are psychologically motivated to pay attention to political news. After all, each party wants to stay vigilant regarding how the other party is trying to destroy America and its entire way of life. Partisan media outlets profit from this fear by spending their time terrifying their audiences. The audience for partisan media sees a nearly uninterrupted—they need to have commercials after all—barrage of attacks painting members of the opposing political party as either intolerant ideologues, or brainwashed sheep blindly following the untrustworthy and downright evil leaders of their political party. This creates a vicious cycle where people watch partisan media and become more afraid, which subsequently causes them to pay more attention, thereby increasing their fear, and so on. Now that we understand the economic incentives of partisan media, let's examine how exposure to their content affects ideology, political hostility, and participation in the political system.

The Effects of Political News

Now we return to the news media's role as an agent of political socialization. Like other agents of socialization, news media have unique effects on ideology, tolerance, and participation. Just like political discussion groups, the news media affects ideology and political tolerance depending on the diversity of viewpoints people encounter. In the modern media environment, people have a great deal of control over their news media sources. People wield that control to either isolate themselves into like-minded echo chambers or to learn about different perspectives. As with many things, the news media can be positive or negative for individuals and democracy depending on how people use it. Fire can heat your house or it can burn it down; it all depends on whether you use it responsibly. In this section, we examine how the effects of news media on ideology, tolerance, and participation depend on where people get their news.

How does partisan media affect ideology? Recent research shows that the more someone pays attention to like-minded partisan media, the more extreme their issue opinions become (de Benedictis-Kessner et al., 2019; Broockman and Kalla, 2023; Levendusky, 2013). For example, Fox News makes Republicans more conservative in their policy preferences and issue opinions, while CNN and MSNBC make Democratic viewers more liberal. This polarization effect occurs regardless of whether people watch partisan television, listen to talk radio, or read like-minded media websites (Jamieson and Cappella, 2008; Stroud, 2011). There is also evidence that partisan media can decrease extremism among opposing partisans (Levendusky, 2013). When Republicans watch MSNBC and Democrats watch Fox News, they both become less extreme in their issue opinions (Dilliplane, 2011; Stroud, 2011). That is, opposing media decreases polarization, while like-minded media increases extremist political opinions.

One interesting study demonstrated the power of partisan media to influence the way voters perceive the world. Broockman and Kalla (2023) had people who usually watch Fox News watch CNN instead. Watching CNN for only a short period made Fox News viewers more moderate on a variety of political issues. In other words, simply switching one's news source can have important effects on political information and beliefs. The dangers of partisan media are not entirely theoretical, or limited to the laboratory, as they can have dire consequences when they spread misinformation. During the COVID-19 pandemic, for example, Fox News was more negative and skeptical toward the vaccine than their competitors. This skeptical coverage made their viewers less likely to take the vaccine (Motta and Stecula, 2023). As this example illustrates, there are times when exposure to partisan media can affect health decisions and potentially cost the lives of viewers and their loved ones.

How do partisan media affect political hostility? There is abundant evidence that paying attention to like-minded partisan media increases negativity toward elected officials and everyday citizens in the other party. Democrats who watch MSNBC or CNN harbor more distrust and animosity toward Republicans, while Republicans watching Fox News feel more hostility toward Democrats (Smith, 2016; Smith and Searles, 2013; 2014). And it's not simply the case that hostility motivates people to watch like-minded partisan media. Experimental research shows that exposure to partisan media increases hostility toward the opposing party (de Benedictis-Kessner et al., 2019; Feldman, 2011). There is also evidence that when partisan media pay more attention to presidential candidates in the opposing party, their viewers become more negative (Smith, 2016; Smith and Searles, 2014). In other words, when Fox News devotes more attention to a Democrat, or CNN spends more time discussing a Republican, like-minded viewers feel more negative toward those candidates the next day and week. Interestingly, Democrats and Republicans who pay *no attention* to partisan media do not become more negative toward opposing candidates during the same periods. This suggests that it was not anything the candidates were doing, but instead how partisan media frame and shape the reality that people see that causes negativity. As discussed earlier, partisan media profit when they make people afraid of the other party. Unlike their effects on political ideology, however, partisan media do not appear to lower negativity among customers in the opposing party (Levendusky, 2013; Smith and Searles, 2013; 2014). That is, while watching oppositional media may make people more moderate in their issue opinions, it does nothing to lower negativity in American politics.

There is at least one type of media that *does* lower negativity, and that is traditional mainstream news outlets. In my research, I found that broadcast news made viewers less negative toward leaders in the opposing Party (Smith, 2017). Furthermore, mainstream news had its largest effects on those who strongly identify as Democrats or Republicans, who are typically more hostile toward opposing partisans. Broadcast news outlets decrease negativity by presenting both Democratic and Republican talking points in their political coverage. So, it is not that mainstream news is nice to political candidates, as research shows they are more negative than positive (Smith and Searles, 2014). Instead, mainstream news provides the best arguments from both candidates. Learning the strongest arguments from the opposing party challenges stereotypes regarding why opposing partisans disagree over political issues.

If mainstream media lowers hostility by challenging stereotypes of opposing politicians, why don't partisan media do the same thing for opposing customers? The answer lies in the nature of partisan media coverage. Remember, partisan media are selling fear, and to that end, they spend more time attacking the opposing party than praising their preferred party. Content analyses show that partisan media are extremely negative toward opposing party presidential candidates, but are not overly positive toward like-minded leaders (Smith and Searles, 2014). For example, research shows that Fox News is overwhelmingly negative when they cover Democrats, but no more positive toward Republicans than you would find on mainstream media. As a result, partisan media have their largest effect on increasing negativity in politics rather than bridging any divides between the political parties.

Despite the overall gloomy picture this paints, partisan media are not all bad. Exposure to like-minded partisan media outlets can *benefit* democracy by motivating viewers to engage in the political system. Fear is a primal motivator for action. When partisan media make customers afraid of the opposing party, they not only boost their profits, but also motivate political activity (Wilson, 2009). Indeed, there is a fairly consistent link between exposure to partisan media and political activity (Wojcieszak et al., 2016). Those paying more attention to like-minded partisan media are more likely to be active in the political system (Dilliplane, 2011; Stroud, 2011). Increasing fear of the opposing party motivates people to do whatever they can to stop that other party from gaining power. While exposure to like-minded media increases political participation, counter-attitudinal news does *not weaken* the motivation to participate (Dilliplane, 2011; Matthes et al., 2019; Wojcieszak et al., 2016). Research suggests that exposure to mainstream news increases political participation, though only when the news presents political information (De Vreese and Boomgaarden, 2006). News programs that rarely cover political topics do not affect political activity.

When it comes to how mainstream news influences political activity, two opposing effects end up canceling each other out. On the one hand, mainstream news increases political information, which research shows consistently increases motivation to participate in the political system (Carpini and Keeter, 1996). Indeed, even so-called soft news programs, which are entertainment programs that occasionally discuss political topics, also increase political information (Baum and Jamison, 2006). Likewise, mainstream news provides political information to their customers, which makes them more engaged, interested, and motivated to affect the political system. On the other hand, mainstream news also increases ambivalence. As we have seen, mainstream news decreases hostility towards opposing party candidates by challenging negative stereotypes (Smith, 2017). Ambivalence toward political candidates occurs when someone has a roughly equal amount of things they like or dislike about the two major political candidates. In other words, if we equally like the two major party candidates (or equally dislike them), we are less concerned with who wins the election. Given that negative partisanship is the prime motivator in contemporary politics, reducing negativity towards the opposing party candidate also weakens motivation to engage in the political system by voting, campaigning, or donating to political causes. Consequently, mainstream news neither increases nor decreases political activity to a substantial degree because the positive effect it has on increasing political information is usually offset by the ambivalence it creates towards the political candidates. The unfortunate result of this is that those who are most extreme, hostile, and hateful of opposing partisans are the most likely to engage in the political system and influence electoral outcomes. Party extremists are also the most likely to vote in party primaries that nominate the candidates. Given that most Congressional elections are not competitive, the primaries are the "real" elections, and are dominated by party extremists. By motivating the most hostile among the population to engage in the political system, partisan media increase the chances political outcomes will reflect extreme views rather than less politically active Americans who hold moderate opinions or feel less animosity toward their fellow Americans. Representative democracies favor the politically active, and this is especially true in America's party nominating system. Partisan media make their customers more extreme and active in the political system, while mainstream media decrease negativity, but do nothing to motivate political participation.

Discussion Questions

1. What can schools do to foster political participation among young people?
2. What are the main obstacles to productive political discussion?
3. Does social media bridge political divides or increase animosity?
4. How might electoral changes increase participation among moderate voters?

References

Alford, J. R., Funk, C. L., & Hibbing, J. R. (2005). Are political orientations genetically transmitted? *American Political Science Review*, *99*(2), 153–167.

American Psychological Association. (n.d.). Political socialization. In *APA Dictionary of Psychology*. Retrieved September 6, 2024, from https://dictionary.apa.org/political-socialization

Archer, A. M. (2023). The effects of elite attacks on copartisan media: Evidence from Trump and Fox News. *Public Opinion Quarterly*, *87*(4), 887–910.

Baum, M. A., & Groeling, T. (2009). Shot by the messenger: Partisan cues and public opinion regarding national security and war. *Political Behavior, 31*, 157–186.

Baum, M. A., & Jamison, A. S. (2006). The Oprah effect: How soft news helps inattentive citizens vote consistently. *The Journal of Politics*, *68*(4), 946–959.

Bobo, L., & Licari, F. C. (1989). Education and political tolerance: Testing the effects of cognitive sophistication and target group affect. *Public Opinion Quarterly*, *53*(3), 285–308.

Bond, R. M., Fariss, C. J., Jones, J. J., Kramer, A. D., Marlow, C., Settle, J. E., & Fowler, J. H. (2012). A 61-million-person experiment in social influence and political mobilization. *Nature*, *489*(7415), 295–298.

Bos, A. L., Greenlee, J. S., Holman, M. R., Oxley, Z. M., & Lay, J. C. (2022). This one's for the boys: How gendered political socialization limits girls' political ambition and interest. *American Political Science Review*, *116*(2), 484–501.

Brader, T. (2005). Striking a responsive chord: How political ads motivate and persuade voters by appealing to emotions. *American Journal of Political Science, 49*(2), 388–405.

Broockman, D. E. and Kalla, J. L. (2023). The impacts of selective partisan media exposure: A field experiment with Fox News viewers. Forthcoming, *Journal of Politics*.

Bulla, D. W. (2015, December 29). *Party press era*. Encyclopedia Britannica. https://www.britannica.com/topic/party-press-era

Campbell, B. A. (1980). A theoretical approach to peer influence in adolescent socialization. *American Journal of Political Science, 24*(2), 324–344.

Cappella, J. N., & Jamieson, K. H. (1997). *Spiral of cynicism: The press and the public good.* Oxford University Press.

Carmines, E. G., and D'Amico, N. J. (2015). The new look in political ideology research. *Annual Review of Political Science, 18,* 205–216.

Carpini, M. X. D., & Keeter, S. (1996). *What Americans know about politics and why it matters.* Yale University Press.

Cooperman, A. (2023, May 10). *Most U.S. parents pass along their religion and politics to their children.* Pew Research Center. https://www.pewresearch. org/short-reads/2023/05/10/most-us-parents-pass-along-their-religion-and-politics-to-their-children/

Dawes, C., Cesarini, D., Fowler, J. H., Johannesson, M., Magnusson, P. K., & Oskarsson, S. (2014). The relationship between genes, psychological traits, and political participation. *American Journal of Political Science, 58*(4), 888–903.

de Benedictis-Kessner, J., Baum, M. A., Berinsky, A. J., and Yamamoto, T. (2019) Persuading the enemy: Estimating the persuasive effects of partisan media with the preference-incorporating choice and assignment design. *American Political Science Review, 113*(4), 902–916.

De Vreese, C. H., & Boomgaarden, H. (2006). News, political knowledge and participation: The differential effects of news media exposure on political knowledge and participation. *Acta Politica, 41,* 317–341.

Dilliplane, S. (2011). All the news you want to hear: The impact of partisan news exposure on political participation. *Public Opinion Quarterly, 75*(2), 287–316.

Domke, D., Watts, M. D., Shah, D. V., & Fan, D. P. (1999). The politics of conservative elites and the "liberal media" argument. *Journal of Communication, 49*(4), 35–58.

Dostie-Goulet, E. (2009). Social networks and the development of political interest. *Journal of Youth Studies, 12*(4), 405–421.

Dvir-Gvirsman, S., Garrett, R. K., & Tsfati, Y. (2018). Why do partisan audiences participate? Perceived public opinion as the mediating mechanism. *Communication Research, 45*(1), 112–136.

Fairleigh Dickinson University. (2024, August 23). *FDU poll finds race and gender push Harris above Trump nationally.* Fairleigh Dickinson University. Retrieved September 12, 2024 from https://www.fdu.edu/news/fdu-poll-finds-race-and-gender-push-harris-above-trump-nationally/

Feldman, L. (2011). Partisan differences in opinionated news perceptions: A test of the hostile media effect. *Political Behavior, 33*, 407–432.

Feldman, L. (2011). The opinion factor: The effects of opinionated news on information processing and attitude change. *Political Communication, 28*(2), 163–181.

Forman-Katz, N., & Jurkowitz, M. (2022, July 13). *U.S. journalists differ from the public in their views of 'bothsidesism' in journalism.* Pew Research Center. https://www.pewresearch.org/short-reads/2022/07/13/u-s-journalists-differ-from-the-public-in-their-views-of-bothsidesism-in-journalism/

Fowler, J. H., Baker, L. A., & Dawes, C. T. (2008). Genetic variation in political participation. *American Political Science Review, 102*(2), 233–248.

Gerber, A. S., Green, D. P., & Larimer, C. W. (2010). An experiment testing the relative effectiveness of encouraging voter participation by inducing feelings of pride or shame. *Political Behavior, 32*, 409–422.

Gerber, A. S., Huber, G. A., Doherty, D., Dowling, C. M., Raso, C., & Ha, S. E. (2011). Personality traits and participation in political processes. *The Journal of Politics, 73*(3), 692–706.

Gibson, J. L., & Bingham, R. D. (1982). On the conceptualization and measurement of political tolerance. *American Political Science Review, 76*(3), 603–620.

Hamilton, J. T. (2004). *All the news that's fit to sell: How the market transforms information into news.* Princeton University Press.

Hansen, G. J., & Kim, H. (2011). Is the media biased against me? A meta-analysis of the hostile media effect research. *Communication Research Reports, 28*(2), 169–179.

Hartig, H., Daniller, A., Keeter, S., & Van Green, T. (2023, July 12). *Republican gains in 2022 midterms driven mostly by turnout advantage.* Pew Research Center. https://www.pewresearch.org/politics/2023/07/12/voter-turnout-2018-2022/

Huddy, L., & Khatib, N. (2007). American patriotism, national identity, and political involvement. *American Journal of Political Science, 51*(1), 63–77.

Huddy, L., Mason, L., & Aarøe, L. (2015). Expressive partisanship: Campaign involvement, political emotion, and partisan identity. *American Political Science Review, 109*(1), 1–17.

Iyengar, S., Norpoth, H., & Hahn, K. S. (2004). Consumer demand for election news: The horserace sells. *The Journal of Politics, 66*(1), 157–175.

Iyengar, S., & Westwood, S. J. (2015). Fear and loathing across party lines: New evidence on group polarization. *American Journal of Political Science, 59*(3),

690–707.

Jamieson, K. H., & Cappella, J. N. (2008). *Echo chamber: Rush Limbaugh and the conservative media establishment*. Oxford University Press.

Jennings, M. K., Stoker, L., & Bowers, J. (2009). Politics across generations: Family transmission reexamined. *The Journal of Politics, 71*(3), 782–799.

Krupnikov, Y., & Ryan, J. B. (2022). *The other divide*. Cambridge University Press.

Ladd, J. M. (2010). The neglected power of elite opinion leadership to produce antipathy toward the news media: Evidence from a survey experiment. *Political Behavior, 32,* 29–50.

Ladd, J. M. (2012). *Why Americans hate the media and how it matters*. Princeton University Press.

Lay, J. C., Holman, M. R., Greenlee, J. S., Oxley, Z. M., & Bos, A. L. (2023). Partisanship on the playground: Expressive party politics among children. *Political Research Quarterly, 76*(3), 1249–1264.

Leppert, R., Desilver, D. (2023, January 3). *118th Congress has a record number of women*. Pew Research Center. https://www.pewresearch.org/short-reads/2023/01/03/118th-congress-has-a-record-number-of-women/

Levendusky, M. (2013). *How partisan media polarize America*. University of Chicago Press.

Matthes, J., Knoll, J., Valenzuela, S., Hopmann, D. N., & Von Sikorski, C. (2019). A meta-analysis of the effects of cross-cutting exposure on political participation. *Political Communication, 36*(4), 523–542.

McIntosh, H., Hart, D., & Youniss, J. (2007). The influence of family political discussion on youth civic development: Which parent qualities matter? *PS: Political Science & Politics, 40*(3), 495–499.

Mendelberg, T., McCabe, K. T., & Thal, A. (2017). College socialization and the economic views of affluent Americans. *American Journal of Political Science, 61*(3), 606–623.

Motta, M., and Stecula, D. (2023). The effects of partisan media in the face of a global pandemic: How news shaped COVID-19 vaccine hesitancy. *Political Communication,* 1–22.

Mutz, D. C. (1992). Mass media and the depoliticization of personal experience. *American Journal of Political Science, 36*(2), 483–508.

Mutz, D. C. (2001). Facilitating communication across lines of political difference: The role of mass media. *American Political Science Review, 95*(1), 97–114.

Mutz, D. C. (2002). Cross-cutting social networks: Testing democratic theory in practice. *American Political Science Review, 96*(1), 111–126.

Mutz, D. C. (2006). *Hearing the other side: Deliberative versus participatory democracy*. Cambridge University Press.

National Archives. (n.d.). *Alien and Sedition Acts, 1798*. U.S. National Archives. https://www.archives.gov/milestone-documents/alien-and-sedition-acts

National Constitution Center. (2023, Nov. 4). *On this day: The first bitter, contested presidential election takes place*. National Constitution Center. https://constitutioncenter.org/blog/on-this-day-the-first-bitter-contested-presidential-election-takes-place

Panagopoulos, C. (2010). Affect, social pressure, and prosocial motivation: Field experimental evidence of the mobilizing effects of pride, shame and publicizing voting behavior. *Political Behavior, 32*, 369–386.

Patterson, T. E. (1994). Out of order: An incisive and boldly original critique of the news media's domination of America's political process. *Vintage.*

Patterson, T. E. (2005). Of polls, mountains: U.S. journalists and their use of election surveys. *Public Opinion Quarterly, 69*(5), 716–724.

Pew Research Center. (2023, November 15). *Social media and news fact sheet.* Pew Research Center. https://www.pewresearch.org/journalism/fact-sheet/social-media-and-news-fact-sheet/

Reid, S. A. (2012). A self-categorization explanation for the hostile media effect. *Journal of Communication, 62*(3), 381–399.

Reifen-Tagar, M., & Cimpian, A. (2022). Political ideology in early childhood: Making the case for studying young children in political psychology. *Political Psychology, 43*(1): 77–105.

Rosenstone, S., & Hansen, J. (1993). *Mobilization, participation and democracy in America*. Macmillian.

Sanders, L. (2022, April 5). *Trust in media 2022: Where Americans get their news and who they trust for information*. YouGov. https://today.yougov.com/politics/articles/41957-trust-media-2022-where-americans-get-news-poll

Sheppard, Si. (2007). *The partisan press: A history of media bias in the United States*. McFarland.

Smith, G. (2016). The timing of partisan media effects during a presidential election. *Political Research Quarterly, 69*(4), 655–666.

Smith, G. (2017). Sympathy for the devil: How broadcast news reduces negativity toward political leaders. *American Politics Research, 45*(1), 63–84.

Smith, G. R. (2010). Politicians and the news media: How elite attacks influence perceptions of media bias. *The International Journal of Press/Politics, 15*(3), 319–343.

Smith, G., & Searles, K. (2013). Fair and balanced news or a difference of opinion? Why opinion shows matter for media effects. *Political Research Quarterly, 66*(3), 671–684.

Smith, G., and Searles, K. (2014). Who let the (attack) dogs out? New evidence for partisan media effects. *Public Opinion Quarterly, 78*(1), 71–99.

Stroud, N. J. (2011). *Niche news: The politics of news choice.* Oxford University Press.

Tucker, D., & Unwin, P. (n.d.). *History of publishing.* Britannica. Retrieved September 12, 2024 from https://www.britannica.com/topic/publishing/Spread-of-education-and-literacy

Tyler, M., & Iyengar, S. (2023). Learning to dislike your opponents: Political socialization in the era of polarization. *American Political Science Review, 117*(1), 347–354.

Verba, S., Schlozman, K. L., and Brady, H. E. (1995). *Voice and equality: Civic voluntarism in American politics.* Harvard University Press.

Watts, M. D., Domke, D., Shah, D. V., & Fan, D. P. (1999). Elite cues and media bias in presidential campaigns: Explaining public perceptions of a liberal press. *Communication Research, 26*(2), 144–175.

West, D. (2001). *The rise and fall of the media establishment.* Palgrave.

Wilson, R. E. (2009, September 23). *The most powerful motivator.* Psychology Today. https://www.psychologytoday.com/us/blog/the-main-ingredient/200909/the-most-powerful-motivator

Wojcieszak, M., Bimber, B., Feldman, L., & Stroud, N. J. (2016). Partisan news and political participation: Exploring mediated relationships. *Political Communication, 33*(2), 241–260.

Interest Groups

Carl D. Cavalli

Learning Objectives

After covering the topic of interest groups, students should understand:

1. The history of and reasons why interest groups exist.
2. Why we join interest groups, and their structure, their organization, and the "free rider" problem.
3. The mythology and reality of interest groups.
4. The influence of interest groups on public policymaking, including the various methods of influence.

Abstract

The framers' hostility to "factions" was addressed not by restrictions but by encouraging proliferation, creating what today is referred to as a pluralist system. While groups offer potential members many social and economic reasons for joining, obtaining active support is often difficult because of the "free rider" problem. Modern literature challenges the popular myth of benevolent groups alleviating inequities in society. Instead E. E. Schattschneider warns of a strong upper-class bias. Data on federal spending by lobbyists support this theory about bias. Groups use many methods to influence public policy. These methods include lobbying, the direct access afforded by "iron triangles," litigation, "going public," and electoral activity. Government regulation of groups' electoral activity has resulted in the formation of many types of organizations, including political action committees, 527 and 501(c) organizations, and, most recently, SuperPACs.

Introduction

The previous chapter discussed political socialization—how our beliefs and values are formed. We learned that our beliefs and values are not just randomly distributed—we develop consistent sets of beliefs known as ideologies. Related to those beliefs are issues that are important to us—issues involving our lives and how society functions (or how we think it *should* function). The chapter also covered the media and public opinion polling—how we learn about what government is doing and how government learns about our positions on the issues of the day. We express our views to others and to the government, often with the hope of changing minds and changing government policies. And so, to help express these views to government and to the public, we form groups of like interests or . . . interest groups.

A Chorus versus a Crowd

Why groups? They are louder than individuals. Consider this thought exercise about the difference between a chorus and a crowd: Suppose you have several people all expressing the same thought regarding a particular issue. But they are all scattered throughout a large population, and within that population, they express their view on this issue in different ways at different times and in different places. They will simply fade into the background noise in the same way that many people in a sports arena, all rooting for the same player or outcome, will get lost in the crowd noise if they are all using different words at different times in different places. Now, if those fans all get together in one place and say the same thing at the same time, like a chorus, their expression is much more likely to stand out among the crowd noises. Similarly, if people with the same view on an issue organize into a group and coordinate their message to say the same thing in the same way, at coordinated times, they will more likely get noticed. That is why people form interest groups. Because government, for better or worse, is more likely to hear an organized interest as opposed to disorganized voices among the larger crowd.

Pluralism

Our system is *designed* to promote groups. It is designed to promote **pluralism**. What is pluralism? The Encyclopedia Britannica (2008) defines it as the belief that "power is (or should be) dispersed among a variety of economic and ideological pressure groups and is not (or should not be) held by a single elite or group of elites." Pluralism in a democratic government is based on the idea that competition among diverse ideas, values, and viewpoints serves the public good. It is based on the idea that competition promotes compromise and moderation. In *Federalist #10*, James Madison promotes the advantages of a large democratic republic (see Chapter 2) over a small direct democracy mainly because the diversity in a large republic helps prevent a single faction assuming controlling power (Madison, 2001, p. 92). In other words, Madison is promoting the advantage of pluralistic competition. The more groups that have input into what government does, the better. So, we have a system that is designed to promote groups.

The Basics

What are Interest Groups and Why Do They Exist?

Quite simply, interest groups organize to influence government. This makes them purely *political* entities, as they seek to affect public policy. However, these groups generally are not interested in all policies. Typically, they focus on a single area, remaining uninterested in others (except to the extent those others may affect their interest). This focus leads many to refer to them as *special-* or *single-* interest groups. In addition, as they are not part of the government, they are also often referred to as *outside* groups.

While the framers' distaste for "factions" included interest groups as well as political parties, this singular focus distinguishes them from political parties, which generally seek to mold policy in *all* areas. Another distinction is that, in general, while interest groups are focused on *influencing* government—largely from the outside—parties want to get their members elected to government in order to *run* it (see Chapter 6).

Democracy, Diversity, and Division

While not an absolute requirement, *democracy* helps explain the existence of interest groups. Democratic governments are set up to listen to public input, and an organized group is more easily heard than a scattered collection of individuals (as discussed earlier).

Another explanation is found in *diversity*. There would be little reason for groups to form if the entire population possessed the same beliefs, desires, and needs. Indeed, in *Federalist #10*, Madison notes that one way of "removing the causes of faction" is to give everyone "the same opinions, . . . passions, and . . . interests," and another way is to destroy liberty (Madison, 2001, p. 92). He quickly dismisses the first as impossible and the second as anti-democratic. So, in a democracy—factions happen! As a large democratic republic, the United States is composed of many diverse factions.

One other less appreciated but equally important explanation for the existence of interest groups is *division*. More precisely, our government is fragmented—divided in many ways. Implementing the constitutional principle of separation of powers leads to a divided government—three branches (executive, legislative, and judicial) in each of three levels (national, state, and local). In addition, each branch at each level usually has multiple agencies with many individuals within it. This diversity creates numerous **access points** for interest groups to contact. In addition to lobbying Congress for favorable legislation, they may also lobby executive agencies for favorable regulations as well as accessing the legal system to affect laws, regulations, and their implementation. All of these may be pursued at the state (governor, state legislature, state courts) and local (mayor, city council, municipal courts) levels as well.

Why Join One?

Writing about his exploration of American society in the early 19th century, historian Alexis de Tocqueville suggested that Americans are joiners—of associations, of societies . . . of groups. He put it this way:

Americans of all ages, all conditions, and all dispositions, constantly form associations. They have not only commercial and manufacturing companies, in which all take part, but associations of a thousand other kinds—religious, moral, serious, futile, extensive, or restricted, enormous or diminutive. The Americans make associations to give entertainments, to found establishments for education, to build inns, to construct churches, to diffuse books, to send missionaries to the antipodes; and in this manner they found hospitals, prisons, and schools. If it be proposed to advance some truth, or to foster some feeling by the encouragement of a great example, they form a society. (Democracy in America, Vol. II, Chapter V, para. 2).

What he observed applies today just as much as when he traversed the young nation two centuries ago. We are a nation of joiners. Joiners of all sorts of groups. So why do we do that? At least in theory, groups form to further the interests of their members (Olson, 1971). That would suggest that people join groups to pursue those collective interests. That is true, but there are other reasons people may join groups.

- People may join groups because they believe in the groups' *goals*. They may wish to see policies changed at the local, state, or national level because they believe it will benefit the greater society. Many who join civil rights groups or other kinds of policy or political groups do so for this reason.
- People may also join groups because those collective interests benefit them *personally*. For example, workers join labor unions because the higher wages and better working conditions fought for by unions will benefit them directly.

- Others may join for *psychological or social* benefits. They may join an environmental group or a local community group to meet and interact with like-minded people—even to form friendships. On the other hand, some may join groups simply because the membership may make them look better to others—even to help them advance their careers.

- Others may join a group for *employment* purposes—to work for the group. That employment may be for reasons directly related to the group's interests, or it may be for reasons related to the individual's skills. So healthcare or environmental groups may hire doctors, scientists, or researchers because of their special skills. On the other hand, every interest group needs communications and legal experts to function and so may hire or contract professionals in those areas.

Keep in mind that the reasons above are not mutually exclusive. It is very likely that most people join groups for several or all the above reasons.

Organization

There are more *potential* interests than most of us may comprehend. Your interests may stem from any number of factors related to you or your surroundings, including sociological factors (race, ethnicity, nationality, religion, sexual orientation), political factors (partisanship, ideology), behavioral factors (activities, personal and consumer habits), demographic factors (gender, age, location, income, occupation, education), and even physical characteristics (height, weight, health issues). However, not all interests gain the attention of government. The key to gaining this attention is *organization*. Organization is what separates interests from interest *groups* (again, recall the earlier chorus versus crowd analogy).

Any interest wishing to influence government must have some sort of structure, consisting most basically of *leadership* and *membership*. The leadership provides direction and (along with the staff) usually accounts for much of the group's activities. The membership may account for some activity (e.g., picketing, protesting, writing to or calling government officials), but in many instances provides mainly financing and popular support.

In general, organized groups cannot achieve significant success without a sound *financial structure*. Most organizations rely on membership dues along with additional contributions from supporters (including charitable foundations and think tanks—i.e., other groups). Many groups also benefit from federal and state funding. This funding is not *supposed* to be used to support their attempts to influence government. However, funding in the form of research or project grants—often providing data in support of a group's aims—may help them succeed nonetheless.

The "Free-Rider" Problem

As noted above, people join groups for many reasons. In general, it makes sense to say that we look to obtain some sort of benefit from our memberships. In turn, groups need our support to function effectively. Yet many groups find it difficult to obtain that support. Interestingly, this difficulty generally increases with the size of a (potential) group. You might think that the broader the interest, the easier it is to organize, collect resources, and act. You would be wrong! Broad interests face a **free-rider problem**. Mancur Olson (1982) describes the logic:

> The successful boycott or strike or lobbying action will bring the better price or wage for everyone in the relevant category, so the individual in any large group with a common interest will reap only a minute share of the gains from whatever sacrifices the individual makes to achieve this common interest. Since any gain goes to everyone in the group, those who contribute nothing to the effort will get just as much as those who made a contribution. It pays to "let George do it," but George has little or no incentive to do anything in the group interest either, so . . . there will be little, if any, group action. The paradox, then, is that (in the absence of special arrangements or circumstances . . .) large groups, at least if they are composed of rational individuals, will not act in their group interest. (p. 18)

In other words, groups that pursue **collective, or public, goods**, cannot limit them only to those who contribute time and resources to the cause (see Samuelson, 1954). National defense is one of the purest examples of a collective good. It is impossible to divide: If it is provided at all, it is provided for everyone. Contrast this with largely private goods—like typical consumer goods—that are bought and sold through individual transactions. You must pay for that iPhone you want! On the other hand, much of the regulations regarding the manufacture and sale of iPhones (material and manufacturing quality, limitations on the use of hazardous materials, required disclosure of radiation levels) are closer to public goods that exist (or not) regardless of your individual actions. If you benefit from these goods whether you contribute or not, it is not rational for you to contribute to any groups seeking these benefits. Groups seeking these regulations often will struggle to build support. You will just "let George do it" (which, of course George will not, lacking any more incentive than you!). In small groups (such as a local union seeking a pay raise for a company's workers), you may quickly realize that if you and George do not act, you may not receive any benefit. This realization may spur you to action. However, in large groups (such as consumer, environmental, social, and issue groups), there are lots of other Georges, at least some of whom (you are likely to assume) will act. Yet again, they have no more incentive than do you. This lack of action is the problem.

Governments may address this problem through compulsory action. National defense is funded through tax revenues. You pay taxes or you go to prison (assuming you are caught). Interest groups, however, do not have that compulsory power. So how do groups overcome this problem? Two words: **selective incentives** (or selective *benefits*). These are benefits that *can* be limited in their distribution. As Olson (1971) says,

> group action can be obtained only through an incentive that operates . . . selectively toward the individuals in the group. The incentive must be "selective" so that those who do not join the organization . . . can be treated differently from those who do. (p. 51)

These are the kind of benefits mentioned earlier, including material benefits like access to or discounts on consumer goods or other resources or information, and social benefits like entertainment, travel, and other group activities. Regardless of what George does, you are more likely to contribute your time and money to the group if it means that you can get a t-shirt with the group's logo on it, or a magazine with information on the group's accomplishments and activities, or a discount on tickets to Yankees games or on an insurance policy, or if you can attend a group party or lecture, or go on a Caribbean cruise with group members.

Myth and Reality: Equality and Biases

Myth: Fighting to Better Our Lives

As noted earlier, the accepted rationale for the formation of groups involves working for the betterment of society or some segment of it. Unions fight for better pay and working conditions for their members and for workers in general. Environmental groups fight for a cleaner and healthier environment. Civil rights groups fight for greater equality. Civil liberties groups fight for more personal freedom. Business and corporate groups fight for legislation and regulations that benefit their bottom line. And so on. In total, this is the type of pluralist democracy described earlier. While this is not wholly untrue, the reality is more complex . . . .

Reality: Upper-Class and Corporate Biases

The analogy of a chorus, organized to stand out among a crowd, helped to explain the formation of interest groups. Over sixty years ago, political scientist E. E. Schattschneider pointed to a problem in the pluralist universe. "The flaw" he said, "in the pluralist heaven is that the heavenly chorus sings with a strong upper- class accent" (1960). What Schattschneider means is that our system of interest groups is dominated by the upper class—the wealthy and well-educated. What accounts for this? Three things:

- *Time and Resources.* The upper classes, or those with a high socioeconomic status (SES) in social science lingo, possess the free time and the resources needed to participate in interest groups to a much greater extent than those with a lower SES. They have the wealth needed to help groups purchase equipment and technology, and to hire others with the skills needed for an interest group to be effective.
- *Awareness.* Because of their greater education levels, those with a higher SES have greater knowledge and awareness of the issues pursued by their groups. They may also have a greater understanding of how to tackle those issues to the group's benefit.
- *Skills.* With greater education levels, those with higher SES are also more likely to have the skills needed to make the group function successfully. This includes technical skills, organizational and leadership skills, and communications expertise among other skills.

In addition, this upper-class "accent" leans in a clearly corporate direction. This leaning can be demonstrated by examining the spending done by lobbyists at the federal level. Compiling data from the U.S. Senate Office of Public Records, The Center for Responsive Politics ranked various sectors of society by how much they spent on lobbying (Center for Responsive Politics, 2024a). In *just the first half* of 2024, definably corporate sectors—health (dominated by pharmaceutical companies), finance/insurance/real estate, communications/ electronics, energy/natural resources, transportation, agribusiness, defense contractors, construction, and other business interests—spent almost $2 *billion* on lobbying while non-corporate interests—ideological, single-issue (e.g., environmental, human rights, social issues), labor, education, public sector, religious interests, lawyers/lobbyists—spent about $263 million. In other words, corporate interests spent about seven times as much as non-corporate interests.

More Groups

We talked about why interest groups form, but it is also important to note that there are far more interest groups in existence today than there were in the past. While groups organized to influence government have existed throughout our history, the number of groups has grown dramatically in the last 50+ years. In 1971, there were 175 registered lobbying firms in Washington, DC. Just a decade later, that had grown to over 2,000 registered firms (Ranalli, D'Angelo, and King, 2018). In the second quarter of 2024, that number has exploded to over 6,000 firms according to United States Senate data—which was *limited* to 6,000 results (United States Senate, 2024). Several factors help to explain such a spectacular growth over the last half century[1]:

- *The Growth of Government*: The 1960s saw a significant growth in the size and activity of the federal government (see Chapter 3). More laws, more regulations, more federal programs have spawned more groups devoted to influencing those laws, regulations, and programs.

- *Groups beget more groups*: Groups devoted to influencing policy to achieve a particular end very often spark the creation of other groups with differing views. The growth of government activity in the 1960s and 1970s was largely progressive in nature, reflective of the era and the groups advocating for those policies. This spawned the creation of more conservative groups in the 1980s and beyond to counter those groups and the policies they supported. There is a certain "Newtonian" quality to group formation: The formation of groups promoting certain issues will undoubtedly lead to the formation of equal and opposing groups fighting those issues.

- *Better Standard of Living*: Especially after World War II, Americans realized a dramatic increase in their standard of living—meaning more people now have the time and resources to devote to participating in interest groups.

- *Higher Levels of Education*: That increase in our standard of living includes an increase in levels of education. Unlike much of our history, high school graduation is now close to universal. More people also attend college now than ever before. These increasing education levels mean that more of us have a greater awareness of issues affecting us. In addition, greater education levels mean more of us possess the skills that are valuable to participate in groups.

---

1   The following list was developed in part from Lowi, Theodore, et al. (2006). *American Government: Brief 2006 Edition*. New York: W.W. North & Company. See Chapter 12 on interest groups, especially the section on the proliferation of groups.

- *More Sophisticated Technology* (especially communications technology): Developments in technology over the last half-century have made it far easier to form interest groups. Computerized databases and instantaneous worldwide communication have both reduced the cost of organizing and made it far easier to communicate with others. In the past, organizing people meant gathering them all in one spot to communicate directly with them, or taking the time to communicate by letter or newsletter that may take days or weeks to distribute to all involved. These methods of communication also had significant costs (printing, publishing, distributing) associated with them. Today, an internet connection, Zoom, and free social media and messaging apps on your phone are all you need to reach dozens or even hundreds (or more?) of people to organize your group in near-instantaneous fashion for little to no cost.

So now that we know about the basics of interest groups, let's look at what they do.

Strategies

Lobbying

Perhaps the most obvious strategy used to influence government policy is direct contact, most commonly referred to as **lobbying**. As noted earlier, the number of lobby groups has dramatically increased in the last half-century. Not only are there thousands of groups in Washington, DC lobbying legislators and their staff in Congress, along with regulators in the executive branch, but there are innumerable groups that do the same thing on the state and local levels.

One of the challenges facing these groups is knowing how to play the game. All the money, expertise, and effort a group has may go to waste if it does not know the whos, hows, and whens of lobbying. To assist them, an entire community of professional lobbying firms line K Street in Washington, DC. These firms are not dedicated to any causes—their value lies in both their knowledge of the policy process and (more importantly) their connections to it. They are populated with highly-paid former members of Congress and ex-congressional and executive branch staffers. What makes these people so valuable is their knowledge of the process and *especially* their connections to current members of the legislative and executive branches. A former member of Congress has access to many places in the Capitol to which others do not. This advantage gives them a chance to buttonhole current members that ordinary interest group members do not have. The "revolving door" of legislators and staffers going from government to lobbying firms (and back again) has become a regular feature in Washington, DC. The high price of these professional lobbyists also limits their availability to upper-class and corporate clients.

Access and Iron Triangles

The "holy grail" of interest groups is the ability to gain direct access to members of Congress and/or the executive branch to develop policies favorable to their interests. The ability of groups to do this is fostered by the development informal but very powerful arrangements often referred to as "**subgovernments**" or "**iron triangles.**" This arrangement was described by Douglas Cater in his groundbreaking work on power in Washington as he describes the sugar industry subgovernment:

> Political power within the sugar subgovernment is largely vested in the Chairman of the House Agricultural Committee who works out the schedule of quotas. It is shared by a veteran civil servant, the director of the Sugar Division in the U.S. Department of Agriculture, who provides the necessary "expert" advice for such a complex marketing arrangement. Further advice is provided by Washington representatives of the domestic beet and cane sugar growers, the sugar refineries, and the foreign producers. (Cater, 1964, p. 18)

These arrangements tightly link the legislative, executive, and interest group actors involved in each policy area in a stable, mutually beneficial relationship. The classic subgovernment or iron triangle is illustrated in Figure 5.1.

Figure 5.1: Iron Triangles

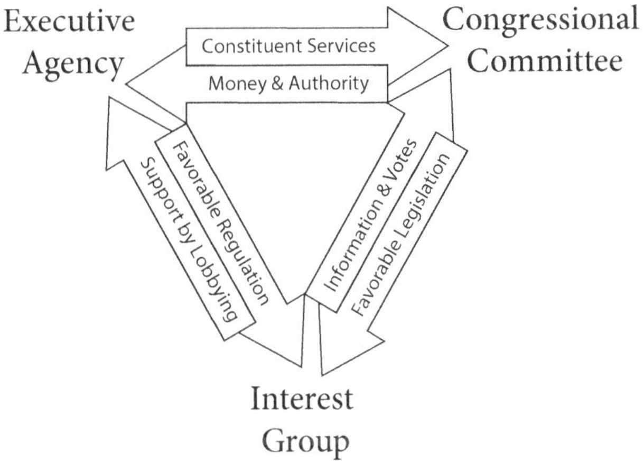

For example, in the policy area of agriculture described by Cater, the partners in the iron triangle are as follows: congressional committees, the Agriculture Committees; executive agency, the Department of Agriculture; and agricultural interest groups representing sugar growers, refiners, and producers. The theory is that these partners take control of policymaking in the relevant policy area while other officials and citizens pay little attention because it is generally viewed as technical, boring "inside baseball" stuff.

- *Congressional committees* need information to help them legislate. They get that information in the form of feedback from *executive agencies* regarding the performance of existing programs and regulations. They also get information from *interest groups* about how existing policies are working along with additional policies to consider. Committees respond by producing legislation based on interest group input, as well as providing budgets for the relevant executive agencies.

- *Executive agencies* are charged with carrying out the policies created by Congress. They need funding from *Congress* to hire the people and open the facilities needed to carry out their legislative mandates. In addition, they need feedback from *interest groups* as to how these policies are working in the real world. Agencies respond by providing feedback to congressional committees to help them develop policy, as well as responding to interest group input with favorable regulations and policy interpretations.

- *Interest groups* want laws from *Congress* and regulations from *executive agencies* that are favorable to their interests. They provide information to congressional committees and feedback on how existing programs are performing to executive agencies—all with the goal of influencing the governmental actors in ways that are favorable to their interests.

No matter what you call them, subgovernments or iron triangles, these arrangements all but guarantee a seat at the policy table for interest groups.

Courts

Many groups—notably **public interest groups**[2]—set out to influence policy by going "over the heads" of the president and Congress and filing lawsuits in the judiciary. This strategy is often used by groups that lack extensive resources. Instead of hiring expensive K Street lobbying firms, they use the courts, filing

---

2 Public interest groups pursue policies that benefit the public in general as opposed to benefiting only a particular segment of the public. Environmental and civil liberties groups are examples of public interest groups.

lawsuits to either enforce policies they feel are not properly carried out, or to stop policies they feel may be harmful or even unconstitutional.

Going Public and Grassroots Activity

Legislators may or may not listen directly to interest groups (who may sometimes be discounted or dismissed as unrepresentative of the general population), but they will *frequently* listen to public opinion. The quest for reelection means constantly pleasing the voters. Recognizing this idea, many groups attempt to influence public opinion in addition to trying to directly influence government. In the age of modern media, "going public"—as it is often called—is an increasingly popular strategy that may take several forms.

- *Advertising*: Trade and issue groups will try to build a favorable public image through advertising. One of the more successful ad campaigns is the dairy industry's "Got Milk?" ads (e.g., see https://www.gotmilk.com/). Look carefully at the ads. They are not designed to sell one company's brand of milk. They are designed to build support for the overall dairy industry. The hope is that these ads will build support for policies favorable to a "popular" industry. Other ad campaigns may involve more naked attempts to pressure governments for favorable action. In 2021, the National Association of Manufacturers (https://www.nam.org) ran a series of ads to pressure the federal government into enacting tax policies favorable to manufacturers. Its ads raised the specter of job losses and other calamities if Congress did not do what it wanted (see: https://www.nam.org/manufacturers-launch-ad-campaign-to-protect-american-jobs-13411/). More recently, they have taken to social media outlets like TikTok to promote manufacturing jobs to "Gen Z" youth (see: https://nam.org/influencers-make-blue-collar-cool-31400/). In addition to broad advertising, groups may try to build support with narrower direct mail, email, or social media campaigns using "big data," where they obtain names, addresses, email addresses, and social media account information from companies or online sites that they believe their potential supporters will patronize, and send out information to those customers (e.g., if you subscribe to the *Wall Street Journal* or frequently access *Fox News* posts on X or TikTok, you are a good target for business, Republican-leaning, and conservative groups).

- *Letters, phone calls, emails, social media posts*: As they build favorable public opinion, groups will also encourage supporters to act. One of the simplest forms of action is to have supporters contact government officials, journalists, or go public in general by mail, phone, email, or social media account. The LGBTQ+ advocacy group PFLAG encourages storytelling to "intrigue a journalist. To inspire a donor to give. To motivate staff to aim higher. To spark an advocacy revolution. To land a corporate sponsorship deal" (https://straightforequality.org/wp-content/uploads/2023/03/2023-PFLAG-Storytelling-Workbook.pdf). They also provide advice and guidelines for developing effective communication (see: https://pflag.org/resource/pao-sharingyourstory/).

- *Rallies and protests*: As with other methods of going public, rallies and protests are a way of turning public support into action. They are often used by groups with fewer resources, as the main costs—time, transportation, bullhorns, and hand-signs—are much less expensive than media ads, billboards, and professional lobbyists. The purpose of most rallies and protests is to gain the attention of government officials *and* the news media in the hopes of building further support for a cause. It should also be noted that, in many instances, these gatherings provide as much of a cathartic experience for their participants as anything else.

MARCH FOR OUR LIVES—AN EXAMPLE: March for Our Lives is a gun control advocacy organization founded by students who survived the 2018 Parkland School shooting in Florida (see: https://marchforourlives.org/). In the spring of 2022, following another school shooting in Uvalde, Texas, the group organized actions across the country to promote gun control legislation. This included "some 450 rallies would be held across the country, including Washington DC, New York, Los Angeles and Chicago" (Usher, 2022, para 6).

Like many groups, March for Our Lives uses many strategies. In addition to rallies and protests, they will use multiple strategies to press their issues:

> Using a diversity of tactics, we're making sure our leaders can't look away from the crisis of gun violence in America. From mobilizing youth voters in elections up and down the ballot to turn out record numbers of young people to vote, to creative activations that force our leaders to face the epidemic of gun violence head on, we're flipping the script on business-as-usual. (https://marchforourlives.org/what-we-do/)

- *"Grassroots" Lobbying*: Sometimes the public seemingly will act on its own, with little or no aid from organizing groups. This type of spontaneity is known as **grassroots** activity (as in, from the bottom up). Grassroots activity generally consists of many of the activities described earlier. New laws or proposed legislation may energize people to contact their legislators in support or opposition. They may gather in public to protest, as March for Our Lives often does. Interest groups may encourage these activities or use them as a springboard for their own activities.

Groups and Election Campaigns

One way in which groups may increase their chances of obtaining favorable policies is to help put the "right" people in office in the first place by getting involved in election campaigns. The further benefit of this is that officials who arguably owe their election to groups' support may feel gratitude for that support. This gratitude, in turn, may influence their policy positions in ways beneficial to the groups.

The most common electoral strategy is campaign spending. This spending may take the form of either contributions to parties, candidates, other outside groups, or direct spending in support of candidates. To address the concern among many progressives in the early 1900s that politicians were "bought" by corporate money, the 1907 Tillman Act outlawed corporate campaign contributions. The 1947 Taft-Hartley Act also outlawed labor union contributions. In addition to those laws, many others in the first half of the twentieth century established a patchwork of regulations on money in elections. Following the 1968 presidential election and during the 1972 election and the Watergate scandal, there was still public concern regarding the influence of wealthy individuals and groups over elections.

Congress enacted a set of laws known as the Federal Election Campaign Acts (FECA) in the early 1970s to:

- Set strict limits on individual and group contributions to parties and candidates.
- Require the public reporting of contributions.
- Require groups to register with the federal government before they can contribute.
- Limit the spending of presidential and congressional candidates.
- Set up a system of public funding for presidential elections.
- Create an independent agency, the Federal Election Commission (FEC), to administer and enforce the regulations.

See Chapter 6 for more details on the FECA.

Political Action Committees

While law forbids corporations and unions from contributing to candidates' campaign committees, the FECA formalized their *members'* ability to create **political action committees** (PACs) for the purpose of raising money to contribute to campaigns. These PACs (the legislation actually refers to them as "multi-candidate committees") must register with the FEC before they can raise and contribute money, and they are limited to contributing a maximum of $5,000 per candidate, per election. To qualify as a PAC, they must support at least five candidates.

The number of PACs has grown dramatically, from over 600 in 1974 to over 6,100 in 2018, with the bulk of that increase coming in trade association and non-connected (ideological and issue-oriented) PACs (Herrnson, 2020). Consistent with the upper-class and corporate biases discussed earlier, the greatest amount of spending on campaigns by far comes from corporate and trade-association PACs. FEC data from the first quarter of 2024 indicate that corporate and trade-association PACs spent almost 62% more than labor and non-connected PACs combined (U.S. Federal Election Commission, 2024).

FOLLOW THE MONEY: PACs differ in their goals and strategies. Paul Herrnson (2020) describes three PAC strategies: access, ideological, and mixed. The bottom-line goal of access PACs is to influence legislation. They like winners, so they contribute most often to incumbents and to sympathetic candidates in close elections (where the extra money may make the difference). They do not wish to waste resources on challengers with little chance of getting elected. Most corporations pursue an access-oriented strategy. Ideological PACs wish "to increase the number of legislators who share their broad political perspective or position on specific, often emotionally charged issues . . ." (Herrnson, 2020, p. 147). Most of their contributions go to sympathetic candidates in close elections, but they are far more likely than access PACs to contribute to sympathetic challengers as well. Most non-connected (issue or ideological) PACs pursue this strategy. PACs pursuing a mixed strategy will make some contributions to candidates sharing their views, and some contributions to incumbents "to improve their access to legislators" (Herrnson, 2020, p. 149). Most unions pursue a mixed strategy.

Beyond PACs: Soft Money, 527 and 501(c) Groups, and Super PACs

Restrictions placed on political-party spending by the Bipartisan Campaign Reform Act (BCRA) of 2002 (see Chapter 6) opened the way for vastly increased spending by groups in recent elections. The law restricted the ability of parties to raise and spend unregulated "soft money," and restricted their ability to run "issue ads." However, no such restrictions were placed on interest groups. Party activists, now restricted by BCRA, simply shifted their activity to outside groups. Given the exponentially growing costs of campaigns, PACs were not an attractive alternative, given their $5,000-per-candidate, per-election limitation. Activists found their answer in tax-exempt "527," "501(c)3," and "501(c)4" groups (named for sections of the Internal Revenue Code). Campaign activity by these groups is either limited or prohibited (See Chapter 6 for more details. Also see: https://afj. org/wp-content/uploads/2018/06/The-Connection_p6_Chart_paywall-2.pdf).

However, FEC and court decisions established that soft money and issue ads do *not* amount to campaign activity if they do not expressly advocate the election or defeat of candidates. What seals the deal is that these decisions also said that candidate names and images could be used in soft-money-funded issue ads without violating the campaign restriction. So, an ad just prior to an election saying, "Vote for Jane Doe!" is an expressly campaign activity forbidden to many of these groups, but one saying "John Smith will cut our taxes!" is *not* (even if it includes a picture of Smith).

In recent years, whole new classes of groups have formed to keep interests involved in the big-money world of modern campaigns. The latest creation is the "Super PAC." These are officially known as independent expenditure-only committees, and they

> may raise unlimited sums of money from corporations, unions, associations and individuals, then spend unlimited sums to overtly advocate for or against political candidates. Unlike traditional PACs, super PACs are prohibited from donating money directly to political candidates, and their spending must not be coordinated with that of the candidates they benefit. Super PACs are required to report their donors to the Federal Election Commission on a monthly or semiannual basis—the super PAC's choice—in off-years, and monthly in the year of an election. (Center for Responsive Politics, 2024b)

In addition, the restrictions placed on corporations (and presumably unions) were upended by the 2010 Supreme Court decision in *Citizens United v. Federal Election Commission* (130 S.Ct. 876). The court said that corporations have a First Amendment right to spend money from their own treasuries to expressly support the election or defeat of candidates, which the BCRA had forbidden (though they are still forbidden from contributing to campaigns, and their members' PACs still face contribution limits).

Other Activities

While spending dominates the election-related activity of interest groups, there are other ways in which members may get involved. Group members may volunteer their time and effort to candidates. Supportive candidates may recruit volunteers for groups to help with information and get-out-the-vote (GOTV) activities. This often involves staffing phone banks, operating computers, or stuffing envelopes. Given their place among the workforce, union members are especially able to help candidates they support by going door-to-door throughout their communities, encouraging residents to vote for their candidates.

Case Studies: Groups in Action

1. Lobbyists Helping Lobbyists

Sometimes, interests and their lobbies form unlikely allies. T. R. Reid (1980) describes a situation in the late 1970s in which railroad lines and environmentalists both favored a waterway user charge for barge lines and opposed funding to rebuild a major Mississippi River Lock and Dam in Alton, Ill. The environmentalists were concerned about the ecological impact while the railroads were battling a competitor in the transportation business. The railroad companies were flush with lobbying cash while the environmentalists were not (see the earlier discussion of the free-rider problem). Yet railroads were hesitant to spend a lot for fear of being dismissed as a self-interested competitor with a financial stake.

They thought that environmental lobbying could have a greater impact because these groups had no direct financial or business interest in the policies. However, the railroads could not contribute funds directly to the environmentalists because they were equally big (if not *bigger*) polluters, as were the barge lines. Environmental groups would not take their money. The railroads' chief lobbyist got an idea.

> He conjured, out of thin air, a new organization, for which he created a name (The Council for a Sound Waterways Policy), an address (a vacant office down the hall in the Western Railroads Building), and a bank account. Each month he transferred some money from the railroads' lobbying fund to the Council, and the Council, in turn, transferred a monthly grant to environmental groups lobbying for waterway charges and against the Alton project. For the environmental groups, this arrangement was just right. They could continue their work without ever acknowledging that they were accepting money from a major polluter. (Reid, 1980, pp. 50–51)

The funding for the non-corporate environmentalists was now coming in large part from a major corporate interest. So, the corporate bias discussed earlier is likely even greater than the data may indicate.

2. Grassroots' Evil Twin, "Astroturf"

Grassroots activities may appear to be democracy at its purest—but sometimes appearances can be deceiving. Knowing the value of public opinion to lawmakers, interest groups may try to artificially generate activity that appears to be grassroots. That is, what look like grassroots letter-writing or emailing campaigns, or spontaneous protests may actually be carefully planned and orchestrated by interest groups. These activities have been derisively (but not inaccurately) referred to as **"Astroturf"** (get it? fake grass!). In a 1996 PBS documentary, Hedrick Smith interviews the head of a professional public relations firm that generates these kinds of campaigns (Smith, 1996):

HEDRICK SMITH [VOICE OVER]: Usually, business is targeting Congress.

JACK BONNER/PRES., BONNER & ASSOCIATES: They want 100 phone calls, 20 calls in to a senator, 25 letters, 200 letters to a particular member of the House.

SMITH: So you have 300 phone lines, that means you can have 300 people out of here at one time?

BONNER: The biggest thing we ever did, we were doing six thousand patch-through phone calls a day to the Hill.

HEDRICK SMITH [VOICE OVER]: Patch-through phone calls are a hot item for Bonner and leading-edge lobbyists. Bonner's staff phones ordinary citizens, sells them on a client's issue, and when successful, immediately patches the call through to their senator or house member, while the mood is hot.

SMITH: If they're on the side of the issue your client wants, they get patched through?

BONNER: Right.

SMITH: If they're on the other side of the issue, what happens to them?

BONNER: What's your guess?

SMITH: They get dropped.

BONNER: That's right.
(https://web.archive.org/web/20220704120835/http://www.hedricksmith.
com/site_powergame/files/uneltrans)

So be wary. What appears to be grassroots activity may be democracy at its purest—or it may be Astroturf at its most artificial!

Discussion Questions

1. Discuss the history of interest groups. Why do they exist at all? What are the benefits of joining one?
2. Tocqueville said that America is a nation of joiners. What did he mean? Investigate other nations to see whether they differ from the United States.
3. Contact a local interest group or the local chapter of a larger group. Many groups may be found at this site: https://justfacts.votesmart.org/ interest-groups. What are their goals? What are their strategies for achieving those goals?
4. Examine the data on the "revolving door" by going to the OpenSecrets. org website. Under the "Lobbying" menu, click on "Revolving Door." On the left-hand menu, click on "Lobbying Firms," and select one of the firms. You will see a list of its lobbyists. Click on the lobbyists' names and examine employment timeline and history. Examine several lobbyists' profiles. What do you see? Did they spend time in government service before their current employment as a lobbyist? If so, explore their time in government. Does it appear related to their expertise and/or their clients? Can you make the case that their past government work constitutes a current asset to their lobbying work?

References

Cater, D. (1964). *Power in Washington*. Random House.

Center for Responsive Politics. (2024a). *Influence & lobbying: Ranked sectors.* Open Secretss. https://www.opensecrets.org/federal-lobbying/ranked-sectors?cycle=2024

Center for Responsive Politics. (2024b). *Super PACs*. Open Secrets. https://www.opensecrets.org/political-action-committees-pacs/super-pacs/2024

de Tocqueville, A. (1945). *Democracy in America*. Alfred A. Knopf, Inc.

Encyclopaedia Britannica. (2008, April 7). *Pluralism*. Encyclopedia Britannica. https://www.britannica.com/topic/pluralism-politics

Herrnson, P. S. (2020). *Congressional elections: Campaigning at home and in Washington*. 8th ed. CQ Press.

Lowi, T. J., et al. (2006). *American government: Brief 2006 edition*. W.W. North & Company.

Madison, J. (1788/2001). The utility of the union as a safeguard against domestic faction and insurrection. *The Federalist #10*. G. W. Carey & J. McClellan (Eds.). Liberty Fund.

Olson, M. (1971). *The logic of collective action: Public goods and the theory of groups*. Harvard University Press.

____. (1982). *The rise and decline of nations*. Yale University Press.

PFLAG. (2024). *Sharing your story to create change (GOTV edition)*. PFLAG. https://pflag.org/resource/pao-sharingyourstory/

Ranalli, B., D'Angelo, J., and King, D. (2018). *The 1970s sunshine reforms and the transformation of congressional lobbying*. The Congressional Research Institute.

Reid, T. R. (1980). *Congressional odyssey: The saga of a senate bill*. W. H. Freeman & Company.

Samuelson, P. A. (1954). The pure theory of public expenditure. *Review of Economics and Statistics, 36*(November), 387–389.

Schattschneider, E. E. (1960). *The semisovereign people: A realist's view of democracy in America*. Holt, Rinehart, and Winston.

Smith, H. (producer). (1996). The unelected: The media & the lobbies. *The people & the power game*. PBS. Retrieved August 2, 2024 from https://web.archive.org/web/20220522142129/https://hedricksmith.com/site_powergame/files/uneltrans.html

United States Federal Election Commission. (2024). *PAC contributions to candidates*. FEC.gov. Retrieved August 1, 2024 from https://www.fec.gov/resources/campaign-finance-statistics/2024/tables/pac/PAC2_2024_15m.pdf

United States Senate. (2024). *Lobbying disclosure: Registrations & quarterly activity*. Senate.gov. Retrieved July 30, 2024 from https://lda.senate.gov/filings/public/filing/search/

Usher, B. P. (2022, June 11). *March For Our Lives: Tens of thousands rally for stricter U.S. gun laws.* BBC. https://www.bbc.com/news/world-us-canada-61772039

Court Cases

Citizens United v. Federal Election Commission, 130 S.Ct. 876 (2010)

Political Parties, Voting, and Elections

Carl D. Cavalli

Learning Objectives

After covering the topic of political parties, elections, and voting, students should understand:

1. The evolution, organization, and functions of the two major political parties.
2. The role of "third" or "minor" parties and the hurdles they face in our system.
3. The history of suffrage in America and the rules governing registration, voting, and elections.
4. The prominent role of money in contemporary elections.

Abstract

As noted in Chapters 1 and 2, our government is a democratic republic, and the centerpiece of all such governments are elections in which eligible voters select candidates to represent them. The organizing of voter preferences through political parties is central to the electoral concept. Not only did the framers not foresee this, but they were actually hostile to the concept.[1] This lack of foresight may have been their biggest failure. A strong case may be made that our two-party system traces its roots to the nation's founding. This system is sustained by our most common electoral rules: single-member district, plurality (or "SMDP") rules. Not only do these rules affect our party system, but there is strong evidence that they can affect the outcome of individual elections. Other rules affecting elections include campaign finance regulations.

---

1   See especially *Federalist #10* (https://guides.loc.gov/federalist-papers/text-1-10#s-lg-box-wrapper-25493273) and George Washington's farewell address (https://www.ourdocuments.gov/doc.php?doc=15&page=transcript).

Introduction

Political parties seek to control government through elections. As such, their existence is closely tied to the electoral process.

Political Parties

What is a political party? It is an organization that *selects* candidates for office to represent the party's ideals, conducts *election* campaigns to get their candidates into office, and *organizes* government to facilitate achievement of its goals. Selection includes recruiting (searching for and encouraging) candidates to run, and then conducting a nominating process to formally select a nominee among all competing candidates. In election campaigns, parties provide services (e.g., advertising, polling) for their nominees, and will also encourage turnout to support them. Examples of organization include majority party leadership in Congress (see Chapter 7) or state legislatures, and presidential or gubernatorial appointments to the executive and judicial branches (see Chapter 8). All of this is toward the goal of implementing a broad *policy* agenda. In addition, political party labels serve as "cues," or shortcuts, to help us as voters decide whom to support in elections.

Unlike other multi-party democracies, we have sustained a system of two major parties for most of our history. This fact is interesting because the framers did not anticipate their formation. Indeed, they were actively hostile to the idea. James Madison devotes *Federalist #10* to a discussion of controlling the effects of factions. He defined a faction as "a number of citizens . . . united . . . by some common impulse of passion, or of interest . . . "—a definition in which all modern interpreters include political parties (Madison, 1787). Additionally, in his farewell address as president, George Washington warned us "against the baneful effects of the spirit of party."

However, the formation of political parties was in the air, and that air portended *two* political parties from the start. Every major issue surrounding the formation of the government provoked two opposing sides: national versus state power, commerce versus agriculture, North versus South, and when it came down to it, pro-Constitution versus anti-Constitution. Moreover, these were not random divisions. Those on one side of any issue tended to be consistently on the same side of each of the other issues. Two *big* factions.

Elections

Why conduct elections? With elections, we can reward elected officials who appear to serve us well (by re-electing them to office) and punish elected officials who fail to serve us well (by kicking them out). That is, we can hold them responsible for their actions. This ability also provides the public with a sense of *influence* (as debated in Chapter 1). One might make the case that voting replaces violence as the main means of political participation (consider: If you cannot vote politicians you dislike out of office, then how do you *get* them out?).

From the viewpoint discussed above, elections represent a bargain, both in the sense that they are (at least in theory) a good deal for us *and* in the sense that they represent an *exchange* between us and the government. What is the bargain from the government's standpoint? They concede our right to participate—to influence their composition—in exchange for gaining *stability* and *legitimacy*.[2] What is the bargain from our standpoint? We concede other means of altering the government (for example, *violence*) in exchange for the sense of influence discussed above.

Basics: Parties

Formation

As noted in the introduction, political parties were neither anticipated nor welcomed by the framers. However, the stage was set from the founding for a two-party system. The two big factions mentioned earlier developed, at first, into the Federalists and the Anti-Federalists.

The Federalists

The better-organized faction at our founding was the **Federalists**. The framers were largely Federalists. They felt the Articles of Confederation was a failure (see Chapter 2) and so wrote an entirely new constitution. They favored national power over local power—in large part because they felt coordination at the national level was required to promote and develop the nation's commerce and industry (e.g., see Wood, 1998). Most were northerners, probably because most of the nation's commerce and industry was located in the North.

The Anti-Federalists

At least as numerous, but less organized were the **Anti-Federalists**. With many located in the agricultural South, they feared a powerful national government and the industrialization it might bring. They wanted to maintain the nation's agrarian roots. Throughout the states, opposition to centralized national power was found most often in areas "in which small, self-sufficient, and often debtor farmers were most numerous" (Main, 2006, p. 112).

---

2   That is, we will respect and obey the laws they create, even if we disagree with them. Disagreement becomes a catalyst for voting (and other forms of participation), and *not* for violence.

From the Anti-Federalists to the Democrats

The Anti-Federalists began to organize into a true political party in the mid-1790s. They recognized the value of coordinating their efforts to win elections throughout the nation and to help bridge our system of separation of powers. Under the leadership of Thomas Jefferson and James Madison, they called themselves Republicans.[3] By the election of 1800, their organizational efforts paid off ,and they began to win huge majorities in Congress (Office of the Clerk, 2010; Senate Historical Office, 2010) as well as an unparalleled seven consecutive presidential elections.

Among intra-party divisions in the 1820s, Andrew Jackson came to lead the party and attempted to preserve its Jeffersonian roots. It was at this time they began to call themselves **Democrats**. Even though some left the party, perceiving Jackson's leadership to be autocratic, they continued to win elections. Including their Jeffersonian Republican forebears, they won all but two presidential elections from 1800 through 1856 and maintained control of Congress for all but a few years during that time.

After a period of dominance by the new Republican Party (see below) in the late 19th and early 20th centuries, the Democratic Party regained its majority in the 1930s under the leadership of Franklin Roosevelt. They maintained this majority largely intact into the 1970s. It was a changed party, however.

From its Anti-Federalist forebears, it came to be the party of the "common man." While the party maintains a similar focus today as the party of workers, minorities, and women, its view of government has changed drastically. Franklin Roosevelt's Democratic Party was quite different from Jefferson's and Jackson's. Gone were the Anti-Federalist fears of national government. Roosevelt's "New Dealers" believed in using the power of the national government to fight economic distress and inequality (e.g., see: https://democrats.org/where-we-stand/party-platform/).

From the Federalists to the Whigs to the Republicans

Though our founding was dominated by Federalists, their dislike of political parties proved to be their downfall. They began organizing into what looked like a political party around the same time as the Anti-Federalists—the mid-1790s. However, as the faction in power, their focus was on policy, not elections. By the time they realized the value of organizing for elections, it was too late. In the elections of 1800, they lost out to their better-organized opponents (see above) virtually everywhere. By the early 1800s, they were finished as an organized group.

---

3   This is not the modern Republican Party (see next section). To distinguish this party from the modern one, the terms "Democratic-Republicans" or "Jefferson's Republicans" are often used.

Their sympathizers did not disappear, however. A combination of former Federalists and Democrats (who feared what they saw as autocratic rule in the election of Democrat Andrew Jackson to the presidency) formed the Whig Party. They were quite successful in the 1830s and 1840s, electing several presidents and building congressional majorities (Office of the Clerk, 2010; Senate Historical Office, 2010). The thorny issue of slavery split and ultimately destroyed the party in the early 1850s.

At that time, a new party arose from anti-slavery elements in both the Democratic and Whig parties. To emphasize their belief that they were truly fulfilling the framers' vision, they called themselves **Republicans**. Under the leadership of John C. Fremont and Abraham Lincoln, they quickly rose to major party status. From the mid-1850s through today, they have competed with the Democrats as one of the two major political parties in America.

Consistent with their Federalist roots, the Republicans have historically been the party of business and commerce. However, unlike their forebears who saw a strong national government as the key to commercial development, modern Republicans often take a dim view of federal power. More like the Anti-Federalists, modern Republicans generally place more trust in local government. The modern Republican Party supports free market commerce (i.e., it opposes much government regulation of businesses and industries), small and localized government, and a socially conservative ideology (e.g., see: https://www.gop.com/about-our-party/).

Three-Part Structure

As noted earlier, parties exist to select and elect candidates and to organize government. This idea suggests a three-part structure to parties as we know them. Not only is there the *party organization* itself, but there is also the *party in government* and the *party in the electorate* (voters) as well (e.g., see Beck, 1997; Key, 1964).

It is the party *organizations* at all levels (national, state, and local) that help to select and elect candidates. They do this by first nominating candidates as their choices for the general election. The process of nominating usually consists of either a *primary*, where voters select a nominee, a *caucus*, where party members gather to agree upon a nominee, a *convention*, where party members gather in one location to formally choose a nominee, or some combination of these methods.

Presidential Nominations

We can see all three of these methods in presidential party nominations. In the mid-to-late summer of presidential election years, the national party organizations (the Democratic National Committee and the Republican National Committee) each hold a national *convention* to formally select their presidential nominees. At the convention, delegates representing all 50 states and many territories vote to select the nominees. Most delegates are bound by state and/ or party rules to vote for particular candidates, so the outcome is rarely in doubt (leading some to talk more of coronations than conventions). So, how are the delegates chosen, and why are they bound to one candidate? This is where the other methods come into play.

All states and territories hold either a primary or caucus to choose their delegates to the national conventions.[4] A *primary* can be either open to all voters or closed to all but registered party members (there are some other variations as well). Voting takes place at polling places around the state, much like any election. A *caucus* involves only party members meeting around the state. They involve more effort as participants must gather in one spot (an auditorium or gymnasium) to openly debate the choices (e.g., see: https:// www.c-span.org/video/?532841-1/iowa-republican-caucus-meeting). Because of the effort involved, caucuses usually involve far less of the electorate than do primaries. The Democratic Party requires all its primaries and caucuses to use **proportional representation** rules, which allocate delegates favoring candidates in proportion to their support in the primary vote or the caucus. The Republican Party allows states to use **winner-take-all** rules, where the top finisher gets *all* the state's delegates, if they so choose.

To win elections, the party organizations help candidates appeal to the *electorate*. The focus of these "get-out-the-vote" (GOTV) efforts is two-fold. First, the organizations want to make sure their supporters—the *party in the electorate* (often called the "base")—turn out to vote. Next, they want to reach out to independent and uncommitted voters to win their support. Particularly strong or popular candidates may even reach out to supporters of other parties. Today, there are high-tech efforts to target and appeal to the public using mailing and email lists, consumer and demographic data, and social networking media (e.g., YouTube, X, Instagram, TikTok, Facebook) in addition to traditional speeches, flyers, rallies, and TV/radio advertisements.

Candidates who win the general election will take their seats in office to become their party's *party in government*. In legislating or administering policy, they will attempt to represent their party and to get its agenda enacted into law.

---

4   Or in some cases, like Kansas and Maine, a combination of both.

Modern Regional Bases

The Democratic and Republican parties have competed head-to-head as our only major parties for over 150 years. Currently, the Democratic Party's regional bases are in the Northeast, the Great Lakes region, and the West. The Republican Party's regional bases are in the South, the Upper Midwest, and in the Great Plains. This distribution is evident in the 2020 presidential Electoral College results (e.g., see https://uselectionatlas.org/RESULTS/). While this distribution is accurate, it is also misleading.

Both parties are *competitive* in many areas. However, while some suggest that a mixed "purple America" is a more accurate portrayal of recent party competition than is red (Republican) versus blue (Democrat) (e.g., see Ansolabehere, Rodden, and Snyder, 2006), others see increasingly stark partisan division in the future (e.g., see Wasserman, 2017).[5]

Realignment

The current alignment of political parties has not always been the case. We have seen many different partisan alignments. At any given time, there is a set of parties competing over the issues of the day. This set of parties competing over these issues comprises a **party system**. New events and new generations with new issues will alter the composition of—and competition between—the parties, leading to a new party system. This change is often referred to as **realignment** (Burnham, 1970). Through much of our history, realignments occur with surprising regularity—approximately every 30 years. Perhaps it is a result of generational change.

In any case, most electoral scholars identify five or six realignments in our history (e.g., see Sundquist, 1983), usually resulting in a dominant party. They are identified here by approximate year:

- *1800*: In a sense, 1800 saw an *alignment* rather than a *realignment* since this was the point at which political parties were developing. Indeed, the very development of parties was the issue. Recall the differing views on organizing between the Federalists and Anti-Federalists. The Federalists disliked factions, believing them detrimental to the public good, while the Anti-Federalists saw organizing as the key to success. The Anti-Federalists' organization into Jefferson's Republicans paid off as they became the dominant party in American politics for many years (and, indeed, the only party for a few years).
- *1828*: A new generation of Americans saw the rapid disappearance of property requirements for voting. This change meant voting and

---

5   For a graphic representation of "Purple America," see: https://purplestatesofamerica.org/.

politics were no longer limited to the wealthy elite. In a more practical sense, it made public campaigning a viable option for election. Andrew Jackson was the first person to run for president by openly campaigning for votes among the public. It was the new issue of the political age—political participation, and Andrew Jackson's Democrats capitalized on the expansion of the vote to ordinary (white, male) citizens to become the dominant party for the next 30 years.

- *1860*: An old issue, slavery, became the issue of the age as the nation debated its expansion into the west. The industrial North—less dependent upon slavery—was the locus of a growing movement to abolish the practice, while the agricultural South was still dependent upon it. The issue fractured both the Whigs and Democrats, destroying the former and leaving the Democrats as a largely Southern, pro-slavery party. In 1854, the abolitionists united to form a new party, the Republicans. The growing anti-slavery movement rapidly catapulted the party to majority status (aided by the secession of largely Democratic Southern states from the union in the 1860s). They would remain the majority party nationally until well into the 20th century.

- *1896*: The late 19th century saw the United States emerge as a major industrial, economic power in what we might today call the *first* age of globalization. The major issue was how far to pursue industrialization and globalization. The Democrats, still located largely in the more agricultural South, resisted the trend while the Republicans embraced it. The nation sided with the Republicans, re-energizing their majority at the dawn of the 20th century.

- *1932*: Perhaps the most iconic realignment occurred in the 1930s as a result of the Great Depression—the greatest period of economic distress the country has experienced. The issue for the age was the extent to which the federal government should actively combat it. While both parties embraced at least some activism (it may be argued that Herbert Hoover, the Republican president at the time the Depression hit in 1929, made greater use of the federal government to address the nation's troubles than any previous president[6]), it was the Democratic Party under Franklin Delano Roosevelt that eventually advocated extensive use of the federal government to actively combat the effects of the Depression (the **New Deal**). An increasingly

---

6   See for example the Reconstruction Finance Corporation, created in 1929 (https://www.archives.gov/research/guide-fed-records/groups/234.html).

distressed public flocked to Roosevelt and the Democrats, who won unprecedented majorities in the 1930s.

- *1960s?* If the 30-year cycle held, we would expect to see another realignment in the 1960s. However, there is scant evidence of any traditional realignment. The Democratic Party maintained a relatively strong majority through the 1970s and weaker majority into the early 1990s. While there were new issues—most notably the **civil rights movement**, and more recently the rise of economic and social issues— they led neither to a new majority, nor to radically reformed parties. To this day, while Democratic support has weakened notably, there is little corresponding increase in support for Republicans. Instead, beginning in the 1970s, people began to leave both parties and identify as independents (e.g., see Gallup Poll data on party identification: https://news.gallup.com/poll/15370/party-affiliation.aspx). This change leaves us with a more competitive two-party system, but not with a "50-50" division of Democrats and Republicans. More accurately we now have a "30-40-30" division that includes independents—leading some to say there has not been a *re*alignment, but rather a *de*alignment, or a movement away from political parties (Nie, Verba, & Petrocik, 1976; Rosenof, 2003).

In the mid-1990s, many proclaimed a Republican realignment. There were similar claims of a Democratic realignment after the 2006 and 2008 elections, and again by Republicans after the 2010, 2014, and 2016 elections. All are wrong. The key to realignments is their establishment of a stable, long-term party system, which means you can never proclaim one after only one or two elections. They may only be designated in retrospect after a decade or more.

Minor Parties

That only two major parties have dominated our politics for over 150 years does not mean no other parties exist. There are dozens and possibly even hundreds of smaller parties, which raises a few questions.[7]

Why Are There Only Two Major Parties?

There are several contributing reasons. First, as noted earlier, we divided into two major factions very early on, leading almost inevitably to our two major parties. Second, though, is that our divisions have never been so vast as to sustain many major parties. We share several universal values (see Chapter 4) that do not

---

7   The site Politics1.com lists 35 others at the time of this printing (see: https://politics1.com/parties.htm).

leave much support for additional parties. Third is our self-fulfilling skepticism of third parties. Most all of us are not so issue driven that we will back parties with little chance of winning, even if we agree with their issue positions. In fact, there is evidence to the contrary—we often adjust our own issue positions to conform to the party we support (Campbell, et al., 1960; Fiorina, 1981; Green, et al., 2002; Karol, 2009). We like to back winners, essentially because the rather reasonable logic is that parties do us no good unless they can win elections. Of course, if we do not support them, they will not win—a vicious cycle for third parties.

Last, and least appreciated, are rules. Rules matter. While we like to think that elections are simply "The candidate with the most votes wins," it is more complicated. Different rules may lead to different outcomes even with the same set of votes. All American elections are state-run; it is a delegated power (see Chapter 3). There are federal regulations and constitutional requirements imposed on the states, but the bottom line is that they run the contests. This in itself is a "rule" that matters! It means 50 states may have 50 sets of differing electoral rules. Since all contemporary state legislatures and governors, who write the rules, are under the control of one major party or the other, those rules are generally favorable to the major parties. The first hurdle third parties must clear is negotiating 50 sets of rules—none of which were written by (or for!) them.

There are two sets of rules that have the greatest effect: voting rules and ballot access rules.

- *Voting Rules*: The most common American voting rules are Single-Member District, Plurality rules—known as **SMDP**. Not all U.S. elections are SMDP, but most are.
  - ▷ As the name implies, **Single-Member Districts** have only one representative. It is how we elect representatives to Congress and state legislatures. For example, the state of Georgia is currently apportioned 14 U.S. representatives based on its population (see Chapter 2). The state does not, however, simply elect 14 people statewide. Federal law requires states to create one electoral district per representative—so Georgia must elect one representative each in 14 separate districts. It is this winner-take-all nature (often referred to as "first-past-the-post") that advantages major parties. You must have enough support to finish first. As such, it may be better to think of *single-winner elections*. Contrast this with **Multi-Member District** systems (or *multi-winner elections*), where each district elects several representatives. If states were allowed to use multi-member systems for Congress, Georgia might hold

a single, statewide election where the top 14 finishers won office. Another possibility might be a handful of districts electing several representatives each. In either case, candidates can finish second, third, or lower and still win office. This procedure gives minor parties a much better chance.

    ▷ In **Plurality** elections, the threshold for victory is simply getting more votes than anyone else. Contrast this to **Majority** elections where the threshold is higher: more than half of the votes cast (or alternatively, more votes than everyone else combined). The advantage of plurality rules to major parties may seem counter-intuitive at first. Since winning requires a lower threshold, it is tempting to think minor parties have a better chance—and they do. However, major parties do, too—and they get, by definition, *more* votes than minor parties (the very meaning of plurality, right?). In addition, they do so without needing help from anyone else. This situation leaves little hope for smaller parties. In contrast, even major parties will not always meet the higher standard of a majority election without help (see the case studies at the end of this chapter). That help may come in the form of coalitions with smaller parties to build the necessary majority—giving those smaller parties at least some influence (and a reason to stick around!).

- *State Ballot Rules*: States control elections, and each sets its own rules. This includes deciding which parties get access to limited ballot space. All states award space to parties who won a significant portion of the vote in previous elections—usually 20-25%. Major parties easily meet that standard, so their candidates appear on virtually all ballots. However, minor parties rarely do that well, so they generally do not get automatic access. They must seek it each time. To do so, states have all manner of requirements: fees (ranging from a few to thousands of dollars), petition signatures (again, ranging from a handful to thousands), paperwork, and legal action. Minor parties must spend precious resources meeting these requirements, while the major parties are already out campaigning. This structure means the major parties can devote all their time and money to campaigning while minor parties must devote a significant portion just to get on ballots.

So Why Do They Bother?

Minor parties bother because they have a message. That message usually involves individuals, issues, or just a better way (or any combination of those things).

Some minor parties are vehicles for a single candidate. The Reform Party of the 1990s was the classic example of a single-person, or cult-of-personality, party (see: https://reformparty.org/). Its lifeblood was two-time presidential candidate Ross Perot, a billionaire who practically bankrolled the entire party from his own pocket. While he was a candidate in 1992 (when the entity was the more loosely organized "United we Stand America") and 1996, the Reform Party was born and rose to become the most formidable third party in decades. In 1992, Perot captured almost 20 million votes—the best showing for a third-party presidential candidate in 80 years. In 1996, he ran for the Reform Party's nomination at a convention that he paid for. In the general election, he captured over 8 million votes—a significant drop, but still one of the best third-party showings in years. After that, Perot began to withdraw from active participation in the party, and in 2000, he declined another bid for president. Without him, public support dropped, and the party fractured among internal fighting. The official party nominated conservative columnist Patrick Buchanan for president. A splinter group nominated Dr. John Hagelin. Combined, they managed to win fewer than 600,000 votes. The party (though it still exists today) was effectively dead.

Some minor parties are, in a sense, super-interest groups. Much like a traditional interest group, they will focus on a single issue (or a small range of related issues). However, they will go beyond merely trying to influence government; they will actively run candidates for office. Perhaps the best known national single-issue party is the Green Party (technically, a collection of parties with international roots). While generally a liberal party, their focus is on environmental issues (see: https://www.gp.org). Green Parties originated in Germany in the 1980s and came to the United States in the 1990s. They gained prominence in 2000 when their presidential candidate, longtime consumer activist Ralph Nader, received over 2 million votes for president. In 2016, their presidential candidate, Jill Stein, receive almost 1.5 million votes. The party continues to function nationally, with over 140 elected officials nationwide as of July 2024 (see: https://www.gpelections.org/greens-in-office/).

Still other minor parties are organized and function just like the major parties with a range of issue positions and fielding candidates throughout the country. They are simply smaller. One of the more prominent of these parties is the Libertarian Party (https://www.lp.org). The Libertarians ran hundreds of candidates nationwide in 2024, including their presidential candidate, Chase

Oliver. While Libertarian philosophy supports minimal government, the party neither focuses on a narrow range of issues (like a single-issue party), nor does it revolve around a single person. In a very real sense, the Libertarian Party functions just like the Democratic and Republican parties; it is just a smaller version.

Minor parties are most successful when their message has two components: 1) it resonates with the public, and 2) it has been ignored by the major parties. The rise of Ross Perot and the Reform Party in the 1990s best exemplifies these components. His 1992 candidacy revolved around concern about growing annual national budget deficits (and their cumulative impact on the national debt). In the 1970s and 1980s, both major parties had campaigned on balancing the federal budget, yet the publicly-held portion of the national debt more than tripled between 1976 and 1985 (Office of Management and Budget, 2010). This lack of action by both parties over many years (despite their rhetoric) led many people to listen closely to Perot when he chided the major parties and focused on reducing the deficit. The Reform Party's success shocked the major parties into action. In 1997, a Democratic president and a Republican-led Congress negotiated a balanced budget that quickly led to budget surpluses into the start of the next decade. This action removed deficits as an issue, leaving little reason for continued public support for the Reform Party.

Basics: Voting and Elections

The basics of voting and elections largely encompass four questions: Who votes? How do we decide? What do the results mean? and What can our vote affect?

Who Votes, Part 1: The History of Suffrage

At our founding, the answer to "Who votes?" was, "Not many!" While the original Constitution did not set voting requirements, most of the states restricted voting to propertied white males (often with additional restrictions based on religion, wealth, and other factors). In some states, free blacks and women could vote, though by the early 1800s no states allowed female suffrage. Since that time—with some notable and unfortunate exceptions—the trend has been toward expanding suffrage:

- In the first third of the 19th century, states dropped most all their property and wealth requirements, opening participation far beyond just the elites in society.
- Following the Civil War and the abolition of slavery, the first constitutional voting requirement was enacted when the 15th

Amendment extended suffrage to otherwise qualified African American males.

- A long-developing women's rights movement produced the next constitutional requirement when the 19th Amendment extended suffrage to otherwise qualified females.
- By the mid-1960s, many "baby-boomers" had reached their late teens. At the time, voting in all states was restricted to those 21 and older. With the Vietnam War raging, many called for increased political rights for the young, arguing that if the government can draft 18-year-olds into the military, then they should be guaranteed the right to vote. In 1971, the 26th Amendment guaranteed just such voting rights to 18-year-olds nationwide.

By the 1970s, the vote was guaranteed (in *theory*—more on that below) to most everyone over 18. The remaining exceptions were (and still are) for convicted felons and those deemed mentally incompetent. Yet all was not well. Turnout rates were dropping significantly. In the 19th century, voter turnout often exceeded 80% of those eligible. As late as the 1960s, 60% of those eligible were voting in presidential elections. By the 1970s, though, that percentage had dropped to around 50% and remained around there through the rest of the 20th century. In recent years, the focus has been more on encouraging voter turnout than on expanding suffrage.

Added Barriers: Some Intended, Some Not

While the trend generally is toward expanding suffrage, that expansion has not been uniform and includes both regulations, depressing turnout (often unintentionally), and deliberate attempts to deny the vote to some—most notably African Americans.

Voting rights extended to former slaves by the 15th Amendment were originally enforced by federal troops during the Reconstruction era in the 1870s. When those troops were removed in the late 1870s, Southern states enacted laws known as **Jim Crow laws** to strip African Americans of social and political rights.[8] These laws included barriers to voting. Among these barriers were:

- *Literacy Tests*: Many states required these tests of potential voters who could not prove their education. They were often administered in an unfair manner, with long, difficult tests given to African Americans (e.g., see examples from Louisiana: https://www.crmvet.org/info/la-littest2.pdf

---

8   For more information on Jim Crow laws, see the 2002 PBS documentary, *The Rise and Fall of Jim Crow* at https://www.pbs.org/wnet/jimcrow/voting_start.html.

and Alabama: https://www.crmvet.org/info/litques.pdf) while similarly educated whites were simply given short words to spell. Some illiterate whites could not pass even the simplified tests. However, these tests affected African Americans to a far greater degree, since the literacy rates for newly-freed slaves (who, as slaves, were legally prohibited from being educated) and their descendants well into the 20th century (who were limited to inferior, segregated schools) were much lower than the rates for whites.

- *Grandfather Clauses*: Even illiterate whites were often allowed to vote if their ancestors had that right prior to Reconstruction. Since most white ancestors had the right while slaves were denied it, African Americans were forced to prove their literacy, while whites were often exempted from any required proof.

- *Poll Taxes*: State laws required potential voters to pay an annual tax to vote. The sums were small but still out of reach for many African Americans and poor whites. They were cumulative—if you could not pay the first time, you likely could never pay, since you had to pay all back taxes as well. While these taxes affected poor whites, enforcement was lax, and the taxes were also subject to grandfather clauses that exempted whites.

- *White Primaries*: Because the Democratic Party dominated the South, almost literally to the exclusion of any Republican participation (e.g., see: https://public.websites.umich.edu/~lawrace/votetour7.htm), winning the Democratic Party nomination for office was effectively the same as winning the general election. Democrats declared their organizations to be private and claimed the right to control their membership. They prohibited African American participation in party primaries, which effectively disenfranchised them.

- *Difficult Registration and Voting Requirements*: In addition to formal restrictions, there were all manner of methods used to discourage African American participation. Michael J. Klarman (2004) describes some discriminatory registration methods:

> Some registration boards . . . registered voters at undisclosed times in secret locations . . . Whites discovered through word of mouth where and when to show up to register, while blacks were kept in the dark . . . Registrars required blacks to fill out their own forms and flunked them for trivial errors, while they filled out whites' forms for them. Blacks but not whites were asked to recite the entire

U.S. Constitution or to answer impossible and insulting questions, such as "How many bubbles are in a bar of soap?" . . . Some registrars did not even bother to indulge in the pretense of legality and informed blacks that they would not be registered regardless of their qualifications. (p. 244)

- There were similarly discriminatory voting practices. Polls were often located in segregated white neighborhoods, meaning the few registered African Americans would have to travel great distances into hostile locations. There were complex procedures developed to facilitate disenfranchisement of African Americans. One notorious example was South Carolina's "eight box" law, "which operated as a literacy test by requiring voters to deposit ballots in the correct boxes" (Klarman, 2004, p. 31). Any mistake would invalidate all ballots. As with the registration procedures described above, whites were usually given assistance as needed, while African Americans were not.

- *Intimidation and Violence*: Threats to the livelihood, safety, health, and even lives of potential African American voters turned voting procedures and requirements that might sound innocuous into very dangerous and discouraging hurdles. For example, some states required the names and addresses of registered voters be published in local papers. While this caused little concern for whites, African Americans knew that being publicly identified as voters often cost them their jobs, and even worse, subjected them and their families to beatings and killings (and their homes to burnings) from local Ku Klux Klan members.

- *Registration and Identification Requirements*: Not all barriers involve deliberate suppression. Early in our history, when only a few prominent citizens could vote, no system of tracking voters was needed. As suffrage expanded and the ranks of eligible voters swelled, states began requiring eligible voters to register with the state to help track who voted (Fischer & Coleman, 2006). The purpose was to curb fraud (e.g., in the 19th century, some states recorded more votes cast than there were eligible voters!). A major effect, however, is a significant decline in turnout. That is, registration is a hurdle to overcome that is especially problematic among:

  ▷ The Less Educated—because it requires awareness and knowledge of elections well before they are held. If we know anything about elections, we are much more likely to know approximately when

Election Day is than to be aware of registration deadlines.

▷ Lower **Socioeconomic** Classes—because voter registration is likely to be a very low priority for someone struggling to maintain food and shelter for their family. Upper classes are much more likely to have the time, ability, and awareness to be involved.

In recent years, several states enacted strict photo identification requirements for voting (e.g., see Georgia's requirements: https://sos.ga.gov/page/georgia-voter-identification-requirements). These laws generally require people to produce a valid photo ID (usually a driver's license, passport, state employee or student card, or something similar) before they can vote. Proponents claim the laws are needed to help prevent voting fraud, while opponents claim the requirements place an undue burden on those—like the elderly, minorities, and the poor— who are otherwise qualified to vote but are less likely to either possess such ID or to be able to obtain them. In 2008, the Supreme Court upheld Indiana's version (*Crawford v. Marion County Election Board*, 2008). As of 2024, 36 states have some form of ID requirement (see: https://www.ncsl.org/research/elections-and-campaigns/voter-id.aspx). In some states, like North Carolina and Texas, federal courts blocked the laws, citing concerns like those noted above (Weber, 2017).

By the mid-1960s, most of the deliberate attempts to suppress African American voting had been removed. In *Smith v. Allwright* (1944), the Supreme Court declared that white primaries were unconstitutional. In 1964, the U.S. Constitution was amended to outlaw all poll taxes. In 1965, the federal Voting Rights Act outlawed many of the remaining discriminatory practices and provided for federal enforcement of voting rights. In 2013, a key enforcement provision of the Act was struck down by the Supreme Court in the 2013 case of *Shelby County v. Holder*. Since then, many states enacted new restrictions, not just around ID requirements, but also regarding the times and places for voting among other things.

Who Votes, Part 2: Making it Easier

Originally, registration meant taking time off to physically travel to a specific location to fill out paperwork. This fact added to the hurdles faced by the less educated and the lower classes, who were not aware of the locations and/ or not able to take the time or travel the distance to register. In recent decades, attempts have been made to ease the burdens of registration. Most notably, the **Motor Voter Act of 1993** requires all states to offer mail-in registration forms and requires them to offer the forms at most state government facilities like schools and many state services locations like motor vehicle bureaus (hence the name "Motor Voter"). In addition, many states have made greater efforts to promote voter registration in high schools, colleges, and among the public in recent years.

Many states have also attempted to make voting itself easier by liberalizing voter registration or absentee ballot rules (which were traditionally used for voters who certified that they could not get to their local polling place to vote) among other measures. As of 2023 there are 23 states that have adopted automatic voter registration (see: https://www.brennancenter.org/our-work/research-reports/automatic-voter-registration-summary). Under an automatic system, voters are registered by the state unless they 'opt-out'.

Also, in the wake of the controversial **2000 presidential election** (which was held up for over a month by voting controversies in Florida), Congress passed the Help America Vote Act. Among other things, it provided money to help states upgrade their voting equipment and required states to allow people to cast provisional votes if their eligibility is in question.[9]

How We Decide: Voting Cues

When we cast votes, we are choosing among alternatives. How do we decide? The answer is that we use **voting cues**, or indicators. Historically, the most important of these is *party identification* (i.e., which candidate belongs to the party we favor?). As information has become easier to obtain in recent decades (at first with the immediacy of radio and television, and now with the information explosion on the internet), *issue positions* (i.e., which candidate's issues do we most like?) have become an increasingly prominent indicator as well. Beware of issues, though (more on that below)! While these are the most prominent cues, there are others. Here is a brief discussion:

- *Party Identification*: Very few Americans are formal (i.e., "card-carrying") party members. That does not mean we lack strong attachments. Americans have very strong personal attachments. Most of us identify with a party. Recent polls say about 60% of the public identifies with a major party—and the number reaches 90% if "leaners" (self-described independents who, when pressed, express some support for a party) are included (see: https://news.gallup.com/poll/15370/Party-Affiliation.aspx). This party attachment begins early in life as part of our political socialization (see Chapter 4).

---

9   Such votes would be counted later, if the voter's eligibility was certified.

Prior to the age of mass media (especially before radio and television), parties were *the* source of political information. Well into the 19th century, most major newspapers were run by one of the major parties and made no pretense of objectivity. Political rallies and speeches were considered social events. With little independent information, party labels served as our primary (and often *only*) cue.

Modern commercial media displaced parties as a prime source of political information. With other sources increasingly available, Americans drifted away from political parties, with independents becoming as common as partisans. By the late 20th century, most observers said parties were "in decline." Even as they have revitalized in the last couple of decades (first as fundraisers, and now as ideological competitors), this decline allowed other cues to rise in prominence.

- *Incumbency*: As parties declined in influence, more candidates appealed directly to the public through radio and television. With little help from the parties, voters searched for other cues, with **incumbency** (who currently holds office?) filling the gap (Mayhew, 1974). The thinking is that, with less party information, voters began to notice who was currently in office (the incumbent) and began voting for them. Incumbents had the finances and organization to take advantage of new media to out-campaign obscure and underfunded challengers.

  Though parties re-emerged as major players, incumbents still enjoy greater support than their challengers. For example, at a time of seemingly great dissatisfaction with the federal government, incumbents running for re-election to the U.S. House of Representatives in 2022 won 94% of the time.

- *Issues*: The mass media age (radio, television, internet) has made information easier for us to obtain. As such, voters focus increasingly on candidate issue positions. It is laudable to say, "I don't vote just for a party label, I want to know where the candidates stand on the issues!"—however, one must beware that issues can be manipulated.

  - ▷ **Valence** (one-sided) **issues** are campaign favorites. Many candidates will carefully emphasize issues they know you will agree with. "Criminals should be punished!" or "I believe in America!" are examples. You might find yourself saying, "I agree with that statement!", but has the candidate actually said anything substantial?

    Next time you hear an issue statement from a candidate, try applying the "stupidity test." Imagine the opposite of the statement.

If the opposite is debatable, then the statement is probably reasonable ("Social Security should be reformed," vs. "Social Security should be preserved"). If the opposite sounds stupid ("Criminals should be punished" vs. "Criminals should go free"), then the statement is absurd.

> ▷ Another favorite is attempting to appease all sides on an issue, particularly on divisive issues. For example, about abortion, a candidate might say, "I am personally opposed to it, but I don't believe government should get involved." There is nothing intrinsically wrong with this kind of issue position, but be aware that it may be designed to appeal to both sides. It says to pro-life supporters that the candidate is on their side, but it also says to pro-choice supporters that they have nothing to fear from the candidate.

- *Candidate Characteristics*: In addition to the major cues, we use any number of others to help us decide. Most common among the remainder are candidate characteristics. We like to think candidates will understand us and help us. *Demographics* like race, gender, and ethnicity help us understand who candidates are and whether they can relate to our concerns. Other *background* characteristics like occupation, education, religion, ideology, childhood, and residence help us understand their experiences and whether they can empathize with our life. Lastly, basic *personality* traits like honesty, competence, friendliness, and intelligence help us understand how approachable they are and how they might handle the responsibilities of office.

What Votes Mean: Rules (Again!)

This consideration may be decisive, yet it is little appreciated. Rules matter. They affect outcomes. In other words, how we translate votes into outcomes is how we know who wins. We tend to take words like "vote" and "election" for granted. However, it is not that easy.

First, different votes do different things. *Party primaries* select nominees to represent the party in a general election. If you vote in a primary, you have exercised an important civic function, but you have not elected anyone to office. *General elections* fill government offices for fixed terms, while *special elections* are used to fill vacancies temporarily. Some states allow *recall elections* that can remove someone from office. Most unusual is the *presidential election* where you do not actually vote for president at all! It is an indirect system where you, in fact, vote for electors for your state, who in turn vote for president.

Second, rules vary from election to election and from state to state. The same set of votes might lead to different winners using different rules. Again, rules matter! Single-Member District, Plurality (SMDP) rules discussed earlier are one example. Elections using SMDP rules can produce different outcomes from Multi-Member District and Majority rules. We discussed earlier how these rules affect political parties. Let us now see how they affect elections.

The following example (based on Ross, 1988) demonstrates the effect of rules on outcomes, even with the exact same set of voter preferences. We start with four candidates: A, B, C, and D. A is supported by 40% of the population, B is supported by 30%, C is supported by 20%, and D is supported by 10%. In a straight, SMDP election, where there is one winner needing only more votes than anyone else, A wins (see Table 6-1, Plurality column). However, if the rule is changed to a multi-member one, with say three winners, then A, B, and C would win. The votes have not changed, only the rules.

In a single-member (or "single-winner") election with a *majority* rule, the same set of votes produces yet another result. Since the initial result, where A leads with 40%, does not produce a majority for anyone, we need a way to force one, which is done with a second, **runoff election** between the top two finishers, A and B. Since the supporters of C and D can no longer vote for them, they must decide between A or B. Table 6-1 lays out the distribution of preferences among all voters. Looking at C's supporters, we see that their second choice is D, their third is B, and their last is A. Thus, we deduce that they prefer B over A. From the table, we also see that D's supporters also prefer B over A. So, the result of the runoff is that A gets their 40% again, and B gets their 30% *plus* the 20% of C's supporters, *and* the 10% of D's supporters for a 60% majority. Again, no votes have changed, only the rules. A plurality rule favors A, but a majority rule favors B.

Yet another possibility is **approval voting**, where voters may cast votes for *each* candidate they like. Proponents argue this is a more accurate representation of our preferences, as it allows us to cast votes for two or more candidates if we cannot make up our mind or if we like two or more equally. The winner of such a vote would be the most widely-approved candidate among the voters. In Table 6-1, we can determine voter approval by observing the vertical bars ("|") among the voter preferences. Voters approve of choices to the left of the bar, and they disapprove of choices to the right. For example, the 40% whose first choice is A also approve of D, but not of C or B. Using this rule, we find that the first 40% cast votes for both A and D. The next 30% vote for both B and C. The next 20% vote only for C (which shows you can still cast a traditional single vote under this rule). The last 10% vote for everyone *except* A. Tallying these votes, we now find that C is the most widely-*approved* candidate. Again, there are no changes in voters or their preferences, only in the rules.

Table 6.1: Distribution of Voter Preferences and Results Using Different Voting Rules

Votes	1st	2nd	3rd	4th	Plurality	Majority	Approval
40%	A >	D > |	C >	B	A = 40 ✓	A = 40	A = 40
30%	B >	C > |	D >	A	B = 30	B = 60 ✓	B = 40
20%	C > |	D >	B >	A	C = 20		C = 60
10%	D >	B >	C > |	A	D = 10		D = 50

The bottom line: Again, rules matter. The same voters with the same preferences produced different results using different rules!

RANKED-CHOICE VOTING: A NEW METHOD? **Ranked-Choice voting** (also called **instant runoff voting**) uses majority rule but asks voters to rank all candidates from first to last preference instead of just casting a single vote. So, how does this work? Using this method on the hypothetical voting from Table 6.1, we arrive at the same majority rule result (B wins with 60 votes) but without the need for a costly and time-consuming second runoff election. Instead of casting one vote for their most preferred candidate, the 100 voters rank the four candidates according to their own preferences—as seen in the table's distribution of preferences. No candidate in the initial vote has a majority (A leads with 40%), so the candidates with the fewest votes—C and D—are eliminated, and their votes are redistributed up to A and B. D's supporters liked B next, so those 10 votes are given to B, increasing the candidate's total to 40— still not a majority. C's supporters like D next, but D was eliminated, so their third choice, B, gets those 20 votes, increasing the B's total to 60—a winning majority! Instead of spending more time and money on a runoff election requiring voters (and poll workers) to return to the polls a second time weeks later, ranked-choice voting can produce a winner as soon as the numbers can be crunched.

As of 2024, 54 jurisdictions over 28 states either currently use or have experimented with ranked-choice voting (Rank the Vote, 2024). For more information on how ranked-choice voting works, see: <u>https://ballotpedia.org/ Ranked-choice_voting_(RCV)#How_RCV_works</u>.

What Voting Affects:

The quick answer to this question is not everything. In other words, we do have some ability to shape our government, but we cannot shape everything. Our reach is limited.

How is it limited? The most obvious answer is that not everything or everyone in government is subject to election. We cannot vote on:

- presidential advisors or other executive branch officials.
- congressional staff members.
- federal judges or Supreme Court justices.
- many state and local administrative and judicial officials.
- federal laws or regulations.
- many state and local laws or regulations.

Even when we can vote, it is often in a limited fashion. For example, since U.S. Senate elections are staggered (see Chapter 7), with only one-third of the Senate up for election every two years, we can only change that much in any single election. In other words, two-thirds of the Senate is insulated from us in every election. In addition, the reach of our vote is limited by geography. We can only vote for U.S. senators in our state and U.S. representatives in our local congressional district (and state and local geography is usually even *more* limited). Those geographic districts also limit our ability to act collectively, since many groups among the public (i.e., racial, ethnic, gender, occupational, ideological, religious, and others) are fragmented among many districts and states.[10]

Too Many Votes?

There are more than a half-million elected officials in the United States (e.g., see Shelley, 1996). Add to that party primaries, runoff elections, recall elections, special elections, judicial elections, sheriff and school board elections among other local offices, and even policy proposals on ballot measures and state constitutional amendments, and it becomes quite clear that Americans have a lot of voting to do! This amount contributes to a phenomenon known as "voter fatigue," which helps account for why turnout rates in the United States are far lower than in similar democracies. Consider this example:

There were five elections conducted in 2010 to determine who Georgia's 9th Congressional District representative to the U.S. House would be. Why five? First, the incumbent—Republican Nathan Deal—resigned his House seat in March 2010 to run for governor of Georgia (spoiler alert: he won). This situation required a special election to fill the seat until the term expired in January of

---

10   Sometimes deliberately so. See "gerrymandering" in Chapter 7.

2011. The special election was held in May. Second, since Georgia's election laws require a majority vote to win, a runoff election was needed because none of the candidates received a majority. The runoff was held in June. So, it took two votes just to fill out the term. Tom Graves was elected to fill the seat.

It does not end there. The regular vote to fill the next term was still scheduled for November 2nd, and the party primary votes for this election were scheduled for July 20th. The Republican primary (there were no Democratic candidates) required a runoff vote, which was held in August. The incumbent, Tom Graves, won the runoff. So, there was a special election in May, a runoff for that special election in June, a party primary in July, a primary runoff in August, *and* the election in November (Graves won)—five elections for one seat in one year! There could even have been a sixth, a November runoff, had any significant opposition kept Graves from getting a majority.

It gets even more interesting. Like many states, Georgia attempted to make voting easier by allowing people to vote up to 45 days before an election at the time. This early voting meant people could vote in the July 20th primary as early as June 7th. It is noteworthy because the special election runoff date was June *8th*, meaning it was possible for voters to vote in the regular election primary at the same time or even before they voted in the special election runoff (Fielding, 2010). Of course, this situation created some confusion. Some voters in the 9th District who intended to vote in the special election runoff accidentally voted early in the primary vote instead (Redmon, 2010)! The state has since reduced early voting down to about three weeks.

Money

In the past, political parties and election campaigns revolved primarily around organizing and energizing people in order to win elections. The focus was on face-to-face gatherings like campaign rallies. Today, things are far more complex. Make no mistake, people are still important. Our votes are, after all, the bottom line. However, as communications technologies (radio, television, internet) and campaign techniques (polling, phone-calling, direct mail marketing, and other public relations methods) develop, parties and campaigns have changed. In addition to the traditional armies of staffers and volunteers spreading out to win over our votes, there are now groups of more elite technology and marketing experts working behind the scenes to win us over as well.

These new experts and their technologies and techniques are far more expensive than the hordes of staffers and volunteers. This in turn pushes money and fundraising to the forefront, requiring parties and campaigns to seek out ever-greater amounts of cash. Candidates and parties naturally turned to wealthy supporters for large donations to meet the demands. By the 1970s, an increasingly uneasy public grew concerned that politicians were being "bought" by these wealthy contributors (that is, that politicians were ignoring the public and focusing on keeping their few, wealthy contributors happy). This situation led to federal regulations (see below) that limited the amount of money individuals could contribute in any election to $1,000 per candidate. Oddly enough, these regulations make fundraising more important because far more contributors were now required to pay for increasingly expensive campaigns.[11]

Campaign Finance Reform

Some campaign finance regulations date back more than a century. The Tillman Act of 1907 prohibited the direct contribution of corporate funds to campaigns. The Taft-Hartley Act of 1947 similarly prohibited direct contributions from labor unions. However, there have been two major waves of reforms in recent decades. The first was in the 1970s. Spurred on by perceived loopholes in the first wave, the second was in the late 1990s and early 2000s.[12]

The Federal Election Campaign Acts of the 1970s (FECA)

In 1971, 1972, and 1974, Congress enacted laws that:
- limited contributions to federal campaigns from individuals ($1,000 per candidate, per election) and from groups ($5,000 per candidate, per election);
- required groups representing various interests (known as Political Action Committees) to register with the federal government before they could contribute to federal campaigns;
- limited both candidate and independent (individuals and groups not connected with any candidate) spending in federal elections (House, Senate, presidency);
- created the Federal Election Commission (FEC) to oversee federal campaign regulations; and
- set up a system of public funding for presidential nominations and elections.

---

11   Where a candidate could once raise $100,000 from a single wealthy donor, they now had to seek out 100 people to get the same amount.

12   A good description and history of campaign finance may be found on the Federal Election Commission website at https://www.fec.gov/help-candidates-and-committees/#Historical_Background.

Opponents of these regulations claimed they violated the First Amendment speech rights of both candidates and potential contributors, and they challenged the laws in court. In the case of *Buckley v. Valeo* (1976), the Supreme Court upheld many of the regulations. However, they struck down the spending limits as unconstitutional, saying that candidate and independent spending amount to protected speech. In addition, they said contribution limits only apply to activities involving "express advocacy"—meaning words that clearly advocate the election or defeat of a candidate. Contribution limits and public funding of presidential campaigns set the tone for federal elections for the next two decades. However, things were changing.

Soft Money and Issues Ads

In 1979, one change in FEC interpretations led to what is called **soft money**. This money is used for non-campaign, "party-building" activities like get-out-the-vote drives or issue advertisements (as opposed to express campaign advertisements). Based on the Supreme Court's "express advocacy" restriction in *Buckley*, soft money contributions are not subject to limitations. Little-noticed at the time, this change, combined with federal court rulings in the 1990s that said candidate images and names used in ads do not amount to express advocacy, had profound consequences as the political parties reinvented themselves as soft money machines. Wealthy supporters were no longer able to donate more than $1,000 to candidates or groups that run ads saying something like "Vote for Smith," but they now could pour unlimited contributions into political parties and groups that run **issue ads** saying, "Smith is good for America" or "Smith supports legislation X while Jones opposes it." (For examples of issue ads in the 2000 presidential campaign, see: https://p2000.us/ads2/partyadlist.html).

The Bipartisan Campaign Reform Act of 2002 (BCRA)

By the late 1990s, as issue ads saturated the airwaves before every election, many saw them as a loophole rendering contribution limits meaningless. The argument was that the average television viewer, in weeks before an election, would not distinguish between ads that say, "Bob Dole will cut our taxes" and ones that say, "Vote for Bob Dole." Calls for new legislation to close the perceived soft money loophole were led by U.S. Senators John McCain (R-AZ) and Russell Feingold (D-WI). Their proposals were debated for several years and finally enacted into law in 2002 as the Bipartisan Campaign Reform Act. This law banned political parties from using soft money in federal elections (and restricted state parties' soft money) so that contributions from wealthy contributors to political parties were once again limited. However, to compensate for 30 years of inflation, the individual contribution limit was doubled to $2,000 and subsequently indexed to the inflation rate (as of 2024, the limit was $3,300). In addition, issue ads featuring candidate names and faces were limited. Ads could not show or mention a candidate 30 days before a party primary or 60 days before a general election.

The new laws were soon challenged, but the Supreme Court in 2003 upheld all but a few minor provisions.

"527" Groups "501" Groups, *Citizens United,* and Beyond

BCRA did little to stem the flow of money in elections. For one thing, the national parties subsequently became very adept at raising record sums of money through good old-fashioned limited contributions. For another, while parties were restricted from using soft money and running issue ads, many types of outside groups were not. Tax-exempt "527" groups (named for Section 527 of the federal tax code) could exploit a difference between tax law and campaign law. Tax law prohibits these groups from engaging in campaign activity but remember *Buckley* and the FEC said issue ads are *not* campaign ads. Therefore, 527s could run all the issue ads, using all the unlimited money, they wanted![13] Traditional interest groups formed 527s. More importantly though, members of political parties that could *not* spend soft money simply went out and formed 527s which could.

In the 2004 elections and beyond, the airwaves were still saturated with issues ads. But they were no longer party ads, they were 527 ads. Then came *Citizens United.*

In addition to the long-standing bans on corporate and union campaign contributions, BCRA also restricted them from using their own funds to engage in "electioneering" (though their members could form political action committees to raise funds and make limited contributions. See Chapter 5). In 2008, a little-known, nonprofit corporation known as Citizens United wanted to broadcast and advertise a documentary titled "Hillary: The Movie," which was critical of presidential candidate Hillary Clinton. A federal court held that doing so would violate the BCRA restrictions on issue ads and on corporate electioneering. The case reached the Supreme Court in 2009, originally simply to determine whether the film and its ads amounted to issue ads or "electioneering." However, the Court ordered the case to be reheard a year later, this time to determine the far more consequential question of whether or not the BCRA restrictions on corporations and unions use of their own funds is constitutional. In a 5-4 vote, the Court struck down the restrictions as unconstitutional violations of the First Amendment's

---

13   Other types of tax-exempt groups, known as 501(c)(3) and 501(c)(4) groups, could run these ads as well.

speech protection (*Citizens United v Federal Election Commission*, 130 S.Ct. 876). This ruling opens the door for corporations and unions to use their own money for any political activity they desire (except for direct contributions, which are still prohibited).

Where will this lead? Will we see multi-million-dollar product marketing campaigns that endorse candidates ("Vote for Smith for president because she uses our product!")? It is trite to say that only time will tell, but surely the issue is not yet resolved. The question remains: What place does money have in our elections?

FOLLOW THE MONEY? NOT SO EASY: What we *have* seen in the last fifteen years is that both traditional corporations and incorporated interests (like *Citizens United*) have become involved in campaigns. However, traditional corporations often wish to remain anonymous (to avoid offending customers or partners). Many incorporated interests also wish to remain anonymous (often just to avoid retaliation or scrutiny). In these cases, the kind of overt spending allowed by the Citizens United decision won't do. To accommodate their wish to remain anonymous, many political organizations, including some quite close to candidates and campaigns (though direct coordination is illegal), are using a two-pronged approach. They form both Super PACs (see Chapter 5) and tax-exempt groups known as 501(c)(4) groups. Why both? Because Super PACs can raise and spend unlimited amounts of money and overtly express support for candidates (though direct contributions are forbidden), but they must disclose their donors. That's where the 501(c)(4)s come in handy. As "Social Welfare" groups, according to the tax code, express political support cannot be their primary function. However, they can accept unlimited donations and they *can* contribute to political organizations like Super PACs. The key is that 501(c)(4)s do not have to disclose their donors! So, corporations and wealthy individuals can contribute unlimited amounts to these 501 groups and remain anonymous. The 501 groups then contribute the money they raise to Super PACs that spend it on express electioneering.

When you ask a Super PAC where they got their money from, they must tell you. If they use the approach described above, they tell you they got it from a 501(c)(4). When you ask the 501(c)(4) where *their* money came from, all they have to say is, "None of your business!" Mission accomplished!

Case Study: Majority Versus Plurality in the Real World—The 2020 U.S. Senate Elections in Georgia

Most U.S. elections use SMDP rules. The state of Georgia is an exception. It requires a majority vote (see: Georgia Code Title 21. Elections § 21-2-501).[14] If no

---

14   However, it exempted local municipalities using other rules prior to the law's adoption.

candidate has captured a majority on election day, a "runoff" is held several weeks later between the top two finishers to determine the winner. This rule affected not one, but *two* U.S. Senate elections in Georgia in 2020—and had repercussions for control of the Senate in 2021. Normally, 33 or 34 states have *one* Senate election in an election year (see Chapter 7). Why only 33 or 34 states, and why only one each for those states? More rules! The Constitution specifies that only one-third of Senate seats are up for re-election every two years, and they are distributed so that no state has more than one seat up in any election cycle. So why did Georgia have *two*?

In the summer of 2019, one of Georgia's incumbent U.S. senators, Johnny Isakson, announced that he would resign at the end of the year due to declining health (Everett, 2019). Governor Brian Kemp appointed business executive Kelly Loeffler to fill the seat until a special election was held concurrently with the upcoming November election. Georgia's other incumbent senator, David Perdue, would also be up for re-election at the same time, as his regular six-year term was expiring.

The *rules* were different for each of these contests. The special election for Loeffler's seat was a "jungle primary", with all eligible candidates competing (i.e., there were no party nominees). Instead of just two major-party nominees dominating the ballot, there could be any number of candidates from both major and minor parties. If no candidate won a majority, then the top two finishers— regardless of party—would compete in a later runoff (Keenan, 2020). The election for Perdue's seat was a more traditional affair with the two major parties nominating candidates to compete in November.

Georgia has been solidly Republican for a couple of decades, though Democrats have made recent inroads. 2018 saw their best results in many years, with a close governor's race and some gains in both the U.S. House and the state legislature. Still, throughout most of 2020, both Perdue and Loeffler were expected to retain their seats (e.g., see: Cook Political Report, 2020; Gonzales, 2020; Silver, 2020).

By late October, both senators' leads were nearly gone. Perdue's lead dissipated at least partly because of missteps by the candidate (Fox News, 2020)—but also because of a well-positioned Democratic nominee, Jon Ossoff, who maintained significant statewide name recognition and support from a strong U.S. House challenge two years earlier. Meanwhile, Loeffler's lead fell victim to a strong challenge from Republican U.S. Representative Doug Collins (who was endorsed by President Trump). Remember, Loeffler was competing in the jungle primary, so there was no party nomination to settle intra-party challenges. Loeffler and Collins were splitting the Republican vote, while on the Democratic side, Rev.

Raphael Warnock had emerged as a singular favorite. Heading into election day, the special election was essentially a three-way race which virtually guaranteed that no candidate would receive the 50 percent needed to avoid a runoff. The other election was a razor-thin race between Ossoff and Perdue, with neither candidate clearly above 50 percent. It looked like both races would result in runoffs.

On election day, neither of the races were settled. In the special election, Warnock finished first, with just under 33% of the vote. Loeffler finished second with just under 26%, and Collins finished third with just under 20%. Warnock and Loeffler were headed to a runoff. In the other election, Senator Perdue's vote total flirted with the 50 percent mark, but as later votes (mostly absentee ballots) were tallied, he fell just short with 49.7%. Ossoff finished with just under 48% of the vote. This race was also headed to a runoff. So . . . rules matter. Under plurality rule, both races would have been settled. However, the state's majority voting rule meant the contests would continue.

Both runoffs were scheduled for January 5th, 2021—a date based on . . . you guessed it . . . Georgia election *rules*. This *mattered* as it occurred two days after Senator Perdue's term expired. So, for two days, Georgia had only one senator, Kelly Loeffler. Her term did not expire until after the special election was resolved.

Runoff elections are usually very low-turnout events. However, because victories by both Democratic candidates would result in a shift in Senate power, these runoffs had national implications and drew a lot of attention, leading to unusually high turnout. This turnout was not uniform across the state. African Americans voted in large numbers in the runoff (Cohn, 2021). This helped the Democratic candidates in both races. In the end, both Democrats won their runoffs. Jon Ossoff defeated incumbent Senator David Perdue 50.6% to 49.4%, and Raphael Warnock defeated incumbent Senator Kelly Loeffler 51% to 49%. For the first time in more than 60 years, a state lost two incumbent U.S. senators in the same election cycle. The last time was in West Virginia in 1958 (Ostermeier, 2021).

Under plurality rule, Republicans would have retained both seats and retained control of the Senate. However, under Georgia's majority rule, Democrats were able to capture both seats and return control of the Senate to their party. Oh, one last rule. Jon Ossoff was elected to a full six-year term. So he will not be up for re-election until 2026. However, Raphael Warnock was elected to finish the full term begun by Johnny Isakson and continued by Kelly Loeffler. That term ended in 2022, so to retain his seat, Warnock ran *again* just two years later in 2022. Once again, neither Warnock nor his challenger, Republican Herschel Walker, received a majority on election day. Yes, that meant yet another runoff, which Warnock again won.

Discussion Questions

1. Why did political parties become such a central part of our political environment if the framers derided them as "factions"? In other words, what do they do that might make them so central?

2. Compare "third" or "minor" parties to the major parties. A list can be found here: https://www.politics1.com/parties.htm. Peruse their websites and compare their goals, organization, and success to that of the two major parties.

3. Compare our largely two-party system to other systems (e.g., Great Britain's three-party system or Israel's multiple-party system). How do their party systems affect their politics?

4. As noted earlier, our history is full of attempts to disenfranchise African Americans (see chapter section: "Added Barriers: Some Intended, Some Not"). Some were obvious (white primaries), but some seemed more innocuous to whites (publishing names and addresses of registered voters). Today, there are still provisions that might not concern whites while they seriously concern blacks. For instance, many states have toughened their identification requirements in the name of combating voter fraud. Why might this concern African Americans? Contact or visit a nearby chapter of the NAACP (https://www.naacp.org) and investigate their concerns with these tougher restrictions.

5. Many campaign finance regulations were enacted in the name of preventing the appearance of elections being "bought" by wealthy contributors. Is there any validity to this concern? Explore campaign contribution data on these sites to investigate the role of money in election campaigns: http://www.cfinst.org/, https://www.fec.gov.

References

Ansolabehere, S., Rodden, J., & Snyder, J. M. (2006). Purple America. *The Journal of Economic Perspectives, 20*(2), 97–118.

Beck, P. A. (1997). *Party politics in America.* (8th ed.). Longman.

Burnham, W. D. (1970). *Critical elections and the mainsprings of American politics.* W.W. Norton.

Campbell, A., Converse, P., Miller, W., & Stokes, D. (1960). *The American voter.* John Wiley & Sons.

Cohn, Nate. (2021). Why Warnock and Ossoff won in Georgia. *The New York Times.* https://www.nytimes.com/2021/01/07/upshot/warnock-ossoff-georgia-victories.html

Cook Political Report. (2020). *2020 Senate race ratings.* The Cook Political Report. https://cookpolitical.com/ratings/senate-race-ratings/230641

Everett, B. (2019). Sen. Johnny Isakson to resign at end of the year. *The Atlanta Journal-Constitution.* https://www.politico.com/story/2019/08/28/sen-johnny-isakson-to-resign-at-end-of-the-year-1476655

Fielding, A. (2010, May 16). Runoff, primary overlap may cause confusion for voters. *The Gainesville Times.* https://www.gainesvilletimes.com/news/elections-archived/runoff-primary-overlap-may-cause-confusion-for-voters/

Fiorina, M. P. (1981). *Retrospective voting in American national elections.* Yale University Press.

Fischer, E. A. & Coleman, K. J. (2006, March 22). *Voter registration systems.* American University. Retrieved September 12, 2024 from https://web.archive.org/web/20130115000000*/https://www.american.edu/spa/cdem/upload/2-Fischer_Coleman-Voter_Registration_Systems-AU.pdf

Fox News. (2020). *Key Senate races begin to tighten two weeks out from election* [transcript]. Special Report with Bret Baier. https://www.foxnews.com/transcript/key-senate-races-begin-to-tighten-two-weeks-out-from-election

Gonzalez, N. L. (2020). *Senate ratings.* Inside Elections with Nathan L. Gonzales, Nonpartisan Analyst. https://www.insideelections.com/ratings/senate/2020-senate-ratings-october-28-2020

Green, D., Palmquist, B., & Schickler, E. (2002). *Partisan hearts and minds.* Yale University Press.

Karol, D. (2009). *Party position change in American politics.* Cambridge University Press.

Keenan, Sean. (2020). What in the world is a jungle primary, and what's in store for Georgia's? *Atlanta Magazine.* https://www.atlantamagazine.com/news-culture-articles/what-in-the-world-is-a-jungle-primary-and-whats-in-store-for-georgias/

Key, V. O., Jr. (1964). *Politics, parties, and pressure groups.* Crowell.

Klarman, M. J. (2004). *From Jim Crow to civil rights: The Supreme Court and the struggle for racial equality.* Oxford University Press.

Madison, J. (1787, November 23/2011). Federalist #10: The same subject continued: The union as a safeguard against domestic faction and insurrection. *The New York Packet.* https://guides.loc.gov/federalist-papers/text-1-10#s-lg-box-wrapper-25493273

Main, J. T. (2006). *The Anti-Federalists: Critics of the Constitution, 1781–1788.* University of North Carolina Press.

Mayhew, D. R. (1974). Congressional elections: The case of the vanishing marginals. *Polity, 6*(3), 295–317.

Nie, N. H.,Verba, S., & Petrocik, J. R. (1976). *The changing American voter.* Harvard University Press.

Office of Management and Budget. (2010). *Table 7.1—Federal debt at the end of year: 1940–2015.* Historical Tables. https://trumpwhitehouse.archives.gov/wp-content/uploads/2020/02/hist07z1_fy21.xlsx

Office of the Clerk of the U.S. House of Representatives. (2024). *Party divisions of the House of Representatives (1789 to Present).* Office of the Clerk of the U.S. House of Representatives https://history.house.gov/Institution/Party-Divisions/Party-Divisions/

Ostermeier, E. (2021). *Georgia democrats record historic rarity.* Smart Politics. https://smartpolitics.lib.umn.edu/2021/01/06/georgia-democrats-record-historic-rarity/

Rank the Vote. (2024). *About ranked choice voting.* https://rankthevote.us/learn/#howrcv

Redmon, J. (2010, July 21). Congressional election redos costly, confusing. *The Atlanta Journal-Constitution.* Retrieved September 12, 2024 from https://web.archive.org/web/20100728204858/https://www.ajc.com/news/georgia-politics-elections/congressional-election-redos-costly-575715.html

Rosenof, T. (2003). *Realignment: The theory that changed the way we think about American politics.* Rowman & Littlefield.

Ross, R. S. (1988). *American national government: Institutions, policy, and participation.* Dushkin Publishing Group, Inc.

Senate Historical Office. (2010). *Party division in the senate, 1789–present.* Senate Historical Office. https://www.senate.gov/pagelayout/history/one_item_and_teasers/partydiv.htm

Shelley, F. M. (1996). *The political geography of the United States.* The Guilford Press.

Silver, N. (2020). *Forecasting the race for the Senate.* FiveThirtyEight. Retrieved June 16, 2021 from https://web.archive.org/web/20200920193754/https://projects.fivethirtyeight.com/2020-election-forecast/senate/

Sundquist, J. L. (1983). *The dynamics of the party system.* (Revised Edition). The Brookings Institution.

Wasserman, D. (2017, March 8). *Purple America has all but disappeared.* FiveThirtyEight. https://fivethirtyeight.com/features/purple-america-has-all-but-disappeared/

Weber, P. J. (2017). Judge again finds discrimination in Texas' voter ID law.

Associated Press. https://apnews.com/3ac028eda56a4cf39c0efd02aab12881

Wood, G. S. (1998). *The creation of the American republic, 1776–1787*. University of North Carolina Press.

Court Cases

Buckley v. Valeo, 424 U.S. 1 (1976).

Citizens United v Federal Election Commission, 130 S.Ct. 876 (2010).

Crawford v. Marion County Election Board, 553 U.S. 181 (2008).

Shelby County v. Holder, 570 U.S. 529 (2013).

Smith v. Allwright, 321 U.S. 649 (1944).

Congress

Carl D. Cavalli

Learning Objectives

After covering the topic of Congress, students should understand:

1. The origins and representative nature of Congress and the roles of individual members.
2. The organization of Congress, including the leadership and the committee system.
3. The functional processes, including legislating and annual budgeting.
4. Influences on the decision-making of members of Congress.

Abstract[1]

The framers created a bicameral congress out of their concern that the legislature is the most powerful branch. Beyond simple division into two houses, they deliberately created differences: different terms and different methods of apportionment. They allowed each house to create its own rules and organization. This separation results in a complex parallel structure of rules and behavior that produces significantly differing views on policy from representatives and senators—even though both are attempting to represent their constituents. The resulting legislative and budgetary processes are difficult, complicated, and more likely to lead to failure than success for any given proposal. In recent decades, the Congress has evolved to meet public demands for greater democracy and openness and has attempted to adapt to increasing polarization between the political parties. This evolution results in even greater complexity and a focus on responsiveness (to constituency) over responsibility.

---

1 Portions of this chapter were originally included in Cavalli, Carl. D. 2000. Congress. Lesson 9 in POLS 1101: American Government. University System of Georgia eCore™.

Introduction

The First Branch

The first branch of government described in the Constitution is the Congress. The framers did this deliberately. If politics is about "who gets what, when, how" (Lasswell, 1936), then it is important to first consider those who *decide* these things—the Congress.

Congress does its work in the Capitol building in Washington, DC. Not surprisingly, the structure of the Capitol itself lends clues to the operation of Congress. The building is divided into three connected segments: two large columned wings on either side, connected in the center by a towering dome. The center dome is vast, decorative, and largely empty (except, of course, for the hordes of gawking tourists). All the action occurs in the two intricate and busy wings. The architecture of the building is a close metaphor for the Congress itself: two complicated, active houses forever linked to one another and to the public (those gawking tourists). Why two? Why linked? And above all, why so busy?

Basics

Bicameralism

Bicameralism is the division of a legislative body into two chambers. In our case, Congress is divided into two houses: the House of Representatives (or simply, "The House") and the Senate. What is the purpose of bicameralism? James Madison (1788) had this to say in *Federalist #51*, "In republican government, the legislative authority necessarily predominates. The remedy for this inconveniency is to divide the legislature into different branches; and to render them, by different modes of election and different principles of action, as little connected with each other as the nature of their common functions and their common dependence on the society will admit."

The framers feared Congress might become the most powerful, and thus dangerous, branch. Their solution to the problem of power was division. With the *legislative* branch, this meant division into two houses. Notice Madison's quote above, though. The focus is not on simply dividing the Congress into two *twin* houses. Rather, it is "to divide the legislature into *different* branches . . . as little connected with each other" as possible. Here are some examples of these differences:

Two Different Branches

- The House is larger, with 435 members apportioned according to the population of each state (states with larger populations have more representatives), while the smaller Senate has 100 members apportioned two per state regardless of population.

Because of this system, representatives in the House generally have fewer constituents than do senators. There are from 1 to 52 representatives per state, whereas both senators in each state represent its entire population.

- The previous point means each representative has about the same number of constituents, whereas senators represent vastly different numbers of constituents. It also means a representative's constituents are usually more homogeneous than a senator's.

- Representatives' terms of office are two years, while senators serve for six years.

- Representatives are generally younger than senators: first, because the Constitution requires them to be at least 25 while it requires senators be at least 30, and second, because the House is often informally considered a stepping stone to the Senate.

- The Constitution designates that all revenue bills originate in the House (but the Senate must still concur), while the Senate has exclusive powers to confirm executive and judicial appointments and ratify treaties negotiated between the United States and other nations.

Why the differences? The answer may come from examining the *effects* of these differences.

With generally smaller constituencies and a shorter term of office, the connection between House members and the public is both closer and more direct. The short two-year term also means representatives are constantly in campaign mode (think about it: They are forever either running for re-election this year, or next year). There is often a got-to-get-it-done-now-because-I'm-up-for-re-election mentality. In addition, the generally smaller, more homogeneous constituency also means representatives are less likely to deal with diverse opinions on any issue.

With larger and more varied constituencies, a longer term of office, and generally older members, the Senate is more "elite"—less directly connected to the public. The mentality in the Senate is often one of going slow and of considering a wide array of views on any issue.

The differences between the houses produce different *perspectives*. The views of senators will *differ* from the views of representatives. They will argue. There is an often-repeated tale that suggests a junior House Democrat once referred to House Republicans as "the enemy." This junior representative was quickly corrected by a more senior member who intoned that the Republicans are simply rivals—"the *Senate* is the enemy!" (e.g., see Ornstein, 2008). What we today refer to as "gridlock" is something to which the framers would not object. They feared quick action far more than they feared delay.

Lawmaker, Representative

What is the role of a legislator? Most people would answer that the basic job is to create laws. This description is correct, but incomplete. Equally important is a focus on representing the public. But what does "representation" mean? There are several ways of defining the term.

Representation

Does Congress truly represent the public? One way to assess representativeness is to see if it shares the same **demographic** characteristics as the public. In other words, does Congress *look* like the public? The answer is clearly no! In 2024, the average ages in the House and Senate are 58 and 64, respectively—more than 20 years older than the average American. Most members are lawyers or political professionals.[2] Also, while there are more women and minorities in Congress than ever, they are still vastly underrepresented compared to the general public. For example, in 2024, 28.6% of Congress was female compared to over 50% of the general public, and about 11.5% of Congress was African American compared to around 13% of the general public (Manning, 2024). In addition, there are far more military veterans and far more Protestants than are found in the general public. So, from a demographic standpoint, Congress does not represent the public at all.

However, demography is not the only type of representation. Another type is known as **agency representation**. Do members of Congress speak for their constituents (in the same way that "agents" in the entertainment and sports professions speak for their clients)? This assessment method yields a far more positive answer. One way to measure agency representation is to see if constituents express their satisfaction with their incumbent representatives by voting to re-elect them. Over the last 25 years, re-election rates in the House average over 90% and have not dropped lower than 87%. Over the same period, rates in the Senate average over 80% and have not dropped lower than 75% (The 2022 rates were 94.5% in the House and 100% in the Senate!). These consistently high re-election

---

2   A "political professional" is someone who has worked most of their lives in political offices, either as legislative or administrative assistants, or as elected officials in local or state offices before their election to Congress.

rates are particularly interesting given the relatively low levels of public support shown for the Congress as a whole in recent decades—currently at or below 20%, and rarely above 50% over the last 50 years (Gallup, 2024). In total, this data suggests that while the public does not often approve of the collective actions of Congress as an institution, they are more than satisfied with their own members of Congress (e.g., see Mendes, 2013).

Indeed, researchers like David Mayhew (1974) find that it is this "electoral connection"—regularly facing the voters—that largely promotes agency representation. It appears to be a conscious design of lawmakers. Their desire for re-election produces a palpable focus on what Richard Fenno (2003) calls "home style." That is, legislators are concerned about how they are perceived by their constituents. As Fenno says,

> there is no way the act of representing can be separated from the act of getting elected. If the congressman cannot win and hold the votes of some people, he cannot represent any people … [T]he knowledge that they will later be held accountable at the polls will tend to make [representatives'] behavior more responsive to the desires of their constituents. (p. 233)

To build support, "[M]embers of Congress go home to present themselves as a person and to win accolade: 'he's a good man,' 'she's a good woman'… And their object is to present themselves as a person in such a way that the inferences drawn by those watching will be supportive" (p. 55). Beyond simply appearing "good," leadership and helpfulness are also part of the presentation: "[T]he core activity is providing help to individuals, groups, and localities in coping with the federal government. … [I]t is a highly valued form of activity. Not only is constituent service universally recognized as an important part of the job in its own right. It is also universally recognized as powerful reelection medicine" (p. 101).

DISTRICTING: WHO IS YOUR "AGENT?" Rules matter. They affect outcomes. Congressional representation is affected by rules for creating congressional districts.[3] As noted earlier, representatives in the House are apportioned by state population (so the most populous state, California, currently has 52 representatives, while the seven least populous states each have only one representative). Federal law requires states with more than one representative to draw individual districts for each. Constitutionally, those districts must be as equal in population as possible. Federal law also requires the creation of districts where

---

3   This is not a concern in the Senate, where both senators in a state represent the *entire* state.

minority groups comprise the majority of the district population where possible.[4] Population shifts and demographic changes are measured by the decennial United States Census. These requirements mean district boundaries must be redrawn at least every decade as indicated by population and demographic shifts detected by the census. How the boundaries are redrawn—**"redistricting"**—can have a decisive effect on who we elect to represent us.

For example, a state with a population large enough to be apportioned three representatives must create three districts. However, state legislatures are free to draw the boundaries as they please, keeping in mind the population and minority requirements. Yet, how those boundaries are drawn can strongly affect who gets elected as the districts' representatives.

Figure 7.1: Districting Possibilities in a Hypothetical State

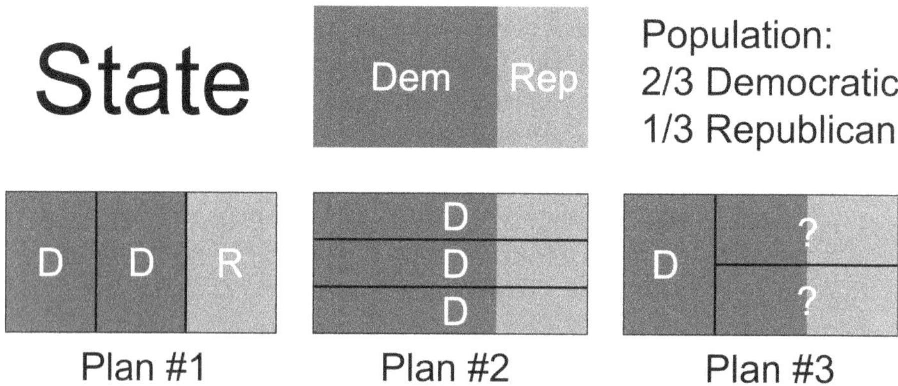

Figure 7.1 provides an example of possible district boundaries in a state with three districts and an evenly-distributed population. Assuming people vote for the candidate of their party, the plans produce a state represented by anywhere from a solidly Democratic delegation (Plan #1) to a potentially majority Republican delegation (Plan #3). In other words, the state's population may be represented by notably different representatives depending upon how the districts are drawn. When you consider not only partisan, but also ideological, racial, ethnic, and other demographic differences within most states, it is easy to see why redistricting often results in heated battles.[5]

---

4   This provision has been challenged in federal court on several occasions but has survived largely intact.

5   For example, see https://www.reuters.com/world/us/court-fights-could-tip-control-us-house-2024-2023-11-14/.

These battles frequently involve **gerrymandering**.[6] The term "gerrymander" has its roots in the districting process used in Massachusetts in the early 19th century under the direction of Governor Elbridge Gerry (where one unusually-shaped district was said to look like a salamander). Today, the term is used to describe districts deliberately drawn to advantage one group of people over another. Most battles have been fought over racial, ethnic, and partisan gerrymandering. Historically, this was one method of disenfranchising African Americans. Concentrations of African Americans were divided between districts to prevent any district majorities. This method of dividing a population is known as "cracking" (see Plan #2 in Figure 7.1) and was used to prevent the election of blacks (or sympathetic whites) to Congress. The method in part explains the lack of *any* black representatives elected from Southern states in Congress from 1901 to 1965 despite black populations often making up 25-50% of the total state population (Gibson & Jung, 2002). As noted above, federal law now prohibits racial/ethnic "cracking" and requires the creation of "majority-minority" districts where possible, though the law has been challenged in court.

Another method of gerrymandering is known as "packing" (see Plan #1 in Figure 7.1). This involves concentrating a group into as few districts as possible. This often guarantees electing someone from (or sympathetic to) that group in those districts but leaves surrounding districts lacking in that group. Critics of majority-minority districts see them as "packing" and note that while they lead to the election of some minority members, they ultimately lead to more racially or ethnically polarized politics while diluting minority influence in more numerous surrounding districts (defeating the very rationale for requiring them).

As the nation has become more politically polarized, partisan gerrymandering has become increasingly common (e.g., see Cooper, 2010). States controlled by one party will draw districts to advantage their party. States under divided control (between state legislative houses and/or the governor) will battle it out. Some states (most recently California) have turned to independent districting commissions. These range in power from mere fig leaves for the legislatures to truly independent bodies.

Delegate v. Trustee

A final point about representation: What exactly does the word mean? Some say the legislator's role as a "representative" is simply to reflect constituents' wishes. This definition is known as the *delegate* theory of representation. Former Rep. Ron Paul (R-TX) seemed to invoke the delegate theory to defend changing

---

6   Pronounced *with a soft "g", as in "jerry."*

his stance on the policy forbidding homosexuals to serve openly in the military (often called "Don't Ask, Don't Tell"). A long-time supporter of the policy, he later voted to repeal it, saying, "I have received several calls and visits from constituents who, in spite of the heavy investment in their training, have been forced out of the military simply because they were discovered to be homosexual . . . To me, this seems like an awful waste" (Weigel, 2010).

Others say their role is to use their knowledge to do what is best for their constituents, regardless of what the constituents say. This idea is known as the *trustee* theory of representation. Former Rep. Eric Massa (D-NY) invoked the trustee theory in voicing his opinion regarding health care legislation to a gathering of liberal activists by saying, "I will vote adamantly against the interests of my district if I actually think what I am doing is going to be helpful" (Pickett, 2009).

Yet, others note that the roles are not necessarily distinct. Consider the words of Rep. Gary Peters (D-MI):

My philosophy is that my sole responsibility is to represent and fight for the people who elected me to serve them. That means seeking out opinions and listening to local residents constantly. I try to listen to as many views and collect as much information as possible, thoroughly read legislation and then vote my conscience based on the answer to this question: Does the proposal improve the lives of people in our community? Representing the people you serve and voting your conscience are not mutually exclusive if your primary goal is to help solve problems people are facing. (Gilbert, 2010)

Philosophers from Edmund Burke in the 18th century to today argue over which role for a representative is proper. At least one entire book has been devoted to the subject (see Pitkin, 1967).

There are additional factors to consider. "Representation" may include political party, ideology, region, religion, race, ethnicity, district interests, and gender as well. Given some of these, sometimes demographic representation *is*, in fact, agency representation!

Organization

The Leadership

There are two types of congressional leadership: institutional and partisan. The institutional leaders are the presiding officers. That is, they preside over the floor of each chamber. With more rules, this means more in the House than it does in the Senate. The partisan leaders are in charge of their respective parties in each house. They develop their party's legislative agenda, and coordinate their positions on issues of the day.

Institutional Leadership

The institutional leader of the House is the **Speaker**. The Speaker is elected by a majority vote of the entire House. The vote is traditionally a party-line vote, so the Speaker is always a member of the majority party. The institutional leaders of the Senate are the **Senate president** and **president pro tempore**. Constitutionally, the Senate president is automatically the vice president of the United States. This rule means the Senate president may or may not be a member of the Senate's partisan majority. The president pro tempore traditionally is the senior-most member of the majority party.[7]

House rules empower the Speaker, who has the authority to decide to which committee(s) bills are referred. Also, as the officer presiding over floor debate, the Speaker has the power to enforce formal limits on floor activity—debating and amending bills—that are set by the House Rules Committee. To add to these powers, the Speaker also has the ability to appoint the majority party members of that committee. Together, these powers mean the Speaker controls the legislative process, almost literally, coming and going! The House legislative process begins with the Speaker, the Speaker significantly shapes the committee that sets the rules for legislative consideration, and the Speaker has the authority to enforce those very rules on the floor.

Here are a couple of views from past Speakers on what it is like to be Speaker (note the similarity):

- "The power of the Speaker of the House is the power of scheduling"—Thomas P. "Tip" O'Neill (D-MA), Speaker 1977–1987. November 15, 1983. Congressional Record, daily ed., 98th Congress, 1st sess.
- "When you are Speaker you get to set the agenda"—Newt Gingrich (R-GA), Speaker 1995–1998, in Rosensteil, Thomas B., and Edith Stanley. November 9, 1994. For Gingrich, It's 'Mr. Speaker'. Los Angeles Times. p. A2.

In the Senate, with very few rules, the president (of the Senate) and president pro tempore have little to do in those roles. In addition, they both have other formal roles to play—the president is the vice president of the United States, and they play increasingly important roles as advisors to modern presidents. The president pro tempore, by virtue of traditionally being the senior-most member

---

7   The speaker and the president pro tempore are second and third in the line of succession to the presidency, respectively, behind the vice president.

of the majority party, is almost always chair of an important Senate committee. The *real* leadership in the Senate falls to the majority party leader (see below).

Partisan Leadership

Each party in each house has its own leadership to coordinate party policy positions and manage the party's voting. The **majority party leader** (the leader of the party with the most seats) in each house is also in charge of scheduling floor activity (mainly, when bills come to the entire house for debate and passage). The **minority party leaders** serve mainly to organize and coordinate their party in opposition to the majority. These leaders are assisted by party "**whips**" (formally, "**assistant floor leaders**"), who act as the eyes and ears of their party. They link the leadership to everyone else. Mostly, they are vote-counters and negotiators. It is their job to keep everyone informed of the legislative schedule and to round up votes in support of their party.

In the House, the majority leader effectively serves *under* the Speaker (who, recall, is always a member of the majority party) as part of a leadership team. In the Senate, however, without a strong institutional leader, it is the majority leader that runs the show. With few formal rules in the Senate, power is exercised informally and strategically.

What follows is an exploration of one past Senate majority leader's method of running the Senate.

THE "JOHNSON TREATMENT" Before he served as vice president of the United States in the 1960s, Lyndon B. Johnson was a United States representative (1937–1949) and senator (1949–1961) representing the state of Texas. He rose quickly to serve in the position of Senate majority (Democratic) leader (1955–1961).

Because of the lack of formal Senate rules, there was never much use for any kind of leadership—institutional or partisan. Johnson, however, transformed the position of majority leader into a powerful one.

He was always interested in acquiring and using power. He wanted to use the position of majority leader to advance the legislative agenda of the Democratic Party during the Republican presidency of Dwight D. Eisenhower (1953–1961). He managed to transform the position on the sheer force of his will and personality—through something that became known as "the Johnson Treatment." The effectiveness of the treatment began with Johnson's thorough and breathtaking knowledge of those with whom he would interact. He knew the likes, dislikes, predilections, and indiscretions of every senator. He then would put this knowledge to use when he needed to build support for legislation. Here is a description of "The Treatment" by journalists Rowland Evans and Robert Novak:

Its tone could be supplication, accusation, cajolery, exuberance, scorn, tears, complaints, the hint of threat. It was all of these together. It ran the gamut of human emotions. Its velocity was breathtaking, and it was all in one direction. Interjections from the target were rare. Johnson anticipated them before they could be spoken. He moved in close, his face a scant millimeter from the target, his eyes widening and narrowing, his eyebrows rising and falling. From his pockets poured clippings, memos, and statistics. Mimicry, humor and the genius of analogy made the treatment an almost hypnotic experience and rendered the target stunned helpless. (Evans and Novak, 1966)

No future Senate leaders possessed Johnson's talents, so "The Treatment" was not seen again. However, the expectation of an active, involved majority leader subsequently became the norm.

The Rank and File

"Rank and file" means everyone else—members not in leadership positions. As noted earlier, Congress is more demographically diverse than ever. In addition, its ranks since the 1950s are increasingly filled with political professionals. These changes have consequences for the functioning of Congress.

Political professionals often see Congress as a career, making re-election important. These careerists will act as "policy entrepreneurs" or "professional legislators"—deliberately seeking issues on which to legislate to demonstrate their value to their constituents. Their growing ranks have transformed Congress into a sort of legislating machine with specialized subcommittees (see "The Committee System" below) and increasing numbers of staff and support agencies (e.g., see the Congressional Budget Office [https://www.cbo.gov] and the Congressional Research Service [https://www.loc.gov/crsinfo]), all geared toward developing legislation on issues of interest to their constituents.

Much of this activity involves *pork barrel legislation*—usually defined as legislation or funding for projects of little to no benefit beyond a single district (the term is loosely related to the idea of "bringing home the bacon" to please local voters). Pork barrel projects take the form of things like research grants for local institutions and funding for highways, bridges, museums, and parks. The process generally involves inserting amendments—or "**earmarks**"—into vital "must-pass'" legislation like the annual federal budget. Mutual support among legislators (or "logrolling") virtually assures their passage.

The public and many legislators decry earmarks as wasteful, and the House of Representatives actually banned them in 2010 (United Press International,

2010). However, eliminating them entirely is tricky. "Pork barrel" is often in the eye of the beholder. One person's wasteful pork barrel spending is another's vital jobs program (an especially likely view within the benefitting district). In 2021, both parties in Congress decided to reinstate earmarks (Zanona & Emma, 2021).

The increasing diversity of Congress has led to the growth of another type of organization: *congressional caucuses.* These are groups of legislators promoting particular interests within Congress.[8] While there have been groups promoting ideological and commercial interests for a long time, recent decades have seen a growing number of caucuses representing demographic interests. Most prominent among these is the Congressional Black Caucus (see: https://cbc.house.gov/).

Taken together, policy entrepreneurism among the rank and file and its attendant effects on staff, structure, and legislating produce tremendous advantages for incumbent legislators. As noted earlier, re-election rates for incumbents have remained consistently high in recent decades. The developments discussed here play a large part in those high rates.

However, below the leadership level, the most prominent organizations in Congress are **committees.**

The Committee System

Long before he was elected president, Woodrow Wilson wrote extensively about our government. Of the congress, he said, "Congress in session is Congress on exhibition, whilst Congress in its committee rooms is Congress at work" (Wilson, 1885/2009, p. 79). Wilson's quote still holds true over 135 years later! In it, Wilson conveys some important points. One is that most of the speechifying, arguing, and blustery debate you may see or hear takes place on the floor of each House. Second, and more important, is that the real work of writing, shaping— some say "crafting"—legislation takes place in the smaller, behind-the-scenes groups we call committees and subcommittees.

Why Committees?

The Constitution allows each house to organize itself in any way it sees fit. Why, then, would both houses choose to organize into committees? It may have something to do with workload and expertise. Consider the alternative of each house working on legislation as one large group as opposed to several smaller groups. There have been about 14,000 pieces of legislation proposed

---

8   For lists of recent House caucuses (formally known as Congressional Member Organizations), see: https://cha.house.gov/congressional-member-and-staff-organizations.

in recent two-year congressional sessions. Without committees, it would be impossible to address anywhere near this number of proposals. In addition, committees are not undifferentiated groups. Each committee focuses on a specific topic. This focus helps to promote expertise within the Congress that further "greases" the process.

Types

If you are familiar with any committees in Congress, they are probably one of the "standing" committees, which are permanent, legislative committees. However, they are not the only committees in Congress. Here are brief descriptions of the four basic committee types:

- <u>Standing</u>: They are permanent and focus on legislating. They contain only members of one chamber.
- <u>Select</u> (or Special, or Ad Hoc): They are temporary and generally used to investigate issues that do not fit neatly into any standing committees. They, too, contain only members of one chamber.
- <u>Joint</u>: They may be permanent or temporary and are generally advisory. They exist to coordinate policy between the House and Senate. As such, they contain members from both chambers.
- <u>Conference</u>: The most temporary and specific of all committees. They are created as needed, solely to resolve differences between House and Senate versions of a single bill. They contain members from both chambers (usually members from the standing committees that developed the bill).

Committee Assignments

Members inform their party's selection committee of their preference for assignments. These preferences are usually based on their own interests, expertise, or on improving their re-election prospects. While the selection committees consider these factors, committee assignments are based mainly on seniority.

Seniority System

Seniority is defined as the length of continuous service. This definition applies to both chamber and committee service. Chamber seniority is a factor in committee assignments, while committee seniority is a factor in determining the committee's leadership. Members with greater chamber seniority may request committee assignments before members with less chamber seniority. Within each committee, a chair is determined largely on the basis of committee seniority.

Majority party committee members with the greatest committee seniority have first choice at chairing the committee.

Using chamber seniority to determine committee assignments is not unlike the registration process used at most colleges and universities (that is, seniors get to register for a class first, while freshmen must settle for whatever classes are still available after everyone else has registered).

Why seniority? While not a formal rule in either chamber, seniority is a strong tradition in both. It is clear that both chambers feel the benefits outweigh the drawbacks. What are the benefits? Chamber seniority tends to promote continuity and legislative expertise by rewarding members for remaining in Congress. Committee seniority also promotes expertise by putting in charge those who have spent the most time on a particular committee. In addition, one of the less-appreciated benefits of committee seniority is that it helps avoid leadership fights—no confusion, no campaigning, no battles, no power struggles; if you are the senior member of the majority party on a committee, you get the chair if you so desire. Case closed!

There are drawbacks. Consider the following questions. Are people necessarily better suited for a committee or for a chair just because they have been around a long time? If someone keeps their chair mainly by seniority, are they more or less likely to listen to anything other committee members may have to contribute?

Seniority has been, and continues to be, the primary basis for selecting chairs. However, not everyone has always considered it to be the wisest of methods for committee assignment and chair selection. Here is the story of some that questioned the value of seniority.

ONCE UPON A TIME, IN A CONGRESS FAR, FAR AWAY . . . In the 1950s, Congress was under the control of a few conservative, southern Democrats. They got their power through seniority. With no Republican opposition in the South, they constantly won re-election (racking up far more seniority than their eastern, northern, or western colleagues). As conservatives, they were resistant to change and opposed most legislation brought before them.

However, society was changing. The Civil Rights Movement was in full swing by the late 1950s. There were many calls for legislation to end racial segregation and promote civil rights and integration. In addition, the Cold War between us and the Soviet Union had evolved into an arms and space race—with many feeling that the Soviets were ahead of us in science and technology. This fear led to many calls for legislation to promote education and develop technology. By 1958, there were so many calls for action that a huge number of Democrats were elected to Congress because of their support for new programs. Because of their proposals for change, they were labeled "programmatic liberal" Democrats. In 1964, another wave of these Democrats was elected. By the mid-1970s, these liberals were gaining seniority, which finally gave them the numbers they needed to challenge the old southern conservatives.

The stage for confrontation was set: The southern conservatives wanted nothing to do with these new proposals—and as committee chairs, they were able to thwart many (though not all) attempts at change. These refusals left the growing ranks of liberals frustrated and vowing to change the way Congress did business.

In 1975, four senior members of the House were denied their committee chairs by the rest of the House Democrats. One was forced out because of a scandal (involving someone known as "Fanne Fox, The Argentine Firecracker"). The other three were forced out because they had not been responsive to other members of their committees. In other words, they were *not* forced out because of specific *wrongdoing,* they were forced out for doing *precisely* what chairs had done all along—running their committees in a dictatorial fashion. This action was the warning shot by the liberals that seniority would no longer be the sole determinant for committee chairs.

The liberals formalized their control through the Subcommittee Bill of Rights, a new set of House rules that steered power away from committee chairs. It stated that committees must follow set rules. They must have subcommittees, and committee chairs could not control what the subcommittees did. The bill also limited the number of chairs anyone could hold, forcing the southern conservatives to give up several chairs to the less senior liberals. It also said that all legislation must be referred to the subcommittees—so there was less chance that a committee chair could kill a proposal by refusing to act on it. Subcommittees, who were often chaired by the younger programmatic liberal Democrats, became the locus of power and activity in the House.

The less formal Senate did not pass any similar changes. However, the influx of programmatic liberals changed the way they did business as well. The result was that, by the late 1970s, power was spread out among many more people than it was just a decade earlier.

When Republicans finally gained control over Congress in 1995, they attempted to reverse the decentralization trend. One of their first acts was to repeal the Subcommittee Bill of Rights. Because the new Republican Speaker, Newt Gingrich of Georgia, had enough support from his party to hand-pick some chairs, he—and not the chairs—was really the beneficiary of this change. By this time, though, the die of decentralization had been cast. Congress operated under "subcommittee government" for a generation by the late 1990s, and was becoming used to it.

While seniority was attacked from the left in the 1970s and from the right in the 1990s, it still survives as a formidable tradition in Congress.

Operation

Once again, Woodrow Wilson is on target with the following passage from his book: "Once begin the dance of legislation, and you must struggle through its mazes as best you can to the breathless end—if any end there be" (Wilson, 1885/2009, p. 297).

The process of creating laws is often referred to as labyrinthine—having lots of twists and turns where proposals can (and do) disappear. To understand the method for this madness, let us explore the process.

The Dance

Proposals may come from anywhere: constituents, interest groups, the president, and yes, even members of Congress come up with ideas now and then! Most proposals come from the president. Why? The executive branch is charged with carrying out the laws, so they are in the best position to make suggestions.

Proposals go round and round through the legislative path. They may or may not emerge at the end. Of the 14,000 proposals typically introduced in recent congresses, only 400–500 become law—and often over 100 of these are ceremonial in nature (Singer, 2008).

Proposals must pass both houses in identical form before being sent to the president to consider. They may begin in either house (or both simultaneously), with one exception: Constitutionally, all bills for raising revenue must begin in the House.

In the House, bills are first submitted to the Speaker's office. The Speaker determines which committee(s) to send the bill. One of the changes made in the mid-1970s was to give the Speaker the power of *multiple referral*, which allows the Speaker to send a bill to several committees at once or to divide pieces of a bill among several committees. Once in committee, bills are first referred to a specialized subcommittee, which is where the action begins. The subcommittee holds hearings to gather information on the bill. They then "markup"—make changes to, or *amend*—the bill based on information from the hearings. They then vote on whether or not to send the bill to the full committee. If the majority of the subcommittee fails to support the bill, it is dead. If they do support the bill, it then goes back up to the full committee for further consideration.

Action in the full committee is the same as in the subcommittee: hearings, mark-up, vote. In a sense, it is a second chance to affect the bill—this time by a somewhat wider circle of actors. If the full committee fails to support the bill, it is dead. If they do support it, it will eventually go before the entire chamber.

In the Senate, bills are first submitted to the office of the majority leader who will, in consultation with the minority leader, refer the bill to one or more committees. The committee and subcommittee process in the Senate is identical to the House process (see above). If the full Senate committee supports the bill, it will also go before the entire chamber. However, at this point the House and Senate paths differ.

In the House, because it is such a large body, there are strict limits on debating and amending legislation on the floor. In the smaller Senate, there are no such limits. Debate and amendments are unlimited and need not be *germane* (related to the issue).

In the House, every bill gets a rule from the Rules Committee before it is scheduled for floor action by the entire chamber. The rule may place limits on floor debate and amendments. House rules specify that the *maximum* allowable debate on any bill is one hour per member. In addition, the rules require all debate and all offered amendments to be germane. The Rules Committee may enact stricter limits on debate (all the way down to no debate at all) and may place limits on amending (all the way down to no amendments at all) as well. These abilities make the Rules Committee a very powerful force in the House. Keep in mind—the Speaker exercises control over it (see the earlier discussion of the Speaker's powers).

With no similar rules in the Senate, there is no similar referral to any rules committee. They consider legislation using *unanimous consent agreements* (UCAs). These are agreements (negotiated between proponents and opponents) on debate and amendment limits that—as the term implies—require the consent of everyone in the chamber. There are no standard rules to enforce UCAs. This lack of enforcement power is often used strategically in the form of a **filibuster**—an attempt to talk a bill to death—or a *hold* (which is basically a *threat* to filibuster). It works this way: To debate legislation, senators seek recognition to speak. When granted, they may engage in discussion and debate. As long as they are recognized, no other action takes place on the Senate floor. Under UCAs, they voluntarily give up that recognition after a while so others may speak. However, a senator wishing to disrupt the process may continue to speak. At this point, the senator is said to be filibustering.

Remember, there are no standard limits on a filibuster—including the content of the discussion. Some filibustering senators have sung songs. Some have read recipes. Some have even read from phone books! All is fair during a filibuster. It is not a tactic used lightly, though. Consider this: If you filibuster my bill today, I just might come back tomorrow and filibuster your bill.

The one way to end a filibuster is through a cloture vote. *Cloture* is essentially a petition among senators to formally limit debate on a bill. However, it is very difficult to invoke cloture because the vote is not determined by a simple majority. Invoking cloture currently requires 60 votes, which is a very high standard.

MODERN FILIBUSTERS: SANITIZED FOR YOUR PROTECTION? In earlier times, filibusters were tiresome and physically difficult—as depicted in the classic film *Mr. Smith Goes to Washington*. In the past, senators wishing to filibuster had to talk continuously—hour after hour. The record for an individual filibuster was set in 1957 by Senator Strom Thurmond (D-SC), who spoke continuously for just over 24 hours in opposition to civil rights legislation. For one person, that may be a long time, but for the entire process, it is really not very long. Some began to realize that one way to elongate a filibuster is to work in concert with others. Teams of senators may filibuster for days, weeks, or longer. When one speaker tires, a sympathizer rises to ask a question—which may take several hours—giving the original speaker a much-needed break (the rules allow a senator to maintain recognition while others are asking questions). Thus, a typical filibuster involves several senators taking turns speaking and asking questions of each other. A classic example of this was the 57 days that several senators held control of the floor during debate over the Civil Rights Act of 1964.

In recent decades, changes in the way the Senate handles debate have led to an explosion of filibustering. First, majority leaders of both parties began scheduling two or more bills for floor action at the same time. They will then bring up one of the bills for debate—but they will seek to invoke cloture *first*—*before* any debate occurs. If the cloture vote fails, the bill is pulled off the floor in favor of one of the others scheduled at the same time. Consequently, bills may now be kept off the floor with simply the *threat* of a filibuster—often called a "hold." A senator will essentially say to the majority leader, "If you bring up this bill, I will filibuster."

In addition, when a traditional filibuster *does* occur, the Senate now acts in a "genteel" manner. Instead of forcing around-the-clock sessions, the Senate will adjourn each evening. When it reconvenes in the morning, the previous speaker is recognized first—to continue the debate (filibuster).

Together, these changes make filibuster/cloture activity the focus of the contemporary Senate. If we use cloture petitions as indicators of the filibuster or hold, we can see a truly massive increase in this activity. In the fifty years before the process changed—from the 1920s through the 1960s—there were a total of 56 cloture petitions. In 2021–2022 *alone,* there were 336 petitions (United States Senate, 2024).

In addition to legislation, presidential nominations to the executive branch and courts were also subject to filibusters. These nomination filibusters increased dramatically as well, from virtually none in the 1950s to over 300 from 2007 through 2011 (Kane, 2013). This led the Democratic majority at the time to change the rules on all but Supreme Court nominations to allow debate to be stopped by a simple majority vote. This so-called "nuclear option" was extended to cover Supreme Court nominees by the Republican majority in 2017. In 2021, Senate Democrats—once again in the majority (see the Chapter 6 case study)—debated eliminating filibusters entirely to prevent Republicans from derailing their ambitious legislative agenda. As of June 2021, Democrats lacked enough votes to once again invoke the "nuclear option."

The End Game

In order for a bill to become law, it must pass both houses in identical form and be submitted to the president. Given the ability of both houses to amend legislation, *if* bills pass both houses, they are almost always different from one another. These differences must be resolved if the legislation is to be presented to the president. One way to resolve any differences is to have one house simply adopt the other's version. Sometimes it happens, but given the different perspectives of the two houses, it is not likely. Often, both houses will call for a *conference committee* consisting of members of each house (usually from the committees that worked on the bills). As noted earlier, conference committees exist solely for the purpose of resolving the differences between the House and Senate versions of a bill. Once those differences are reconciled, the committee disbands.

The reconciled version is presented to both houses for an up-or-down vote (conference reports may not be amended). If it passes both houses, it is presented to the president, who may sign it into law (or allow it to become law without signing it) or veto it. If it is vetoed, it is returned to the Congress, where both houses may try to override the veto with a two-thirds vote in favor from each house.[9] If such a vote is successful, the bill becomes a law without the support of the president.

The dance must begin anew with each new Congress. If a bill has not become law by the time Congress adjourns before the next congressional elections,

---

9   Except for "pocket vetoes," which are vetoes occurring while Congress is not in session. Pocket vetoes may not be overridden.

it must begin the process all over again at the start of the new Congress the following January.

The Budget

In addition to legislating, Congress also keeps the federal government running by passing an annual budget. The rules governing this process have a profound effect on both the functioning of Congress and the distribution of power within it.

The process is relatively simple. Early every year, the president submits a budget proposal to the Congress. It consists of requests from all federal agencies and organizations for operating funds, as well as requests from the president for funding new programs and policies. Congress then molds these proposals into a budget for the following year.

From February through mid-April, Congress works on *authorizing* legislation. This step is the typical legislative process described above. While there are many exceptions, in general, for laws to take effect the following year, they must be authorized by mid-April of the current year. This legislation includes a budget for the program/policy (the maximum funding it may legally withdraw from the U.S. Treasury). Authorization must be completed by April 15th, when Congress must approve a preliminary budget resolution.

While budgets have now been authorized, not a single penny has been allocated yet. The process of actually doling out money to each policy/program is known as the *appropriations* process. From May through mid-June, two huge committees—the Appropriations Committees in each house—do this work. They decide how much funding each policy/program actually gets. Appropriations must be completed by June 15th, at which point Congress must approve another—binding—budget resolution.

Not every policy/program gets everything it wanted. Difficult economic times or less-than-expected revenue may mean some items get appropriations that fall short of their authorized maximum. In many instances, this shortfall requires rewriting the authorizing legislation to accommodate the newer budget realities. Orders from the Appropriations Committees to rewrite are known as *reconciliation orders*. These orders mean standing committees must return to work legislating. They must complete their work by the end of September. The new budget ("fiscal") year begins on October 1st.

This relatively straightforward process—authorization, appropriation, reconciliation—sounds as though it can be carried out simply and completely every year. Is it? No. Modern budget realities mean frequent funding shortfalls, and that means fights over every penny. The process is *rarely* completed in time for the new fiscal year. The government cannot operate without a budget (even if the money exists, it cannot be withdrawn from the Treasury without the proper legislation). To avoid a shutdown, Congress will pass a *continuing resolution*, which is a joint resolution (which must be signed by the president, like regular legislation) that allows the government to continue spending at current levels. Continuing resolutions may last anywhere from a few hours to several months or longer.

CONTINUING ALL YEAR The budget for 2007 was never completed. This marked the first time since the budget process was adopted in 1974 that the government failed to finish the process. By the end of 2006, the outgoing Congress had completed work on funding for only two areas: defense and homeland security.

After losing seats in the 2006 elections, the outgoing Republican majority passed a continuing resolution that left the remaining work to the new Democratic majority taking office in 2007. Once the Democratic majority assumed control of both houses in January 2007, they quickly realized that they could not complete work on the 2007 budget while simultaneously working on the 2008 budget. They simply passed another continuing resolution to fund the remainder of the government through the end of the fiscal year (September 2007) at the 2006 levels.

2008? You guessed it! Congress did not complete a budget in time, so they had to pass yet another continuing resolution. This lasted through December of 2007—marking the first time the government operated for more than an entire year under continuing resolutions. Since then, the government has operated under resolutions about as often as under formal budgets as Congress, the president, and the two political parties continue to push very different priorities. The PBS *Frontline* documentary "Cliffhanger" covers some of the battles between Congress and the Obama administration (see https://www.pbs.org/wgbh/pages/frontline/cliffhanger/).

Congressional Evolution[10]

The 1970s and beyond were a time of great change in the Congress. The changes in the membership and operating rules discussed earlier went hand-in-hand with changes in the legislative process and the functioning of Congress. What emerged is a far more complicated institution using far more "unorthodox" processes (Sinclair, 2017).

---

10   Much of this section is based on Sinclair, Barbara. 2017. *Unorthodox Lawmaking*. 5th ed. Washington DC: CQ Press.

The "Traditional" Process

Prior to the institutional reforms of the mid-1970s, when committee chairs still ruled the show, the legislative process was relatively simple and open. Bills were referred to a single committee in each house. In the House, the rules for debate and amendments were generally open—allowing members the maximum amount of debate and relatively unrestricted ability to propose amendments. The amendments were often supportive, and they usually passed. In the Senate, the process was similarly open. Unanimous consent agreements were relatively simple, and filibusters were rare. House-Senate differences in legislation were often minor and were resolved in small conference committees.

The Modern Process

Beginning in the 1970s as congressional power became more dispersed, but especially in the 1980s and later as the parties became increasingly polarized, the process grew far more complex. To allow the growing ranks of policy entrepreneurs many avenues to tend to their constituents, bills were often referred to several committees in each house. This led not just to action within each committee, but also to negotiations *between* committees as well. To keep fragile coalitions together in the House, floor rules became more restrictive. These rules left little time for members to speak. Complex rules limiting amendments became the norm. In the Senate, unanimous consent agreements became more complex and limiting. Negotiations among senators to avoid potential filibusters became commonplace. Yet, even with these negotiations, the amount of filibustering increased significantly. Prior to the 1970s, the number of filibusters (as measured by cloture votes) in each two-year Congress usually numbered in the low single digits. From the 92nd Congress (1971–72) through the 99th Congress (1985–86) the number fell below 20 only twice. From the 100th Congress (1986–87) to the present, the number has fallen below 40 only once, and topped 100 for the first time in the 110th Congress (2007–08). In the 113th through 118th congresses (2013–24) the number has reached an astounding 200+ four times (United States Senate, 2024).

Negotiation rules the day not only within the Senate, but between the houses as well, as ever-larger conference committees (often containing over 100 representatives and dozens of senators) discuss major changes in legislation—often, in effect, rewriting bills. Furthermore, negotiations occur not only within Congress itself, but between Congress and the president too, as presidents try to secure votes for passage of their programs and as Congress tries to avoid presidential vetoes.

What Happened, and Why?

The changes in membership and operating rules discussed earlier had a profound effect on the behavior of the institution and its members. Barbara Sinclair (2017) notes three factors involved in the increasingly complex legislative environment:

- <u>Internal reforms</u>: Changes in the composition of the Congress in the 1960s and beyond (especially the influx of "programmatic liberals" discussed earlier) and changes in the media landscape (especially the increased imagery of television) led to a greater focus on individuals. In the Senate, this meant extended debate and a greater number of amendments to legislation. Passing legislation increasingly required 60 votes to stop the growing number of filibusters. In the House, there were shifts in power to accommodate these changes—downward to increasing numbers of subcommittees and upward to the Speaker—reducing the power and autonomy of the standing committees. This made legislating more difficult for the majority party.

- <u>The budget process</u>: As part of the reforms in the 1970s, a formal, annual budget process was created by the 1974 Budget and Impoundment Act. This new process provided Congress with a mechanism for comprehensive policy change. In other words, policies must now fit into a single annual budget. Congress can no longer simply pass laws and worry about the budgetary consequences later (as it could before the 1974 law was passed).

- <u>The political environment</u>: From the 1960s onward, three things became more common in the political environment—adding to the complexity of the legislative process: divided government, partisan polarization, and budget deficits. From 1911 to 1961 there were only 14 years of divided government (where the majority party in one or both houses of Congress is not the president's party). From 1961 to 2011, that number more than doubled to 30 years.[11] At the same time, the two parties have become more polarized as conservative southern Democrats defected to the Republicans and liberal northeastern and western Republicans defected to the Democrats. This left Democrats largely moderate to liberal and Republicans largely moderate to conservative by the 1990s (e.g., see Kohut et al., 2010).[12] At the same

---

11 Including the unprecedented year of 2001, where the government went from divided to unified and back to divided (because of a single party defector) in the space of six months.

12 For an illustration of this increasing polarization in Congress, see Keith Poole's NOMINATE

time, increasingly common budget deficits create a "zero-sum game" where new policies become more difficult to fund. All of this makes the widespread cooperation needed to work the legislative process more and more elusive.

Other "Stuff"

How Members Decide

Just as voters use cues (see Chapter 6) in elections, so do members of Congress use them to decide whether or not to vote for legislation. Though written 30-plus years ago, John Kingdon's (1977, 1981) research on congressional voting is still considered the standard. According to Kingdon, there are several "actors" that influence congressional voting: constituents, fellow legislators, party and committee leadership, interest groups, the executive branch, congressional staff, and media.

As Kingdon says, the obvious place to start is with *constituents*—the voters. It is all too easy to say legislators should simply represent their constituents. Reality is far more complicated. For one thing, most votes cast by members of Congress involve regulatory, budgetary, or arcane procedural issues about which, as one representative bluntly said, "[m]ost of my constituents don't care" (Kingdon, 1981, p. 32). When voters *do* care, though, even the most homogeneous constituencies may not possess a single, obvious opinion. A related complication is the intensity of voter preferences. Many voters may hold an opinion on an issue, but they may not feel strongly about it. Should a legislator vote with an apathetic majority, or with an intense minority?

Because constituents are not always the best source, legislators also look to other actors.

- *Fellow legislators*, including *party and committee leaders,* can sometimes provide direction. Fellow legislators provide a trusted and convenient source whereas the leadership is often a strategic source—especially to the ambitious legislator.
- Despite our jaundiced view of *interest groups*, they are often a valuable source of information regarding an issue. This makes them valuable at times when there is no constituency consensus and/or when legislators lack detailed knowledge of the issue at hand.

---

data at https://voteview.com. To view the changes from the 1960s, examine the graphic here: https://voteview.com/static/articles/party_polarization/voteview_party_mean_diff.png. Notice that after a period of relatively low polarization in the middle of the 20th century, the measured distances between the parties ("polarization") in each house began to increase again in the 1960s.

- While *presidents* often possess "a store of credit" with their *own* party, Kingdon finds remarkably little reliance on the executive branch as a source (Kingdon, 1981, p. 186). This is most likely because of both partisan and institutional competition. That is, at any given time, a large portion of Congress is not from the president's party (often a majority). In addition, Congress is fiercely protective of its constitutional power and position. This interinstitutional rivalry sometimes keeps even fellow party members from relying on the president. Also, local constituencies are often at odds with the president's national concerns. What appears to be executive influence may better be explained by partisanship.

- While rarely credited by members of Congress as a source, their own staff commonly provide significant direction:

  > Adequate staff, the argument runes, could considerably ease the information burdens and the claims on the congressman's time. In the process the staff could be expected to be an influence on congressmen's decisions of considerable importance, since they work with the legislators day in and day out, presumably have their confidence, and supposedly are in a position to furnish and withhold information, suggestions, and advice. (Kingdon, 1981, p. 201)

- The *media* and *other sources of information* also provide direction to members of Congress. Traditional media and ever-expanding Internet sources (including blogs, Facebook, and Twitter) may affect members both directly and through their influence on many of the other cues noted above. Members of Congress also have access to information not available to the outside public. This extra information includes committee and staff reports, executive branch reports, and in some cases, classified information.

Other Activities

Lastly, while the basic job of Congress is legislating, and the main focus of that job is representation, there are other tasks Congress performs.

- Perhaps the most important is **oversight**. Oversight may take two related forms. First, it is the review of existing laws and programs to see if they are functioning as Congress intended, which is often closely connected to the budget process to see if existing laws and programs require budgetary adjustments. The second form involves investigations into businesses, industries, or other aspects of society—

often in the wake of crimes, scandals, natural disasters, or economic distress—to see if government action is warranted.

- As noted earlier, the Senate has exclusive powers to confirm executive and judicial appointments and ratify treaties negotiated between the United States and other nations. This authority gives the Senate an increasingly important source of input into the other two branches of government, as it acts as a check on presidential power. In addition, the 25th Amendment requires the House join the Senate in confirming appointments to fill vice presidential vacancies.

- In extreme instances, Congress also has the ability to discipline and even remove its own members and to impeach and remove members of the other two branches. Each house may *expel* a member upon a two-thirds vote of that house. **Impeachment** and removal from office of an executive or judicial official is similar to indictment and conviction in the court system. Constitutionally, the House has the sole power of impeachment. When impeached, an official is then tried by the Senate (with the chief justice of the Supreme Court presiding), which requires a two-thirds vote to convict and remove from office.

Discussion Questions

1. Do the nature of Congress and the roles of its members make it a truly representative body?

2. Explore how parliamentary systems function and compare them to our congressional system.

3. Attend a state legislative or city council meeting or visit the local office of a U.S. representative or senator. After doing so, consider: Do legislatures actually function as textbooks suggest they do?

4. Are interest groups *vital* to democracy, or do they *distort* democracy? You can research one of the largest and most controversial influences on Congress at these and other sites:

   ▷ UShistory.com: *Interest Groups* (https://www.ushistory.org/gov/5c.asp)

   ▷ OpenStax: *What Are the Pros and Cons of Interest Groups?* (https://openstax.org/books/introduction-political-science/pages/8-2-what-are-the-pros-and-cons-of-interest-groups)

   ▷ University of Michigan Open Library: *Lobbying: The Art of Influence* (https://open.lib.umn.edu/americangovernment/chapter/9-2-lobbying-the-art-of-influence/)

> ▷ Open Secrets: *Top Interest Groups Giving to Members of Congress, 2024 Cycle* (https://www.opensecrets.org/industries/mems)
> ▷ The Center for Public Integrity: *Lobby Watch* (https://publicintegrity.org/topics/accountability/lobby-watch)

References

Cooper, M. (2010, September 5). How to tilt an election through redistricting. *The New York Times.* https://www.nytimes.com/2010/09/26/weekinreview/26cooper.html

Evans, R., & Novak, R. (1966). *Lyndon B. Johnson: The exercise of power.* The New American Press.

Fenno, R. F., Jr. (2003). *Home style: House members in their districts.* (Longman Classics ed.). Longman.

Gallup. (2024). *Congress and the public.* Gallup. https://news.gallup.com/poll/1600/congress-public.aspx

Gibson, C., & Jung, K. (2005). *Historical census statistics on population totals by race, 1790 to 1990, and by Hispanic origin, 1970 to 1990, for the United States, regions, divisions, and states.* Census. https://www.census.gov/content/dam/Census/library/working-papers/2002/demo/POP-twps0056.pdf

Gilbert, G. (2010, March 27). Trustee or delegate? Congress' role up for debate. *The Oakland Press.* https://www.theoaklandpress.com/2010/03/27/trustee-or-delegate-congress-role-up-for-debate/

Kane, P. (2013). Reid, Democrats trigger 'nuclear' option; eliminate most filibusters on nominees. *The Washington Post.* https://www.washingtonpost.com/politics/senate-poised-to-limit-filibusters-in-party-line-vote-that-would-alter-centuries-of-precedent/2013/11/21/d065cfe8-52b6-11e3-9fe0-fd2ca728e67c_story.html

Kingdon, J. W. (1977). Models of legislative voting. *The Journal of Politics, 39*(3), 563–595.

Kingdon, J. W. (1981). *Congressmen's voting decisions,* (2nd ed.). Harper & Row.

Kohut, A., et al. (2010). *Voters rate the parties' ideologies.* Pew Research Center for the People & the Press. https://www.pewresearch.org/politics/2010/07/16/voters-rate-the-parties-ideologies/

Lasswell, H. D. (1936). *Politics: Who gets what, when, how.* Whittlesey House.

Madison, J. (1788, 2011, November 23). Federalist #51: The structure of the government must furnish the proper checks and balances between the different departments. *The New York Packet.* https://guides.loc.gov/

federalist-papers/text-51-60#s-lg-box-wrapper-25493427

Manning, J. E. (2024). Membership of the 118th Congress: A profile. *Congressional Research Service Report R47470*. https://crsreports.congress. gov/product/pdf/R/R47470

Mayhew, D. R. (1974). *Congress: The electoral connection*. Yale University Press.

Mendes, E. (2013). *Americans Down on Congress, OK With Own Representative*. Gallup. https://news.gallup.com/poll/162362/americans-down-congress-own-representative.aspx

Ornstein, N. (2008). Our broken Senate. *The American: The Journal of the American Enterprise Institute, 2*(2).

Pickett, K. (2010, August 16). Rep. Massa: I will vote against the interests of my district. *The Washington Times*. Retrieved September 12, 2024 from https:// web.archive.org/web/20121014152254/http://www.washingtontimes.com/ weblogs/watercooler/2009/aug/16/video-rep-massa-i-will-vote-against-interests-my-d/

Pitkin, H. F. (1967). *The concept of representation*. University of California Press.

Sinclair, B. (2017). *Unorthodox lawmaking*. (5th ed.). CQ Press.

Singer, P. (2008, December 1). *Members offered many bills but passed few*. Roll Call. https://rollcall.com/2008/11/26/members-offered-many-bills-but-passed-few/

United Press International. (2010). *McConnell switches, backs earmark ban*. United Press International. https://www.upi.com/Top_News/ US/2010/11/15/McConnell-switches-backs-earmark-ban/UPI-21901289846681/

United States Senate. (2024). *Senate action on cloture motions*. United States Senate. https://www.senate.gov/legislative/cloture/clotureCounts.htm

Weigel, D. (2010, May 28). Ron Paul: Constituents changed my mind on 'don't ask, don't tell'. *The Washington Post*. Retrieved September 12, 2024 from https://web. archive.org/web/20210508132454/https://voices.washingtonpost.com/right-now/2010/05/ron_paul_constituents_changed.html

Wilson, W. (1885/2009). *Congressional government: A study in American politics*. Transaction Publishers.

Zanona, M, and Caitlin, E. (2021). House GOP votes to embrace the return of earmarks. *Politico*. https://www.politico.com/news/2021/03/17/house-gop-ends-earmark-ban-476696

The Presidency

Carl D. Cavalli

Learning Objectives

After covering the topic of the presidency, students should understand:

1. The origins and executive nature of the presidency and the roles played by presidents.
2. The sources of presidential power.
3. The organization of both the White House and the larger Executive Branch.
4. The growth of presidential power and how that power has changed over the past century.

Abstract[1]

The framers envisioned a presidency that left them concerned about what they termed "energy in the executive." In other words, they thought the presidency would not be powerful enough. Contemporary politicians and scholars present a very different view. They often debate whether or not the presidency has in fact become too powerful. Related to this shift in the views about power is a shift in what is perceived to be the main sources of presidential power. The framers created an office empowered by, and limited by, the Constitution. However, modern analysts see the office empowered by a very different—and extra-constitutional—source: the public.

Introduction

The Second Branch?

On January 20th, 2025, Donald Trump took the oath of office for the second time. In doing so, he became only the second person to serve two non-consecutive terms as president (Grover Cleveland was the first). In returning to the office, what

---

1 Portions of this chapter were originally included in Cavalli, Carl D. 2000. The Presidency. Lesson 10 in POLS 1101: American Government. University System of Georgia eCore™.

is Trump becoming (again)? The president is the head of the Executive Branch. By executive, we mean that it is the branch designed to carry out (or *execute*) policy. The framers clearly treated the executive as a secondary branch. It is discussed in Article II of the Constitution. Article I covers the Legislative Branch largely because they felt it would be the most powerful branch. It seems more the opposite today. How can this be so?

Basics

Presidential Roles

It is best to begin exploring this question by reviewing the expectations placed on presidents. That is, what roles do they play in our system? Generally, they play two roles: Chief of State and the head of government.

Chief of State

One role the president plays is that of **chief of state**, or national symbol. The presidency is the only office in this country elected by the entire nation. Presidents have come to embody their symbolic role in many ways.

The night Joseph Biden was formally declared the winner of the 2020 presidential election, he said "We must restore the soul of America." Is "we" his family? The White House? The federal government? No. His use of the term is a reference to the nation. Presidents often claim to be a voice for the American people (e.g., see Barger, 1978; Teten, 2007). True or not, their priorities do become our priorities—when a president suggests the nation focus on an issue (like civil rights or health care), we do engage in debate. We may not always *agree* with the president, but we do wind up *discussing* these issues as a nation.

In addition, presidential involvement in international affairs is the equivalent of American involvement. When the president signs an international agreement, America is committed to that agreement. When the president receives another nation's ambassador, it is *America* recognizing the existence of that country.

Consider the following private presidential conversations that were recorded on Dictabelts in the White House. Is the president speaking as an *individual*, or speaking for the *nation*?

- Following the space flight of Major Gordon Cooper on May 16, 1963, President John Kennedy called him and said, "*We're* very proud of you, Major" (Miller Center, 2010a, emphasis added).
- On the birthday of famed poet Carl Sandburg, January 6, 1964, President Lyndon Johnson called Sandburg and said he wanted "to tell

you how fortunate *America* was to have you with *us*" (Miller Center, 2010b, emphasis added).

These conversations were not intended for public consumption, and so they provide us with evidence that presidents often speak for all of America even in private moments. Of course, a glance at most public presidential addresses reveals the same character. You can see this by perusing White House video (https://www.youtube.com/whitehouse) and briefing (https://www.whitehouse.gov/briefing-room) sites.

Head of Government

The other role of the president is that of **chief executive** or chief operating officer of the United States. In this role, the president is recognized as the person atop the federal government's policy-making team.

In a sense, the president as the head of government is in charge of the day-to-day operations of the United States government. The president is, of course, the person charged with carrying out the laws of the land (as noted earlier). The president is also charged with evaluating the laws and recommending changes.

Most of the legislative proposals that Congress works on actually originate in the Executive Branch. The executive departments and agencies charged with carrying out the laws will also evaluate those laws: Are the laws having their intended effect? Are any changes needed? If so, what? All of this information eventually flows back up to the president, who will in a very real sense act as chief *legislator* in addition to being the chief executive.

Shortly after speaking to Carl Sandburg, President Johnson also called Minnesota Senator Eugene McCarthy regarding civil rights legislation in the Senate. He said, "I want you to pull together those other Democrats and make them attend the meetings, make them keep their mouths shut, make them vote down the amendments, and get me a bill out on that floor!" (Miller Center, 2010c). Though seated in the White House, Johnson is clearly acting as a legislator during this phone call.

Chief Legislator entails more than just evaluating and recommending laws. The president also has the constitutional power to veto legislation. Congressional legislation must be submitted to the president for approval. The president can either sign it into law or veto it. If the president vetoes a bill, it is dead unless two-thirds of each house of Congress votes to override the veto (see Chapter 7). This action would enact the bill into law without presidential approval. It is hard enough to get sufficient votes to pass a bill in the first place, so you can imagine the difficulty of trying to get two-thirds of each house to override a veto. The consequence is that, generally, nothing becomes law without the president's approval![2]

These roles are a lot to invest in one person. How does this compare to other nations? Who plays these roles in other countries? Compare the United States to the United Kingdom. In the United Kingdom, these roles are separated. The King acts as the ceremonial Chief of State, and the Prime Minister acts as the day-to-day head of government. In the United States, we combine them into one person, which would seem to make our presidents very powerful people. This statement is true, but the framers designed a system where one powerful executive does not go unchecked. We tether our presidents (that is, we limit their independence). They are tethered to Congress and the courts through checks and balances (see Chapter 2), and they are tethered to the public through elections (and politically through measures of public approval). In the United Kingdom, the Prime Minister is tethered only to the majority party in the House of Commons, and the King is not tethered to anyone.

In some instances, we can actually see a combination of these two roles. Our recognition of presidents as national leaders leads us to allow them substantive powers.

Executive Orders

As the head of government, the president supervises the Executive Branch. This responsibility includes deciding how to execute the laws of the land.

Bolstered by the role of Chief of State, the president has a lot of authority. That authority is exercised through the issuance of **executive orders**. If, for example, the Executive Branch is charged with carrying out various programs called for by legislation, the president may issue executive orders directing whom to hire and how to disburse the appropriate funding. While divorced from formal congressional authorization, these orders carry the same official weight as laws and at times may be used by presidents in place of legislation in the face of an uncooperative Congress.

The effects of this kind of order may have profound consequences, not only for the Executive Branch, not only for the program involved, but also for the individuals hired and for the society at large.

The situation was true for one of the most famous executive orders in the post-World War II era: Executive Order #10952. With this order, President

---

2　There is a third possibility—the president may let a bill become law without signing it by letting it sit for 10 days. This option essentially says, "I don't like this bill, but I don't want to fight it." It is not a commonly exercised option.

John F. Kennedy created the Equal Employment Opportunity Commission in 1961. It was charged with ensuring that, in all contracts using federal funds, the contractors must take affirmative action to ensure that applicants are employed, and employees are treated fairly during employment, without regard to race, creed, color or national origin. This marked the first time the term "affirmative action" was used by the federal government, putting its weight behind the cause of civil rights with consequences (and controversy) still felt today.

Executive Agreements

An **executive agreement** is an agreement between the President of the United States and the head of another country. While the president has the constitutional power to negotiate treaties with other countries, such treaties require the approval of two-thirds of the Senate. Executive agreements, on the other hand, do not require any congressional approval (although any money or changes in the law that may be required to fulfill an agreement must be approved by Congress through the normal legislative process), yet they are recognized as having the same force of law as treaties. This recognition has been granted—and upheld by the courts— precisely because of the president's standing as Chief of State. In other words, the president has the power to speak for the country and to commit its resources in an agreement with other nations. For example, despite an official policy of neutrality, President Franklin Roosevelt took it upon himself to reach an agreement with the United Kingdom to exchange U.S. warships for British bases during the opening months of World War II. At the time, there was no specific legal or constitutional provision empowering the president to do so. He justified his actions on the *commander-in-chief* and *executive* powers found in the Constitution, as well as a minor law permitting the president to dispose of obsolete military equipment. Congress eventually acquiesced to this by passing the Lend Lease Act of 1941, which permitted the president to lend "defense articles" to any government "whose defense the president judges vital to the defense of the United States."

Executive Privilege

Executive privilege is the claim by presidents of their right to refuse to hand over information requested by Congress. The logic is that the constitutional provision for separation of powers means that the Congress has no right to force the president to turn over information to them. It is most often used with the rationale of maintaining secrecy for purposes of national security.

In his battle with Congress over materials related to the Watergate scandal, President Richard Nixon tried to exert an absolute claim of executive privilege. In the case of *United States v. Nixon*, 418 U.S. 683 (1974), the Supreme Court ruled that, while presidents do have a right under the separation of powers to claim executive privilege, the right is not absolute.

In 1998, Federal Judge Norma Holloway Johnson ruled that executive privilege does not cover presidential conversations with White House aides absent any national security claims. In so ruling, she compelled reluctant presidential advisers to testify in the investigation into President Clinton's affair with Monica Lewinsky.

More recently, the administration of President George W. Bush invoked claims of executive privilege on a number of occasions, including its refusal to disclose documents relating Vice President Dick Cheney's meetings with energy company executives during the administration's development of energy policy proposals and its refusal to allow White House personnel to testify before Congress during the investigation into the firing of U.S. attorneys (e.g., see Holding, 2007).

What Makes a President Powerful?

In one of the most famous explorations of presidential power, Richard Neustadt (1990) claims that the constitutional powers of the president amount to no more than the powers of a clerk.

Remember, the framers designed the presidency as an office which merely carries out the laws passed by Congress. Yet, modern presidents are often referred to as the most powerful person on Earth. During the Cold War, presidents were referred to as "the leaders of the free world." This description sounds like a lot more than just a clerk. How can it be?

If Neustadt is correct, most presidential power does not come directly from the Constitution. It must come from somewhere else. An exploration of presidents' constitutional and legal sources of power, along with their more political sources, may help clarify this confusion.

Constitutional and Legal Power Sources

These sources of power stem from either the Constitution itself or from federal law.

The Vice President

The vice presidency is established in both Articles I and II of the Constitution. Our first vice president, John Adams, said, "I am nothing. I may be everything." The first part of Adam's lament is based on the lack of formal duties for vice presidents. This case was especially true in Adams's day, because vice presidents were then the second-place finishers in the presidential elections—which meant they were the opposition as far as the new president was concerned. So, vice presidents were then largely isolated from their presidents. The 12th Amendment changed this situation by providing for the separate election of vice presidents, which grew into a system where vice presidents are largely elected with their own party's presidential nominee.

The second part of Adams's quote, "I may be everything" is based on the vice president's position as first in the line of presidential succession. Should a president die, resign, or become incapacitated, it is the vice president who takes over as president. It has happened eight times in our nation's history (more, if you count the times that recent vice presidents temporarily took charge as their presidents underwent medical procedures).

Today, vice presidents are on much friendlier terms with their presidents. They are often trusted advisers. Vice presidents are increasingly charged with leading various presidential initiatives. For example, George W. Bush's Vice President, Dick Cheney led many administration policy initiatives, including those regarding energy and anti-terrorism policy. Cheney was described by many as the most powerful vice president ever (Kuttner, 2004; Walsh, 2003), though some speculated that his successor Joe Biden may have been as or more powerful (Hirsch, 2012; McDuffee, 2013; Rothkopf, 2013). Biden was also a trusted adviser to President Obama, especially in the area of foreign policy. He led many administration initiatives, especially those involving the budget and gun control. President Biden's Vice President, Kamala Harris was a close advisor. President Trump's second term Vice President, JD Vance, will likely play a similar role.

As noted in Chapter 7, vice presidents are also formally charged with presiding over Senate floor debate, but since that debate is essentially unregulated, this duty is without true power. Oftentimes, the vice president is mainly an electoral resource—someone to help a presidential candidate pull in votes in an area of the country where that person might be weak.

The White House Staff and The Executive Office of the Presidency

Positions and organizations in these two entities may be based on direct presidential creation or on congressional statutes (or some combination thereof). They act as personal/political and policy advisers to the president, respectively.

- The **White House Staff** are the people who most immediately surround the president. They act as *personal* advisers. These people advise the president on what to say, when to say it, what to do, who to meet, and when. The president's Chief of Staff coordinates this group, which includes people like speech writers, press and appointment secretaries, and political advisers.

- Members of **Executive Office of the President** (or E.O.P.) act as *policy* advisers to the president. They advise the president on what policies to pursue and propose and assist with management of the federal bureaucracy. This group includes economic advisers, legislative advisers, and domestic and foreign policy advisers, among others.

The president appoints members of the White House Staff and top E.O.P officials. Many do not require Senate confirmation because they are advisers without any true operational responsibility. In addition, they serve "at the president's pleasure." This phrase means they serve only as long as the president wants them. The president may fire them at any time without cause.

Because of their advisory role, presidents often place some of their closest acquaintances in these positions. New presidents generally replace all of the previous occupants with people they want and trust. Information on White House offices and agencies may be found on the White House website (see: https://www. whitehouse.gov/administration).

Cabinet Departments and Executive Agencies

These are the organizations created by congressional statutes. They actually carry out policy. In this capacity, they both assist the president in fulfilling the roles of the chief executive, and they also provide the president with advice on future policies to pursue. These departments and agencies are grouped according to substantive topics, much like the committee system in Congress. Examples include the departments of Agriculture, Commerce, Defense, and Homeland Security, The Small Business Administration, and NASA (see Chapter 9).

The president nominates the heads of these organizations, but unlike the advisers, they require Senate confirmation. The reason for this distinction is that, these organizations have operational responsibilities (in other words, unlike advisers, they actually do something). They carry out the will of Congress (in the form of laws), so Congress has a say as to who heads these departments and agencies.

Like the advisers, department and agency heads serve at the president's pleasure. Generally, incoming presidents will replace most or all department and agency heads with their own people. Everyone below the few top levels in these organizations are neither appointed nor fired by the president. They are hired under provisions of the Civil Service (see Chapter 9) based on merit and cannot be fired except for cause. As such, lower-level department and agency employees often serve in their positions as careers which cross two or more administrations. Information on cabinet departments and executive agencies may be found at the USA.gov website (see: https://www.usa.gov/federal-agencies/).

It is clear from all this information that cabinet departments and executive agencies are more independent and removed from the president than are the White House Staff and E.O.P.

WHO DO YOU TRUST? Presidents have many sources of advice. Members of the White House Staff and the E.O.P. are hired as advisers, but cabinet secretaries and agency heads are also in a good position to provide advice—especially since they are the ones actually out there carrying out laws and policies.

Since members of the White House Staff and the E.O.P. depend on the president for their jobs, they sometimes become "yes people" and shield the president from bad news. Understandably, this characteristic makes them potentially poor advisors[3]. The **Cabinet** may actually be in a better position to give advice. After all, they know if policies are working or not because they are running them! But will presidents listen to them?

Cabinet departments and executive agencies are less dependent on the president for their jobs (since the heads of these organizations require congressional confirmation and everyone else is a civil service hire). As such, they are much more likely to say no to the president. Is there potential here for a president to become isolated in a "White House Fortress" favoring those White House aides who are least likely to be honest over the cabinet and executive officers who have real-world experience? Is there any evidence that recent presidents favored their advisors over their department and agency heads?

Appointment Power

The Constitution empowers the president to appoint all federal judges and Supreme Court justices, and top-level cabinet and executive agency personnel (including the ambassadors who represent the United States around the world), subject to Senate confirmation (see Chapter 7). In addition, presidents may hire White House staff as they see fit. These appointments amount to over 6,000 people by recent estimates. This ability is considered a source of power, because it gives the president the ability to shape the Executive Branch. The president has the power to appoint area and issue experts and/or to reward loyal supporters with jobs ("**patronage**"). Also, while judicial appointments

---

3   When she was President Reagan's Assistant for Public Liaison, Elizabeth Dole once ironically remarked, "The president doesn't want any yes-men and yes-women around him. When he says no, we all say no" (Werthheimer & Gutgold, 2004).

serve for life, Executive Branch appointments (except for those in regulatory agencies) serve "at the president's pleasure" (meaning they may be fired at any time, without cause). As mentioned earlier, this power is best illustrated at the start of each new administration, especially if the new president is not from the same party as the outgoing one. At that time, most, if not all, incumbent department and agency heads resign to allow the incoming president to nominate "friendly" replacements[4].

Legislative Power

Though not part of the Legislative Branch, many consider the president our "chief legislator" (Cavalli, 2006; Rossiter, 1956, p. 14). The president is an important actor throughout the legislative process. The presidency is the primary source of legislative proposals. In fact, in some instances, such as with the federal budget, the president is required by federal law to submit proposals[5]. The Constitution even requires the president to recommend legislation "from time to time" (Article II, Section 3). This process became institutionalized as the president's annual "State of the Union Address." This **agenda-setting** function gives the president a lot of influence over Congress's legislative work (e.g., see Light, 1999).

Modern presidents tend to live or die by the success of their campaign proposals (Cavalli, 2006), which almost always involve legislative proposals. So, once proposals are submitted to Congress, presidents have a natural interest in taking steps to ensure their passage. Much of their time is spent building support for their proposals both publicly and with members of Congress.

The constitutional **veto** power (Article I, Section 7) also gives presidents influence at the end of the process. All legislation must be presented to the president who may sign it into law (or allow it to become law without signature after ten days) or reject it with a veto, which the Congress may try to override and enact into law on its own[6] (see Chapter 7).

---

4   Though rarely admitted, there is evidence that most presidents ask new appointees to submit a standing letter of resignation. Presidents will pull out these letters when they want to replace someone but wish to avoid the distasteful act of firing them (which sometimes leaves the impression that the president erred in their hiring).

5   The Budget Act of 1921 requires the president to submit a budget to Congress every year. A related example is the Employment Act of 1946 which requires the president to submit an annual economic report to Congress that includes direction on how to achieve future economic goals.

6   Except for "pocket vetoes," which occurring while Congress is not in session and may not be overridden.

So, the head of the Executive Branch is actually one of the most influential players in the legislative process at all stages: The beginning (recommends legislation), the middle (builds support), and the end (signs or vetoes).

Chief Diplomat and Commander-in-Chief

The president is also our chief diplomat and **commander-in-chief** of our armed forces. The president effectively manages our relationship with the rest of the world. As chief diplomat, the president meets with foreign heads of state, negotiates treaties, and enters into executive agreements with them, and receives foreign ambassadors in recognition of their government. As commander-in-chief, the president oversees the nation's military establishment:

In times of peace he raises, trains, supervises, and deploys the forces that Congress is willing to maintain. With the aid of the Secretary of Defense, the Joint Chiefs of Staff, and the National Security Council—all of whom are his personal choices—he looks constantly to the state of the nation's defenses. (Rossiter, 1957, p. 11)

In [times of war] the President's power to command the forces swells out of all proportion to his other powers. All major decisions of strategy, and many of tactics as well, are his alone to make or to approve. (Rossiter, 1956, p. 12)

WHO LET THE DOGS OUT? Though the Constitution makes the president the commander-in-chief of our armed forces (Article II, Section 2), it gives the power to declare war to the Congress (Article I, Section 8). The power to, as Shakespeare put it, "Cry 'Havoc,' and let slip the dogs of war" (*Julius Caesar*, Act III, Scene I) is actually divided between the two branches. This division has generated a long-lasting tension between them that particularly flared up during the Vietnam War. As with all post-World War II military actions, this "war" was never declared by Congress. Presidents simply began committing troops into military action without seeking a formal declaration from Congress. The escalation of the Vietnam War by presidents Lyndon Johnson and Richard Nixon in the face of drastically declining public and congressional support led Congress to pass the **War Powers Resolution** in 1973. The act limits the president's ability to commit troops into hostile action without the express consent of Congress (see Chapter 14). Though never challenged in court for fear of losing, all presidents since its passage have considered the act an unconstitutional infringement on their power as commander-in-chief. Congress, also fearing that they would lose a court challenge, has never fully insisted on the act's enforcement. Instead, the two sides seem to have reached a mutual understanding where presidents will continue to commit troops to action without any formal war declaration by Congress. In place of a formal declaration, though, presidents will seek some sort of consent (e.g., see CNN Politics, 2002), and Congress, not eager to appear unpatriotic or unsupportive of the military, will most always grant that consent.

These constitutional and legal sources of power are available to all presidents. As such, they would not explain variations in presidential power. In addition, in and of themselves, they have changed little over time. The size of the executive branch has grown tremendously, especially during the 20th century. However, the appointment power has actually been curtailed—largely through the Civil Service Act. As noted earlier, Richard Neustadt claims all these resources make the president nothing more than a clerk (with a really top-notch support staff!). They do not, according to Neustadt, explain the modern transformation of the presidency into something often regarded as the most powerful position on earth. To explain that, we must move beyond these sources.

Political and Other Power Sources

These sources of power are not formally specified either in the Constitution or in federal law. However, Neustadt and others say they are responsible for much of the power of the modern presidency.

Support: Election and Approval

Whether through election or through ever-present public opinion polls, a president with the support of the public can accomplish a lot. For example, presidents often suggest legislation to Congress. Congress is more likely to act on those suggestions if the president can claim that the American people support such legislation. After all, the American people collectively comprise the voters who put members of Congress in office (and can take them out as well!). A president who claims a popular mandate because of a landslide electoral victory and/or high public approval ratings can claim such support. One without such a mandate cannot.

Support: Party and Groups

Political party is a source of loyalty and cooperation that can bridge the separation of powers built into our system. This was the original intent of the Anti-Federalists as they organized themselves into the first American political party (see Chapter 6). Presidents can often count on their fellow partisans to support their initiatives and proposals. In Congress, this support translates into votes. There, it helps even more if the president's party is the majority—more able to control the process and to deliver a victory for the president. Obviously, a Congress controlled by the other party can severely constrain a president's influence over policy.

Groups can work to build public support for presidents. This support in turn, can bolster a president's influence over Congress when seeking legislation. Democratic presidents will often seek to work with labor unions like the AFL-CIO, while Republican presidents will often seek to work with business groups like the Chamber of Commerce.

Leadership

When the president raises an issue, it becomes the topic of discussion for many, if not most, Americans. For example, if the president says we should debate reforming Social Security or access to affordable health care, the country debates those issues. We may or may not agree with the president's position, but if it is an issue to the president, then it is an issue to us. In fact, we expect presidents to do this.

Think about what you look for in a presidential candidate. Do you look for one who says "I promise to do the best I can to execute the laws of the land" or one who says "I want to change this law or create that policy?" You probably prefer the latter. It gives the president the opportunity to set the nation's agenda. That is, to lead the way on the issues upon which we will focus our energies.

Media

When the president says it, it is news. It is as simple as that. The White House is simply required coverage for any major news organization. This means that presidents can rely on media to convey their ideas to the public. In fact, with the development of the Internet, presidents have far more avenues to advance their ideas than ever before. Ironically, many presidents often distrust the media, seeing them as the enemy rather than as an ally (Nelson, 2000). However, presidents who see the benefits can use the media as a conduit to exercise the leadership discussed earlier. In the television—and now, Internet—age, presidents are increasingly "going public" to sell their policies directly to the people (Kernell, 1986). The Internet especially allows presidents to communicate directly with the public, avoiding the scrutiny and punditry of news media (for example, see: https://x.com/potus).

Presidential Power Redux

The contention among presidential scholars like Richard Neustadt is that presidents' constitutional and legal powers add up to no more than that of a servant to Congress. Yet, we know that the president is thought of oftentimes as the most powerful person on earth. Neustadt and many others claim that *real* presidential power stems from persuasive abilities backed up by public support and skillful use of other political resources (Jacobs, 2010; Neustadt, 1990; Tichenor, 2010; Tulis, 1987).

THE "JOHNSON TREATMENT" COMES TO THE WHITE HOUSE: Shortly after the assassination of President John F. Kennedy in November 1963, the new president, Lyndon Johnson, formed a commission to investigate the murder. One person he asked to serve on the commission was Senator Richard Russell of Georgia, one of the most senior and powerful members of Congress at the time.

Sen. Russell tried to decline the appointment. Yet, Johnson took the audacious step of simply announcing that Russell, among others, had been appointed to the commission. In a conversation recorded on the evening of November 29, 1963, President Johnson tells Sen. Russell that the announcement has already been made (Miller Center, 2010d). Russell protests, "I just *can't* serve on that commission!"

Over the course of many minutes, Johnson simply wears Russell down. Russell is relentlessly bombarded with a mixture of flattery ("I've got one man that's smarter than the rest…"), patriotism ("You're going to serve your country and do what is right!"), loyalty ("I'm begging you!", "…your president's asking you to do these things…because I can't run this country by myself!"), and conspiracy theories ("The Secretary of State…[is] deeply concerned…about this idea that [Soviet Premier] Kruschev killed Kennedy.").

Eventually, a resigned Russell says, "We won't discuss it any further, Mr. President, I'll serve."

The Growth of Presidential Power

As noted earlier, the Executive Branch was not first on the minds of the framers. They clearly felt Congress would be the more dominant branch. Their vision held true through the 19th century and into the 20th. Then, things began to change.

The Legislative Branch is designed to discuss and debate. These are essential abilities for law-making in a democratic society. The Executive Branch is designed to execute, in other words, to *do* things. It is designed for *action*. In the 20th century, a series of major—indeed international—crises touching several generations of Americans began to permanently shift our main expectation of the federal government from one of democratic deliberation to one of action.

The Great Depression of the 1930s, the Second World War in the early 1940s, and the Cold War of the late 1940s through the late 1980s all required action—often immediate action—often on a massive scale. We began to *expect* the federal government to secure our well-being from threat after threat. The government responded by taking unprecedented action to manage the economy during the Great Depression, and to beef up our military capabilities and international involvement throughout the Second World War and the Cold War. These responses are now permanent areas of government activity. Concerns over domestic and international terrorism in the early 21st century have perpetuated this activity.

So how do these things empower the presidency? Quite simply, all this activity required legislation, and each new law and program required another executive agency and more presidential advisers.

"The President Needs Help"

So said the Brownlow Committee on Administrative Management in its 1937 report following President Roosevelt's attempts to cope with expanded government in the face of the Great Depression. The committee recommended a formal structure to help manage the growing number of agencies and the laws and programs they administer. Over time, most of their recommendations were adopted as the Executive Office of the Presidency. This management assistance in turn allowed the pursuit of a broader array of policies, further empowering the Executive Branch.

Congressional Accomplices

In some instances, the Congress actually ordered the president to take action. For example, in recent decades, presidents were required to monitor and manage levels of national inflation and unemployment. They have also been required to certify which foreign countries are worthy of our highest levels of trade.

The more laws, the larger the Executive Branch. The larger the Executive Branch, the greater the effect of presidents and presidential decisions on our lives. As of 2023, the Executive Branch employs over 2.1 million civilian personnel (see: https://www.bls.gov/oes/2023/may/naics4_999100.htm). There are yet another 1.3 million active duty military personnel under the Department of Defense. These numbers make the Executive Branch the largest single employer in world history!

Case Study: Presidential Power in the Trump and Biden Eras

By Carl Cavalli and Hayden Lathren (with additional research provided by Antonia Ramirez)

Presidential Power established Richard Neustadt as the leading presidential scholar of our time. The book has had a "greater effect than any other book about a political institution." (Charles O. Jones quoted in Nelson, 2010, para. 21).

To Neustadt, presidential power is "the power to persuade" (1990, p. 11). Success is conditioned upon the ability to persuade others that their interests coincide with the president's, especially as those whom presidents must persuade will have at least some means to resist. Because everyone has some measure of status and authority, presidents derive persuasive abilities (aside from any innate talents) from their status and authority relative to others. The greater degree of these possessed by presidents, relative to others, the greater is presidential persuasiveness.

Presidents accrue status and authority from their professional reputation and personal prestige, that is, their standing with both those in power and the public. The building blocks of both—and the *foundation* of Neustadt's formula—are a president's *choices*. A good foundation consists of choices made with power stakes in mind and those that help enlighten the public (Neustadt, 1990).

Later editions of *Presidential Power* suggest that presidents most effectively gain power by starting at the end and working backward, what Neustadt calls "backward mapping" (1990, p. 215). So, presidents should focus on their *choices*. Even before taking office, newly elected presidents have crucial decisions to make, on organization, staffing, and priorities. New incumbents must address these with very little guidance. As Neustadt says, "No continuity of pattern, no stability of doctrine, and precious little lore survives from one Administration to the next . . ." (1990, p. 228).

This is true especially of transitions involving partisan change. As Donald Trump begins a second term a review of both his first term and the term of his successor, Joseph Biden can provide insight into the importance of choice and persuasion.

Donald Trump and Presidential Power

In 2016, Donald Trump ran a fiery campaign promising "transformational policy change" (Edwards, 2018, p. 475) since as he memorably claimed that only he could fix a broken nation (Applebaum, 2016).

Trump deliberately tried to distinguish himself from his predecessors and defied convention at every turn. He "differed significantly…in his management of the White House staff, domestic cabinet appointments" (Pfiffner, 2018, p. 153). His West Wing was described as "an unstructured workspace governed by [his] moods" (Karni & Haberman, 2019, para. 6).

So, was Donald Trump an outlier in Neustadt's universe, or was he another example of the still-relevant framework of *Presidential Power* as "merely an extension of trends that have long been in place" (Jordan & Pennebaker, 2017, p. 312)?

President Donald Trump: Persuasive? Successful?

Was Trump's unusual style successful? How do we clarify the meaning of "success"? Behind the exploration for the answers is always the underlying question of Neustadt's ongoing relevance.

A Mixed Bag

Early in Trump's first term, George C. Edwards III (2018) said that

[t]he most notable fact about Trump's legislative record to this point is the relative absence of passage of significant legislation. Although tax cuts did pass, prominent among the legislation that did not pass were bills dealing with health care reform, infrastructure spending, and immigration—policies central to Trump's presidential campaign. In 2018, Congress simply ignored large sections of the president's budget proposals. (p. 456)

Edwards implies that his success rate was low because he chose not to press for support. Matthew Glassman (2019) suggests that "[t]hroughout the first two years of the Trump presidency, Republican leaders in Congress skillfully used a variety of tactics to minimize the president's influence and maximize their own control over public policy" (p. A23).

Politifact points out that at the midpoint of his term, "almost half of his promises from the 2016 campaign have been blocked or dropped." (Tobias 2019a, para. 2), while "close to a third of his goals were achieved or saw partial progress" (Tobias 2019a, para. 2).

By comparison, only about a quarter of the promises of Trump's predecessor, Barack Obama, were blocked or dropped (Tobias 2019b, para. 6).

While Trump's team "proudly points to a number of first-year successes", as Lewis, Bernhard, and You (2018) conclude, his critics say "that the administration's achievements have occurred *despite* the president's management performance rather than because of it" (p. 495, emphasis added).

Those critics might point to the executive order prohibiting refugees and immigration from several countries with large Muslim populations. According to James Pfiffner (2018), high-ranking Trump officials emphatically denied that the ban intended to prevent Muslims from traveling to the U.S. However,

> President Trump undercut them when he tweeted, "People, the lawyers and the courts can call it whatever they want, but I am calling it what we need and what it is, a TRAVEL BAN!" (p. 156)

Pfiffner goes on to say that "cabinet members were not consulted or informed about important policies" and "often publicly disagreed with the president or had to backtrack or explain his changes of mind", indicating "a lack of communication" (p. 162).

Critics may also point to the 2017 tax cuts that Edwards (2018) suggests were the "most important legislative victory" for Trump (p. 467). As Edwards notes, this was

> the area of policy on which [Trump and Congress] have the most agreement. Thus, cutting taxes is easier than virtually any other legislative task for Republicans. "If we fail on taxes, we're toast," said Republican Senator Lindsey Graham. (p. 467)

Such a legislative victory arguably does *not* exemplify presidential power, since the Republican majority in Congress was predisposed to support such cuts (Cavalli, 2006).

Trump's *choices* as president did indeed affect his power, just as Neustadt suggests.

President Trump, Persuader

Perhaps the best example of *Presidential Power*'s continued relevance is the passage of criminal justice reform in the First Step Act, characterized as "a significant victory for Trump" (Rodrigo, 2018, para. 5).

While it had bipartisan support in both houses, Senate Majority Leader, Mitch McConnell was an opponent. He initially refused to schedule the bill for a vote (Kim & Dawsey, 2018, para. 2). Persistent, vocal, and public support for the bill from the President and his surrogates (e.g., see: Fandos & Haberman, 2018; Levine & Everett, 2018; Offutt, 2018; Trump, 2018) eventually convinced McConnell to schedule a vote: "Trump's support for the bill was key last month for advocates, and he repeatedly pushed Senate GOP leadership to bring it up for a vote this month." (Rodrigo, 2018, para. 10).

Trump's *choice* to vocally support the bill had a direct effect on its eventual passage.

Joseph Biden and Presidential Power

Joseph Biden defeated Donald Trump in 2020 to become the 46th President of the United States, as Democrats also gained control of both chambers of Congress. However, Ruy Teixeira and Yuval Levin suggest that these successes were more-so the result of a country focused on Trump's "misdeeds," and that more traditional Republican candidates may have been more successful (2024, p. 30). While Biden "likely came to the presidency with more legislative, executive, policy, and leadership experience than any chief executive before him" (Goodsell, 2023, p. 179), could he succeed in the current political climate?

Upon taking office in January 2021, Biden hung a portrait of Franklin Delano Roosevelt over the Oval Office fireplace. A silent, but powerful move to indicate "how he planned to govern" (Sargen, 2024, para. 1). This connection to Roosevelt is noteworthy as the Roosevelt presidency marks the beginning of Richard Neustadt's "modern" era of presidential leadership (Neustadt, 1990, p. xiv).

What defines a president's success? Did Biden's extensive career in politics help him succeed? Is Richard Neustadt's *Presidential Power* still relevant over six decades after its original publication?

Another Mixed Bag

Charles T. Goodsell says Biden is a multi-layered president, whose lifelong service to the American people shaped him into the perfect candidate for the American presidency (Goodsell, 2023). He further suggests that one reason for Biden's likely success

> is the occupant's range of role diversity. His multiple forms of leadership allow him to present himself as the situation warrants at a moment's notice. The skill refers not just to varied speaking styles but wholly different personae. (p. 175)

Elizabeth Bomberg (2022) suggests that, if persuasion is important, then Biden is well-situated:

Successful presidents overcome institutional constraints through their power to persuade—including persuading members of Congress. Biden should be in a good position to do so. He himself served for decades in Congress and campaigned in part on his ability to persuade. (p. 32)

As they did with Trump, *Politifact* tracked the progress of Biden's 2020 campaign promises (The Poynter Institute, n.d.). Of his many pledges, the *Politifact* scorecard indicates that as of December 2024 he kept 32% of his pledges and compromised on 19%. Although 14% of Biden's pledges are categorized as "in the works," *Politifact* concludes that 31% have been broken or stalled. These numbers compare favorably to Trump's term, but do they make Biden a "successful" president? There are assessments on both sides.

Some suggest that "history will remember him as one of the most effective presidents of his era" (Foer, 2024, para. 2), citing legislative accomplishments like the American Rescue Plan, The CHIPS Act, the Inflation Reduction Act, and the Infrastructure and Investment Act, and pointing to successes in dealing with crime rates, health care coverage, and job creation (Bloomberg Opinion Columnists, 2024).

Others point to a deeply unpopular president who's "choices put an extra millstone around Democrats' collective necks" (Blumenthal, 2024, para. 3). Critics point to a president who was saddled with high inflation rates throughout much of his term, who was responsible for a disastrous Afghan troop withdrawal and who struggled with a persistent immigration issue (e.g, see: Alexander, 2021).

Can Neustadt help us understand these differing views? Below are two examples of President Biden's policy efforts that we can use to assess the ongoing value of *Presidential Power*.

First, we examine Biden's role in the Afghan troop withdrawal.

During an Oval Office meeting in April of 2021, President Biden alerted his senior national security advisors of his decision to withdraw all American troops from Afghanistan. When describing Biden's go-to-zero order, Defense Secretary Lloyd Austin said "This is not the decision that we wanted, but this is what we got. Now we have to execute it." (p. 56).

Troop withdrawal plans were not new. Shortly after Trump lost the 2020 election, he ordered a full troop withdrawal from both Somalia and Afghanistan that Joint Chiefs Chair Gen. Mark Milley described as "nonstandard" and "potentially dangerous" (Shane, 2022, para. 6). The order was not carried out as the senior staff doubted its legality. After assuming office, Biden ordered a similar withdrawal, against the advice of Gen. Milley and other senior military and State

Department officials, who still considered the move dangerous (Sciutto, Liptak, & Atwood, 2021).

On August 26, 2021, amid the withdrawal, the Abbey Gate terrorist attack "killed 13 U.S. servicemembers, wounding another 45, and killed more than 170 Afghan civilians" (Foreign Affairs Committee, 2024, p. 8). Addressing the House Foreign Affairs Committee, Colonel Seth Krummrich recalled that "[t]he president decided we're gonna leave, and he's not listening to anybody" (Foreign Affairs Committee, 2024, p. 52). A State Department review of the withdrawal faulted the Biden administration for "damning shortcomings . . . that led to the deadly and chaotic U.S. withdrawal" (Hansler & Atwood, 2023, para. 1).

President Biden's *choice* had major implications. His choice to ignore the advice of senior officials had disastrous results that marred the rest of his presidency. His public approval declined from 56% in June of 2021 to 43% by September of 2021, and never topped 50% again (Gallup.com, 2024).

Next, we examine Biden's role in the passage of the Infrastructure Investment and Jobs Act of 2021.

The U.S. economy "relies on a vast network of infrastructure to keep it afloat. But the systems currently in place…were built decades ago and are struggling to keep pace" (McBride, Berman & Siripurapu, 2023). Previous administrations, including Trump's had failed to deliver on promises to improve the nation's infrastructure. Biden made similar promises and delivered. How did he succeed?

Biden faced a "deeply divided U.S. Congress" as he worked to get his infrastructure bill passed (Shalal & Holland, 2021, para. 1). The President made the choice to pursue "centrist Republicans and Democrats for months in hopes of forging an agreement" (Tankersley, 2021, para. 7).

> [A]ides said, he requested multiple daily briefings on negotiations, personally directed administration strategy on policy trade-offs and frequently phoned moderates from both parties to keep the pressure on for a final deal. (Tankersley, 2021, para. 7)

Biden's actions succeeded. On November 15, 2021, he signed the $1 trillion infrastructure bill into law. The bill disperses billions of dollars to state and local governments "to fix crumbling bridges and roads and by expanding broadband internet access to millions of Americans" (Shalal & Holland, 2021, para. 2).

According to Neustadt, "[p]ower is persuasion, and persuasion becomes bargaining" (1990, p. 33). A president's persuasiveness stems from *choices*. He says they "are the only means in his own hands by which to shield his sources of real power" (1990, p. 90). President Biden chose to bargain with an extremely partisan Congress to pursue infrastructure legislation. This *choice* paid off.

Conclusion: The Continuing Relevance of *Presidential Power*

The wins and losses of both presidents suggest that, over 60 years after the initial publication of *Presidential Power*, "we need presidents to persuade" (Shaefer, 2021, p. 109).

Matthew Glassman (2017) notes that when Trump chose to ignore "Neustadt's strategic advice" he made "simple errors that have damaged his professional reputation and public prestige—and ultimately his power" (para. 15), leading to several policy failures.

On the other hand, when Trump applied Neustadt's advice—as with his active promotion of the First Step Act—he scored a policy victory over some significant opposition within his own party. To paraphrase Neustadt, persuasion (criminal justice reform) succeeds, command (travel ban) does not.

Similarly, Biden's choice to proceed with a troop withdrawal from Afghanistan against the advice of many senior officials hurt both his professional reputation and his public standing, putting his "reputation for foreign-policy expertise at risk" (Bernstein, 2021, para. 4). On the other hand, his choice to relentlessly pursue congressional support for his infrastructure legislation paid off with a significant policy victory.

Neustadt described our governmental system as "separated institutions *sharing* power" (1990, p. 29). Former Presidential Assistant Roger Porter recently pointed out that this is evolving into separate institutions *competing* for power (Kennedy School, 2019, 00:32:32). As such, former Harvard Provost Harvey Fineberg—who worked with Neustadt—stresses the importance of persuasion in the presidency alongside the importance of learning about history (Kennedy School, 2019, 00:25:26).

"Backwards mapping", staffing the presidency, and other *choices* presidents make were crucial to Trump and Biden, and will continue to be so as Trump returns. Presidents still benefit from Neustadt. Following the initial publication of *Presidential Power*, Neustadt said:

There is reason to suppose that in the years immediately ahead the power problems of a President will remain what they have been in the decades just behind us. If so there will be equal need for presidential expertise of the peculiar sort this book has stressed. Indeed, the need is likely to be greater.

The President himself (and with him the whole government) is likely to be more than ever at the mercy of his personal approach. (Neustadt, 1990, p. 156)

It appears that, more than sixty years later, those "power problems" still challenge presidents.

Discussion Questions

1. Discuss the nature of executive power and the framers' intentions for the presidency.

2. From where do other nations' leaders derive their power? For example, compare the source of power in both the British monarch and Prime Minister to our presidents.

3. Visit or contact either your state governor's office or a state executive agency, or if possible, the White House or a federal agency or cabinet department and explore the "every-day" meaning of executive power.

4. Perhaps the most famous modern study of the presidency is Richard Neustadt's *Presidential Power*. Contrary to earlier views, Neustadt suggested the main power source is *not* the Constitution (as the best known work at the time–Edward S. Corwin's *The President: Office and Powers*–suggested), but rather presidents' persuasive abilities, as affected by their situation relative to others ("status and authority"). His work is still celebrated today (e.g., see Michael Nelson's tribute in *The Chronicle of Higher Education*: "Neustadt's 'Presidential Power' at 50," https://chronicle.com/article/Neustadts-Presidential/64816/). Later research built on his ideas:
    ▷ Aaron Wildavsky's 1966 "The Two Presidencies" (*Trans-Action*, vol. 4, iss. 2, pp 7-14)
    ▷ Graham Allison's 1971 *Essence of Decision* (Boston: Little, Brown, and Co.)
    ▷ James David Barber's 1972 *Presidential Character* (Englewood Cliffs, NJ: Prentice-Hall)
    ▷ Samuel Kernell's 1986 *Going Public* (Washington, DC: CQ Press)
    Use these classic works as a starting point to research changing views on the nature of presidential power.

References

Alexander, L. (2021). Joe Biden's growing list of failures. *Newsweek*. https://www. newsweek.com/joe-bidens-growing-list-failures-opinion-1654002

Applebaum. (2016). 'I alone can fix it'. *The Atlantic Monthly.* https://www.theatlantic.com/politics/archive/2016/07/trump-rnc-speech-alone-fix-it/492557/

Barger, H. M. (1978). The prominence of the chief of state role in the American presidency. *Presidential Studies Quarterly, 8*(2), 127–139.

Bernstein, J. (2021). *Joe Biden can't escape fallout from Afghanistan.* Bloomberg. https://www.bloomberg.com/opinion/articles/2021-08-13/joe-biden-can-t-escape-fallout-from-afghanistan

Bloomberg Opinion Columnists. (2024). *What have Biden and Harris accomplished? Look at these 10 metrics.* Bloomberg. https://www.bloomberg.com/graphics/2024-opinion-biden-harris-accomplishment-data/

Blumenthal, P. (2024). How Biden's critical failure gave Trump another shot at the White House. *The Huffington Post.* https://www.huffpost.com/entry/biden-failure-2024-election-trump_n_6735056be4b07b3c59486360

Bomberg, E. (2022). Joe Biden's climate change challenge. *Political Insight,* April 2022, 30–33.

Cavalli, C. D. (2006). *Presidential legislative activity.* University Press of America.

CNN Politics. (2002, September 4). *Bush to 'seek approval' from Congress on Iraq.* CNN. https://www.cnn.com/2002/ALLPOLITICS/09/04/congress.iraq/index.html

Edwards, G. C., III. (2018). "Closer" or context? Explaining Donald Trump's relations with Congress. *Presidential Studies Quarterly, 48*(3), 456–479.

Fandos & Haberman. (2018). Trump embraces a path to revise U.S. sentencing and prison laws. *The New York Times.* https://www.nytimes.com/2018/11/14/us/politics/prison-sentencing-trump.html

Foer, F. (2024). Biden's greatest strengths proved his undoing. *The Atlantic.* https://www.theatlantic.com/politics/archive/2024/07/bidens-greatest-strengths-proved-his-undoing/679179/

Foreign Affairs Committee. (2024). *Willful blindness: An assessment of the Biden-Harris administration's withdrawal from Afghanistan and the chaos that followed.* Foreign Affairs Committee. https://foreignaffairs.house.gov/wp-content/uploads/2024/09/WILLFULL-BLINDNESS-An-Assessment-of-the-Biden-Harris%20Administrations-Withdrawal-from-Afghanistan-and-the-Chaos-that-Followed.pdf

Gallup. (2024). *Presidential Job Approval Center.* Gallup. https://news.gallup.com/interactives/507569/presidential-job-approval-center.aspx.

Glassman, M. (2017). *Donald Trump is a dangerously weak president.* Vox. https://www.vox.com/the-big-idea/2017/12/4/16733450/donald-trump-weak-president-neustadt

———. (2019). How republicans erased Trumpism. *The New York Times.* https://www.nytimes.com/2019/02/01/opinion/how-republicans-erased-trumpism.html

Goodsell, C. T. (2023). Joseph R. Biden as a multi-layered president. *The American Review of Public Administration, 53*(5–6), 175–181. https://doi.org/10.1177/02750740231171686

Hansler, J., and Atwood, K. (2023, June 30). *U.S. State Department report details damning failings around chaotic Afghanistan withdrawal.* CNN. https://www.cnn.com/2023/06/30/politics/state-deparment-afghanistan-withdrawal-report/index.html

Hirsch, M. (2012, December 31). Joe Biden: The most influential vice president in history? *Atlantic Monthly.* https://www.theatlantic.com/politics/archive/2012/12/joe-biden-the-most-influential-vice-president-in-history/266729/

Holding, R. (2007). Privileged positions. *Time, 170*(4), 57–8.

Jacobs, L. R. (2010). The presidency and the press: The paradox of the White House communications war. In Nelson, Michael (Ed.), *The presidency and the political system* (9th ed.). CQ Press.

Jordan, K. N., and Pennebaker, J. W. (2017). The exception or the rule: Using words to assess analytic thinking, Donald Trump, and the American presidency. *Translational Issues in Psychological Science 3*(3), 312–316.

Karni & Haberman. (2019). Clinton's White House faced impeachment with discipline. Trump's approach is different. *The New York Times.* https://www.nytimes.com/2019/09/27/us/politics/clinton-trump-impeachment.html

Kennedy School Institute of Politics. (2019). *The American presidency in the 21st century: What would Dick Neustadt say?* Harvard University. https://iop.harvard.edu/forum/american-presidency-21st-century-what-would-dick-neustadt-say

Kernell, S. (1986). *Going public: New strategies of presidential leadership.* CQ Press.

Kheel, R. (2019). Mattis: Trump is 'an unusual president'. *The Hill.* https://thehill.com/policy/defense/459419-mattis-trump-is-unusual-president

Kim, S. M., and Dawsey, J. (2018, December 31). McConnell tell White House little chance of vote on criminal justice bill. *The Washington Post.* https://www.washingtonpost.com/politics/mcconnell-tells-white-house-little-chance-of-senate-vote-on-criminal-justice-bill/2018/12/06/7084c654-f9a2-11e8-863a-8972120646e0_story.html

Kuttner, R. (2004, February 25). Cheney's unprecedented power. *The Boston Globe*. https://archive.boston.com/news/globe/editorial_opinion/oped/articles/2004/02/25/cheneys_unprecedented_power/

Levine, M. and Everett, B. (2019). White House makes last-ditch push on criminal justice reform bill. *Politico*. https://www.politico.com/story/2018/11/27/white-house-criminal-justice-reform-bill-1021119

Lewis, D. E., et al. (2018). President Trump as manager: Reflections on the first year. *Presidential Studies Quarterly, 48*(3), 480–501.

Light, P. C. (1999). *The president's agenda: Domestic policy choice from Kennedy to Clinton*. The Johns Hopkins University Press.

McDuffee, A. (2013, January 15). Joe Biden a more powerful vice president than Dick Cheney? *The Washington Post*. https://www.washingtonpost.com/blogs/thinktanked/wp/2013/01/15/joe-biden-a-more-powerful-vice-president-than-dick-cheney/

Miller Center of Public Affairs. (2010a). *John F. Kennedy—Dictabelt recordings 19A.3—Kennedy and Gordon Cooper (May 16, 1963)*. [Audio recording]. https://web2.millercenter.org/jfk/audiovisual/whrecordings/dictabelts/conversations/jfk_dict_19a3.mp3

______. (2010b). *Lyndon B. Johnson – January 1964 Tape #6401.06, Citation #1198, Carl Sandburg*. [Audio recording]. https://millercenter.org/presidentialrecordings/lbj-wh6401.06-1198

______. (2010c). *Lyndon B. Johnson – January 1964 Tape #6401.06, Citation #1204, Eugene McCarthy*. [Audio recording]. https://millercenter.org/presidentialrecordings/lbj-wh6401.06-1204

______. (2010d). *Lyndon B. Johnson – November 1963 Tape #K6311.06, Citation #14, Richard Russell*. [Audio recording]. https://web2.millercenter.org/lbj/audiovisual/whrecordings/telephone/conversations/1963/lbj_k6311_06_14_russell.mp3

Nelson, M. (2000). Why the media love presidents and presidents hate the media. *The Virginia Quarterly Review, 76*(2), 255–68.

______. (2010, March 28). "Neustadt's 'Presidential Power' at 50. The Chronicle of Higher Education. https://www.chronicle.com/article/Neustadts-Presidential/64816

Neustadt, R. E. (1990). *Presidential power and the modern presidents*. Free Press.

Offutt, L. (2018). *Trump endorses criminal justice reform legislation*. The Jurist. https://www.jurist.org/news/2018/11/trump-endorses-criminal-justice-reform-legislation/

Pfiffner, J. P. (2018). Organizing the Trump Presidency. *Presidential Studies*

Quarterly, 48(1), 153–167.

Rodrigo, C. M. (2018). *Trump signs criminal justice overhaul.* The Hill. https://thehill.com/homenews/administration/422517-trump-signs-criminal-justice-reform-bill

Rothkopf, David. (2013, January 14). The Bidenization of America. *Foreign Policy.* https://www.foreignpolicy.com/articles/2013/01/14/the_bidenization_of_america

Rossiter, C. (1956). *The American Presidency.* Harcourt, Brace, and Company.

Sargen, N. (2024, November 1). *Opinion – Why the public dismisses Biden's legislative accomplishments.* The Hill. https://www.yahoo.com/news/opinion-why-public-dismisses-biden-113000863.html.

Schaefer, T.M. (2021). Conclusion: What Trump's presidency teaches us about presidential power (and *Presidential Power*). In *Presidential Power meets the Art of the Deal: The evolving American presidency.* Palgrave Pivot.

Sciutto, J., Liptak, K., and Atwood, K. (2021, April 14). *How Biden went his own way on Afghanistan withdrawal.* CNN. https://www.cnn.com/2021/04/14/politics/biden-overrules-advisers-afghanistan-withdrawal/index.html

Shalal, A., & Holland, S. (2021, November 15). Biden signs $1 trillion infrastructure bill into law. *Reuters.* https://www.reuters.com/world/us/biden-needing-boost-sign-1-trillion-infrastructure-bill-2021-11-15/

Shane, L., III. (2022, October 13). Trump ordered rapid withdrawal from Afghanistan after election loss. *Military Times.* https://www.militarytimes.com/news/pentagon-congress/2022/10/13/trump-ordered-rapid-withdrawal-from-afghanistan-after-election-loss/

Stolberg, S. G. (2017, November 29). Republicans, entering homestretch on tax cuts, are calm and cooperative. *The New York Times.* https://www.nytimes.com/2017/11/29/us/politics/republicans-tax-cuts-success-analysis.html

Tankersley, J. (2021). How Biden got the infrastructure deal Trump couldn't. *The New York Times.* https://www.nytimes.com/2021/07/29/business/economy/biden-infrastructure-deal.html

Teixeira, R., & Levin, Y. (2024). *Politics without winners: Can either party build a majority coalition?* American Enterprise Institute.

Teten, R. L. (2007). "We the people": The "modern" rhetorical popular address of the presidents during the founding period. *Political Research Quarterly.* 60(4), 669–682.

The Poynter Institute. (n.d.). *Biden Promise Tracker.* Politifact. https://www.politifact.com/truth-o-meter/promises/biden-promise-tracker/

Tichenor, D. J. (2010). The presidency and interest groups: Allies, adversaries, and policy leadership. In Michael Nelson (Ed.), *The presidency and the political system*, (9th ed.). CQ Press.

Tobias, Manuela. 2019a. *At halfway mark, Donald Trump's campaign promises hit roadblocks*. Politifact. https://www.politifact.com/truth-o-meter/article/2019/jan/16/halftime-donald-trump-promises-hit-roadblocks/

______. 2019b. *Comparing progress on Trump, Obama campaign promises at two-year mark*. Politifact. https://www.politifact.com/truth-o-meter/article/2019/jan/17/comparing-trump-obama-campaign-promises-two-years/

Trump, D. J. 2018. *President Donald J. Trump calls on Congress to pass the FIRST STEP Act*. White House. Retrieved November 3, 2019 from https://www.whitehouse.gov/briefings-statements/president-donald-j-trump-calls-congress-pass-first-step-act/

Tulis, J. K. (1987). *The rhetorical presidency*. Princeton University Press.

Walsh, K. T., et al. (2003). The man behind the curtain. *U.S. News & World Report*. 135(12), 26–32.

Wertheimer, M. M., & Gutgold, N. D. (2004). *Elizabeth Hanford Dole: Speaking from the heart*. Praeger.

Court Cases

United States v. Nixon, 418 U.S. 683 (1974)

The Federal Bureaucracy

Jaimie Edwards-Kelly

Learning Objectives

After reading this chapter, students will be able to:

1. Explain the role of the federal bureaucracy in policy making and implementation and their role in administering laws passed by Congress.
2. Describe the various institutions that make up the federal administrative state as well as the growth of the federal bureaucracy over time.
3. Evaluate the relationship between the American people, federal agencies, and other branches of government at the federal, state, and local levels of government.

Abstract

The federal bureaucracy is the largest and arguably the most powerful part of the federal government. Though mentioned as an afterthought by the framers in Article 2 of the Constitution, federal agencies have the discretion to execute laws, implement policy, adjudicate disputes, and impact the day-to-day lives of citizens, all without being democratically elected. This chapter seeks to provide an overview of the administrative state, the history of its growth, the sources of its power, and the implications of its responsibilities on Americans.

Introduction

The framers, based on Article II of the Constitution, suggested that there might be a need for the president to have an executive branch capable of administering laws. After all, they had granted the president executive power, or the responsibility to "take Care that the Laws be faithfully executed..." (Article II, Section 3). Yet it is unlikely that these men envisioned fifteen **Cabinet departments**, more than 2,000 federal agencies, and almost three million unelected individuals working in what is sometimes called the "fourth branch" of government. Yet as the functions of government grow, so too does the need for this administrative state.

Woodrow Wilson, our 28th President, and more importantly for this chapter, the "Father of Public Administration," argued that it was "getting to be harder to *run* a constitution than to frame one" and imagined an administrative state with both great power and great discretion to help shape policy in a way that was both efficient and effective (Wilson, 1887, p. 200; p. 213). Wilson (1887) believed that "there is no danger in power, if only it be not irresponsible. If it be divided, dealt out in shares to many, it is obscured; and if it be obscured, it is made irresponsible" suggesting that great deference to the administrative state was necessary (p. 214–215).

As the federal bureaucracy grows, so too do the critiques of its existence. On the pragmatic side, it is often argued that the bureaucracy is inefficient, wasteful, and arbitrary in the way that it operates. Many, including Ronald Reagan, Pat Buchannan, and Donald Trump have all made calls to "Drain the Swamp" to reduce the ineffectiveness and swell of the federal bureaucracy. And any of us who have spent time waiting in line at the Department of Motor Vehicles (DMV) have complained about the lack of efficiency and surplus of **red tape** necessary to secure or change a driver's license.

Still others would argue that the administrative state, in its very existence, goes against the democratic principles in that it is full of decision makers who are unelected by and often unaccountable to the electorate. Wilson argued that these bureaucrats were in fact politically neutral in their decision-making capacity; however, others, like Dwight Waldo (2017), argued that expertise is not necessarily a claim to neutrality, but rather a claim to power. In this argument, he muses about how much democracy the public is willing to give up in the name of expertise. For those unsure of this argument, the COVID-19 pandemic is a notable example of where Americans were willing to give up their freedoms (and often rightly so) based on the guidance of the experts.

So how, then, do we reconcile both the necessary and evil in conducting the functions of government? In this chapter, we will discuss the administrative state's structure and its functions and goals, while not shying away from the true critiques of such a system of bureaucracy. Through a greater understanding of the administrative state, the hope is that you will come to understand that, like most things in government, the bureaucracy is both flawed and brilliant in its design.

A Brief History of the Federal Bureaucracy

While the founders may not have thought to say much on the role of the federal bureaucracy, the executive branch and the legislature have surely taken advantage of the opportunity to delegate authority and increase both the size and responsibilities of the administrative state. This growth has occurred in four main phases over the past two hundred years (Baron, 2015).

Phase 1: Creation of the Administrative State. 1787-1863

With the creation of the first three cabinet departments, the Department of State, the War Department, and the Department of Treasury, the federal bureaucracy came into being. Initially, these departments had little power, except the Department of the Treasury. The State Department, including the secretary, had nine employees, and the Department of War had a few thousand troops and an administrative staff in the double digits (Wilson, 1991). The Treasury Department had more responsibility as it was tasked with running the national bank, collecting taxes, and managing the federal debt, but because of its power, was closely watched and regulated by Congress (Wilson, 1991). In 1849 and 1862 respectively, the Department of the Interior and the Department of Agriculture[1] were added. The Department of the Interior split the duties of the Department of State, focusing on domestic policy, and reassigned the Indian Affairs office from the War Department. The Department of Agriculture was created under the Lincoln administration for the purpose of providing resources to farmers through research, improving rural development, and improving human nutrition (7 U.S. Code 2201). Despite the administrative state's growth during this period, before the Civil War, the main employer within the federal bureaucracy was the Post Office.

Phase 2: Post Civil War and Reconstruction. 1863-1932

Following the Civil War and during Reconstruction, three more cabinet departments and several regulatory agencies were added to help with the country's recovery. These included the Department of Justice (1870), Department of Commerce (1903), Department of Labor (1913), Interstate Commerce Commission (ICC), the Federal Reserve, and the Federal Trade Commission (FTC). These agencies were primarily focused on helping to regulate the fast-growing U.S. economy, specifically the railroad, small business, and banking industries.

Phase 3: The New Deal Era. 1932-1952

Passed to help the U.S. recover from the Great Depression, Roosevelt's New Deal was a group of initiatives that expanded both the services provided by the

---

1 Though the Department of Agriculture was created in 1862, it did not achieve full "cabinet status" until 1889

federal government and the size and scope of the administrative state. In fact, between 1933 and 1953, the size of the administrative state went from one public administrator for every 280 citizens to one civil servant for every 80 Americans (Bowles, 1998). During this period, the only changes in the cabinet were the creation of the Department of Health and Human Services and the reorganization of the Department of Defense into a single department that included the various branches (Army, Navy, and eventually the Air Force) as well as various intelligence agencies. However, many other agencies, such as the Tennessee Valley Authority (focused on infrastructure projects and the creation of jobs in Appalachia) and the Social Security Administration (which provides financial assistance to elderly and disabled Americans) were created. In addition, the Security and Exchange Commission (SEC) was created to regulate the stock market and prevent collapses as seen on Black Thursday in 1929.

Phase 4: The Post-War Era and the Great Society. 1952-Present

The Great Society was Lyndon B. Johnson's call to Congress to end discrimination and poverty in the United States. He hoped that through a variety of programs, he would be able to provide "aid to education, attack on disease, Medicare, urban renewal, beautification, conservation, development of depressed regions, a wide-scale fight against poverty, control and prevention of crime and delinquency, [and] removal of obstacles to the right to vote" (Friedel, 2006). As with all expansion of government programs, Johnson's tenure saw an increase in the administrative state. This included the addition of the Departments of Housing and Urban Development, Transportation, and later on during Jimmy Carter's administration, Energy, and Education.

Additionally, phase four saw the creation of the Department of Veteran Affairs which transformed the Veteran's Administration into a cabinet level position responsible for providing medical care to veterans through the Veterans Health Administration and administering benefits such as the GI Bills for education and housing assistance for veterans.

The most recent cabinet creation occurred in response to 9/11. The Department of Homeland Security was formed in 2003 to serve as the umbrella organization for national security and includes the Transportation Security Office (TSA), U.S. Customs and Border Protection, and the Federal Emergency Management Agency (FEMA), among others.

As we citizens ask the government to do more, indirectly we are asking for growth of the federal bureaucracy. Other factors, such as changes in technology, increased interaction on the world stage, and increased population have led to an administrative state that the framers would not recognize. However, despite this, every new initiative requires a public administrator to implement and run it.

The Move from Patronage to Merit

The federal bureaucracy was not always run by professional public administrators the way that it is currently. Rather, "to the victor belong the spoils" was the law of the land in assigning persons to employment within the administrative state. Thomas Jefferson was the first president with the ability to "switch" the employees of the federal bureaucracy when he was elected in 1801, but it was not until the election of Andrew Jackson twenty-eight years later that citizens began to question the patronage system. Jackson brought many of his supporters with him to Washington and set them up with jobs in the federal bureaucracy (Morey, 1898). Jackson believed that running the government was "so plain and simple" that it did not require a merit-based system (White House Historical Association, 2024). Many disagreed, finding the practice of giving jobs to your political supporters made the government less efficient.

The **Pendleton Civil Service Reform Act of 1883** was passed as a way to reform the **spoils system** and ensure that civil servants were given jobs based on their qualifications, or **merit**. This civil service reform initially only covered a small number of government jobs; today, most public administrators in the federal government have job protection because of the Pendleton Act. The Act required competitive exams for many of the jobs offered, ensuring that candidates met certain qualifications before being hired.

In addition to creating a merit-based, rather than spoils-based system of hiring federal employees, the Pendleton Act also led to the creation of the Civil Service Commission. In 1978, the Civil Service Reform Act replaced the Civil Service Commission with the Office of Personnel Management. Passage of these two laws, as well as the commissions they created, served to move the role of the civil servant from one of "friendship" with the party in power to a profession of government leaders trained in the tasks of running a government.

The Federal Bureaucracy's Structure and Institutions

Before we move on, we need to define some terms. First, the **federal bureaucracy** is the group of institutions organized within the executive branch to carry out laws. They are hierarchical in structure and have clear delineations of authority. The **administrative state**, which we often use interchangeably with the term bureaucracy, has come to connote not just these bureaucratic institutions but also the power possessed by them. Finally, we will also talk about **public administration** (the study of the bureaucracy) and **public administrators** (the professionals who work in the bureaucracy).

The structure of the federal bureaucracy is complex but can be best understood by looking at the four major entities. These include **executive departments**, **executive agencies**, **independent regulatory agencies**, and **government corporations**. Each of the four groups provides the executive branch with the ability to execute the laws passed by Congress.

- *Executive Departments*, also known as cabinet departments, are critical for the running of the federal bureaucracy. These departments were initially created in 1789 (Departments of State, Treasury, and Defense—formerly War) and served to advise the president on issues related to foreign relations, monetary policy, and defense of the nation. Since the initial three executive departments were created, twelve additional departments have been added, with the Department of Homeland Security being the most recent. Each of these departments is headed by a "secretary" nominated by the president and confirmed into office by the Senate.

- *Executive Agencies* are part of an executive department, but they are treated separately in that they have their own leadership and budget independent of the department. In part, this is because unlike executive agencies, which regulate large swaths of American policy, executive agencies are typically more focused in their missions. Examples of executive agencies include the Central Intelligence Agency (CIA)—the intelligence arm of the federal government, and the National Aeronautics and Space Administration (NASA)—the space and aeronautics research agency of the United States.

- *Independent Regulatory Agencies* are agencies established by Congress with a level of independence for the executive branch. These agencies have the power to create rules and regulations to govern specific areas or industries within the private sector. The power is delegated to them from Congress and allows them to be at once quasi-legislative since they can create and enforce regulations, quasi-executive in their ability to issue summonses, and quasi-judicial when they hold hearings to resolve issues. Examples of Independent Regulatory Agencies include the Federal Communications Commission, which regulates radio, television, and wire communications, and the Securities and Exchange

Commission, which protects investors and helps to safeguard the stock market.

- Finally, *Government Corporations* are organizations within the federal bureaucracy that function as public enterprises. These corporations sell products and provide services to consumers. The intent of these corporations is for them to pay for themselves through institutional revenue; however, they often end up being funded in part by taxpayer dollars. Examples of government corporations include the United States Postal Service (USPS) and AMTRAK.

The Role of the Federal Bureaucracy

As we touched on briefly in the previous section, the federal bureaucracy has three major functions: the implementation of laws, the creation and enforcement of rules, and the adjudication of disputes. In this next section, we will discuss how the administrative state impacts public policy and how.

When Congress passes a law, it may often offer vague prescriptions on the implementation and execution of the policy. Congress lays out in legislation an overarching expectation and delegates authority to administrative agencies to interpret the statute and implement it. This delegation of authority is called the **bureaucratic authority.** Congress delegates authority to bureaucratic agencies for assorted reasons. First, members of Congress often lack the time or staff needed to properly implement the policies they pass. Second, Congress lacks the experience to implement these policies. Public administrators, unlike members of Congress, are subject matter experts, both in the actual carrying out of the policy and in the details of the policy itself.

As an example, Congress passes legislation aimed at reducing carbon emissions. They then delegate the power to implement this policy to various agencies, such as the Environmental Protection Agency (EPA). It is the EPA that is staffed with scientists who can measure carbon emissions, engineers who can design systems to help businesses meet new carbon emission standards, and regulators who can provide oversight of various industries, and lawyers who resolve disputes in the law. The EPA, not Congress, has the power to ensure that the laws are followed. By delegating this authority to the EPA, Congress ensures that the legislative goals are met.

Congress places a great deal of trust in the administrative state to perform the essential function of policy implementation. With this delegation of authority, Congress must maintain oversight to avoid bureaucratic drift. **Bureaucratic drift** occurs when members of the administrative state interpret policy in a way that strays from the initial legislative intent to meet the needs of the individual bureaucrat or agency. It is important for public administrators to stay true to the legislative intent and not insert their own political leanings.

Conclusion

The role of the federal bureaucracy is vast, and its power is delegated, rather than clearly defined in the Constitution. As the government is asked to do more by the citizens, the administrative state will continue to grow to meet these demands. Through administrative discretion, Congress allows the federal bureaucracy to oversee many aspects of our lives. There are arguments about how much power should be given to the bureaucracy, as well as how oversight is conducted by Congress, the President, and the Judicial Branch. Oversight, however, is immensely important given the power and the undemocratic nature of the administrative state.

Discussion Questions

1. From where does the federal bureaucracy derive its power?
2. How has the federal bureaucracy contributed to the increased size of the federal government?
3. What is the role of the administrative state?

References

Baron, P. (2015). *Is the federal bureaucracy out of control?* Political Investigations. https://peped.org/politicalinvestigations/handout-federal-bureaucracy-independent-study-booklet/

Bowles, S. and Gintis, H. (1998). Efficient redistribution: New rules for markets, states and communities. In E. O. Wright (Ed.) *Recasting egalitarianism: New rules for communities, states and markets, 3*, 1.

Freidel, F. (1998). *Presidents of the United States of America*. DIANE Publishing.

Morey, J. S. (1898). The spoils versus merit system. *Vassar Miscellany, 27*, 9. https://newspaperarchives.vassar.edu/?a=d&d=literary18980601-01.2.5

Waldo, D. (2017). *The administrative state: A study of the political theory of American public administration*. Routledge.

White House Historical Association. (2024). *Andrew Jackson: The 7th president of the United States*. The White House. https://www.whitehouse.gov/about-the-white-house/presidents/andrew-jackson/

Wilson, J. Q. (2019). *Bureaucracy: What government agencies do and why they do it*. Hachette UK.

Wilson, W. (1887). The study of administration. In J. M. Shafritz & A. C. Hyde (Eds.), *Classics of public administration* (5th ed.). Thomson Wadsworth.

The Federal Judiciary

Brian M. Murphy

Learning Objectives

After covering the topic of the federal judiciary, students should understand:

1. The relationship of state courts to the federal judiciary.
2. The jurisdiction of federal courts.
3. The structure of the federal judicial system.
4. The procedures of the U.S. Supreme Court.
5. The powers of the federal judiciary.

Abstract

The judicial system in the United States is based on the doctrine of federalism. Two court systems exist side-by-side, national and state, and each has a distinct set of powers. State courts, for the most part, are responsible for handling legal issues that arise under their own laws. It is primarily when a federal question is presented that the federal judicial system can become involved in a state court. Otherwise, state judiciaries are generally autonomous even from one another. The Constitution precisely outlines the types of cases that can be heard by federal courts, yet it is almost impossible to force a federal court to hear a case that falls under its jurisdiction if the judge(s) wants to avoid it. The authority of the U.S. Supreme Court has slowly grown over time, largely through the power of judicial review. Nonetheless, federalism has managed to remain a significant barrier against federal courts becoming too powerful. The judicial system designed by the framers continues to survive and function after 200 years.

Introduction

The federal judicial system is the least known and least understood branch of American government. In fact, in a 2015 survey, 32 percent of Americans did not even know the Supreme Court is one of the three branches of the federal government (Bomboy, 2016). This lack of knowledge is largely because judicial work is conducted out of the limelight. Only 43 percent could name *any* member of the Supreme Court (Green and Rosenblatt, 2017, p. 9), while 9.6 percent of college graduates believe TV's Judge Judy is one of the justices (American Council of Trustees, 2016, p. 5). Anonymity has worked to the Supreme Court's advantage by building confidence in the institution. Recently, however, an erosion of public confidence has occurred as the Supreme Court has handed down a series of controversial decisions on topics like abortion, affirmative action, and LGBTQ rights. The Court's favorability rating as a result declined 26 points since 2020 and now, for the first time, its public support is more negative than positive (Lin and Doherty, 2023). Questionable ethical lapses by members of the Supreme Court have further undermined reliance about its objectivity in decision-making. It was discovered that Justice Clarence Thomas, for example, did not disclose the payment by wealthy friends of private school tuition for his grandnephew, private jet trips, and vacations on a superyacht. Justice Samuel Alito similarly failed to report a trip on a private jet involving a donor who later had cases before the Court. Additionally, political activity by the spouses of Justices Thomas and Alito created skepticism about their neutrality on cases that dealt with the issues championed by their wives.

In an effort to quell concerns about the behavior of the Supreme Court's members, the justices voluntarily adopted a Code of Conduct to guide their actions. It should be noted that all other federal judges "are subject to the Judicial Conduct and Disability Act, a federal law that allows people to file ethics complaints and sets out a mechanism for their review. The penalties include public censures and reprimands. It does not apply to Supreme Court justices" (Liptak, 2023). When the Supreme Court developed its own Code of Conduct, five "ethical canons" were included (Lampe, 2023):

1. A justice should uphold the integrity and independence of the judiciary.
2. A justice should avoid impropriety and the appearance of impropriety in all activities.
3. A justice should perform the duties of office fairly, impartially, and diligently.
4. A justice may engage in extrajudicial activities that are consistent with the obligations of the judicial office.
5. A justice should refrain from political activity.

Critics complain that no enforcement mechanism exists if a justice violates a provision of the code, meaning that compliance depends entirely upon the honor system. No punishment, in other words, is imposed for open defiance by a member of the Court.

It is clear the framers believed the federal judiciary would be the weakest of the three branches since, as Alexander Hamilton wrote, it "has no influence over either the sword or the purse" (Hamilton, 1961, p. 465). Put another way, courts cannot command an army (or even the police) to enforce their decisions or allocate money to implement one of their rulings. Judges must depend on the other branches to get anything done, and this level of dependence on the other branches has not changed over time. According to an oft-repeated story, President Andrew Jackson supposedly mocked a decision by Chief Justice John Marshall with the words, "John Marshall has made his decision, now let him enforce it" (Schwartz, 1993, p. 94). But times and the role of the federal judiciary have not remained static. The federal judiciary has evolved beyond what Hamilton initially contemplated. One scholar even concluded that the United States is now operating under a "government by judiciary" because the U.S. Supreme Court can revise the Constitution by how it interprets the wording (Berger, 1997). As Chief Justice Charles Evans Hughes once quipped, "We are under a Constitution, but the Constitution is what the judges say it is" (Hughes, 1916, p. 185).

The actual power of federal courts lies between these two extreme viewpoints. While the federal judiciary remains dependent on Congress and the president to enforce judicial rulings, the courts are not powerless in the tussle over checks and balances. This chapter examines judicial power and defines the powers and limitations of federal courts. What must be kept in mind, however, is that relatively few cases ever end up in federal courts. Most judicial decision-making takes place at the state level. The old adage that "I'll fight all the way to the U.S. Supreme Court" is legally impossible in the overwhelming majority of cases. State courts handle most of the legal action in the United States, so that is where we will start our discussion of the judicial system. Federalism quite clearly applies to the country's judicial system as well.

State Court Systems

In the United States, two court systems exist—federal and state—and there is remarkably little overlap between the two. In most situations, decisions on matters of state law are resolved by state courts, and no federal court, not even the U.S. Supreme Court, can overrule, which means state courts usually render the final judgment on most cases involving state law. The principal way cases from state courts can end up in the federal judiciary is when a **federal question** is involved in a dispute. A federal question is defined as a legal issue that concerns a federal law, federal treaty, or federal Constitution.

Consider the following example. Suppose an African American walks into a restaurant in a small town and is forcibly thrown out by the owner, breaking the visitor's arm. This scenario presents several potential legal claims, including aggravated assault and the violation of federal civil rights laws. The first issue, aggravated assault, constitutes a question of state law, while the civil rights claims are federal in nature. Where will this case be heard? Since state law is at stake, the case will go to a state trial court. What about the federal questions? Contrary to what some believe, state courts have the authority to decide federal questions when they are mixed with state law.

Judges in state courts are bound by two constitutional constraints in deciding cases that combine state and federal issues. First, Article VI, Section 2 of the U.S. Constitution, called the **Supremacy Clause**, declares the following:

This Constitution, and the Laws of the United States ... and all Treaties ... shall be the supreme Law of the Land; and the Judges in every State shall be bound thereby, any thing in the constitution or Laws of any State to the contrary notwithstanding.

As such, judges at the state level must swear to obey the federal Constitution, laws, and treaties regardless of state law. If there is a conflict between the two, the Supremacy Clause requires a state judge to enforce federal law over state law. The second legal constraint on state judges involves the interpretation of federal law. Does the state's supreme court, for example, have the authority to instruct lower courts in its state how to interpret a federal law? In 1816, the U.S. Supreme Court ruled that state courts are bound by its holdings on federal questions (*Martin v. Hunter's Lessee*, 1816) no matter what the state's highest court has decided on the issue. In short, state judges must apply the rulings of the U.S. Supreme Court in deciding federal questions and should ignore any state law or state court ruling that is in contradiction.

Now, let us take another look at the restaurant dispute. At trial, the state court can rule on both the aggravated assault and civil rights issues. The judgment on aggravated assault, however, should be based on state law while the civil rights controversy should follow the rulings of the U.S. Supreme Court. Will a jury be used? In a state case, the right to a jury trial varies depending on whether a criminal or civil case is involved. A jury trial in a criminal case is available under the Sixth Amendment when a jail term of six months or more is a possible outcome of a trial

(*Duncan v. Louisiana*, 1968). A civil case differs from a criminal case in several ways: (1) a criminal case involves either jail time or a fine as an outcome while a civil case is seeking either monetary damages (e.g., to cover injuries suffered like in an auto accident) or a declaration of rights (e.g., to decide who owns a piece of property or who has custody of a child); (2) the government is always a party in a criminal case while a civil case is a lawsuit between private parties; (3) the government's **burden of proof** in a criminal case requires establishing guilt beyond a reasonable doubt while the burden of proof in a civil case is the **preponderance of evidence** (i.e., the winning side is the one with the majority of evidence in its favor); and (4) states are under no constitutional mandate to provide juries in any civil case, although states are not forbidden from allowing them (*Minneapolis & St. Louis R.R. v. Bombolis*, 1916).

The famous O.J. Simpson murder case illustrates the differences between criminal and civil trials. Simpson was charged criminally with the murder of his ex-wife (Nicole Brown) and Ronald Goldman. While Simpson was acquitted of both murders in 1995, a few years later in 1997 he lost a civil suit to the families of Brown and Goldman for battery (touching without consent) and for wrongful death (causing death without legal justification)—the latter a civil parallel to murder. What must be understood is that the outcome of a criminal case has no bearing on a civil case involving the same act—like the death of Brown and Goldman—because the burdens of proof are not the same. Consequently, Simpson was found *liable* (the term guilty does not apply in a civil case) for $33.5 million for the wrongful death of Goldman, battery against Goldman, and battery against ex-wife Brown. In other words, O.J. Simpson was not guilty of murder but liable for causing the wrongful death of the same person!

Since all states guarantee the right to one appeal, a higher court can review a trial court's decision. It should be noted that the U.S. Constitution has no specific provision that requires the right to an appeal, even in cases heard in federal courts. An appeal is possible solely because every state as well as the federal government have enacted this right into law and, at least in theory, the right could be taken away.

It is important to note that an appeal cannot be based on the fact that the loser is unhappy with the outcome of a trial. Nor can a person appeal claiming innocence. Rather, appeals can only be based on a **question of law** that alleges an error(s) in procedure or application of a law occurred at the trial (e.g., evidence that should have been excluded was allowed or a juror was biased and should not have been permitted to serve). In practical terms, an appeal is contending that the judge made a mistake during the trial that could have impacted the outcome.

Since an error in legal procedure or law is the basis of the claim, no juries exist in appellate cases because the average person has no background to know whether a judge committed a legal error. Juries are only found in trial courts and are used to determine questions of fact, such as guilt or innocence. Judges decide all questions of law during a trial. If a person declines a jury trial, the judge acts as both judge and jury (known as a **bench trial**).

In a criminal case, only the defendant can appeal if convicted. The government cannot appeal an acquittal. Either party, however, can appeal after the verdict in a civil case. Why would the winning party want to appeal? Consider Ward Churchill, a tenured professor at the University of Colorado. On the day after the destruction of the World Trade Centers on September 11, 2001, he wrote an essay comparing some of the workers in the buildings to Adolf Eichmann, who coordinated the Holocaust for Nazi Germany. Outrage emerged on a national level as the essay slowly worked its way across the internet. Churchill was eventually investigated by the university for this writing as well as on allegations of plagiarism. The University of Colorado Board of Regents fired him in 2007 for repeated and intentional academic misconduct. In 2009, a jury decided that Churchill had been fired in retaliation for his article, but he was only awarded $1 in damages. Although Churchill won the civil case, he might contemplate appealing in an effort to collect a higher settlement.

Another popular misconception is that a person can be found innocent on appeal. It cannot happen, of course, because an appeal only involves questions of law, not questions of fact. If a person wins on appeal, the usual result is that a new trial is conducted before a different judge and jury, with the legal error from the first trial being corrected. Take the famous case of Ernesto Miranda, who was convicted at trial for sexual assault. Miranda appealed to the U.S. Supreme Court, which held that Miranda's confession could not be used as evidence because he was never warned about his right to refuse to answer police questions. Miranda was not set free but was given a new trial in which he was again convicted because enough evidence of guilt existed without his confession. Thus, a person on re-trial after a successful appeal can still lose again and even receive a harsher sentence than the original penalty. Appeals are certainly not without risk.

Once a trial is over, a decision must be made whether to appeal. All states allow only a certain number of days to make this decision or the opportunity is forfeited. In the restaurant case, let us assume the **plaintiff** (the person bringing the case) lost on both issues at the trial court. Specifically, the jury decided that no aggravated assault took place because the restaurant owner (the **defendant**, or the person being sued) was defending himself and that no civil rights violation occurred since the plaintiff was kicked out for being unruly. Where will the appeal be heard? Let's find out.

Most states have three levels of courts in their judicial system:

- Trial courts determine questions of fact (a conclusion about the evidence).
- Intermediate appellate courts (found in most, but not all, states) sit without juries and handle questions of law made by judges at trial.
- State supreme courts (not called "supreme" in all states) generally hear appeals from intermediate appellate courts. In states with no intermediate appellate court, (https://www.appellatecourtclerks.org/links.html), an appeal from a trial court's decision is taken directly to the state's highest court.

In our example, let us assume that the intermediate and state supreme courts both upheld the decision of the trial court. Now what? The decision on state law (aggravated assault) is over and no further appeal is possible. The decision of the state's highest court will be the final word because aggravated assault is a matter of state law. With respect to the federal question (a possible civil rights violation), the losing party can appeal directly to the U.S. Supreme Court. No other federal court has the authority to take the appeal.

Aside from an appeal from a state's highest court to the U.S. Supreme Court, there are two other ways in which federal courts can become entangled with state courts. Upon conviction in a criminal case and an unsuccessful appeal to the state's highest court, a prisoner can file a **habeas corpus** petition to a federal trial court (called a U.S. District Court) claiming that a violation of a federal constitutional right took place (such as not being allowed to cross-examine a key witness). If granted, the federal judge will issue a *writ of habeas corpus*—which translates into "you have the body"—to the jailor requesting that the prisoner be brought before the U.S. District Court to determine the legality of detention. In this way, *habeas corpus* serves as "the fundamental instrument for safeguarding individual freedom against arbitrary and lawless state action" (*Harris v. Nelson*, 1969). Much like an appeal, a new trial at the state level will generally be ordered if the federal judge finds that a federal constitutional right was indeed denied. The new trial is designed to correct whatever error happened at the initial hearing.

The final way federal and state courts interact is through a **diversity suit**. These cases arise when citizens of different states (hence the word "diversity") are involved in a civil case. The framers were concerned that an unbiased court would not exist in a diversity suit because state judges might favor citizens from their own state. Consequently, the Constitution (Article III, Section 2) empowered

Congress to grant federal courts the authority to handle such cases, and in the Judiciary Act of 1789, this jurisdiction was assigned initially to federal circuit courts. Nonetheless, certain cases are exempt from diversity jurisdiction since they would be inappropriate for federal courts to decide. These cases include divorce, alimony, custody, wills, and the administration of estates. In deciding a diversity case, a federal judge will actually apply the appropriate state—not federal—law that governs the situation.

Over time, the number of diversity cases exploded to the point where the federal judiciary became overwhelmed. Congress responded by shifting less important diversity cases (currently defined as a lawsuit with less than $75,000 at stake) to state courts. If the amount in controversy exceeds $75,000, the defendant (the person being sued by the plaintiff) has a choice between taking the case to state court or to a U.S. District Court.

The relationship between state and federal courts can be summarized as follows:

- State judges must apply federal law over state law if the two are in conflict.
- Appeals from a state's judicial system are submitted from the state's highest court directly to the U.S. Supreme Court but only the parts of the case that concern federal questions.
- *Habeas corpus* petitions from prisoners convicted of a state crime can be reviewed by U.S. District Courts if the breach of a federal constitutional right is alleged.
- U.S. District Courts may hear a civil suit between citizens of different states if $75,000 or more is at stake and the defendant elects federal over state court.

While separate, state and federal courts do interact on a narrow but important range of issues.

State court systems, in contrast, are entirely independent from each other. This means that the decision of a state court rarely has an impact outside its own borders. The lone exception—mandated by Article VI, Section 1 of the U.S. Constitution—requires each state to give **full faith and credit** to the judicial decisions of other states. Thus, a decision issued in one state must be respected by all other states (*Mills v. Duryee,* 1813). The Full Faith and Credit Clause is intended to prevent a person who loses a case to avoid compliance by moving elsewhere. For example, if a defendant loses a civil case in Pennsylvania and is ordered to pay $15,000, the defendant cannot escape the decision by changing residence to Georgia. The plaintiff merely has to file suit in Georgia to have the judgment enforced against the defendant. There is no need for a new trial since a valid and final decision was already rendered. The clause is frequently used in marriage and divorce situations. If people marry in a state with lower age requirements and return to their home state, the marriage must be honored even though it would be illegal if performed in that state. The Full Faith and Credit Clause, in short, protects the integrity of each state's judicial system in making its own judicial decisions.

Federal Jurisdiction

Two conditions must be met in order for a case to be heard before a federal court: jurisdiction and justiciability. **Jurisdiction** simply means that a court has the authority to decide a case. Article III of the U.S. Constitution outlines the kinds of cases federal courts are eligible to handle, but leaves it up to Congress actually to assign each potential area of jurisdiction. Congress can only provide federal courts with the powers allowed by the Constitution; it cannot expand federal judicial jurisdiction to cases beyond those specifically authorized in the Constitution. Moreover, Congress can change federal jurisdiction at any time by removing authority it had previously awarded to federal courts (Ex *Parte McCardle*, 1869). An effort to remove an area of federal jurisdiction is typically intended to deny federal judges the power to decide controversial issues. In the past, members of Congress have introduced bills to deny federal courts the jurisdiction to hear cases involving abortion, prayer in the school, and busing to desegregate public schools. Such efforts almost always fail in Congress because they are driven by politics rather than legitimate legal concerns. The independence of the judiciary is too deeply a part of the American political culture to allow the politics of emotional causes to interfere.

The jurisdiction of federal courts can be established in one of two ways. First, the Constitution identifies certain topics (**subject matter jurisdiction**) as appropriate for federal courts: federal questions (issues arising under federal laws, treaties, and Constitution) as well as **admiralty and maritime** law (disputes involving navigation and shipping on navigable waters). The second way the Constitution allows jurisdiction to be established in federal courts is where cases are brought by certain parties (**party jurisdiction**). There are four parties with this constitutional privilege: (1) the U.S. government, (2) one of the states, (3) citizens of different states (diversity cases), and (4) foreign ambassadors and counsels. If a case involves either a subject matter or party that falls under federal jurisdiction, a judge will next examine whether the issue is justiciable.

Justiciable means that a dispute is a matter appropriate for a court to resolve. In other words, courts should not be bothered with problems where a judicial decision is not necessary. Why waste a court's time? Judges look at five factors in making this determination, any one of which could render a case not relevant for judicial consideration.

- *Case or controversy:* The dispute must involve parties with a genuine conflict. Federal courts will not answer hypothetical questions. When George Washington sought advice about American neutrality during the European wars of the 1790s, the Supreme Court in a letter (not in a judicial ruling) declined to give an advisory opinion. Until an actual controversy arose about Washington's policy on neutrality, the justices believed that federal courts would not know what was to be decided.

- *Finality:* A federal court's decision must be final. The concept of separation of powers would be violated if another body should have the authority to review and modify a judicial decision. Judges alone make judicial rulings. When a congressional statute allowed the Secretary of War to review pension decisions made by federal courts, the Supreme Court held that the federal judiciary should not become involved because the Secretary of War could overturn whatever a judge decided on an issue involving a federal pension (*Hayburn's Case,* 1792).

- *Standing:* The plaintiff must suffer personal damage to a right protected under federal law or the U.S. Constitution. When Congress enacted a law requiring mandatory drug testing to land a job at the U.S. Postal Service, the union representing postal employees sued on the grounds that the statute violated privacy rights. A U.S. Appellate Court ruled that the union lacked standing because the drug testing policy applied only to job applicants who were not yet members of the union (*American Postal Workers Union v. Frank,* 1992). The union itself, therefore, had not suffered any damage and thus had no standing.

- *Political Questions:* A federal court will not hear an issue that can be better handled by another branch of government. Consequently, the U.S. Supreme Court refused to rule on the constitutionality of the Vietnam War by claiming that foreign policy decisions should be made by Congress and the president (*Massachusetts v. Laird,* 1970). A majority of justices argued that judges have no expertise that qualifies them as experts on international relations. The Vietnam War, accordingly, was not a legal question but a political one.

- *Timeliness*: Cases must reach federal courts at a time when the outcome of a decision could make a difference. Judges will not take cases that arrive too early (**ripe**) or too late (**moot**). When a white applicant was denied admission into the University of Washington Law School even though minority applicants with lower test scores had been admitted, a court ordered the white applicant to be enrolled pending resolution of the lawsuit. By the time the issue reached the U.S. Supreme Court, the white applicant was in the final quarter of school and would graduate no matter what happened in the case. For this reason, the lawsuit was declared moot and no ruling was made (*DeFunis v. Odegaard,* 1974). Ripeness is the reverse of moot in the sense that a case is considered premature for decision. When a federal law prohibited federal civil service employees from taking part in political campaigns, a complaint by employees was thrown out because no one had yet been arrested (*United Public Workers v. Mitchell,* 1947). According to the Supreme Court, the threat of arrest does not mean anyone would actually be arrested under the law, so that there was nothing yet to decide.

Only the requirement of a "case or controversy" is mentioned in the Constitution (Article II, Section 2); the remaining four factors have been created by the U.S. Supreme Court and are frequently used by federal courts as an excuse to dodge controversial cases. Take the Vietnam War lawsuit that was evaded for being a "political question." Justice William Douglas challenged the majority opinion in a dissent complaining the case did indeed present a justiciable issue— whether the president had the constitutional power to engage in a military action without congressional approval. Was the legality of the Vietnam War truly a "political question" or was the Supreme Court merely avoiding a problem because it was too controversial? Justiciability is clearly an ambiguous concept that can be interpreted quite freely by federal judges.

Once jurisdiction is established and a judge rules an issue justiciable, a case is eligible for a federal court to hear.

The Structure of Federal Courts

Article III of the U.S. Constitution directly mentions only the U.S. Supreme Court, but it empowers Congress to create additional federal courts as needed. Like most state systems, the federal judiciary today is divided into three levels: trial court, intermediate appellate court, and Supreme Court. The first step in bringing a case to federal court is identifying the correct trial court in which to file suit. Congress has created a host of options, with the selection of the specific trial court depending upon the issue at stake in the lawsuit. Here is a partial list of the complex alternatives: Contract claims against the federal government go to the U.S. Court of Federal Claims, international trade and customs issues are handled by the U.S. Court of International Trade, bankruptcy cases belong to U.S. Bankruptcy Courts, and federal income tax disputes are taken to the U.S. Tax Court. These courts are designed to handle narrow, highly technical issues and the judges are chosen on the basis of their background in these specialized areas of law. As shall be discussed, the trial courts with the broadest federal jurisdiction are called U.S. District Courts.

At this point, an important distinction must be made between different types of federal courts. Except for the U.S. Supreme Court, all other federal courts have been created by Congress but not under the same constitutional power. The first, and most important type, of federal courts were authorized under Article III, the section of the Constitution that deals with the judicial branch, and they are limited to exercising only judicial powers (i.e., deciding legal cases and controversies). These courts are the following: U.S. District Courts, U.S. Circuit Courts of Appeal, U.S. Supreme Court, U.S. Court of Claims, and U.S. Court of International Trade. The president nominates judges to serve on these courts, and appointment depends upon approval by the U.S. Senate. Article III judges "hold their Offices during good Behaviour," meaning they cannot be removed except by death, resignation, or impeachment by the House of Representatives and conviction by the Senate. Even senility and incompetence are not grounds that justify dismissal of an Article III judge. It is interesting to note that Article III does not spell out any specific qualifications that must be possessed to be a federal judge; not even a law degree is a necessity. Justice Hugo Black even argued that at least one non-lawyer should serve on the Supreme Court because many cases involve more politics than law.

Congress also created a second type of federal courts under Article I, the section of the Constitution dealing with the legislative branch. This section enables Congress more flexibility in setting up courts because it is not restricted by the provisions of Article III in terms of powers and tenure. So-called Article I, or **legislative courts,** are typically assigned certain non-judicial duties, such as administrative roles, and the judges do not have a lifetime appointment. Most, but not all, Article I judges are nominated by the president and approved by the Senate to serve a specific term (8–15 years). The current list of legislative courts is the following: U.S. Magistrate Courts, U.S. Bankruptcy Courts, U.S. Court of Appeals for the Armed Forces, U.S. Tax Court, and U.S. Court of Appeals for Veterans Claims. In the past, Congress has changed the status of an Article I court to an Article III court to give the judges more independence.

The workhorses at the federal level are the 94 U.S. District Courts. These trial courts (courts of original jurisdiction) hear all crimes against the U.S., most federal civil actions, and certain diversity cases. Each state has at least one U.S. District Court and, based roughly on population, a state may be allocated extra court(s). Georgia, for example, has three U.S. District Courts while California has four. The number of judges assigned to a district ranges from two to twenty-eight. U.S. District Courts can also be found in the District of Columbia, Puerto Rico, and in three U.S. territories: The Virgin Islands, Guam, and The Northern Mariana Islands. To relieve the heavy caseload (almost 400,000 cases are filed annually with U.S. District Courts), Congress in 1968 created magistrate judges to deal with minor matters such as preliminary hearings, warrants, bail, and lesser criminal offenses. In 2024, the practice of "judge shopping" was ended in which challenges to state or federal policy were filed in courthouses staffed by judges with well-known ideological preferences. Most famously, District Court Judge Matthew Kascmaryk in Amarillo, Texas frequently received cases involving conservative attacks on issues like abortion pills in the belief that he would likely narrow or overrule anything in a liberal direction. Now, "lawsuits seeking to block state or federal laws (are) to be assigned a judge randomly throughout a federal district and not be heard just by judges in a specific courthouse, or division, within the larger district" (Raymond, 2024).

As a trial court, U.S. District Court judges decide cases either alone or with a jury. Federal law requires District Court judges to write an opinion explaining their decision when sitting without a jury. The Sixth Amendment awards the right to a jury trial in all federal criminal cases, but $20 must be involved under the Seventh Amendment for the right to a jury trial to apply in a federal civil case. Most federal cases are resolved at the District Court level. Only about 10 percent of decisions are appealed on the basis of a question of law.

Congress created twelve U.S. Courts of Appeal that have jurisdiction over a set of U.S. District Courts and federal agencies within a defined geographic region (called a **circuit**). Each circuit, in turn, is numbered (see Figure 10.1). Thus, the U.S. Court of Appeals for the Eleventh Circuit takes all appeals from the U.S. District Courts located in Georgia, Florida, and Alabama (nine District Courts in total). As noted, federal agencies (like the Social Security Administration) can render decisions, and these too are appealed to the appropriate U.S. appellate court. A thirteenth appellate court, the Court of Appeals for the Federal Circuit in Washington, D.C., was launched in 1982 to manage appeals involving patents from anywhere in the country as well as appeals from decisions by the Court of International Trade and the Court of Federal Claims.

Figure 10.1: U.S. Courts of Appeals and Georgia District Courts

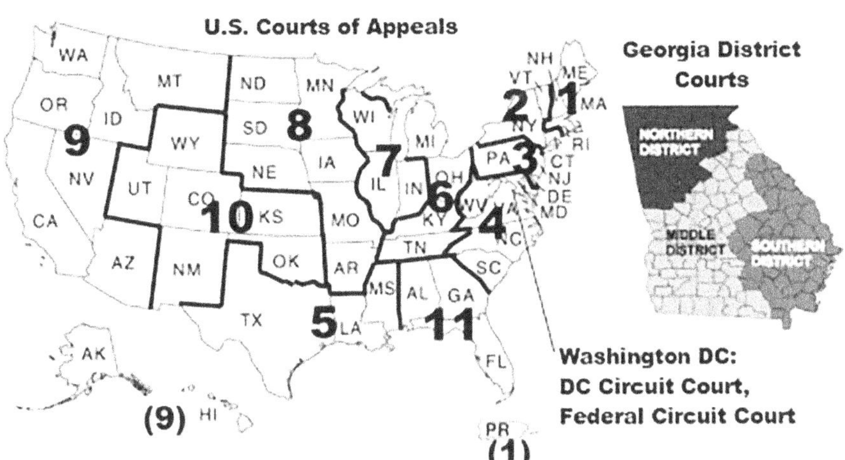

A federal appellate court has from six judges (First Circuit) to twenty-eight judges (Ninth Circuit). The appellate judge in the circuit with the most seniority serves as chief judge until the age of 70, although the person can continue as a regular member of the court after reaching that age. Individual cases are generally heard in three-judge panels without juries, with judges normally assigned to a panel by the chief judge. The winning party is determined by a majority vote. In rare cases (less than 1% of the total), all judges in a circuit—a requirement relaxed by Congress for appellate courts with 15 or more members—will be present for a case in what is known as an *en banc* hearing. Such hearings tend to take place either to deal with a controversial case or to review a panel's ruling in the circuit on an important case. The fact that all, or almost all, appellate judges in the circuit are deciding the case is intended to give more weight to the eventual judgment. An *en banc* hearing may be requested by any member of an appellate court and is convened when at least a majority of judges are in favor (some circuits require less than a majority vote).

The decision by a U.S. Court of Appeal is binding on all U.S. District Courts and federal agencies in its circuit. An appellate court does not have the authority to issue compulsory orders outside its geographic jurisdiction. As a consequence, the interpretation of a federal law may vary across the nation when different U.S. Courts of Appeals deliver conflicting rulings on a law. These contradictions can only be ironed out by the U.S. Supreme Court, if it chooses to do so. Only about 15% of decisions by U.S. Courts of Appeal are appealed to the Supreme Court.

U.S. Supreme Court

Congress determines the number of justices on the Supreme Court. Historically, the size of the Court has ranged from 6 to 10 members. The current size of nine justices was set in 1869, although President Franklin Roosevelt (FDR) in the 1930s famously threatened to increase the membership by "packing" the Court with a majority who would support his programs. FDR became frustrated when his New Deal legislation kept being declared unconstitutional by a 5-4 vote. Congress, however, was reluctant to support a proposal that would enable judicial decisions to be manipulated for political purposes, and it dropped the court-packing plan when one justice suddenly stopped opposing New Deal laws in a move sometimes called "a switch in time that saved nine." Two characteristics of the justices are worth noting. First, they tend to remain on the Supreme Court a long time, with the average tenure being seventeen years (Bialik & Gramlich, 2017). And second, they have similar backgrounds, with all but one current justice graduating from either Harvard or Yale law school. The outlier is Justice Amy Coney Barrett who attended law school at the University of Notre Dame.

One member of the Supreme Court is nominated by the president to serve as Chief Justice of the United States[1]. The other eight members are known as associate justices. The chief justice has only a few formal powers not possessed by the other justices. In particular, the chief justice votes first on cases, assigns the author of the court's opinion if voting with the majority (if the chief justice is in the minority, the writing assignment is doled out by the associate justice in the majority with the most seniority), and heads the Judicial Conference of the United States that administers all federal courts.

At least six justices are needed to decide a case. If a tie vote occurs (3–3 or 4–4), the ruling of the last court to decide the case—usually a U.S. Court of Appeals or a state's highest court—is allowed to stand. It does not mean, however, that the Supreme Court is agreeing with the ruling of the lower court. It merely means that the Supreme Court itself was unable to reach a decision.

While the U.S. Supreme Court is commonly considered to take cases solely on appeal, the U.S. Constitution (Article III, section 2) assigns a limited **original jurisdiction**. In these instances, a case goes directly to the Supreme Court, and the justices serve as the trial court. The decision by the justices is final on these cases and no further appeal is possible. Four types of cases constitute the Supreme Court's original jurisdiction:

- Cases between two or more states.
- Cases between a state and the United States.

---

1   This position is often mistakenly referred to as "Chief Justice of the Supreme Court".

- Cases involving ambassadors and foreign counsels.
- Cases in which a state is suing a citizen of another state or a foreign nation.

Since the Supreme Court has little time to devote to an actual trial, Congress (28 U.S.C. section 1251) awarded U.S. District Courts **concurrent jurisdiction** over the last three types of cases. Concurrent jurisdiction denotes that a particular type of case can be heard by more than one court. In practical terms, most of the Supreme Court's original jurisdiction is shared with U.S. District Courts to the point where it is a waste of time to request the justices to consider a case that falls in these categories (with an appeal through U.S. Courts of Appeal to the U.S. Supreme Court still feasible). Moreover, the last category of original jurisdiction was restricted by the Eleventh Amendment (1795) to prevent a state from being sued by a citizen of another state or a foreign country under the doctrine of **sovereign immunity** (i.e., the concept that a government cannot be sued without its consent).

Only cases between two or more states remain within the Supreme Court's exclusive original jurisdiction. These cases most often involve disputes over borders or water rights, such as a dispute between New York and New Jersey over ownership rights to Ellis Island (*New Jersey v. New York*, 1998). Even here, the tradition is for the Supreme Court to appoint a **master** (usually a retired federal judge) to examine the evidence and recommend an outcome to the justices. It is seldom that more than one or two cases annually will be heard under original jurisdiction.

By far, the caseload of the Supreme Court comes from its appellate jurisdiction—over 5,000 appeals annually. Remember that, under the Constitution (Article III, Section 2, Clause 2), federal appellate jurisdiction is assigned with "such exceptions and under such regulations, as the Congress shall make." Currently, appellate cases are taken from the 13 U.S. courts of appeals, from the U.S. Court of Appeals for the Armed Forces, from U.S. District Courts (in exceptional circumstances), and from the highest state courts when a federal question exists. There are three avenues of appeal to the U.S. Supreme Court: (1) **writ of appeal** (when federal law gives the automatic right to have a certain type of case reviewed by the Supreme Court), (2) **writ of certification** (when a lower federal court requests instructions on a point of law never before decided), and (3) **writ of certiorari** (when a writ of appeal is not available). The first two avenues generate few cases, especially since Congress severely cut back on the availability of the writ of appeal in 1988.

Today, the writ of certiorari (or more commonly, *writ of cert*) is the primary means of appealing to the Supreme Court. According to Supreme Court Rule 10,

"Review on writ of certiorari is not a matter of right, but a judicial discretion. A petition for writ of certiorari will be granted only for compelling reasons" (Supreme Court of the United States, 2019, p. 5). The Supreme Court uses the *rule of four* to determine which appeals are granted; that is, the Court considers an appeal if four justices vote to accept (only three votes are necessary if six or seven justices are present). Only about 100 cases are taken annually. Denial of a writ does not mean the justices agree with the previous ruling by a court, only that not enough justices believe a substantial question was raised that is worthy of review. The justices simply do not have time to correct every error that occurred in lower courts. Moreover, the granting of the writ provides no indication of how the Supreme Court will ultimately rule on the case. The losing party in the lower court may still lose.

The Supreme Court begins its regular session on the first Monday in October and continues until late June or early July. When petitions are received, the chief justice creates the Supreme Court's agenda and places each petition either on the "discuss list" or "dead list." Petitions assigned to the dead list will routinely be denied unless any justice requests a particular petition to be shifted to the discuss list. The justices meet together in conference on Wednesdays and Fridays and, by tradition, begin with a handshake. Since 1910, only justices are allowed in the room. The associate justice with the least seniority must respond to knocks at the door or to collect books or papers sought by the other members. The chief justice is allowed to speak first on whether to accept or deny petitions on the discuss list and is followed by the associate justices in order of seniority, with voting taking place in the reverse sequence. Again, four votes are required to schedule a hearing on a case.

Oral arguments are conducted Mondays through Wednesdays beginning in early October and running through late spring. Two-week breaks are periodically arranged to enable the justices an opportunity to research and write. During oral arguments, each side is typically allocated a half-hour, and justices can interrupt at any time—cutting into a lawyer's time. The **Solicitor General**, nominated by the president and confirmed by the Senate, argues cases in which the federal government is a party. Public access to oral arguments is permitted on a limited basis.

During conference, the justices discuss and vote on the cases heard at oral argument. A majority vote determines the winning party. The chief justice assigns the opinion writer only if a member of the majority side (which happens over 80% of the time). When the chief justice is on the losing side, the associate justice in the majority with the most seniority has the duty of determining the author of the court's decision. Justices circulate drafts of their opinions and must take great care to ensure that their wording does not alienate members of the majority. It has happened that an opinion begins as the majority decision but, due to the way in which the decision is written, may end up the losing side. Justices are allowed to alter their votes on a case up to the moment a decision is announced to the public.

Justices on the losing side have the option of writing a **dissenting opinion**. Since a dissenting member is speaking for no one else (although other justices can support the dissent), these opinions tend to be more candid and sometimes insulting. Even justices in the majority can write separate **concurring opinions,** and these must be read carefully to determine the extent to which the Court's opinion is supported. In a concurring opinion, a justice may merely want to elaborate on the reasons for agreeing with the majority, but a justice may also express concerns about aspects of the decision. A common situation is when a justice agrees as to the winning party but does not support the rationale behind the Court's opinion. For example, five justices could rule that a conviction should be overturned, with four believing evidence was improperly admitted while the fifth believes a juror was biased. Where concurring opinions have been written, it sometimes becomes complicated in understanding what the Supreme Court actually decided.

If a majority (five justices) does not endorse both the outcome *and* the rationale for a decision, the Supreme Court issues what is called a **judgment** (Cross, 2009, p. 323). Such opinions only identify the winning and losing parties and do not establish precedent that is binding on lower courts. A **precedent** requires judges to follow the ruling of a higher court in their jurisdiction when dealing with a case that presents similar facts. This doctrine (known as **stare decisis***)* was created to ensure that people are treated the same in applying legal standards. An appellate court's precedent binds only the courts and agencies within its jurisdiction (circuit). The U.S. Supreme Court alone binds all courts, state and federal, when it decides a federal question.

Precedent is established when a majority agrees on the outcome as well as the rationale behind a decision. Here, the Supreme Court issues an *opinion* that is binding on all federal courts. The relationship with state courts is more complex. State judges, of course, must obey the precedents of the U.S. Supreme Court on federal questions. When a case originating in state court is decided, the Supreme Court typically **remands**, or sends the case back, to the highest court in the state to enforce its ruling. At this point, however, state courts will occasionally evade a U.S. Supreme Court ruling because a state can always "impose higher standards . . . than required by the Federal Constitution" so long as they are not interfering with a federal interest (*Cooper v. California*, 1967). One study found that 12 percent of the cases remanded to state courts by the U.S. Supreme Court reversed winning and losing parties (Evasion of Supreme Court mandates, 1954).

Consider an example. In 1976, the U.S. Supreme Court held a police search of an impounded car was permissible under the Fourth Amendment even though no probable cause existed that contraband was located inside the vehicle (*South Dakota v. Opperman*, 1976). On remand, the state's supreme court ruled the search unconstitutional under the state's constitution (*State v. Opperman*, 1976). In other words, the state court was able to sidestep a direct ruling by the U.S. Supreme Court by giving the citizens of South Dakota more protection than allowed under the U.S. Constitution. Police need a warrant to search an impounded car in South Dakota—but nowhere else in the country—in the absence of probable cause. The Supreme Court of the United States may not be the last word after all!

Powers of the Federal Judiciary

Aside from deciding cases and controversies, the Constitution is silent on the powers to be exercised by federal courts. This lack of clarity differs from the careful attention devoted to the enumeration of powers belonging to Congress and the president. Accordingly, the authority of federal courts had to develop over time in response to issues as they arose. It is not surprising that service on the Supreme Court was not viewed initially as too significant a position. John Jay, the first chief justice, stepped down to become governor of New York, something that surely would not happen today.

Marbury v. Madison (1803) and the Power of Judicial Review

The landscape began to change when John Marshall became chief justice in 1801, and he continued serving until 1835. His influence vastly expanded the power of all federal courts. The key decision was issued in *Marbury v. Madison*, 5 U.S. 137 (1803). The case would make a good soap opera. In the 1800 election, the Federalist party lost control of the presidency and both houses of Congress. Two developments resulted from this loss that led to the *Marbury* decision. First, the chief justice of the Supreme Court resigned, and President John Adams immediately nominated Marshall, his Secretary of State, to the position. Adams requested Marshall to continue as Secretary of State for the little time remaining in his term. And second, the Federalists moved quickly to create a host of new judicial posts to which members of the party would be appointed before the new administration took office under Thomas Jefferson. The goal was to pack federal courts with Federalists who would frustrate Jefferson in any way possible. Forty-two new

Justice of the Peace positions were created for the District of Columbia. President John Adams nominated and the Senate confirmed all forty-two appointments the day before Jefferson was to assume office. Adams signed the commissions, and it fell upon Secretary of State Marshall to deliver them. Marshall worked throughout the night and managed to give out all but four of the commissions before midnight. Since the papers had been signed and sealed, Marshall assumed James Madison, the new Secretary of State, would complete the project. Jefferson, however, instructed Madison to ignore the undelivered commissions.

William Marbury, and the other three promised recipients of a judgeship, filed suit directly before the U.S. Supreme Court under a federal law enacted in 1789 that expanded the Supreme Court's original jurisdiction to allow suits against federal officials to perform their legal duties. Marbury, in other words, was alleging that Madison had no choice but to give him his commission since it was required by federal statute. Marshall, who was responsible for the mess, was now in position to decide the dispute as Chief Justice. The situation suddenly became even more complicated when Jefferson asserted he would not provide Marbury his commission no matter what the Supreme Court ruled. Several members of Congress additionally threatened Marshall with impeachment if Marbury won. It now seemed that Marshall was in a box with no way out. If he decided in favor of Marbury, Marshall would be defied by Jefferson and could even be impeached. On the other hand, if he decided against Marbury (who deserved to win), Marshall would be publicly humiliated for having no backbone and would also lower the prestige of the court system. The drama was made more compelling because Jefferson and Marshall were second cousins, and the controversy was splitting apart the family. In a brilliant maneuver, Marshall managed not only to escape the dilemma but to enhance the power of the federal judiciary at the same time!

Marshall wrote the opinion in *Marbury v. Madison* for a unanimous Supreme Court. While acknowledging that Marbury deserved the commission and admonishing Madison for not performing his legal duty, Marshall nonetheless lamented that the Supreme Court lacked authority to order Madison to comply. The reason is that the 1789 federal law that enabled Marbury to file suit directly before the Supreme Court was not one of the four types of cases listed in Article III as part of its original jurisdiction. That is, Congress added a fifth type of case to the Supreme Court's original jurisdiction. Could a law of Congress override the Constitution? Marshall answered in the negative because "all those who have framed written constitutions contemplate them as the fundamental and paramount law of the nation." Put differently, the Constitution is superior to congressional statutes.

Only one important question remained: are courts required to follow a federal law that is inconsistent with the Constitution? In a famous sentence, Marshall concluded: "It is emphatically the province of the judicial department to say what the law is." If a law violates the Constitution, federal courts are empowered to strike down the law. Separation of powers entrusts courts with the authority to interpret laws, and the Constitution should be interpreted like any law. Consequently, Marbury was in the wrong court and would have to file suit elsewhere, an option that would not be worth his time since his term as Justice of the Peace was soon to expire. Thus, Marshall succeeded in publicly rebuking Jefferson and in making the Supreme Court a feared institution that could nullify acts of Congress. As might be expected, the decision stirred a storm of controversy, and the Supreme Court waited fifty-four years before daring to strike down another congressional statute.

Marshall, without using the term, claimed the power of **judicial review** for the court system. As it has evolved, the concept of judicial review has come to include the following elements:

- It is a power possessed by all courts, state and federal.
- It enables acts of Congress or of any public authority to be challenged.
- If found to be in violation of the federal Constitution, the law or action is voided and does not have to be obeyed.

Keep in mind that only the U.S. Supreme Court has national jurisdiction so that it alone can exercise judicial review that applies across the country. The use of judicial review by other courts is limited to the geographic area within their jurisdiction: a U.S. Court of Appeals has controls over its circuit; a state's highest court controls courts in the state, etc. Moreover, it is not only legislative bodies that can be challenged but executive officials as well. It was the U.S. Supreme Court, for example, that forced President Richard Nixon to turn over the recordings made in the Oval Office in the Watergate controversy. The Court rejected Nixon's argument that a president—unlike other citizens—could withhold information demanded by a court (*United States v. Nixon*, 1974). Thus, Nixon's claim of presidential power was in violation of the Constitution, and he resigned fifteen days after the Court's decision.

Judicial review is a hotly debated topic for several reasons. First, the power is not mentioned in the Constitution itself. Marshall found the power a logical extension of the judiciary's authority to interpret laws, but the Constitution's failure explicitly to mention the power renders the rationale open to questioning. If the framers wanted the courts to utilize judicial review, critics contend that the power would have been written directly into the Constitution, especially since the issue was discussed at the Constitutional Convention. Second, opponents warn that the power is subject to abuse with little oversight. Woodrow Wilson once described the Supreme Court as a constitutional convention in continuous session. A majority on the Supreme Court can interpret the Constitution to say almost anything, and the only way to reverse is by the grueling process of amending the Constitution. In fact, a number of amendments (Eleventh, Fourteenth, Sixteenth, Nineteenth, and Twenty-Sixth) have been adopted specifically to override decisions of the Supreme Court, although hundreds of proposals to do so have been introduced into Congress over the years. Finally, judicial review has been blamed for undermining the Doctrine of Separation of Powers by enabling courts to write what amounts to legislation. It could be argued, for example, that the Supreme Court "legislated" when it required police to inform detained individuals of their rights before questioning them. Since the Fifth Amendment only declares that no person "shall be compelled in any criminal case to be a witness against himself," the Supreme Court could be accused of adding words to the amendment.

Judicial Activism and Judicial Restraint

Judicial review is surely a potent weapon that will survive if for no other reason than its use is inevitable. The judiciary must have some way under checks and balances to protect its authority. The real debate focuses on when the exercise of judicial review is appropriate. **Judicial activists** consider the proper role of courts to include "filling in the holes" left by the Constitution's vague language. They believe it is the duty of judges to minimize potential social disruption caused by the lack of clear policy guidelines, such as when public schools were ordered to integrate flowing from the words "equal protection" in the Fourteenth Amendment. To them, the Constitution should be considered a living document that changes with society. Judicial activists, however, have been accused of promoting ideological agendas. Controversial decisions on abortion (*Roe v. Wade*, 1973), contraception (*Griswold v. Connecticut*, 1965), and contracts (*Lochner v. New York*, 1925) have been faulted for imposing the personal values of judges on society without any direct support in the language of the Constitution.

Advocates of **judicial restraint**, in contrast, contend that judges should decide cases on the basis of precedent and overturn laws only when a conflict with the Constitution is unmistakable. They believe this approach is best accomplished when judges try to remain within the original intent or meaning of the framers to avoid making up policy. While logical in theory, judicial restraint is almost impossible to practice consistently. Justice John Paul Stevens, for example, could not resist chiding Justice Antonin Scalia, the Supreme Court's most vocal champion of judicial restraint, for overturning long-standing precedent to achieve what many considered an ideological result on the Second Amendment: "It is, however, clear to me that adherence to a policy of judicial restraint would be far wiser than the bold decision announced today" (*District of Columbia v. Heller*, 2008). The public, for its part, is slightly in favor of a more activist role for the Supreme Court. When surveyed in 2018, fifty-five percent believed the Supreme Court should interpret the Constitution on what it "means in current times," rather than what it "meant as originally written" (Bialik, 2018).

Statutory Interpretation

Aside from judicial review, federal courts are frequently called upon to engage in **statutory interpretation** where they attempt to understand the meaning of a law enacted by a legislature. Here, judges are not examining a law for its conformity with the Constitution but are merely trying to make sense of it (Cross, 2009). If Congress enacts a law requiring all "able bodied" males aged 18 to be subject to the military draft, for example, it is unclear whether a male is "able bodied" if having flat feet. Typically, courts decide such cases by seeking to identify the legislature's intent when the law was enacted and applying this intent to the circumstances presented by the situation. Laws are hardly written with a great deal of precision, and the opportunity for courts to interpret statutes is quite frequent. Unlike judicial review, however, Congress is able to alter court interpretations of statutes more easily. Since the courts are not interpreting the Constitution, Congress can reverse the judicial interpretation of a statute simply by re-writing the law. One study found that Congress overturned 124 Supreme Court decisions based on interpretations of federal law in a 23-year period (Eskridge, 1991, pp. 335–341). The doctrine of checks and balances is alive and well!

Discussion Questions

1. Is the Supreme Court the "least dangerous branch," as once described by Alexander Hamilton? Justify your answer on the basis of the material in the chapter.
2. From the reading, what are the checks on the powers of the judiciary? Are the checks adequate to prevent the abuse of judicial power? Explain.
3. Which position makes the most sense to you, judicial activism or judicial restraint? Justify your position. Is a Republican or Democratic judge more likely to favor judicial restraint? Explain your answer.

4. The chapter makes a case that federalism is "alive and well" in the relationship between state and federal courts. What evidence is available to support this position?

Civic Exercise

Interview a lawyer who has argued cases before both state and federal courts and ask the following questions:

1. Do you prefer taking a case to state or federal court? Explain why.
2. Did any of your state cases involve federal questions? If so, to what extent was the state judge knowledgeable about federal law?
3. Do you prefer arguing cases before juries or judges alone? Explain why.
4. Discuss whether civil cases or criminal cases are more difficult to litigate.
5. Have you ever argued an appellate case? If so, how does the experience differ from a trial court? Explain the concept of "perfecting the record."
6. In your opinion, do federal courts have too much power? Cite examples.
7. Federal judges, for the most part, are appointed while state judges are elected. Is there a difference in the quality of judges in comparing the two selection methods?
8. In your experience, did a federal judge use the doctrine of "justiciability" to avoid hearing a case that should have legitimately been taken? Discuss the incident(s).
9. Does the option of taking a diversity case to a federal court still make sense since the original justification was the fear of not being able to find a fair forum in state court?
10. Do the decisions of the U.S. Supreme Court regularly impact your daily practice of law? Justify your response.

References

American Council of Trustees and Alumni, (2016), *A crisis in civic education.* https://www.goacta.org/images/download/A_Crisis_in_Civic_Education. pdf

Berger, R. (1997). *Government by judiciary: The transformation of the Fourteenth Amendment.* (2nd ed.), Liberty Fund.

Bialik, K. (2018). *Growing share of Americans say Supreme Court should base its rulings on what Constitution means today.* Pew Research Center. https://www. pewresearch.org/fact-tank/2018/05/11/growing-share-of-americans-say-supreme-court-should-base-its-rulings-on-what-constitution-means-today/

_____, and Gramlich, J. (2017). *Younger Supreme Court appointees stay on the bench longer, but there are plenty of exceptions.* Pew Research Center. https://www.pewresearch.org/fact-tank/2017/02/08/younger-supreme-court-appointees-stay-on-the-bench-longer-but-there-are-plenty-of-exceptions/

Bomboy, S. (2016). *Surveys: Many Americans know little about the Supreme Court.* National Constitution Center. https://constitutioncenter.org/blog/surveys-many-americans-know-little-about-the-supreme-court/

Cross, F. B. (2009). *The theory and practice of statutory interpretation.* Stanford University Press.

Eskridge, W. (1991). Overriding Supreme Court statutory interpretation decisions. *The Yale Law Journal, 101*(2), 331–341.

Evasion of Supreme Court mandates in cases remanded to state courts since 1941. (1954, May 8). *Harvard Law Review,* 1251–1253.

George, J. J. (2006). *Judicial opinion writing handbook.* (5th ed.), William S. Hein & Co., Inc.

Green. R. and Rosenblatt, A. (2017). *C-SPAN / PSB supreme court survey 2017.* C-SPAN. https://static.c-span.org/assets/documents/scotusSurvey/CSPAN%20PSB%20Supreme%20Court%20Survey%20COMPREHENSIVE%20AGENDA%20sent%2003%2013%2017.pdf

Hamilton, A. (1788/1961). Federalist Paper 78. In Clinton Rossiter (Ed.), *The federalist papers* (pp. 352-357). The New American Library.

Hughes, C. E. (1916). *Addresses* (2nd ed.). Putnam.

Lampe, J. (2023). *The Supreme Court adopts a code of conduct.* Library of Congress. https://crsreports.congress.gov/product/pdf/LSB/LSB11078

Lin, K. and Doherty, C. (2023). *Favorable views of Supreme Court fall to historic lows.* Pew Research Center. https://www.pewresearch.org/short-reads/2023/07/21/favorable-views-of-supreme-court-fall-to-historic-low/

Liptak, A. (2023). Supreme Court's new ethics code is toothless, experts say. *The New York Times.* https://www.nytimes.com/2023/11/14/us/politics/supreme-court-ethics-code-clarence-thomas-sotomayor.html

Raymond, N. (2024). U.S. federal judiciary moves to curtail 'judge shopping' tactic. *Reuters.* https://www.reuters.com/world/us/us-federal-judiciary-adopts-policy-curtail-judge-shopping-2024-03-12/

Schwartz, B. (1993). *A history of the Supreme Court.* Oxford University Press.

Supreme Court of the United States. (2019). *Rules of the Supreme Court of the United States.* Supreme Court of the United States. https://www.supremecourt.gov/ctrules/2019RulesoftheCourt.pdf

Court Cases

American Postal Workers Union v. Frank, 968 P.2d 1373 (1992).

Cooper v. California, 386 U.S. 58, 62 (1967).

DeFunis v. Odegaard, 416 U.S. 312 (1974).

District of Columbia v. Heller, 554 U.S. 570 (2008).

Duncan v. Louisiana, 391 U.S. 145 (1968).

Ex Parte McCardle, 74 U.S. 506 (1869).

Griswold v. Connecticut, 381 U.S. 479 (1965).

Harris v. Nelson, 394 U.S. 286, 290–91 (1969).

Hayburn's Case, 2 U.S. 409 (1792).

Lochner v. New York, 198 U.S. 45 (1925).

Marbury v. Madison, 5 U.S. 137 (1803).

Martin v. Hunter's Lessee, 14 U.S. 304 (1816).

Massachusetts v. Laird, 400 U.S. 886 (1970).

Mills v. Duryee, 11 U.S. 7 (1813).

Minneapolis & St. Louis R.R. v. Bombolis, 241 U.S. 211 (1916).

New Jersey v. New York, 523 U.S. 767 (1998).

Roe v. Wade, 410 U.S. 113 (1973).

South Dakota v. Opperman, 428 U.S. 364 (1976).

State v. Opperman, 247 N.W.2d 673 (1976).

United Public Workers v. Mitchell, 330 U.S. 75 (1947).

United States v. Nixon, 418 U.S. 683 (1974).

Civil Liberties and Civil Rights

K. Michael Reese and Brian M. Murphy

Learning Objectives

After covering the topic of civil liberties and civil rights, students should understand:

1. The defining characteristics of civil liberties and civil rights.
2. The sources of civil liberties and civil rights.
3. The importance of civil liberties and civil rights in a functioning democracy.
4. The roles of the U.S. Supreme Court and the Congress in expanding and limiting, the scope of civil liberties and civil rights.
5. The process by which most provisions of the Bill of Rights were applied to the states.

Abstract

A representative democracy is more than governmental processes. It exists to protect certain fundamental freedoms known as "civil liberties" and "civil rights" because these freedoms are what make democracy possible. This chapter examines the sources, scope, and nature of American civil liberties and civil rights. Specific federal statutes and U.S. Supreme Court cases are cited to enrich the discussion.

Introduction

Civil Liberties and Civil Rights: Definitions and Distinctions

There is no accepted definition of what constitutes the civil liberties of American citizens. Some scholars limit these freedoms to the rights listed in the First Amendment, such as freedom of speech, freedom of press, and free exercise of religion (Wasserman, 2004, p. 152), while others include the first ten amendments to the Constitution, called the Bill of Rights (Rush, 2003, p. 59). In this chapter, the term **civil liberties** will refer to all freedoms and protections provided anywhere in the Constitution. The term **civil rights** is narrower and applies to the rights of individuals to be free from discriminatory treatment, both public and private, based on such characteristics as race, national origin, or gender. Where civil liberties act as a shield to protect specific freedoms, civil rights are more like a sword that promote fair treatment and equality (Stephens and Scheb, 2008, p. 3). This chapter will survey the civil liberties and civil rights of American citizens.

Civil Liberties: Original Constitution

The original Constitution included a number of references to civil liberties. Article I, Sections 9 and 10 prohibit federal and state governments from passing bills of attainder and *ex post facto* laws. A **bill of attainder** is a law that declares an individual or a group guilty of a crime and imposes punishment without a trial in court. For example, the Supreme Court struck down a law that made it a crime for members of the Communist Party to serve as officers or employees of a labor union because such individuals constituted a threat to national security (*United States v. Brown*, 1965). The law was a bill of attainder since members of the Communist Party were assumed criminals prior to committing any illegal act. An *ex post facto* law is "passed after the occurrence of a fact or commission of an act, which retrospectively changes the legal consequences or relations of such fact or deed" (Black, 1968, p. 662). Laws of this kind can occur in several ways. It typically occurs when an action is made a crime that was previously legal and people who committed the act could now be prosecuted. Along the same line, *ex post facto* laws also include increasing the seriousness or punishment of a crime and altering the rules of evidence to the detriment of a criminal defendant. The right of **habeas corpus** is another civil liberty found in Article I, Section 9, and, as explained in the previous chapter, it allows an incarcerated person to challenge in court the legality of that incarceration. A final civil liberty in Article VI of the original Constitution prohibits the federal government from requiring **religious tests** for public office.

The Bill of Rights and Civil Liberties

The Original Formulation

The Founders debated whether to list, one-by-one, the rights citizens of the new national government should possess. After the experience under British rule, many at the Constitutional Convention were fearful that a strong national government would be in position to trample personal liberties (Kommers, Finn & Jacobsohn, 2010, p.111). James Madison, however, persuaded the Convention not to attempt to do so because there is no way to identify every right a citizen could potentially need. If a right was omitted, Madison argued, the government would be justified in believing that citizens were not entitled to it. So why was the Bill of Rights added almost immediately after the Constitution was adopted? The reason is that several states refused to ratify the document until it was clear what basic rights could not be violated by the new government. A compromise was reached in which the First Congress would propose amendments addressing specific fundamental rights upon ratification of the Constitution (Epstein & Walker, 2010, p.67). The task of drafting possible amendments fell to Madison. Congress eventually submitted twelve amendments to the states and ten of them—the Bill of Rights—were adopted in 1791. Madison sought to address his concern that certain important rights would be omitted through the Ninth Amendment. It reads: "The enumeration in the Constitution, of certain rights, shall not be construed to deny or disparage others retained by the people." This means, in simple terms, that American citizens have more rights than those mentioned in the Constitution. It would not be until 1965 that the Supreme Court would use the Ninth Amendment to find a right not contained in the Bill of Rights. But another battle had to be fought prior to this controversial step.

One question left unanswered after the adoption of the Bill of Rights was whether its protections applied to both national and state governments. The Supreme Court initially ruled that only the national government was forbidden from violating the rights listed in these amendments (*Barron v. Baltimore*, 1833). The Court reasoned that the language of the First Amendment, which begins with "Congress shall make no law...," clearly indicates the Founders did not intend for the Bill of Rights to apply to state governments. As such, there was no constitutional ban against states violating any of the protections in the Bill of Rights, such as free speech or the exercise of religion. States could, of course, provide similar freedoms through their own constitutions and laws, but they were not required to do so by the Bill of Rights. It was not until the twentieth century that the Supreme Court's position began to change, but the process occurred slowly and incrementally.

Selective Incorporation: Application of the Bill of Rights to the States

In 1868, the Fourteenth Amendment was added to the Constitution. One section, called the **due process clause**, stated the following: "No state . . . shall deprive any person of life, liberty, or property, without due process of the law." Since the clause declares that states cannot deny a person liberty, did it mean they could no longer violate the Bill of Rights? The Supreme Court, at first, ruled against this interpretation by holding that the due process clause of the Fourteenth Amendment did not apply the Bill of Rights to the states (*Hurtado v. California*, 1884). In 1925, the Court partially reversed direction by acknowledging that freedom of speech and press constituted "fundamental personal rights and 'liberties' protected by the due process clause of the Fourteenth Amendment from impairment by the States (*Gitlow v. New York*, 1925)." It is important to note that the Supreme Court refused to apply all provisions of the Bill of Rights to the states. This hesitation caused confusion since it was no longer certain whether states had to obey any other of these rights. It became cloudier when several more rights were quickly imposed against the states again through the due process clause: freedom of press (1931), right to counsel in capital crimes (1932), free exercise of religion (1934), and right to assembly (1937). It soon became necessary to provide greater clarity about what provisions of the Bill of Rights states are required to protect.

The process by which the Supreme Court applied provisions of the Bill of Rights one-by-one to the states became known as **selective incorporation**. Although certain justices, like Hugo Black and William Douglas (Epstein and Walker, 2010, p. 81), supported "total incorporation" in which all provisions of the Bill of Rights should be included in due process, a majority of the Court rejected this approach in favor of a case-by-case analysis. In determining which rights should be incorporated, the Court came to assess whether a particular provision was essential to "ordered liberty and justice" (*Duncan v. Louisiana*, 1968; *Palko v. Connecticut*, 1937). Even today, however, not every protection in the Bill of Rights has been incorporated. Those that remain unenforced against the states are the following: the Third Amendment prohibition against nonconsensual quartering of soldiers in peace time, the Fifth Amendment right to a grand jury hearing, the Fifth Amendment right to due process of law (because the due process clause of the Fourteenth Amendment makes this unnecessary), the Sixth Amendment right to a jury selected from residents of the state and district where the crime occurred, and the Seventh Amendment right to a jury trial in civil cases. Selective incorporation continues to this day, with the Eighth Amendment's protection against excessive fines incorporated as recently as 2019.

The incorporation doctrine has been used solely with respect to the rights and liberties contained in the first eight amendments rather than to the entire Bill of Rights because: (1) the Ninth Amendment, as discussed earlier, makes no reference to any specific rights and (2) the Tenth Amendment is equally vague by awarding the states all powers not explicitly given to the federal government by the Constitution. Once a provision has been incorporated, however, states must enforce it in every case that occurs afterwards. They have no choice because

Supreme Court interpretations of the Constitution are the supreme law of the land under Article VI, trumping state laws to the contrary. Nonetheless, states may provide greater freedoms and protections to their citizens if based on their own laws and constitutions, but *never less* than the Supreme Court's minimum.

Let's take a look at the key incorporated rights. Keep in mind that no civil liberty is unconditional. At some point, the government can constitutionally deprive citizens of any liberty in the Bill of Rights. For example, there are times when a person can be forced against religious convictions to submit to a blood transfusion even when against a person's religious beliefs. Supreme Court decisions, therefore, are about defining the point at which an individual's freedom can be restricted. While 87 percent of the American public believe it is the government's responsibility to protect these cherished liberties, 54 percent do not think the government is doing a good job at fulfilling this role (Carr Center, 2020). After reviewing the material in this chapter, what do you think?

Survey of Incorporated Civil Liberties
First Amendment

The First Amendment protects freedom of speech, freedom of press, the right to peaceably assemble, and the right to petition the government for redress of grievances. Collectively, these freedoms and rights can be described as the **freedom of expression**. The Supreme Court has given a great deal of protection to freedom of expression, and that protection has on occasion been extended to **symbolic speech and symbolic actions**, often called speech plus. Examples include burning a flag (*Texas v. Johnson*, 1989), wearing a black armband to school (*Tinker v. Des Moines Independent Community School District, 1969*), and adorning one's clothing with offensive sentiments (*Cohen v. California*, 1971).

While fiercely protected, the Court has sometimes allowed freedom of expression to yield in the public interest. As Justice Oliver Wendell Holmes famously put it, "The most stringent protection of free speech would not protect a man in falsely shouting fire in a theatre and causing a panic" (*Schenck v. U.S.*, 1919). The Supreme Court has employed various tests in determining when speech could constitutionally be curtailed. Holmes got the ball rolling in *Schenck* with the **clear and present danger test**. That is, words can be punished if they are likely (clear and present) to produce harm (danger) in light of the circumstances. Thus, there is nothing dangerous in uttering the word "fire" unless said in a context—like a crowded theater—where it could lead to injury. This test has been revised over time, but its basic framework remains largely the same (*Brandenburg v. Ohio*, 1969). The right to free speech also embraces the corollary right *not* to speak. Accordingly, state law could not compel the creation of a website for a same-sex marriage which the designer considered morally objectionable (*303 Creative LLC v. Elenis*, 2023).

The Supreme Court has identified three kinds of expression—**obscenity** (lewd, filthy, or disgusting words or pictures), **defamation** (a false statement that harms reputation), and **fighting words** (words likely to incite immediate violence)—as having no protection of any kind under the First Amendment. Yet even here, judges have found it difficult to decide whether expression is obscene or merely offensive, whether it is defamatory or just unflattering, and whether it amounts to fighting words or simply unpopular opinions. Quite clearly, the scope of free expression is wide for American citizens across-the-board.

Freedom of press, including the broadcast medium, is somewhat different than oral speech due to the possibility of **censorship**. Censorship can occur when governmental approval is needed prior to publication. Oral speech, in contrast, is punishable only after communication has taken place. Censorship of the press is rarely upheld by the courts. When the *New York Times* began publishing top-secret documents on the Vietnam War, the Justice Department sought to censor release of further files. Even though the material was classified, the Supreme Court supported continued publication (*New York Times Co. v. United States*, 403 U.S. 713, 1971). Censorship is most likely to be tolerated, if it is tolerated at all, in a public-school environment.

The First Amendment also contains two clauses on religion, the free exercise clause and the establishment clause. The **free exercise clause** protects the freedom to worship as one sees fit, or not to worship at all. While people have the right to hold any religious belief no matter how offensive or harmful, the government may prevent the practice of the belief if a "compelling" need to do so can be demonstrated. For example, the Supreme Court allowed the government to ban the practice of polygamy for religious reasons (*Reynolds v. United States*, 1878) as well as requiring Amish employers to pay into the social security system despite religious objections (*United States v. Lee*, 1982). The **establishment clause** prohibits governments from supporting a particular religion. Examples include faculty-orchestrated prayer in public schools or a government grant to a private organization to purchase bibles. On the other hand, reasonable government *accommodation* of religion is constitutional (Schultz, Vile, and Deardorff, 2011, p. 78). In order to withstand an establishment clause challenge, the government's policy must have a secular (non-religious) purpose, must have a primary effect that neither advances nor inhibits religion, and must avoid excessive entanglement between the state and religion (*Lemon v. Kurtzman*, 1971). The **Lemon** tests were satisfied in a case where a city's Christmas display in a public park included a nativity scene because the display contained other symbols of the holiday like Santa Claus and thus merely celebrated a holiday in traditional fashion (*Lynch v. Donnelly*, 1984). Lower courts have experienced difficulty in applying the vague language of *Lemon* in concrete cases, with decisions of the Supreme Court being criticized for inconsistency. Confusion was deepened when the Supreme Court "abandoned Lemon" and instead adopted "an analysis focused on original meaning and history" but declined specifically to overrule *Lemon* itself (*Kennedy v. Bremerton School District*, 2022). This situation leaves courts without any coherent guidance on how to handle Establishment Clause cases in the future.

Second Amendment

The Second Amendment gives people the right to bear arms, and for a long time this right only limited the federal government. States and local governments frequently imposed restrictions on the possession and sale of guns. The Supreme Court reversed direction by ruling that the right to defend oneself was fundamental, making the Second Amendment applicable to state governments as well (*McDonald v. City of Chicago*, 2010). But this right is not absolute. Thus, when a court determines that a person constitutes a threat to the safety of others, the Second Amendment does not prevent disarming the individual at least on a temporary basis (*United States v. Rahimi*, 2024).

Fourth Amendment

The Fourth Amendment protects individuals from **unreasonable searches and seizures** by governments. A search is unreasonable when a person's **reasonable expectation of privacy** is violated (*Katz v. United States*, 1967). For example, the Supreme Court has ruled on multiple occasions that no such expectation arises in connection with aerial surveillance (*California v. Ciraolo*; *Dow Chemical Co. v. United States*, 1986) but not when government agents conduct searches using thermal-imaging technology (*Kyllo v. United States*, 2001), obtain cell tower location information from a mobile phone (*Carpenter v. United States*, 2018), or bring drug-sniffing dogs onto a suspect's front porch (*Florida v. Jardines*, 2013). A seizure involves the government taking control over a person or thing. Both searches and seizures require governmental involvement. There is no Fourth Amendment protection against private searches and seizures.

A valid warrant generally makes a search or seizure acceptable under the Fourth Amendment. Nonetheless, most searches and seizures are conducted without warrants, such as when a person gives consent or after a lawful arrest. A valid

search warrant is issued by a judicial officer and must be supported by probable cause, describe the place to be searched and the persons or things to be seized with particularity, and include the oath or affirmation by the government agent. Let's unpack these terms. **Probable cause** means sufficient information exists to lead a reasonable police officer to conclude that evidence of a crime can be found at a location. **Particularity** means enough detail is provided about what to search for and where to search for it. The **oath or affirmation** is the officer's sworn statement that the information is, to the best of the officer's knowledge and understanding, truthful and correct. A judicial officer, such as a magistrate, will determine if these requirements are met and either issue or refuse to issue the warrant. Unless these standards are fulfilled, evidence seized in violation of the Fourth Amendment—pursuant to the **exclusionary rule**—is inadmissible to prove the guilt of the individual whose rights were violated (*Mapp v. Ohio*, 1961; *Weeks v. United States*, 1914). There are exceptions to this rule. Under the **good faith exception**, evidence is admissible even if a warrant is later determined to be deficient so long as the officer acted upon the warrant with reasonable belief it was valid (*U.S. v. Leon*, 1984). Georgia, it should be noted, gives its citizens greater protection by not recognizing the good faith exception to the exclusionary rule (*Gary v. State*, 1992).

Fifth Amendment

The Fifth Amendment contains several important rights. The **privilege against self-incrimination** prevents an individual from being forced to testify if any statements could lead to his or her criminal prosecution. For example, a person could "plead the fifth" when called as a witness in a trial or a hearing, or when questioned by government agents while restrained from leaving (**custodial interrogation**). Indeed, the famous *Miranda* warnings are based primarily on the privilege against self-incrimination (*Miranda v. Arizona*, 1966). These four warnings (You have the right to remain silent. Anything you say can and will be used against you in a court of law. You have the right to an attorney. If you cannot afford an attorney, one will be provided for you) are required if, and only if, a suspect is interrogated while in custody. The warnings are not required if there is custody without interrogation or interrogation without custody. If the warnings are not delivered when required, any incriminating statements made by a suspect will be inadmissible at a subsequent trial. Under the **public safety exception**, however, these warnings do not have to be read when a threat exists to the public well-being (*New York v. Quarles*, 1984).

The **double jeopardy** clause prohibits multiple prosecutions for the same offense. Otherwise, a state could prosecute a criminal defendant over and over for the same crime in hopes of finally getting a conviction or of obtaining a harsher punishment than what was previously imposed. In most cases, the government has one opportunity to obtain a conviction. There are some exceptions to double jeopardy. For example, the government may retry a case when the first trial ended in a mistrial, such as a "hung jury" where the jury could not agree on a verdict. The state may also retry a case if a defendant is initially found guilty but the conviction is reversed on appeal since a reversal on appeal voids the first trial due to a legal error. The same act, however, can violate the laws of two states and lead to two prosecutions and punishments without violating double jeopardy (*Heath v. Alabama*, 1985). This could happen if a person stole a car in Alabama and drove it to Georgia. Alabama could prosecute for stealing the vehicle while Georgia could prosecute for possession of a stolen vehicle. There was one theft but two prosecutions. Each state and the federal government are considered "sovereigns" with the authority to enforce their laws under a concept known as **dual sovereignty**.

The Fifth Amendment additionally contains what is known as the **takings clause.** States, under the power of **eminent domain**, are allowed to confiscate private property from unwilling sellers. To be permissible, the takings clause requires that the property must be used for a **public** purpose and **just compensation** must be paid to the owner. The right to a grand jury is the final Fifth Amendment protection to be discussed. A **grand jury** is a group of people summoned by a government (state or federal) to consider evidence against a person charged with a crime. These juries do not convict individuals but determine whether enough evidence exists to conduct a trial. A government prosecutor presents its evidence to the grand jury in a private hearing. If the grand jury agrees that the accused likely committed the crime in question, an **indictment** (sometimes called a **true bill**) is issued against the accused. As previously noted, the requirement for a grand jury has not been incorporated. Thus, the Supreme Court has required use of grand juries only in federal felony crimes. States are under no constitutional obligation to provide grand juries in criminal prosecutions, although many have chosen to include such a requirement in their own constitutions.

Sixth Amendment

Most of the rights associated with the trial of a criminal defendant can be found in the Sixth Amendment. These include the right to counsel, the right to a speedy trial, the right to a public trial, the right to a jury trial, the right to confront the accuser, and the right to compulsory process. Concerning the **right to counsel**, there is usually no issue when the defendant is financially able to pay for a private attorney. The problem arises when an **indigent defendant**—one unable to pay for a lawyer—is accused of a crime. In this latter case, the rules vary depending on whether the crime is a felony or a misdemeanor. A **felony** is a crime punishable by a fine and/or a year or more in prison, while a **misdemeanor** is a crime punishable by a fine and/or up to twelve months in jail. The Supreme Court ruled that states must appoint counsel for indigent defendants in all felony cases (*Gideon v. Wainwright*, 1963), but only in misdemeanor cases when incarceration occurs (*Alabama v. Shelton*, 2002; *Argersinger v. Hamlin*, 1972; *Scott v. Illinois*, 1979). It is important to note that the right to counsel will sometimes apply in various pre-trial and post-trial procedures.

The Sixth Amendment provides no explanation about how quickly the right to a **speedy trial** must be scheduled. Delays are quite common between an arrest and a trial due to factors such as a psychiatric evaluation or scheduling conflict. There is no bright-line rule when a delay violates the Sixth Amendment. Rather, the Supreme Court considers four factors in making a determination: the length of the delay, the reason for the delay, the defendant's assertion of the right, and any negative impact to the accused because of the delay (*Barker v. Wingo*, 1972). Perhaps for greater clarity, the federal government and most states have enacted laws that define how quickly a trial should be scheduled. The **Federal Speedy Trial Act of 1974**, for example, requires that a trial for a federal crime should commence within 100 days of an arrest or receipt of a summons.

The right to a **public trial** was a response to the old practice of conducting trials behind closed doors in which a defendant could be tried, convicted, and sentenced without anyone knowing what happened. The goal of this provision is to ensure a fair trial by allowing spectators to observe that the process operates according to the law.

The **right to a jury trial** is one of America's treasured legal traditions. It is based on the belief that ordinary citizens are better at judging innocence or guilt than those with a stake in the outcome. Although the Sixth Amendment provides for this right in "all criminal prosecutions," the Supreme Court has ruled that the right attaches only when a defendant is charged with a "serious offense" in which a **potential punishment of more than six months imprisonment** is possible (*Baldwin v. New York*, 1970). The size of a jury in criminal cases varies depending on where the trial occurs. At the time of the Constitutional Convention, a jury customarily consisted of twelve people and criminal trials at the federal level continued the practice. It was not until 1968 that the right to a jury trial was incorporated against the states (*Duncan v. Louisiana*, 1968). Two years later, however, the Supreme Court ruled that criminal cases in state courts could contain as few as six jurors (*Williams v. Florida*, 1970). In order to convict, federal juries must be unanimous, but it was not until 2020 that the Supreme Court required unanimous verdicts in state criminal trials at least for "serious offenses" (*Ramos v. Louisiana*, 2020).

Defendants have the right to confront their accusers through the **confrontation clause** of the Sixth Amendment. This right is afforded so that cross-examination can occur allowing jurors to evaluate the reliability of witnesses. While a face-to-face confrontation is typical, the Supreme Court has relaxed the requirement in certain circumstances when in the best interest of a party, such as using a one-way closed-circuit television in a molestation case where the child is in one room while the defendant, judge, and jury observe from the courtroom (*Maryland v. Craig*, 1990).

The final aspect of the Sixth Amendment worth noting is the **right to compulsory process**. This gives a defendant the power to subpoena witnesses to testify. A **subpoena** is a summons by a court to appear and testify so that defendants have an opportunity to present their side of a case. The prosecution has a similar power of subpoena in order for its case to be fully heard as well.

Eighth Amendment

The Eighth Amendment is a single sentence, but it includes multiple provisions in protecting against excessive bail, excessive fines, and cruel and unusual punishment. Just recently (*Timbs v. Indiana*, 2019), all provisions have been incorporated against the states. Nonetheless, there is still no constitutional right to bail. The purpose of bail, if it is allowed, is to insure the appearance of a defendant at the trial. In determining whether bail is excessive, the courts consider such things as the seriousness of the crime, the risk of flight, and the community ties of the defendant.

The protection against **cruel and unusual punishment** has generated substantial case law. Punishments can be cruel and unusual in two different ways. One possibility would be a punishment that is barbaric or inhumane. Examples would be cutting the hand off of a convicted thief or poking the eyes out of a convicted "peeping Tom." On the other hand, the Court held that the Eighth Amendment is not violated when cities prevent homeless people from sleeping outside in public places even when shelter space is unavailable (*City of Grants Pass v. Johnson*, 2024). Punishments can also be cruel and unusual, even if they are not barbaric, if they are excessive or too severe for the crime. In many situations, the death penalty falls into this category. The Supreme Court has never ruled that the death penalty is cruel and unusual, but this punishment has been considered excessive for most crimes. For example, the Court has held that the imposition of the death penalty for the crime of rape would violate the Eighth Amendment (*Coker v. Georgia*, 1977; *Kennedy v. Louisiana*, 2008). Clearly, it would be unconstitutional to impose the death penalty for less serious crimes, such as theft or forgery. Today, there seems to be a narrow range of crimes for which the death penalty could be imposed. These include certain criminal homicides, treason, and air piracy. The debate over the appropriateness of imposing the death penalty has been longstanding and will no doubt continue into the foreseeable future.

Civil Liberties: Beyond the Bill of Rights
Fourteenth Amendment

After the Civil War, the Fourteenth Amendment was added to the Constitution in an effort to protect the rights of former slaves. It not only grants national *and* state citizenship to all persons born or naturalized in the United States, but it also contains three clauses intended to provide additional layers of protection: the privileges and immunities clause, the due process clause, and the equal protection clause. The **privileges and immunities clause** prohibits states from infringing upon the rights of U.S. citizens. The exact meaning of the words is unclear, but many hoped they would apply the provisions of the Bill of Rights to the states. The Supreme Court rejected this interpretation by distinguishing between national citizenship and state citizenship and holding that the privileges and immunities clause only protected rights of U.S. citizenship already listed in the Constitution, such as travel between the states (*Slaughterhouse Cases*, 1873). In other words, the clause in no way imposed new limitations on state authority.

The **due process clause** has, over time, proven a powerful tool in the hands of courts. The clause forbids states from depriving any person of life, liberty, or property without due process of law. It has been used in two different ways. Under **procedural due process**, courts examine whether the steps required by law and the Constitution have been followed when denying a person life, liberty, or property, such as the right to cross-examine witnesses or the opportunity to be represented by counsel. The greater the potential deprivation, the more elaborate the protective procedures must be. Under **substantive due process**, governments are prevented from interfering with fundamental rights even if proper legal procedures are followed. It is a highly controversial concept because judges have been accused of imposing their own values in determining what constitutes a fundamental right.

A well-known example of substantive due process involves abortion. In 1965, the Supreme Court reasoned a constitutional **right to privacy** exists through the Ninth Amendment that allows individuals access to contraceptives (*Griswold v. Connecticut*, 1965). More recently, the Supreme Court expanded the right of privacy by focusing on the word "liberty" in the due process clause of the Fourteenth Amendment. In *Roe v. Wade* (1973), a majority concluded: "This right of privacy . . . is broad enough to encompass a woman's decision whether or not to terminate her pregnancy." This decision, however, was overturned about 50 years later when states were permitted to regulate or even ban abortion entirely (*Dobbs v. Jackson Women's Health Organization*, 2022), and many states quickly enacted policies severely restricting access to abortion. The upshot is that some states will continue allowing abortion while others will make it almost impossible to acquire. Despite this decision, the right to privacy has been applied broadly to other areas of intimate familial matters, such as marriage, rearing children, and sexual orientation, once the door was opened through the due process clause.

To sum up, substantive due process focuses on what the state *intends* to do to a person, while procedural due process focuses on *how* the state intends to do it. Both, nonetheless, share a concern about ensuring fundamental fairness.

The final protection in the Fourteenth Amendment prohibits states from denying any person equal protection of the laws. In particular, the **equal protection clause** examines whether state governments have acted in a discriminatory fashion by treating **similarly situated groups** differently. Initially applied against allegations of racial discrimination, such as terminating segregation in public school systems (*Brown v. Board of Education*, 1954), the Supreme Court eventually allowed the clause to challenge discrimination more widely in areas like gender, age, and marital status.

Since the equal protection clause was adopted to safeguard the rights of newly freed slaves, the Supreme Court provides greater protection to racial groups than to claims of discrimination against other groups. The **strict scrutiny test** is used in cases involving race and later to national origin as well. Known as **suspect classifications**, the Court considers any unequal treatment in these two categories to be *presumed* unconstitutional unless a "compelling government interest" can be demonstrated justifying the unequal treatment. Racial discrimination was allowed to occur, for example, during World War II when Japanese Americans were detained in relocation centers (*Korematsu v. United States*, 1944). The Supreme Court agreed that the possibility of sabotage and espionage constituted compelling government interests supporting the detention even though German Americans were not treated similarly. The strict scrutiny test is also used when the alleged discrimination abridges fundamental rights—those rights expressly or implicitly granted by the Constitution. Voting and the right to travel between states are two such fundamental rights and, under the strict scrutiny test, are almost impossible for a state to abridge.

The Supreme Court uses the **rational basis test**, sometimes called the traditional test, in cases involving alleged discrimination outside of the two suspect classifications (*Dandridge v. Williams*, 1970). A state government has a much better chance of winning a lawsuit under this test than it does under the strict scrutiny test. Under the rational basis test, a law could be discriminatory and still be constitutional if a rational connection exists between what a government wants to accomplish (does it have a legitimate interest?) and how the state goes about accomplishing its interest (what was the means used?). Consider the case of Robert Murgia, a uniformed patrol officer, who was forced to retire at age 50 under state law (*Massachusetts Board of Retirement v. Murgia*, 1976). The state justified the mandatory retirement age because the physical abilities of individuals decline with age to the point where a police officer might not be able to adequately protect public safety at 50. Although Murgia tested physically capable of performing the job four months before his birthday, the Supreme Court ruled Massachusetts could reasonably conclude a typical person experiences physical decline at 50, making the means (mandatory retirement) permissible. In *Murgia*, the state had a rational way of protecting public safety even though a better means—such as physical tests of all police officers turning 50—could have been used. Unlike under strict scrutiny, laws under the rational basis test are *presumed* constitutional and given the benefit of doubt by courts.

The Supreme Court complicated analysis under the Equal Protection Clause by adding an intermediate level of scrutiny when discrimination is based either on gender or illegitimacy (children born out of wedlock). The reason is that these **quasi-suspect classifications** were not afforded enough protection under the rational basis test while the strict scrutiny went too far by presuming a law unconstitutional if impacting one of these groups. Under intermediate scrutiny, discrimination is permissible if the government is furthering an "important interest" in a way that is "substantially related" to its interest. Take the provision in the Military Selective Service Act that requires males to register for military service but not females (*Rostker v. Goldberg*, 1981). The Supreme Court upheld the law because the government had an important interest (to prepare for a possible military draft) and excluding women was substantially (not merely rationally) related to the interest because women are legally excluded from combat. The adoption of an intermediate level in equal protection has been criticized for creating unnecessary confusion, especially since the Supreme Court has not been consistent in how it has decided gender and illegitimacy cases itself.

Voting

Three constitutional amendments protect the right to vote. The **Fifteenth Amendment** was ratified in 1870. It forbids denying the right to vote based on "race, color, or previous condition of servitude." For a long time, nonetheless, states and local governments particularly in the South invented barriers that acted to prevent African Americans from voting, such as requiring literacy tests, without denying the right outright. The **Voting Rights Act of 1965** finally tackled the inventive ways developed to hinder racial minorities from voting. The two major provisions of the law outlawed the use of literacy tests and required approval by the U.S. Department of Justice before voting laws could be changed in areas where less than 50 percent of the non-white population had not registered to vote. The Supreme Court later voided the requirement of advance federal approval as contrary to the Tenth Amendment and no longer needed after almost forty years (*Shelby v. Holder*, 2013).

The **Nineteenth Amendment** was adopted in 1920 and granted women the right to vote. The amendment produced a significant impact on elections, with females voting at higher rates than males and with different issue priorities than men. The **Twenty-Sixth Amendment**, ratified in 1971, is closely connected to the Vietnam War. The voting age in most states at the time was 21 and much protest occurred over 18-year-olds risking their lives in battle without any opportunity to have a political voice. The amendment reduced the legal voting age to 18 across the country but, unlike suffrage for women, younger voters have never exercised the right with much frequency.

Civil Rights

The Supreme Court made it clear early on that the Fourteenth Amendment did not prevent discrimination by private citizens (*Civil Rights Cases*, 1883). According to the Court, the amendment is specifically addressed to state governments, not to private individuals, and this interpretation has never been overruled to this day. Hotels, restaurants, theaters, and other public spaces could constitutionally continue to discriminate on the basis of race despite the amendment. It took almost a century before another avenue was developed by which the federal government could curtail discriminatory behavior other than by the government.

The change in direction occurred in a case involving a motel in Atlanta that denied access to African Americans in defiance of the recently enacted Civil Rights Act of 1964 that forbade discrimination in public accommodations (*Heart of Atlanta Motel v. United States*, 1965). The motel owners argued that Congress had no authority over private business, but a unanimous Supreme Court ruled that the Constitution gave Congress the power to regulate business that crossed state borders (interstate commerce). Since the motel served people from out-of-state, it is considered an interstate business subject to congressional authority. In turning away individuals from outside the state, the motel would be deterring others from travelling across the country thereby hurting the national economy. This decision meant that almost no public accommodation could legally discriminate any longer.

Congress used the interstate commerce clause to end discrimination in a wide variety of areas beyond public accommodations:

- The **Equal Pay Act of 1963** prohibits unequal pay between men and women for comparable work.
- **Title VII of the Civil Rights Act of 1964** forbids employment discrimination for refusing to hire or promote on the basis of race, sex, religion, or national origin.
- The **Age Discrimination in Employment Act of 1967** protects workers forty and older from discriminatory actions.
- The **Civil Rights Act of 1968** prohibits discrimination in housing on the basis of race, sex, national origin, or religion.
- The **Americans with Disabilities Act of 1990** eliminates barriers to persons with disabilities in such areas as employment, education, and transportation.

Several civil rights statutes rely upon federal financial assistance as a way to reach private organizations and institutions. The acceptance of the money is deemed an agreement to accept its terms. **Title VI of the Civil Rights Act of 1964** bans racial discrimination in any program or activity receiving federal funding. For example, a private college that received a federal grant for scientific research would also be prevented from rejecting admission to students on the basis of race. **Title IX of the Education Amendments of 1972** prohibits sex discrimination by educational programs or activities that receive federal funding, including in athletics, housing, admission, and harassment. Similarly, **Section 504 of the Rehabilitation Act of 1973** bars federally funded programs from discriminating against an individual solely on the basis of a handicap.

These are but a few of the many civil rights laws enacted over the years. A controversial issue called **affirmative action** arose when Congress sought to compensate for past discrimination. It has taken a number of different forms such as hiring preferences, minority set-asides (a portion of a contract must be reserved for minority-owned businesses), and quotas (numerical targets for hiring, promoting, and admitting members of racial groups). Affirmative action coverage was extended to apply to women as well. The controversy over affirmative action centers around whether it constitutes **reverse discrimination** especially toward white males. It is difficult to know exactly when affirmative action is permissible because the Supreme Court has not followed a consistent path in handling these cases. It did, however, slam the door on using race-based criteria in college admissions as a violation of the Equal Protection Clause of the Fourteenth Amendment (*Fair Admissions, Inc. v. President and Fellows of Harvard College*, 2023). It remains possible, if not likely, the Supreme Court will curtail affirmative action across-the-board at a later date based on the same line of reasoning.

It Depends Scenario

Suppose Congress disagrees with a Supreme Court decision. Does Congress have the power to reverse that decision? Well, it all depends on the basis for the Court's ruling. If the ruling involves an interpretation of the Constitution, the answer is no. In *Texas v. Johnson,* the Court held that burning of the American flag is protected under the First Amendment. Congress attempted to override the decision by passing the Flag Protection Act of 1989, which made it a federal crime to desecrate the flag, but the Court voided the Act as a violation of the First Amendment (*United States v. Eichman*, 1990). Since Congress cannot override the Constitution, the Supreme Court prevailed in this conflict between the two branches. On the other hand, if the Court's decision involved the interpretation of a congressional statute, the answer is yes. In *Grove City College v. Bell*, the Court interpreted the Education Amendments of 1972 on sex discrimination to apply to private colleges if any of their students received federal loans even if the college itself took no federal money. The Supreme Court's decision was narrow by limiting the law only to areas of an institution which actually received the federal funds, but this interpretation of the law did not sit well with Congress. The Civil Rights Restoration Act was therefore enacted that made an entire institution subject to the 1972 amendments and not merely the area where funds were directed. Congress prevailed in this situation because its law did not transgress the Constitution.

Case Study: Civil Liberties for Native Americans

Native Americans enjoy the same freedoms, protections, and rights as anyone else in the United States. Yet many Native Americans are confronted by another tier of authority—their tribal governments. While state and federal governments must respect the civil liberties of Native Americans, tribal governments were not legally required to do so because (1) they are not part of the federal government and (2) selective incorporation only applies to states. Consequently, the basic rights and liberties of individual Native Americans had little or no protection in relation to their own tribal governments.

Congress enacted the **Indian Civil Rights Act of 1968** granting many of the freedoms and protections found in the Bill of Rights and the Fourteenth Amendment to tribal members. At least two noteworthy exceptions exist, however: the right to counsel in criminal cases and certain aspects of religious freedom. Remember that the Sixth Amendment requires appointed counsel for indigent (poor) defendants in all felony cases and many misdemeanor cases. The Indian Civil Rights Act provides a right to counsel, but only at the defendant's own expense (Reese, 1992, p. 37). In terms of religion, the Indian Civil Rights Act includes a free exercise provision but not one for establishment issues. This omission means that individual Native Americans are free to worship as they choose, but it also means that tribal governments can support a specific religion. In other words, there can be a tribal religion, but the tribe cannot coerce anyone into embracing that religion.

A controversial issue arose over the use of peyote, which is a hallucinogenic drug derived from a cactus, in religious rituals. The ceremonial use of peyote in the Native American Church has a long history, dating back about two centuries. Many states, nonetheless, began making the use of peyote illegal even in religious ceremonies. In dealing with this restriction on free exercise rights, the Supreme Court deviated from its prior decisions that employed the compelling interest test under which restrictions almost always were struck down as unconstitutional (*Sherbert v. Verner*, 1963; *Wisconsin v. Yoder*, 1972). For the first time in decades, the Supreme Court did not apply the compelling interest test by ruling that "a generally applicable and otherwise valid" state criminal law did not violate the free exercise clause (*Employment Division v. Smith*, 1990). Put simply, a law that did not target religion but applied to everyone (generally applicable) was acceptable under the First Amendment. Congress in the Religious Freedom Restoration Act of 1993 tried to force the Supreme Court to use the compelling interest test in all free exercise cases, but the Supreme Court held that the law violated separation of powers (*City of Boerne v. Flores*, 1997). A frustrated Congress amended the Act by limiting its coverage to the federal government, and the Supreme Court upheld the legislation with this narrowed scope (*Gonzales v. O Centro Espirita*, 546 U.S. 418, 2006). To sum up, the rights of Native Americans to practice their religion were cut back by revising long-established legal precedent.

Conclusion

The sojourn into the world of civil liberties and civil rights is done. You are now acquainted with many basic constitutional freedoms and at least a sampling of civil rights legislation. You had occasion to consider the interaction between Congress and the Supreme Court in the development of these rights and freedoms. You had the opportunity to evaluate the ebb and flow of civil liberties and civil rights as they were refined over time. Thus, you are now in position to understand how important these rights have been in protecting the nation's democracy. Two points should be emphasized in closing. First, this chapter is a survey, or a mere summary, of some critical freedoms and rights. There is so much more to learn. Second, the liberties and rights discussed in this chapter belong to you. These are your freedoms, your rights, your choices. Use them. Take care of them. Keep them safe.

Discussion Questions

1. Distinguish between civil liberties and civil rights.
2. Identify the constitutional right that you most treasure, and discuss why you feel so passionately about that particular right.
3. Concerning civil liberties, how would you change the Constitution? What would you add to it, or take from it, to make it more relevant and meaningful for you?
4. Discuss how a state might constitutionally take a criminal defendant to trial without first providing that defendant with a grand jury hearing.
5. How is it possible that a defendant in a state criminal trial could have rights that are not required by the U.S. Constitution?
6. Concerning the civil rights statutes explored in this chapter, identify and discuss any that you would modify or eliminate.

References

Americans with Disabilities Act of 1990, 42 U.S.C. §§ 12101–12213 (2006).

Black, H. C. (1968). *Black's law dictionary*. West Publishing Company.

Carr Center for Human Rights Policy, *2020 national poll on reimagining rights and responsibilities in the U.S.* Harvard Kennedy School. https://www.hks.harvard.edu/centers/carr/programs/reimagining-rights-responsibilities/2020-poll#:~:text=Americans%20express%20surprisingly%20strong%20support,affordable%20health%20care%20(89%25).

Civil Rights Restoration Act of 1987, 42 U.S.C § 2000d–4a (2006).

Epstein, L., & Walker, T. G. (2010). *Constitutional law for a changing America,* (7th Ed.). CQ Press.

Equal Pay Act of 1963, 29 U.S.C. § 206 (d) (2006).

Flag Protection Act of 1989, 18 U.S.C. § 700 (1989).

Indian Civil Rights Act of 1968, 25 U.S.C. §§ 1301–1303 (2006).

Kommers, D. P., Finn, J. E., & Jacobson, G. J. (2010). *American constitutional law: Liberty, community and the Bill of Rights,* (3rd Ed.). Rowan & Littlefield.

Reese, K. M. 1992. The Indian Civil Rights Act: Conflict between constitutional assimilation and tribal self-determination, *Southeastern Political Review 20*(91), 29–61.

Religious Freedom Restoration Act of 1993, 42 U.S.C. §§ 2000bb *et seq.* (2000).

Rush, G. E. (2003). *The dictionary of criminal justice.* Dushkin/McGraw-Hill.

Schultz, D., Vile, J. R., & Deardorff, M.D. (2011). *Constitutional law in contemporary America: Civil rights and liberties.* Oxford University Press.

Section 504 of the Rehabilitation Act of 1973. 29 U.S.C. §§ 701–796 (2006).

Stephens, O. H., Jr., and Scheb, J. M. II. (2008). *American constitutional law: Civil rights and liberties* (4th Ed.). Thomson Wadsworth.

Title VI of the Civil Rights Act of 1964, 42 U.S.C. §§ 2000d–2000d–7 (2006).

Title VII of the Civil Rights Act of 1964, 42 U.S.C. §§ 2000e–2000e–17 (2006).

Title VIII of the Civil Rights Act of 1968, 42 U.S.C. §§ 3601–3631 (2006).

Title IX of the Education Amendments of 1972, 20 U.S.C. §§ 1681–1688 (2006).

Voting Rights Act of 1965, 42 U.S.C. §§ 1973–1973gg–10 (2006).

Wasserman, G. (2004). *The basics of American politics,* (11th Ed.). Pearson Longman.

Court Cases

303 Creative LLC v. Elenis, 600 U.S. 570 (2023).

Alabama v. Shelton, 535 U.S. 654 (2002).

Argersinger v. Hamlin, 407 U.S. 25 (1972).

Baldwin v. New York, 399 U.S. 66 (1970).

Barker v. Wingo, 407 U.S. 514 (1972).

Brandenburg v. Ohio, 395 U.S. 444 (1969).

City of Boerne v. Flores, 521 U.S. 597 (1997).

City of Grants Pass v. Johnson, 603 U.S. ___ (2024).

Barron v. Baltimore, 7 Pet. 243 (1833).

Brown v. Board of Education, 347 U.S. 483 (1954).

California v. Ciraolo, 476 U.S. 207 (1986).

Carpenter v. United States, 585 U.S. 296 (2018).

Civil Rights Cases, 109 U.S. 3 (1883).

Cohen v. California, 403 U.S. 15 (1971).

Coker v. Georgia, 433 U.S. 584 (1977).

Dandridge v. Williams, 397 U.S. 471 (1970).

Dobbs v. Jackson Women's Health Organization, 597 U.S. 215 (2022).

Dow Chemical Co. v. United States, 476 U.S. 227 (1986).

Duncan v. Louisiana, 391 U.S. 145 (1968).

Employment Division v. Smith, 494 U.S. 872 (1990).

Fair Admissions, Inc. v. President and Fellows of Harvard College, 600 U.S. 181 (2023).

Florida v. Jardines, 569 U.S. 1 (2013).

Gary v. State, 262 GA. 573 (1992).

Gideon v. Wainwright, 372 U.S. 335 (1963).

Gitlow v. New York, 268 U.S. 652 (1925).

Gonzales v. O Centro Espirita, 546 U.S. 418 (2006).

Griswold v. Connecticut, 381 U.S. 479 (1965).

Grove City College v. Bell, 465 *U.S. 555* (1984).

Heart of Atlanta Motel v. United States, 379 U.S. 241 (1964)

Heath v. Alabama, 474 U.S. 82 (1985).

Hurtado v. California, 110 U.S. 516 (1884).

Katz v. United States, 389 U.S. 347 (1967).

Kennedy v. Bremerton School District, 597 U.S. 507 (2022).

Kennedy v. Louisiana, 554 U.S. 407 (2008).

Korematsu v. United States, 323 U.S. 214 (1944).

Kyllo v. United States, 533 U.S. 27 (2001).

Lemon v. Kurtzman, 403 U.S. 602 (1971).

Lynch v. Donnelly, 465 U.S. 668 (1984).

Mapp v. Ohio, 367 U.S. 643 (1961).

Maryland v. Craig, 497 U.S. 836 (1990).

Massachusetts Board of Retirement v. Murgia, 427 U.S. 307 (1976).

McDonald v. City of Chicago, 561 U.S. 742 (2010).

Miranda v. Arizona, 384 U.S. 436 (1966).

New York v. Quarles, 467 U.S. 649 (1984).

New York Times Co. v. United States, 403 U.S. 713 (1971).

Palko v. Connecticut, 302 U.S. 319 (1937).

Ramos v. Louisiana, 590 U.S. 83 (2020).

Reynolds v. United States, 98 U.S. 145 (1878).

Roe v. Wade, 410 U.S. 113 (1973).

Rostker v. Goldberg, 453 U.S. 57 (1981).

Schenck v. United States, 249 U.S. 47 (1919).

Scott v. Illinois, 440 U.S. 367 (1979).

Shelby v. Holder, 570 U.S. 529 (2013).

Sherbert v. Verner, 374 U.S. 398 (1963).

Slaughterhouse Cases, 83 U.S. 36 (1873).

Texas v. Johnson, 491 U.S. 397 (1989).

Timbs v. Indiana, 586 U.S. 146 (2019).

Tinker v. Des Moines Independent Community School District, 393 U.S. 503 (1969).

United States v. Brown, 381 U.S. 437 (1965).

United States v. Lee, 455 U.S. 252 (1982).

United States v. Leon, 468 U.S. 897 (1984).

United States v. Rahimi, 602 U.S. ___ (2024).

Weeks v. United States, 232 U.S. 383 (1914).

Williams v. Florida, 399 U.S. 78 (1970).

Wisconsin v. Yoder, 406 U.S. 205 (1972).

Public Policy

Joseph Gershtenson

Learning Objectives

After covering the topic of public policy, students should understand:
1. The meaning of public policy and types of public policy.
2. The major actors in public policy and the contexts in which those actors operate.
3. The policy tools and instruments used by the government.
4. Major theories of public policy.
5. The steps in the policymaking process.
6. The role of ethics and values in public policy.

Abstract

As a representative democracy, the government in the United States is supposed to serve the American people. The most basic way in which it does so is by acting, or not, on perceived public problems. These outputs of the political system are called public policy. The complex governmental apparatus in the U.S. has significant implications for policy, often making quick and unified action challenging. Furthermore, in addition to government officials, policymaking involves informal actors like interest groups, the public, and the media, and it takes place within an elaborate environment. Complexity also exists with the range of tools government uses to pursue policy aims, from threatening fines and incarceration for non-compliance to providing information in the hopes of encouraging desired behavior. Before determining what tools to use, decisions must be made about what issues to even tackle. This first stage of the policy process is followed by consideration of alternatives, picking a direction, putting the policy into effect, and assessing it. The nature of policymaking and resulting policy makes understanding it challenging. As a result, there are a variety of theoretical perspectives from scholars in the field that focus on the role of societal elites, interest groups, institutions, and other determinants of policy. Ultimately, this chapter aims to deepen awareness of, and appreciation for, the ways in which government actions that affect our lives come into being.

Introduction

While you may not think about it regularly, government decisions can have a profound effect on the lives of college students. You or someone you know likely receives financial assistance through federal work study, Pell Grants, or student loans. Such assistance may be necessary because of tuition rates and other fees which are determined by government. In addition, the number of credit hours you must complete to earn a degree, how credits can transfer across institutions, and specific courses you need to take are products of government decisions. Government policies can also influence your opportunities to participate in sports and what you can and cannot say to fellow students. The government even has a role in the snack you grab from a vending machine on your way to class—check out the nutrition facts.

All these ways in which the government shapes the experiences of college students are aspects of public policy. While there is no single accepted definition of public policy, we can think of it as "what public officials within government, and by extension the citizens they represent, choose to do or not to do about public problems" (Kraft & Furlong, 2021, p. 5). So, if we consider tuition costs and citizen knowledge about food they consume to be problems, government actions or lack thereof, related to these issues represent public policy.

Of course, public policy extends well beyond those things that directly affect the lives of college students and includes a huge array of things like the tax code, environmental regulation, assistance to the needy, interstate construction and maintenance, and trade with foreign countries. Arriving at policy decisions is a complex process that involves many actors. Each of the three branches of the federal government has a role, but so do state and local governments and informal actors such as interest groups and the public. Furthermore, there are myriad ways in which policy occurs such as the passage of laws, the creation of rules and regulations by the bureaucracy, the issuing of executive orders, and decisions of the courts. Understanding public policy is therefore challenging, but it is vital because policy is the central function of government.

The Policy Arena: Actors and Environment

As part of their efforts to guard against tyranny, the founders created a complex and fragmented governmental system. They divided powers of the federal government across three constitutionally independent branches and further divided power between the federal and state governments (see Chapters 2 and 3). This fragmentation has both advantages and disadvantages. It can be difficult to coordinate efforts and arrive at policy coherence. American politics can be subject to gridlock, and different governments can adopt varying and conflicting policies. On the other hand, obstacles to policymaking mean a certain degree of deliberation and consensus is often necessary to reach decisions. The political system also offers citizens and groups multiple access points to influence policy. Policymakers not only face a complex government apparatus, but they carry out their functions in an environment with multiple contexts.

Federalism

The distribution of power between the national government and state governments is an enshrined feature of the United States. The Constitution outlines this with its supremacy clause in Article VI and powers reserved to the states (and people) in the Ninth and Tenth Amendments. Together, however, these provisions offer rather minimal guidance for the nature of federalism and relations between the national and state governments have evolved considerably over the country's history. Whereas spheres of authority were originally relatively distinct, in a model referred to by Grodzins (1960) as layer cake federalism, the two levels of government have been more intertwined for most of the last century in a marble cake model.

Within the system of intergovernmental relations with overlapping authority, the general trend has been toward centralization. The national government provides considerable resources to the states and their constituent local governments, often with specific requirements on use of the funds as with categorical grants. Furthermore, the federal government creates mandates on state governments such as equal educational opportunities for individuals with disabilities and standards for air and water quality. At times, these mandates can be unfunded, creating significant burdens on state and local governments.

While expansion of the federal government means it is now involved in policy realms well beyond the more limited vision of the framers (centered around national defense and relations with other countries, regulating trade, and printing and issuing money), state and local governments still have considerable authority. They have primary responsibility for policies related to education, public health and safety, incorporating businesses, transportation (speed limits, driver's licenses, etc.) and more. They also have concurrent powers with the national government such as taxation and administering justice systems.

In recent decades, many officials have advocated increasing state powers. Supporters point to the flexibility of decentralization. States differ in their cultures (e.g., Elazar, 1984), history, size, economies, etc., and the wants and needs of constituents are not uniform across states. A greater role for states allows them to tailor policies to their residents. In addition, it may lead to more experimentation in policy and promote policy diffusion like witnessed with the Affordable Care Act reforming health care largely modeled on Massachusetts.

Of course, more policymaking authority for states also has potential pitfalls. There are some problems like air and water pollution that do not respect state borders. Some states, given discretion, may choose not to provide adequate protection of human rights or health standards. States also vary in their policy capacity, or ability to address issues, even if they would like to do so.

Separation of Powers with Checks and Balances

In addition to division of powers across the national and state governments, authority is fragmented within the national government. The Constitution creates three branches, the legislative, executive, and judicial, following Montesquieu's (1748/1899) thinking. Yet, the framers also gave each branch a stake in the others as a means to guard against tyranny. For example, while Congress may pass legislation, the president can veto measures. Like federalism, this design has important implications for policy.

Checks and balances complicates policymaking, requiring negotiation and cooperation to act. Most notably, initiating major policy through legislation means navigating congressional committees, forming majorities in both chambers of Congress (often a supermajority in the Senate given the possibility of filibusters), and getting presidential approval. Courts can then interpret laws and even use judicial review to rule measures unconstitutional. This process can help guard against capricious decisions and actions harming constituents. On the other hand, it can inhibit efforts to address public problems, stifling any action or allowing only for incremental change. This may be especially true under divided government.

In the national government, both the legislative and executive branches have considerable resources and expertise. Congress has a division of labor and specialization with the committee system and the president has a White House staff and the Executive Office of the President at their disposal in addition to the vast federal bureaucracy. Thus, both branches can generate policy proposals. In addition, the executive branch can have considerable leeway in implementing policy. Legislation often lacks specificity, allowing for bureaucratic discretion in carrying out law, and bureaucratic entities also have authority to make rules and regulations.

Other Policy Actors

Government officials have the primary responsibility for enacting and implementing public policy. Yet, they are not the only actors involved in policymaking. Officials, particularly those holding elected positions, must consider the wishes of their constituents. Thus, public opinion can be important. The public has a role in monitoring policy outcomes and providing feedback that can guide policy change. Public opinion can illustrate perceptions of public problems and offer ideas on policy direction. In particular, opinion plays a larger on issues that are more visible to people, about which they care more strongly, and on which attitudes are more stable over time. It is true that the public often has limited interest in, and knowledge of, policy questions. Nevertheless, there is evidence of broad policy responsiveness to public mood (Erikson, Wright, & McIver, 2010; Page & Shapiro, 1992). At the local level, public influence can be more direct and pronounced (Berry, Portney, & Thomson, 1993).

Much of what the public knows about politics comes from the media, be those traditional outlets such as cable or broadcast television news or from content on social media. Consequently, the media influences policy through the public. Media coverage can help dictate what issues are on the agenda and the ways they present stories can help steer public attitudes on issues. The media also report on government actions and keep policymakers accountable.

A third non-governmental actor in the policy arena is interest groups and non-profit organizations. These groups represent business interests, labor, professions, single issues such as abortion or guns, and a host of other topics. They are active in politics by lobbying policymakers directly, mobilizing members to pressure policymakers, working to influence public opinion, and participating in political campaigns. Like congressional committees, subcommittees, and bureaucratic agencies, interest groups are experts in their areas of concern. Many conduct research, issue reports and news releases, and convey information to policymakers more generally. The number of groups has exploded in the last 50 years (Nownes, 2023) and their role is undeniable, with some scholars portraying them as the very essence of American politics (e.g., Key, 1964). For more information on interest groups, see Chapter 5.

The Environment of Policymaking

Policy actors do not operate in a void. Rather, they are subject to a range of influences from the state of the economy to relative party power in institutions to the general public mood.

The Economy

The state of the economy directly affects economic policy, decisions on taxing, spending, and the money supply. For example, the government may refrain from major expansionary spending programs when inflation is high for fear of stoking even greater inflation. Economic conditions can place restraints on budget decisions more generally. This is especially true for state governments since, unlike the federal government, they have balanced budget requirements. Economic conditions can also affect other policy areas. Times of economic boom facilitate attention to other issues and problems such as the environment.

Institutions and Politics

As outlined above, the American governmental system is complicated and fragmented. Federalism and the separation of powers with checks and balances mean authority is spread across various actors and that responsibilities often overlap. This system means generating policy can be time consuming and confusing. While the institutional structure is relatively static, power in the structure is more dynamic. Especially in recent years, party control in the House and Senate has changed frequently and divided government has been the norm. At the same time, both the Democrats and Republicans have become more internally unified and more ideologically distinct from one another. Such polarization often exacerbates institutional obstacles to major policy initiatives and quick action.

Society and Culture

Demographic characteristics of the public also impact policy. The American public has been aging as birth rates decline and life expectancy increases. At the same time, the proportion of citizens who are non-Hispanic whites continues to decline. These and other changes can force greater attention to programs like Social Security or diversity, equity, and inclusion policies. Demographics intersect with political culture. The United States has a general commitment to a capitalist economy and individualism. Within this broad national culture, however, there are differences across states and locales (e.g., Elazar, 1984; Erikson, Wright, & McIver, 1994). Political values and public opinion are not identical in California and Mississippi or in Massachusetts and Texas. As a result, we witness variation in policies on issues like unhoused populations, labor unions, income taxes, and abortion.

Policy Tools and Instruments

Having defined public policy as what public officials within government choose to do or not to do about public problems, we must identify what the government can do about problems when it chooses to do something. Actions taken by the government in addressing issues are known as **policy instruments or tools**. The government has a wide array of tools it might use in attempting to put policies into place, to translate objectives into results. Understanding these tools is important precisely because the policy instrument used can significantly impact the success or failure of a policy initiative. For example, if the government wishes to improve public health outcomes by reducing smoking, it might launch a public information campaign about the dangers of smoking, it could require manufacturers to put additional warnings on cigarette packages, it could raise taxes on tobacco products, or it could outright ban the sale of cigarettes. While there is no universal agreement on how to categorize policy instruments, we can provide some guidance. It is also worth noting that the government often uses combinations of different policy instruments in tackling complex problems. Returning to efforts to curb smoking, rather than choosing a single instrument, the government could employ multiple tools, perhaps from each of the categories described below. A public information campaign highlighting the dangers of smoking would represent an information instrument. To complement the information campaign, the government could use command and control to require manufacturers to include new, more explicit, warning messages on cigarettes. Policymakers could finally employ economic instruments through increasing taxes on tobacco products.

Command and Control Instruments

One of the most visible and common tools the government uses is command and control or regulatory instruments. These are legal tools that typically require or prohibit specific behaviors or practices as with banning child pornography. Regulation includes laws passed by the legislature, executive orders, and rules adopted by bureaucratic agencies. All of these are legally binding, and non-compliance can bring punishment through fines or even imprisonment. Regulation can be inflexible and costly as an approach, but it does create clear and uniform standards and typically leads to elevated levels of compliance.

Economic Instruments

Economic instruments allow the government to influence behavior and reach policy goals through intervention in the economy and markets. The most obvious way the government does so is through taxing and spending. For example, to discourage consumption of high sugar drinks, the government could impose taxes on soda. Rather than specific products, taxing can target certain segments of the population, businesses, or activities. Entrance fees for national parks and toll roads both impose financial requirements on individuals accessing the parks or roads and are commonly referred to as user fees. The national income tax differentiates according to individuals' earned income and business taxes depend on how the businesses are structured. Combined with taxing, spending can promote transfers across individuals and groups in society. So, revenue from income taxes may help fund programs to assist the needy. Spending can also take the form of incentives. For example, the Inflation Reduction Act of 2022 provided tax credits as incentives for use of renewable energy. Finally, the government may allow the market to operate more freely to pursue policy objectives. One of the most notable examples of this is discussion of creating a cap-and-trade system that would create limits on greenhouse gas emissions but permit companies to sell allotments to one another.

Information Instruments

The final broad category of policy instruments involves the provision of information designed to educate and persuade. As part of efforts to decrease distracted driving, the government might contract with an advertising agency to develop a series of television commercials featuring compelling stories from family members of distracted driving victims. Information can also be used to encourage individuals to engage in certain behaviors. The United States Department of Agriculture created a food pyramid in 1992 and currently uses "MyPlate" to provide facts about different food groups and guidance on how much of each people should eat. In a similar vein, food labeling, a form of regulation, also aims at educating consumers. Appeals to the public, what Schnieder and Ingram (1990) call hortatory tools, can also be used to mobilize people to do things like provide assistance to families impacted by natural disasters or mass shootings.

Types of Public Policy

In making public policy, government officials employ tools or instruments described above to try to achieve desired objectives. In addition to instrument choice, considerations of policy include the nature or type of policies. The most widely used policy typology comes from Theodore Lowi (1964). Lowi proposed that types of government policy can be understood by considering how concentrated or diffuse costs and benefits are distributed. Doing so, Lowi arrived at three policy categories: **distributive**, **redistributive**, and **regulatory**. In a subsequent extension of his thinking, Lowi (1972) focused on how government coercion would be used and how likely coercion would be needed. This led him to introduce a fourth policy type, **constituent policy**. Using this typology helps thinking about policy in several ways. It assists analysis of the potential impacts and political feasibility of proposed policies, it provides insight into the different strategies governments employ to achieve various objectives, and it allows for more nuanced discussions about the role of government in society. At the same time, greater complexity of policy means that the government often adopts hybrid approaches that do not easily belong in a single category (Peters, 2021). More generally, like any typology, the distinctions between Lowi's categories of policies can be blurry at times, with real-world policies often having elements of more than one category and not being easily classified.

Distributive Policy

Distributive policies involve the allocation of resources or benefits to specific segments of the population or particular geographic areas. Thus, the benefits are narrowly targeted and there is typically little to no direct competition for the benefits. Meanwhile, the costs of distributive policies are spread widely, often across all of society. As a result, distributive policies tend to be less visible and controversial than other policy types (Ripley and Franklin, 1991). Some examples include infrastructure projects like highways, bridges, or dams, money to rural areas to support access to broadband internet, and subsidies for corn farming. Because members of Congress promote measures benefitting their constituents, distributive policies are also called pork barrel projects/spending by many.

Redistributive Policy

Unlike distributive policies, redistributive policies more directly and obviously have identifiable "winners" and "losers." That is to say, both the groups bearing the costs and those reaping the benefits are known and visible, and the groups are distinctive—benefits go to one group while another bears the costs. Since these types of policies are zero-sum, they are usually controversial and generate significant interest and efforts on both sides of the issue. Redistributive policies shift resources from one group to another, often with the aim of helping a group deemed to be at some type of societal disadvantage. So, for example, a progressive income tax (where the tax rate increases as taxable income increases) whose revenue is used to fund need-based programs like Medicaid or food assistance, is a redistributive policy based on economic status. Of course, this is a case where distinctions between types of government instruments and types of policies may oversimplify the actual situation. While a progressive income tax may have redistributive intent and effects, the policy itself involves regulatory tools (command and control instruments) and hence regulatory policy. After all, the tax code is a complicated set of provisions designed at least in part to influence individual and corporate behavior.

Regulatory Policy

As might be expected, regulatory policy is associated with the policy tool regulation. This category of policy contrasts with distributive policy by having costs narrowly targeted and benefits widely spread. The government uses regulatory policy most often in efforts to protect the public. So, rules and regulations dictating behavior "serve to keep conduct from transcending acceptable bounds" (Meier, 1993, p. 82). Embedded in this idea is the assumption that, left to their own devices, individuals and businesses may choose to behave in ways that harm others. For example, companies might wish to employ child labor or might release toxins into waterways to earn greater profits. Thus, regulatory policy typically shelters individuals from harm they might suffer from unrestrained capitalist practices.

Constituent Policy

The final category is constituent policy. Constituent policies center around creating, modifying, or maintaining governmental structures and procedures. This includes things such as changing election rules, creating new bureaucratic agencies, restructuring the committee system and committee jurisdiction, and the nature of citizen input in policy like the use of ballot initiatives. These policies can be especially important because of their impact on other policies. Quite simply, they can affect the relationships between policymakers and how they operate, thereby shaping the framework in which other policies are made and implemented (e.g., Spitzer, 1987).

Views of Public Policy: Influence and Analysis

Theories are mechanisms to promote understanding of complex phenomena. For public policy, theories provide frameworks to help account for how governments make decisions, why they choose certain policies, how they implement programs, and how they evaluate outcomes. In doing so, theories typically involve assumptions and derive expectations about how politics, including public policy, operates based on the assumptions. This invariably involves some simplification of complicated processes in the real world, but it assists discussions of policy and can promote meaningful insights. There are many policy theories of which I outline four general approaches: **elitism** and **sub-governments**, **groups** and **advocacy coalitions**, **institutionalism** and **rational choice**, and **bounded rationality** and **incrementalism**.

Elitism and Sub-Governments

Elitism, as a theory of public policy, posits that a small group of individuals, by virtue of their power, wealth, and/or expertise, wields disproportionate influence over policy-making processes and outcomes. Elitist ideas emerged in classical political thought, including Plato advocating for rule by enlightened kings. In the context of American politics, sociologist C. Wright Mills (1956) suggested that decisions were driven by the overlapping interests of people in dominant positions in three institutions, the military, major corporations, and government. Mills argued that the elites might not consciously recognize their positions and collude to operate in counter-democratic fashion. Nevertheless, many elitist scholars maintain that policymaking is not a neutral process reflecting the will of the majority, but rather a mechanism through which elites maintain and exercise their power. Elite preferences differ from those of the public at large, and policy reflects the values and preferences of elites (e.g., Dye and Zeigler, 2009; Gilens and Page, 2014). As Dye (2001) depicts, policymaking is primarily a top-down process in which special-interest groups, think tanks, political campaign contributors, special-interest groups, lobbyists, law firms, and other entities permit elites to dominate policy and allow them to shape mass opinion on policy questions more than masses shape elite opinion.

In addition to elites shaping public opinion, there are simply many issues about which the public cares and knows little. This facilitates elite dominance of policymaking. Technical issues that require significant expertise and specialization are especially likely to illustrate this pattern. On such issues, policymaking may occur through the cooperation of congressional (sub)committees, executive branch agencies, and interest groups. This triumvirate of actors has been called subgovernments (e.g., Lowi, 1979) and **iron triangles** (e.g. Adams, 1981). In this arrangement, each actor has a stake in the policy and gains from cooperation. For example, consider the sugar industry. Sugar farmers/producers, represented by groups such as the American Sugar Alliance might advocate for industry support. One common mechanism would be a commodity support program that maintains a minimum price for sugar. In fact, the U.S. initiated this policy beginning with the 1981 farm bill. Members of both the House and Senate Agriculture Committees have continued to protect these supports, likely understanding that they benefit some constituents (those in the industry) and can help gain financial backing for election campaigns. The sugar program is administered by the U.S. Department of Agriculture. Like members of Congress, bureaucratic officials gain outside support for their agency, thereby helping protect its budget and influence. Issue networks are similar to iron triangles but can involve more conflict between actors and be more transitory (e.g., Heclo, 1978). For more on iron triangles, see Chapter 5.

Groups and Advocacy Coalitions

Group theory, as its name implies, focuses on the role of organized groups in public policy. However, scholars in this tradition depart from the view of interest group involvement in subgovernments, instead viewing politics as a struggle between various groups that seek to influence policy by providing input to policymakers. Groups employ lobbyists to directly communicate with government officials, they mobilize their members to contact policymakers, they work to influence public opinion, and they are involved in political campaigns. While the groups may not represent majority preferences, as indicated by the common reference to "special" interest groups, group theorists typically envision multiple groups active on any issue that have differing perspectives and desires. Thus, no group tends to be dominant. Of course, not all groups are equally influential since they vary in financial resources, their numbers of members, their relationships with other groups, and other factors (Baumgartner and Jones, 2009). Though groups countering one another on issues are not necessarily equally powerful and influential.

Like earlier group theory, the advocacy coalition framework (ACF) focuses on the interactions of actors involved in various issue areas. The issue areas are known as policy subsystems (Jenkins-Smith et al., 2014). Within the subsystems, advocacy coalitions composed of policy actors that share ideals and preferences about government policy work together in attempting to steer policy (Sabatier & Weible, 2007). So, in thinking about water projects like the building of a new dam, we might witness an environmental protection coalition with actors such as the Sierra Club, governmental wildlife management agencies, and environmentally-minded members of Congress pitted against a pro-development coalition of land developers, local public officials, and business-oriented committees in the national and state governments. ACF envisions such coalitions as relatively stable, and its advocates devote special attention to policy change as subsystems experience external and internal learning.

Institutionalism and Rational Choice

In the earlier section on policy actors, I discussed the structure of American government including the separation of the national government into three branches with checks and balances. Institutionalism focuses on such governmental structures or institutions. The approach posits that institutions are critical in shaping policy outcomes, that their legal authority, their rules, and their behavioral norms all influence decision-making processes and outcomes. In doing so, institutions are not simply objective arbiters of political conflict. Instead, they are inherently important actors themselves, and their structures and behaviors are not neutral (March and Olsen, 1984).

Early institutionalism was legalistic and descriptive in nature (Peters, 2019). However, new institutionalism expanded conceptions of institutions to include interactions between organizations and how organizations promote behavior in accordance with internal norms (March and Olsen, 1984). Thus, for example, in considering the U.S. Senate and policymaking, we would recognize both its relationship with the House of Representatives and the president, the existence of chamber rules such as the filibuster, and norms of behavior like individual prerogatives.

While often regarded as its own theoretical perspective, rational choice shares institutionalism's focus on institutions, particularly in how institutions provide information, and establish structure and incentives for strategic behavior. This approach is called rational choice because it has roots in economics and the idea that individuals are primarily self-interested and act rationally to maximize their utility (think maximizing benefits versus costs) (Shepsle, 1989). Rational choice's application to public policy emphasizes deriving expectations about policymakers' actions based on their priorities such as reelection or achieving policy aims. It is also helpful for analyzing reactions to policies such as effects on smoking rates with increased taxes on cigarettes.

Bounded Rationality and Incrementalism

One of the critiques of rational choice theory is that it involves unrealistic expectations and assumptions about information that actors possess and their cognitive limitations. Herbert Simon (1957) introduced the notion of bounded rationality to address this, arguing that individuals engage in rational decision making, but do so facing constraints. Constraints mean that policymakers often engage in satisficing behavior rather than maximization (e.g., Gigerenzer & Selten, 2002). In other words, policymakers typically are unable to analyze completely and fully all possible policy actions and do the best they can under the circumstances.

In this view, policymakers "muddle through" as they formulate policy, typically comparing a limited number of alternatives that differ only marginally from existing policies (Lindblom, 1959). In addition to bounded rationality, institutional and political constraints often promote incrementalism. American government has multiple veto points and negotiations between the two parties, especially under divided government, create barriers to quick action and major change (though occasional instances of this do occur as discussed by Baumgartner and Jones, 1993). Thus, for example, annual budget proposals typically use the previous year's allocations as their starting point and involve only slight changes (Wildavsky, 1964). In a related vein, the garbage can model of Cohen, March, and Olsen (1972), depicts decision-making as organized anarchy. In this model, policy problems, solutions, and participants operate largely independently, being tossed into the garbage can with policy choices made being rather unpredictable.

The Policymaking Process

The discussion above reveals complexity in policymaking actors and the environment in which they operate, an array of instruments governments use for pursuing policy aims, different types of policies, and multiple perspectives on how best to understand policymaking. This indicates that policymaking is a dynamic and complicated process that involves several steps as officials seek to identify, analyze, and address public problems. While there is no uniform agreement on the steps in the policymaking process, a common approach is to portray the process as a cycle involving five distinct but interconnected stages (e.g., Anderson, Moyer, and Chichirau, 2023): problem identification and agenda setting, formulation, adoption, implementation, evaluation. Figure 12.1 depicts this model. The policy process model provides a framework for understanding activities involved in policymaking and the flow of such activities. At the same time, it is important to note that policymaking is not always as linear as the model suggests—stages may be skipped, an earlier stage may be revisited at some later stage, and policymaking in general is never ending.

Figure 12.1: The Stages of the Policy Process

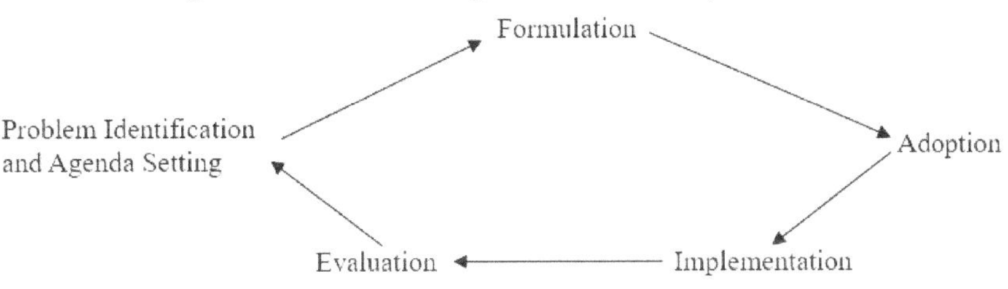

Problem Identification and Agenda Setting

The policy process begins with problem identification and **agenda setting**, getting a commitment to examining an issue and considering ways to tackle it. In modern societies, there are numerous conditions that can constitute public problems. A very abbreviated list could include climate change, gun violence, immigration, drug addiction, mental health, crime, and unemployment. The initial stage in policymaking involves determining which issues deserve attention, which the government will seek to address (Cobb and Elder, 1972).

Assuming that an issue is to get attention, the problem identification aspect of this stage includes defining and **framing** the problem. Consider undocumented immigration for example. There may be agreement that it is a problem, but what exactly is the problem and what are its causes? The answers to these questions necessarily involve values and choices about language and images. That is to say, the process is inherently political rather than neutral and objective, and how problems are defined carries important consequences for policy (Kingdon, 1995). Returning to undocumented immigration, the problem might be framed in terms of security and health concerns such as immigrants bringing transmissible diseases with them or joining gangs and committing violent crime. Alternatively, it might be framed in terms of poor economic conditions and lack of opportunities in home countries. These differing conceptualizations of the problem would point to differing policy approaches, enhanced border security with the first problem definition and increased foreign aid with the second.

Regardless of how a problem is defined, there are no guarantees that it makes it on the policy agenda. Competition to make it on the agenda is fierce and many problems may be overlooked as a result. Earning a place on the agenda depends on several factors, including public opinion, interest group activities, media coverage, efforts by public officials, and crises (Kingdon, 1995). Ultimately, it requires a confluence of activities for an issue to rise to a level where the government is likely to act. In one of the most influential works on agenda setting, Kingdon (1995) posits that the problem stream, policy stream, and political stream need to converge for policy windows to open. The problem stream refers to information regarding an issue including things like investigative journalism stories or think tank or governmental reports. In addition, "focusing events" such as crises like a nuclear plant meltdown can promote visibility and elevate an issue (Birkland, 1998). The policy stream is about ideas to address the issue, alternative policy approaches and proposals. As the name suggests, the political stream refers to public opinion and the political climate. In other words, does the public support action on an issue and is there interest among policymakers.

Policy Formulation

Once an issue is on the agenda, policy formulation begins. This stage involves developing potential solutions to the identified problem. Some alternative approaches will already have been forwarded as part of the policy stream and will now be more carefully analyzed along with additional possible actions. Interest groups, think tanks, and government officials develop proposals. Actors suggesting policies and policymakers considering them apply multiple criteria in assessing proposals, including the likelihood that the policy will achieve its objectives, the economic costs and benefits, support from the public and public officials, and the ability of the government to carry out the policy (Sidney, 2007). A contemporary issue that policymakers understand may need to be addressed in artificial intelligence (AI). AI's presence and influence has exploded in recent years and it is likely to continue having significant societal impact in the future. Among other consequences, AI may lead to workforce displacement and/or transformation in the nature of many jobs, and create new national security concerns. Thus, policymakers may face questions of how to regulate new and emerging technologies and ownership of companies developing and distributing the technology.

Policy Adoption

The adoption stage is where proposed policies are debated, refined, and ultimately accepted or rejected. It concludes with action being taken by legal authorities such as Congress passing legislation or a bureaucratic agency creating a rule. The adoption process is mostly political and often involves negotiations and compromises to generate necessary support. Some policy process models refer to this stage as policy legitimation. This terminology captures the idea that formal choice of policy actions, while important, is not the sole element. Instead, policymakers must consider legitimacy regarding consistency with existing laws and the Constitution, alignment with overarching political culture, and popular sentiment (Kraft and Furlong, 2021).

Policy Implementation

Implementation is the stage where adopted policies are put into practice, where the actual activity by designated actors like bureaucratic agencies takes place. This involves allocating necessary resources, developing procedures and guidelines, and enforcing the new policy (Pressman and Wildavsky, 1973). For example, consider the scenario of Congress passing legislation to create universal healthcare. Adopting the policy through law does not magically make it occur.

Implementation is the process of taking the law and figuring out a myriad of things such as how individuals enroll in the system, guidelines regarding what doctors they can see (e.g., would they need to see a general practice doctor before visiting specialists), how doctors are chosen, and how the system is financed. Effective implementation requires coordination among various government agencies and faces challenges like resource constraints, resistance from those affected by the policy, and administrative capacity.

Policy Evaluation

Debating various policy proposals, adopting a policy, and implementing it, does not automatically mean the targeted problem will be solved. The final stage in the policy process then is evaluation, where the effects and outcomes of the implemented policy are assessed. This involves collecting data on policy outcomes, using accepted criteria to analyze the policy, and identifying areas for improvement or modification (Vedung, 1997). Among the most common criteria for evaluation are effectiveness, efficiency, and equity. Effectiveness involves assessing if the policy accomplished its intended aims. Limited government resources and accountability to the public makes efficiency an important consideration. Efficiency compares the costs and benefits of the policy. Equity looks at not just the overall costs and benefits, but how each of those are distributed across different groups.

Ideally, evaluation has practical applications with the results evaluations informing policymakers. Thus, policymakers may decide to end a policy, to expand on it, or to try a modified approach. It is in this way that the policy process is cyclical in nature and most policymaking entails revising existing policy (Carter, 2012). Hopefully, in the quest to fulfill its function of addressing social problems, this process allows the government to be more successful.

Non-Linear Policymaking

As noted, policymaking is often cyclical. More generally, the policy process is not as neat and simple as the model of the five stages may suggest. Sometimes stages may be very abbreviated or skipped altogether. Similarly, stages may proceed simultaneously or with significant overlap, or, policymakers may return to an earlier stage prior to moving forward. To help illustrate ways in which the process can be non-linear, one can consider a couple examples. First, take the case of policies to address drug addiction. Assume the government used information instruments in the form of public education campaigns through social media on addiction support services. However, in evaluating the program, officials discovered that the policy was ineffective for men over the age of 40. This finding, then, led policymakers to reconsider the program, redefining the problem and formulating additional/alternative actions to target older men, perhaps through television advertising during sporting events.

As a second example, consider the case of energy policy and government regulation of fossil fuel energy, specifically regulations on geographic areas open to oil and gas exploration. A change in central actors in policymaking might lead to policy change that did not follow the five stages. For example, an incoming president may have campaigned on promoting oil and gas production. On entering office, the issue could already be on the policy agenda by virtue of the new president's election victory, even if it was not actively discussed among other policy actors. Policy formulation might also essentially be skipped with movement directly to policy adoption in the form of an executive order to open new federal lands to exploration.

Ethics, Values, and Public Policy

The introduction to this chapter suggested that you or someone you know probably gets financial aid for your education through federal work study, Pell Grants, or student loans. It is easy to think of such policies strictly in economic terms. However, economic assistance for higher education also has moral or ethical aspects and involves consideration of values. More generally, public policy, or what the government does or does not do about perceived public problems inherently involves judgments about social values and priorities and how to allocate limited resources. Furthermore, assessing public policy often includes attention to equity and other ethical issues.

Ethical Frameworks

Attention to ethics in public policy derives from differing political philosophers and traditions. For example, utilitarianism as developed by scholars such as Bentham and Mill, envisions maximizing overall/aggregate societal welfare as policy's ultimate aim. Examining policy through this lens tends to emphasize cost-benefit analyses and can result in subjugating individual rights (e.g., Sandel, 2010). For example, utilitarianism might lead policymakers to undertake infrastructure projects such as highway construction that require displacement of individuals living in the proposed highway path.

A second influential tradition reflects Kant's focus on absolute moral necessities, his moral imperative. The moral imperative suggests that all individuals should be guided by pure reason and should act in accordance with principles they believe should be universal law. Thus, for example, policies should always respect basic human rights. Advocates of universal healthcare access might rely on this perspective, arguing that all individuals, regardless of their economic status, have a fundamental right to basic medical care.

A third major tradition emerges from Rawls's veil of ignorance idea. The veil of ignorance suggests that people should consider policy without regard to their societal position, including their wealth, power, or abilities. This approach emphasizes an unbiased and impartial assessment of justice. As such, it has had significant influence on social policy (e.g. Sen, 2009). Like the Kantian tradition, policymaking guided by the veil of ignorance could likely lead to universal healthcare access. However, the policy outcome would not be due to regarding medical care as a basic human right, but by individuals imagining what it would be like if they were to be among society's least advantaged and not having healthcare as a result.

Ethical Principles

In addition to overarching philosophical approaches to ethics in public policy, there are several more specific ethical principles to consider in policy development and analysis. These include, among others, equity and fairness, accountability, transparency, prevention of harm, and respect for autonomy. Transparency means that the processes by which policies are developed, considered, and selected are open, that the public can see and know about them. Accountability involves monitoring implementation of policies to ensure they are carried out as intended. It also involves evaluating policy effects and outcomes. Prevention of harm captures the idea that government action should minimize potential risks and negative effects to individuals. In essence, it suggests that individuals' liberties be infringed upon only when necessary to prevent harm to others. Respect for autonomy similarly emphasizes the individual control over their own lives and suggests that policy should treat individuals capable of self-determination and permit individual choice provided it is not at the expense of others. Finally, among this non-exhaustive list of ethical principles, is equity. As discussed earlier, equity is often used as a criterion for assessing policy proposals. It involves considerations of how policies might affect different groups of people and typically encourages efforts to reduce inequalities.

Challenges and Tradeoffs

As one might suspect, the different ethical frameworks and the multiple ethical principles are not always perfectly compatible. As a result, policymakers consistently face challenges reconciling and prioritizing values. They are often forced to weigh individual liberties against promoting equity or make other difficult decisions that involve tradeoffs. Furthermore, policymakers' personal beliefs, ideological orientations, and political considerations all may influence the approaches they deem most appropriate. Two examples help illustrate these dilemmas. First, consider the case of climate change. Policymakers have an array of policies they might adopt to address this. As one among these, they might propose increasing minimum fuel efficiency (miles per gallon) standards for gasoline-powered vehicles. Such a policy might adhere to utilitarian ideals of overall social benefit. However, it can simultaneously inhibit personal choice by consumers if it leads to dramatic decreases in the production of trucks and large SUVs. It could also exacerbate inequalities if vehicle prices rose and individuals with lower incomes became even less able to purchase cars.

Finally, let us return to the issue of governmental support for higher education. The government has supported higher education through grants, work opportunities, and other financial aid. Nevertheless, education costs have continued to rise, outpacing inflation on most other goods and services. Consequently, recent decades have witnessed increases in student loans and student debt. In some cases, debt accrued as a student cripples individuals after they graduate. Motivated at least in part by this, some policymakers, including former President Biden, have made efforts to forgive some student loans. Doing so would certainly benefit those having their loans forgiven. Because of the demographics of individuals with greater debt, loan cancellation could promote economic equity—Black and Latino borrowers would likely have more debt forgiven. More generally, loan forgiveness could potentially stimulate the economy and result in spending and growth exceeding costs to the government in cancelling the debt. However, there are competing arguments as well. While forgiveness could promote economic equity, it could be regarded as unfair to those who have made their loan payments. In other words, it could be construed as punishing individuals who acted most responsibly. Furthermore, the costs for such a policy would presumably fall broadly on the shoulders of taxpayers, including those who never attended college themselves and don't have children or other family members who would have debt forgiven.

Discussion Questions

1. Should there be a greater role for the public in policymaking? Does it depend on the nature of the issue in question, on the level of government responsible for the policy, on other factors? If the public

role is to be increased, how might we amplify the quantity and quality of public input?

2. Pick two of the theories that you feel best explain current federal policy regarding guns. Very briefly explain the theories (in your own words, don't just quote from the textbook) and how you think they explain current policy.

3. Consider the issue/program of free and reduced-price meals in public K-12 schools. What actors might be involved in an issue network for this issue? How about actors in advocacy coalitions for and against expansion of the program? Identify actors and explain why you think they would be involved.

4. Visit the websites of 3-4 media outlets such as CNN.com (CNN), Foxnews.com (Fox News), nytimes.com (*New York Times*), wsj.com (*Wall Street Journal*), etc. Looking at stories on the sites, what public policy issues seem to be on the policy agenda right now? Explain your answer and explain how you think the issues got on the agenda.

5. Assume you are concerned about climate change and would like to see the U.S. move toward greater reliance on renewable energy sources. What policy tools/instruments do you think would be most effective in achieving your policy goals and why?

6. Public policy change often occurs in small steps, with only small alterations at the edges of current policy. Do you think this is a sensible way to act on public problems? Why or why not? Are there issues/ problems or conditions when it is more sensible than others? Explain.

7. Assume that you have some concerns about social media and mental health of younger individuals in the United States. Consult sources as necessary to answer the following questions: How might you define the problem? What is the scope of the problem? Are there any differences in the problem across groups/characteristics of individuals? When did the problem arise? What are the causes of the problem?

8. How do policymakers consider and weigh competing values and priorities that have ethical implications? Consider the issue of crime policies such as sex offender laws, minimum sentences for nonviolent drug offenses, and treatment of juveniles as adults.

9. How can public policies be used to promote equal opportunity and reduce disparities in income, wealth, health, and education? What are the challenges and limitations of using public policy to address social inequality?

References

Adams, G. (1981). *The iron triangle: The politics of defense contracting.* Council on Economic Priorities.

Anderson, J. E., Moyer, J., & Chichirau, G. (2023). *Public policymaking: An introduction* (9th ed.). Cengage.

Baumgartner, F. R., & Jones, B. D. (1993). *Agendas and instability in American politics.* University of Chicago Press.

Baumgartner, F. R., & Jones, B. D. (2009). *Lobbying and policy change: Who wins, who loses, and why.* University of Chicago Press.

Berry, J. M., Portney, K. E., & Thomson, K. (1993). *The rebirth of urban democracy.* Brookings Institution.

Birkland, T. A. (1998). Focusing events, mobilization, and agenda setting. *Journal of Public Policy, 18*(1), 53–74.

Carter, P. (2012). Policy as palimpsest. *Policy & Politics, 40*(3), 423–443.

Cobb, R. W., & Elder, C. D. (1972). *Participation in American politics: The dynamics of agenda-building.* Allyn and Bacon.

Dye, T. R. (2001). *Top down policymaking.* Chatham House Publishers.

Dye, T. R., & Zeigler, H. (2009). *The irony of democracy: An uncommon introduction to American politics* (14th ed.). Wadsworth Cengage Learning.

Elazar, D. J. (1984). *American federalism: A view from the states* (3rd ed). Harper and Row.

Erikson, R. S., Wright, G. C., & McIver, J. P. (2010). *Statehouse democracy: Public opinion and policy in the American states.* Cambridge University Press.

Gigerenzer, G., & Selten, R. (Eds.). (2002). *Bounded rationality: The adaptive toolbox.* MIT press.

Gilens, M., & Page, B. I. (2014). Testing theories of American politics: Elites, interest groups, and average citizens. *Perspectives on Politics, 12*(3), 564–581.

Grodzins, M. (1960). The federal system. In *Report of the president's commission on national goals: Administered by the American assembly.* The American Assembly.

Heclo, H. (1978). Issue networks and the executive establishment. In A. King (Ed.), *The new American political system* (pp. 87–124). American Enterprise Institute.

Jenkins-Smith, H. C., Nohrstedt, D., Weible, C. M., & Sabatier, P. A. (2014). The advocacy coalition framework: Foundations, evolution, and ongoing research. In P. A. Sabatier & C. M. Weible (Eds.), *Theories of the policy process* (3rd ed., pp. 183–223). Westview Press.

Key, V. O., Jr. (1964). *Politics, parties, and pressure groups.* Crowell.

Kingdon, J. W. (1995). *Agendas, alternatives, and public policies* (2nd ed.). HarperCollins.

Kraft, S. E., & Furlong, S. R. (2021). *Public policy: Politics, analysis, and alternatives* (7th ed.). CQ Press.

Lindblom, C. E. (1959). The science of "muddling through". *Public Administration Review, 19*(2), 79–88.

Lowi, T. J. (1964). American business, public policy, case-studies, and political theory. *World Politics, 16*(4), 677–715.

Lowi, T. J. (1969). *The end of liberalism.* Norton.

Lowi, T. J. (1972). Four systems of policy, politics, and choice. *Public Administration Review, 32*(4), 298–310.

March, J. G., & Olsen, J. P. (1984). The new institutionalism: Organizational factors in political life. *American Political Science Review, 78*(3), 734–749.

Mills, C. W. (1956). *The power elite.* Oxford University Press.

Montesquieu (1748/1899). *The spirit of laws* (T. Nugent, Trans.). The Colonial Press.

Nownes, A. J. (2023). *Interest groups in American politics: Pressure and power* (3rd ed.). Routledge.

Page, B., & Shapiro, R. Y. (1992). *The rational public: Fifty years of trends in Americans' policy preferences.* University of Chicago Press.

Peters, B. G. (2019). *Institutional theory in political science: The new institutionalism* (4th ed.). Edward Elgar Publishing.

Peters, B. G. (2021). *Advanced introduction to public policy* (2nd ed.). Edward Elgar Publishing.

Pressman, J. L., & Wildavsky, A. (1973). *Implementation: How great expectations in Washington are dashed in Oakland.* University of California Press.

Ripley, R. B., & Franklin, G. A. (1991). *Congress, the bureaucracy, and public policy.* Brooks/Cole Publishing Company.

Sabatier, P. A., & Weible, C. M. (2007). The advocacy coalition framework: Innovations and clarifications. In P.A. Sabatier (Ed.), *Theories of the policy process* (2nd ed., pp. 189–220). Westview Press.

Schneider, A., & Ingram, H. (1990). Behavioral assumptions of policy tools. *Journal of Politics, 52*(2), 510–529.

Shepsle, K. A. (1989). Studying institutions: Some lessons from the rational choice approach. *Journal of Theoretical Politics, 1*(2), 131–147.

Sidney, M. S. (2007). Policy formulation: Design and tools. In F. Fischer, G. J. Miller, & M. S. Sidney (Eds.), *Handbook of public policy analysis: Theory, politics, and methods* (pp. 79–87). CRC Press.

Simon, H. A. (1957). *Models of man: Social and rational.* Wiley.

Spitzer, R. J. (1987). Promoting policy theory: Revising the arenas of power. *Policy Studies Journal, 15*(4), 675–689.

Vedung, E. (1997). *Public policy and program evaluation.* Transaction Publishers.

Wildavsky, A. (1964). *The politics of the budgetary process.* Little, Brown.

State and Local Government

Ross C. Alexander

Learning Objectives

After covering the topic of state and local government, students should understand:

1. The structure, functioning, and common components of state governments in the U.S.
2. The structure and functioning of the various types of local governments in the U.S.
3. The degree to which state and local government affects the lives of citizens on a daily basis.
4. How states and local governments experience continually evolving and difficult funding pressures and priorities.
5.

Abstract

There are over 89,000 (U.S. Census Bureau, 2012) governments in the United States—one federal government, 50 state governments, and tens of thousands of local governments (cities, townships, counties, special districts, etc.), yet we often overlook these vital governmental entities that impact our lives on a daily basis. In addition to exploring the basic composition, administration, and functioning of state and local government, this chapter explains how individuals can become more involved and engaged in the public policy decisions of their communities. Then, this chapter addresses the various funding strategies that states, counties, and cities have had to devise and employ to deliver services in the current economic crisis, many of which are innovative, non-traditional, and driven by necessity.

Introduction

Former Speaker of the U.S. House of Representatives Thomas "Tip" O'Neill once famously quipped that "All politics is local." Whether or not this statement is entirely accurate is open to debate, but the notion that state and local government has an effect on the daily lives of citizens is undisputable. Most government exchanges and interactions are with agents of state and local government and include such offices and officials as: public school teachers, police officers, social workers, county commissioners, city councilors, city and county managers, building inspectors, city planners, parks and recreation directors, firefighters, tax assessors, code enforcers, economic developers, city engineers, city and county clerks, state regulators, park rangers, bus drivers, and more. Elected and appointed officials at the state and local level make policy decisions in the areas of education, transportation, taxation, land use, growth and development, health care, emergency management, social services, immigration, and environmental protection, among others. They shape and control budgets and expenditures ranging from the small (tens of thousands of dollars) to the large (tens of billions of dollars).

Increasingly, as citizens clamor for more government services delivered more efficiently and effectively (without tax increases), state and local governments must devise strategies to generate revenue and meet citizen demands. Voter turnout for state and local elections is less than turnout in national level, especially presidential, elections. Traditionally, the lower the level of government, the lower the rate of voter turnout, which is unfortunate considering that these "lower" levels of government are closest to the people. It is not uncommon for voter turnout for primary elections at the local level to be in the single digits (Holbrook and Weinschenk, 2013).

State Governments
Constitutional Authority

The Tenth Amendment to the United States Constitution reads, "The powers not delegated to the United States by the Constitution, nor prohibited by it to the States, are reserved to the States respectively, or to the people." This so-called **Reserved Powers Clause**, although simply-written, is the constitutional basis for federalism and has resulted in a great deal of controversy and strained relations between the federal government and the states (as described in detail in earlier chapters). Nevertheless, state governments were created as co-equal entities by the framers of the Constitution and are therefore constitutionally-legitimate. Article I, Section Eight of the U.S. Constitution explains in detail powers given to the federal government (specifically Congress), powers shared by the federal government and state governments (called **concurrent powers**), and powers given exclusively to the states. Examples of powers given to the federal government and Congress solely include regulating interstate commerce, coining money, declaring war, raising an army, and making laws "necessary and proper." Examples of concurrent powers that the federal government shares with the states include collecting taxes, establishing courts, borrowing money, making and enforcing laws, and chartering banks and corporations. Finally, powers that states possess exclusively include establishing local governments, regulating intrastate commerce, conducting elections, and ratifying amendments to the U.S. Constitution. As society has become more complex and as citizens have demanded more services, government has expanded exponentially at all levels. Today, states make policy decisions affecting millions of people, concerning potentially billions of dollars.

State Constitutions

Because of federalism, states are constitutionally-legitimate entities and each state, therefore, has its own constitution. Many **state constitutions** (such as those of Virginia, South Carolina, and New Hampshire) existed prior to the writing of the U.S. Constitution in 1787 and were models and guides for the delegates to the Constitutional Convention. James Madison, in fact, utilized the Virginia constitution of 1776, written by Thomas Jefferson, as a template for the Virginia Plan which greatly influenced the U.S. Constitution. The U.S. Constitution is brief (roughly 7,400 words including the Bill of Rights) in comparison to most state constitutions, which are longer and more detailed, averaging roughly 26,000 words, and therefore less flexible. For example, Alabama's constitution adopted in 1901 is over 300,000 words. Even Vermont's constitution, which is the shortest, is over 8,300 words—longer than the U.S. Constitution (Hammons, 1999, p. 840). While the hallmark of the U.S. Constitution is its flexibility and endurance, having only been amended 17 times since 1791, state constitutions are amended much more frequently (115 times on average), or as is the case with many states, re-crafted altogether.

Most states have had several constitutions since 1776. An exception is the Massachusetts constitution, ratified in 1780, which is the longest-enduring written constitution in the world (Kincaid, 1988, p. 13). The current Georgia constitution was ratified in 1983, is the "newest" state constitution, and, in fact, is the 10th constitution in the state's history. The original U.S. Constitution has endured since it was ratified in 1789. On the contrary, there have been 145 different state constitutions since 1776 (Hammons, 1999, p. 838). Louisiana has had 11 constitutions; Georgia 10; South Carolina 7; Florida, Alabama, and Virginia 6; and Arkansas, Texas, and Pennsylvania 5 (Hammons, 1999, p. 841). Another primary difference between the U.S. Constitution and state constitutions is the location of the Bills of Rights. In the national version, the Bill of Rights is not a formal component of the document itself, but rather the first 10 amendments. In most state versions, the Bill of Rights is found in the beginning and often in the very first section (which is true for the Georgia Constitution). Because state constitutions are longer, more detailed, amended more frequently, and less flexible, they can provide additional protections for citizens, something which has led to judicial evolution at the state level, influencing the actions of lawmakers and the decisions of judges (Kincaid, 1988).

How Institutions Function in the States

Like the federal government and the U.S. Constitution, state governments and constitutions outline separate branches of government with checks and balances that share power. In every state, the chief executive is the governor. The lawmaking body is the state legislature, often called the General Assembly. 49 states utilize a bicameral legislature. Nebraska's unicameral legislature is the only exception. The highest courts in the states are referred to collectively as "courts of last resort" because not every state refers to its highest court as the "supreme" court (the Georgia Supreme Court is the highest court in the state). Just as the framers intended that Congress be the strongest branch of government, state legislatures, as described by most state constitutions, are intended to be the strongest entity in state governments. However, just as has been the case with the evolution of presidential power, governors in the states have gained a tremendous amount of power at the expense of state legislatures over time. As a result, governors today are probably much stronger than intended in many cases.

The traditional powers of **governors**, those usually listed explicitly in state constitutions, are similar to the powers of the president (Beyle, 1968). Governors traditionally possess the power to appoint officials in the Executive Branch, oversee state agencies, veto legislation, call the state legislature into general session, dispatch the National Guard in times of crisis and emergency, and craft the budget, among others. In an informal sense, governors also serve as chief of their respective parties, spokespersons and ambassadors for their states, and chief lobbyists with their state legislatures, putting pressure on members to enact their agendas and policies. In terms of length of gubernatorial terms and re-eligibility, states vary tremendously. Most governors serve four-year terms, but a few serve two-year terms, as is the case in New Hampshire and Vermont. Governors in 38 states are limited to two terms of office, the Governor of Virginia is limited to one term of office, and the remaining are not term-limited (National Governors

Association, 2024). The Governor of the State of Georgia is limited to two four-year terms.

As the federal government has devolved power back to the states since 1980 or so, governors have become more powerful, many even possessing name recognition on a national and international scale. Governors today are proactive policy entrepreneurs (Beyle, 1995), aided in no small part by the power of the **line-item veto**, whereby they can veto parts of legislation, but not the entire bill (44 governors possess this power). The president does not possess the line-item veto. Since the 1930s, one path to the U.S. presidency was through the Senate (Harry Truman, John F. Kennedy, Lyndon Johnson, Barack Obama), however many presidents and presidential candidates during this era previously served as governor (Franklin Delano Roosevelt, Jimmy Carter, Ronald Reagan, Bill Clinton, George W. Bush), demonstrating their ability to oversee state agencies, manage budgets, handle crises, and win elections on a smaller scale, yet fulfilling duties similar to that of the president. Not surprisingly, gubernatorial elections can cost tens of millions of dollars, looking very much like presidential elections and are marked by extensive television advertising, usage of professional campaign advisers, and negative campaign ads.

The composition, functioning, and especially size of **state legislatures** vary tremendously across the states. Nebraska's unicameral legislature has 49 members. The smallest bicameral legislature is Alaska's with 60 members. The Georgia legislature has 236 members with 180 in the lower house and 56 in the Senate. Oddly enough, the largest state legislature is found in one of the smallest states—New Hampshire—which has a 424-seat body with 400 members serving in the lower house and has one representative per approximately 3,000 citizens. Contrast that with California, which has 80 members in its lower house, each representing roughly 500,000 people (National Conference of State Legislatures, 2024). Most states utilize four-year **terms of office** for both the lower and upper houses of their legislatures, although 12 states utilize two-year terms. All members of the General Assembly in Georgia serve two-year terms. Since 1990, many states have enacted **term limits** for state legislators; 15 states currently do so. Legislators in these states are limited from 6 to 12 years in office, depending on the state. State legislators in Georgia are not term-limited (National Conference of State Legislatures, 2024).

There is also a tremendous amount of variation among the states with regard to full-time versus part-time legislatures (or "hybrid"), which is determined by both compensation and number of days in session. Many states pay legislators well over $60,000 per legislative session, with California providing the highest pay at over $114,000. Conversely, many states pay their legislators less than $20,000 per legislative session, including Georgia, where legislators are paid $15,607 for the forty-day session (a decrease due to budget cuts). Not surprisingly, those states with longer legislative sessions (several months) provide greater compensation and more staff to its members. (National Conference of State Legislators, 2024). All states except Texas meet in yearly sessions. Women are better represented in state legislatures than in the U.S. Congress, where women currently comprise roughly 29% of the 535-member body. In 2023, there were 2,397 women serving in state legislatures (33%), including a low of 11.4% in Alabama, to a high of 57% in Nevada (in Georgia, women comprise 29% of the legislature). This overall 33% number represents an all-time high (National Conference of State Legislatures, 2024).

The financing of state legislative campaigns does not reflect the campaign finance model at the national level. Campaign contribution limits vary greatly across the states; seven states have no limits on campaign contributions whatsoever. In Georgia, candidates for state legislature can receive $2,600 for primary and general elections. Limits on **campaign contributions** (or lack thereof) can have implications, most notably the degree to which special interests have access to lawmakers and the extent to which they influence public policy. Furthermore, states with low campaign contribution limits tend to have more competitive elections with challengers winning at a higher rate (Hamm and Hogan, 2008).

In terms of daily functioning and policymaking, state legislatures function very similarly to the U.S. Congress, working primarily in **committees**. Legislators will serve on several permanent or standing committees and perhaps other ad hoc or temporary committees as well. Traditionally, seniority rules with longer-serving members holding positions on the more prestigious committees. These long-held legislative traditions and folkways may erode as state legislators are subjected to term limits.

The operation of the **judicial system** (the courts) differs somewhat throughout the states. As mentioned previously, not all states refer to their highest court as the Supreme Court. In some states, judges are elected on partisan ballots, in others on non-partisan ballots. Other states appoint their judges to all levels of courts, while others still utilize the Missouri Plan, which involves a combination of appointments and elections. The primary difference is that judges who must run for election, especially those on partisan ballots, must concern themselves with political issues and variables like those governors and legislators face, most notably fundraising. Today, competition for judicial seats is fierce and can cost candidates hundreds of thousands or even millions of dollars per election cycle

(Bonneau, 2007). What is common among all the states is the amount of judicial business or cases heard by state courts in comparison with the federal court system. State courts are busier, including the state courts of last resort, which hear many more cases per year than the U.S. Supreme Court.

Local Governments
Authority

Local governments (counties, townships, cities, school districts, etc.) are not mentioned in the U.S. Constitution and, therefore, their power and authority is not constitutionally-based. Rather, as the U.S. Supreme Court decision that came to be known as **Dillon's Rule** clarified in 1868, local governments are creations of the state, subject to the authority and oversight of individual states, not the federal government. However, as counties, townships, cities, and other units of local government have expanded, they have become responsible for delivering more services to more people. As a result, they function almost as a third level or layer in the system of American federalism, even if they lack authority from the U.S. Constitution. It should be remembered that almost all units of government are local units of government.

Counties

Counties are subdivisions of states delivering state services at the local level including, but not limited to record-keeping, licensing, transportation, economic development, law enforcement, water management, elections, planning and zoning, child protection, education, and parks and recreation. Counties exist in 48 states, with county-like entities called boroughs found in Alaska and parishes found in Louisiana. Texas boasts the most counties with 254. There are only three counties found in both Hawaii and Delaware. There are 159 counties in Georgia, the second-most of any state (National Association of Counties, 2020). Counties vary tremendously in size, from less than 100 square miles to over 10,000 square miles. Arlington County, Virginia, the smallest county in the United States, is only 26 square miles. Conversely, San Bernardino County, California, the nation's largest, is over 26,000 square miles. In terms of population, many rural counties throughout the United States have less than 5,000 residents while many urban counties have over a million people, including over five million in Cook County, Illinois and over 10 million in Los Angeles County, California (National Association of Counties, 2020). This urban/rural distinction is important for counties because people living in rural areas rely more so on county government and the services it provides because those services are not provided or duplicated by other governments, most notably cities. Many people live in rural, unincorporated areas where government services are provided solely by the county.

Historically, counties have been governed by an elected **commission**, which served as the legislative, policymaking entity for the county as well as the executive entity. In effect, each elected commissioner was responsible for overseeing a particular policy area. Relatively few counties still utilize this arrangement today due to the complex nature of modern county government and the potential for corruption that occurred before the era of professionalization spurred by the institution of the merit system at the county level in the early 20th century. Rather, the commission system of government has evolved over the years and today, counties are governed most often by the **commissioner-administrator** or **commission-manager** system whereby the elected commission chooses a professional manager or administrator to oversee the day-to-day operations of the county. In this system, the commission fulfills its traditional legislative, policymaking function, but the manager or administrator is responsible for budget oversight, personnel administration, strategic planning, and other daily government functions. The commissioner-administrator/commissioner-manager system is the most commonly used system of county governance today because of its relative efficiency and professionalism (Svara, 1993).

Yet other counties employ a **commission-executive** whereby the county executive is a separately-elected official functioning similarly to a county manager or administrator. The advantage to the commission-executive system is true separation of powers (National Association of Counties, 2020).

The least-utilized system of county governance is the **sole commissioner** model, found in only seven counties in Georgia and nowhere else. In these rural Georgia counties, the commissioner is a single person who functions as both the legislative and executive body for the county. As counties have grown, this system of government has become less appropriate and therefore rarely used. County commissioners and executives run on partisan ballots in most cases.

Finally, over 30 cities and counties in several U.S. states have consolidated into one governmental entity. **Consolidated governments** deliver services as one government, rather than duplicating city and county services, theoretically increasing efficiency of service delivery and saving money. New York City, Philadelphia, Indianapolis, Louisville, Nashville, and Jacksonville, FL all operate as consolidated governments. Three consolidated governments are found in Georgia—Columbus-Muscogee, Athens-Clarke, and Augusta-Richmond (U.S. Census Bureau).

Townships

Just as counties are subdivisions of states, **townships** are subdivisions of counties, providing similar services to people living in mostly rural, unincorporated areas. Townships are found in 20 states primarily in the eastern United States and throughout the Midwest. Many states in the South and West do not utilize townships as a separate government entity (there are no townships in Georgia). Townships are traditionally governed by a Board of Trustees or Board of Supervisors serving as the legislative body and may utilize a town manager or administrator to oversee the daily operation of the township (National Association of Towns and Townships, 2020). Townships, like other units of government, function most effectively when their actions and delivery of services is well-coordinated with other levels of government in the region, including counties and cities. Otherwise, their mere existence can be viewed by groups and citizens alike as duplicitous in nature, providing services that are already administered by counties, cities, or states (Visser, 2004).

Cities

There are over 19,000 municipal governments in the United States (U.S. Census Bureau), referred to here as **cities**. Cities vary tremendously in size and population, from literally a few dozen people to several million. Over 60% of all Americans live in cities (National League of Cities, 2020). Cities are "incorporated" or established by receiving a **charter** from the state legislature.

"A city charter is the basic document that defines the organization, powers, functions and essential procedures of the city government. It is comparable to the State Constitution and to the Constitution of the United States. The charter is, therefore, the most important single legal document of any city" (National League of Cities, 2020). Charters differ somewhat from state to state, depending on individual state constitutions, but traditionally, there are three different types of municipal charters: **special or specific charters**, **general or classified charters**, and **home rule charters**. Cities are granted a charter depending on population, proposed government structure, and other variables (National League of Cities, 2020). Those cities with **home rule** can make minor changes to their charters without receiving approval from the state legislature, most notably adjusting the local income tax rate. All cities in Georgia possess home rule.

Like counties, cities are governed by various systems, depending on tradition, era of incorporation, and state and regional political climate. The oldest form of city government is the **mayor-council** form of government whereby the mayor functions as the chief executive and the city council functions as the legislative body. A distinction in the mayor-council form of government is the "strong mayor" versus "weak mayor" classification. In those cities possessing "strong" mayors, the executive possesses greater authority with regard to budgetary and personnel decisions. Atlanta functions as a "strong" mayor system. Candidates for mayor and city council in mayoral systems tend to run on partisan ballots with candidates declaring a party affiliation. Other cities, albeit very few, utilize a **commission system** that looks similar to the county commission system, where the commission functions as both the legislative and executive entity. The most common form of city government is the **council-manager** or **council-administrator** system where the elected city council functions as the legislative policymaking body but selects a professional manager or administrator to oversee the day-to-day operation of the city (similar to the county commission-manager or administrator system described above). Candidates for city council in council-manager systems tend to run on non-partisan ballots, which usually results in lower voter turnout. Finally, the **town meeting** form of government exists only in New England and is not pervasive throughout the region. In a municipality utilizing the town meeting form of government, the entire electorate is allowed to participate in an annual meeting, the primary purpose of which is to pass the budget for the upcoming fiscal year. Policy administration is undertaken by select people, chosen by the electorate (DeSantis and Renner, 2002). The town meeting form of government is hampered by very low voter turnout.

Arguments exist on both sides for **partisan** and **non-partisan** elections. Advocates for partisan elections contend that party labels guide or aid voters in making candidate decisions and voter turnout is usually higher in partisan elections. Advocates for non-partisan elections contend that party labels are antiquated and do not aid professionals in providing city services to the public. The trend is towards non-partisan elections as the council-manager system of government becomes more pervasive, even in large cities that have traditionally possessed the mayoral form of government (Svara, 1999). With regard to term length and term limits of office-holders serving in city government, the overwhelming majority serve four-year terms of office and are not term-limited; less than 10% of cities limit the terms of office-holders (Svara, 2003, p. 14). It should also be noted that minority representation on city councils is higher for communities utilizing the council-manager form of government (Svara, 2003, p. 7).

Other Local Governments

Myriad other local governments exist in the United States and are too numerous to address in detail, although a few merit further investigation.

Councils of Governments (COGs) are voluntary associations of communities in metropolitan areas and exist to address issues and concerns that may affect several jurisdictions in a given region, such as land use, traffic and congestion, transportation, water use, and emergency management. COGs have little formal power but can be effective for strategic, long-term planning. The most successful COG is the one in the Minneapolis-St. Paul area (National League of Cities, 2020). **School districts** are an important unit of local government that make policy for schools in a given jurisdiction, such as a county, township, or city. School districts are governed by the school board, which functions as the legislative, policy-making body. The school board chooses a superintendent to oversee the daily operation of the district. School board members usually run on non-partisan ballots and serve four-year terms. School board politics can become contentious at times because boards oversee the curriculum for school children, making decisions about what children will learn, who will teach it to them, and which subjects should be emphasized (Land, 2002). There are over 13,000 school districts in the United States. The largest is the New York City district, which has nearly a million students (Selected statistics on enrollment, teachers, dropouts, and graduates in public school districts enrolling more than 15,000 students, by state: 1990, 2000, 2006, 2020).

Finally, about one-third of all local governments are **special districts**. Special districts are created to regulate and manage specific services such as water and resources, fire prevention, emergency services, transportation, and even stadiums. These special districts encompass a defined geographic area and have significant taxing and regulating authority, their primary purpose being raising funds. For example, if a city desires to build a new professional sports franchise, a special stadium district will be created and businesses and individuals owning property or buying goods in that geographic area will pay "tax" to fund that endeavor.

State and Local Government Financing Options in the Modern Era

Unlike the federal government, states cannot pass a yearly budget with a deficit and incur debt over many years or even generations. 49 states have some type of **balanced budget** requirement in their state constitutions (National Conference of State Legislatures, 2024). During times of business and economic prosperity and boom, states often produce a surplus, allowing them to increase funding for existing programs and creating new programs, even refunding taxpayers some of their contributions on rare occasions. Conversely, during economic recessions, depressions, and crises, states are often faced with a budgetary shortfall, resulting in deep, dramatic, and permanent cuts to state programs; the result is less money for such things as education, transportation, public health services, and law enforcement. This situation has been the case nationwide since the Great Recession of 2008 and the COVID-19 pandemic of 2020. While states have undergone difficult economic times previously, these recent crises are unmatched since the Great Depression of the 1930s. In previous downswings in the economy, states began to devise non-traditional methods of raising revenue to fund government services. Beginning in the 1980s and 1990s, several states instituted first a state-sanctioned lottery and later state-sanctioned, legalized casino gambling as a means of generating much needed revenue. The results of these measures have been mixed, although the lottery in Georgia is the primary funding mechanism for the HOPE Scholarship (Alexander, 2008; Alexander and Paterline, 2005).

Case Study: Abortion as a State Issue

In 2022, the U.S. Supreme Court issued the *Dobbs v. Jackson Women's Health Organization* decision (see Chapter 11), overturning both *Roe v. Wade* (1973) and *Planned Parenthood v. Casey* (1992), both of which codified and then strengthened women's reproductive rights, including abortion access. After *Dobbs*, the 50-year precedent of *Roe* was overturned, thus devolving or returning the issue of abortion access to the states for the first time in 50 years, creating great political turmoil and controversy. As a result, states (including Georgia) were then empowered to implement their own reproductive rights and abortion access laws that differed greatly in many cases from the *Roe* standards, resulting in further confusion, controversy, and even judicial action at both the state and federal level. The result has been tremendous variation in laws from state-to-state and region-to-region across the country, with mostly "red" (conservative) and "blue" (liberal) state political distinctions. Many public health officials have argued that restrictions in abortion access have placed undue burdens upon the more disadvantaged in society who may not have the means to travel to those states with less restrictive laws and thus accessible healthcare options. The controversy rages and will not be quelled anytime soon.

The abortion issue or case is indicative of a larger and more long-standing "push-pull" power struggle between the federal and state governments that can be traced back to the Founding period of our nation's history, with Constitutional precedent, as we have learned (see Chapter 2). Abortion has been a political "litmus test" for candidates and officeholders for over a half-century, and due to these recent events and decisions, it will only continue to be a divisive issue.

However, it will not be the only flashpoint in the power relationship between the national and state governments. In addition to abortion, other potential issues of controversy include voting rights/access, Medicare expansion, and natural resource usage, among others.

A Civic Engagement Challenge: Becoming Involved in Local Government

One of the basic themes of this chapter has been that it is easier for citizens to get involved in "lower" levels of government, which is true for students as well. Students often have difficulty applying theories, themes, and lessons of government to their daily lives. One way in which they can better understand how government affects them is to become more involved. The civic engagement challenge for this chapter is for students to get involved with a local campaign in one of two ways: either by volunteering for a candidate for city council, county commission, school board, or another local office, or by running themselves. While the first option may be less difficult, the second option is certainly realistic. In many college towns, students have gained election to the city council or county commission. Students underestimate their political power. In a small or mid-sized college community, students comprise an overwhelming portion of the electorate. In most states, including Georgia, students can register to vote in the cities where they go to school. As a result, a candidate for office who is able to harness the political power of the campus and motivate students to vote would have a very good chance of winning an election. City council elections tend to have low voter turnout, and a few dozen votes could very well determine the outcome. A successful student-candidate would have to make sure he or she filed for the election on time, established his or her residency in the community, and drummed up support on campus. So, get going!

Discussion Questions

1. How do state constitutions differ from the U.S. Constitution? Which format is better? Why?

2. How does the composition and functioning of state legislatures differ across the states? In terms of size, term length, and structure, which model is best? Why?

3. Compare and contrast the various forms of local government structure. Which offers the best service delivery to citizens? Why?

4. How can and should states generate much needed revenue to fund essential programs and policy priorities during economic downturns?

References

Alexander, R. C. (2008). The feasibility of legalized casino gambling in Georgia. *Proceedings of the Georgia Political Science Association.* (2007 ed.).

Alexander, R. C., & Paterline, B. A. (2005). Boom or bust: Casino gaming and host municipalities. *International Social Science Review, 80*(1,2), 20–28.

American Gaming Association. (2017). https://www.amcricangaming.org/

Barr, A. and Turner, S. E. (2013). Expanding enrollments and contracting state budgets: the effect of the Great Recession on higher education. *Annals of the Academy of Political and Social Sciences,* 650, 168–193.

Barrett, P., Gaskins, J., and Haung, J. (2019). Higher education under fire: implementing and assessing culture change for sustainment. *Journal of Organizational Change Management, 32*(1), 164–180.

Bauman, D. (2020, May 11). Public regional colleges were already struggling. COVID-19 may push some to the brink. *The Chronicle of Higher Education.*

Beyle, T. (1968). The governor's formal powers: A view from the governor's chair. *Public Administration Review,* 540–545.

______, T. (1995). Enhancing executive leadership in the states. *State and Local Government Review, 27*(1), 18–35.

Bonneau, C. W. (2007). The effects of campaign spending in state Supreme Court elections. *Political Research Quarterly, 60*(3), 489–499.

Danziger, S. (2013). Evaluating the effects of the Great Recession. *Annals of the Academy of Political and Social Sciences,* 650, 6–24.

DeSantis, V. S., & Renner, T. (2002). City government structures: An attempt at clarification. *State and Local Government Review, 34*(2), 95–104.

Ellis, L. (2018). How the Great Recession reshaped higher ed. *The Chronicle of Higher Education, 65*(4), 32.

Friga, P. (2020, April 20). Under COVID-19, university budgets like we've never seen before. *The Chronicle of Higher Education.*

Georgia Lottery Corporation. (2017). https://www.galottery.com/

Hamm, K. E. & Hogan, R. E. (2008). Campaign finance laws and candidacy decisions in state legislative elections. *Political Research Quarterly, 61*(3), 458–467.

Hammons, C. W. (1999). Was James Madison wrong? Rethinking the American preference for short, framework-oriented constitutions. *American Political Science Review, 93*(4), 837–849.

Holbrook, T. M., & Weinschenk, A. C. (2013) Campaigns, mobilization, and turnout in mayoral elections. *Political Research Quarterly, 67*(1), 42–55.

Kincaid, J. (1988). State constitutions in the federal system. *Annals of the*

American Academy of Political and Social Science, 496, 12–22.

Land, D. (2002). Local school boards under review: Their role and effectiveness in relation to students' academic achievement. *Review of Educational Research, 72*(2), 229–278.

Leonard, W. P. (2014). Higher education's flawed recession response. *International Journal of Educational Management, 28*(2), 257–264.

National Association of Counties. (2020). https://www.naco.org/Pages/default.aspx

National Association of Towns and Townships. (2020). https://www.natat.org/

National Conference of State Legislatures. (2024). https://www.ncsl.org

National Governors Association. (2024). https://www.nga.org/portal/site/nga/menuitem.b14a675ba7f89cf9e8ebb856a11010a0

National League of Cities. (2020). https://www.nlc.org

Seltzer, R. (2019, June 5). Public higher education continues to feel pinch from Great Recession a decade later. *Inside Higher Ed.*

Svara, J. H. (2003). *Two decades of continuity and change in American city councils.* National League of Cities.

_____, J. H. (1999). The shifting boundary between elected officials and city managers in large council-manager cities. *Public Administration Review, 59*(1), 44–53.

_____, J. H. (1993). The possibility of professionalism in county government. *International Journal of Public Administration, 16*(12), 2051–2080.

United States Census Bureau. (2012). *Census Bureau reports there are 89,004 local governments in the United States.* United States Census Bureau. https://www.census.gov/newsroom/releases/archives/governments/cb12-161.html

University System of Georgia Board of Regents (2020). *Board of regents provides authority for potential reductions due to COVID-19.* University System of Georgia Board of Regents. https://www.usg.edu/news/release/board_of_regents_provides_authority_for_potential_reductions_due_to_covid_1

Visser, J. A. (2004). Townships and nested governance: Spoilers or collaborators in metropolitan services delivery? *Public Performance & Management Review, 27*(3), 80–101.

Whitford, E. (2020, May 5). Public higher education in a 'worse spot than ever before' heading into a recession. *Inside Higher Ed.*

U.S. Foreign Policy

Jonathan S. Miner and Craig B. Greathouse

Learning Objectives

After covering the topic of U.S. foreign policy, students should understand:

1. The general elements of a foreign policy, and why every country has a specific policy that serves their best interests.
2. The important political and social actors who make U.S. foreign policy.
3. How history and current domestic and international issues shape U.S. foreign policy.
4. How the conflict in Iraq is a result of U.S. foreign policy.

Abstract

One of the most important areas of public policy in which the American government must engage is relations with other countries in the international system. U.S. foreign policy entails developing and advancing American national interests abroad by using all the tools and abilities of government and society. This chapter fits well toward the end of this volume as many of the subjects studied so far (the presidency, Congress, judiciary, bureaucracy, state and local governments, political parties, mass media and general public) have a prominent role in the process of making U.S. foreign policy. In this chapter, a discussion of the nuts and bolts of foreign policy is coupled with an analysis of the specific actors who make and implement U.S. foreign policy, a survey of its prominent historical themes, and a contemporary application of this process to the current war in Ukraine.

Introduction

For much of the last two decades, the media has detailed explosions in Iraq and Afghanistan which kill United States military personnel and innocent civilians. As people watch these reports, many ask obvious questions, such as, why are we there? What does the United States have to gain that justifies fighting two wars in Iraq and Afghanistan that cost billions of dollars and the lives of Americans? The short answer is simple—September 11, 2001. Since the attacks on New York, Washington, and Pennsylvania, the United States has been in the Middle East fighting terrorism and protecting the homeland from those who wish to attack once again. As President Bush declared in his first address to the nation on September 20, 2001, "Tonight, we are a country awakened to danger and called to defend freedom. Our grief has turned to anger and anger to resolution. Whether we bring our enemies to justice or bring justice to our enemies, justice will be done" (Avalon Project, 2008).

While this short and definitive explanation may make logical sense, the long answer as to why the United States is involved in the Middle East is much more complex. A more complete explanation involves answering some of the following questions, such as, how does a response to the 9/11 tragedy become a U.S. foreign policy? What reasons could the U.S. possibly have to send troops so far away to such an unstable place for more than a decade? Who makes these decisions, and why do I not feel involved in making them? Why is this important to me anyway? How can I have my thoughts and opinions known and noticed by policy makers? This chapter answers these questions by bringing together many of the concepts and ideas you have learned in this reader and applying them to events that happen outside the United States. It also helps answer them by explaining how issues important to Americans at home become U.S. foreign policy abroad, what foreign policy actually is, who makes it, what it tries to accomplish, and why it is extremely important to each and every American citizen.

The final part of the chapter helps illustrate the making of U.S. foreign policy by applying these ideas to American involvement in the conflict between Russia and Ukraine. The decision to become involved was based upon a number of long-standing core values and priorities American foreign policy makers have applied to events all over the world throughout our history: **security, democracy, freedom, military superiority, trade** and **international leadership** (Greathouse and Miner, 2008). By understanding the connection between these ideas and the actions taken involving Russia and Ukraine, students will be able to better understand how American political issues become U.S. foreign policy and will have the tools to understand any U.S. foreign policy implemented in any part of the world.

What is foreign policy?

Foreign policy can be explained as "the scope of involvement abroad and the collection of goals, strategies, and instruments that are selected by governmental policymakers" (Rosati and Scott, 2007, p. 4). In other words, foreign policy represents the different needs, interests, and reasons for United States involvement abroad and the ways and means chosen to achieve those goals. Foreign policy is based upon the interests of a particular country, in this case the United States. Whether these interests involve the export of products made in the U.S. or the importation of oil, a worry about terrorism, global pollution, or the drug trade, the foreign policy of the United States is determined by the issues and concerns most important to our country as a whole (Greathouse and Miner, 2010).

U.S. foreign policy is made by the government, but not the government alone. The president often leads in foreign policy making, but is influenced and supported by Congress, the military, the media, the State Department, intelligence community, interest groups, the bureaucracy, and the public, among others. It is a bargaining process in which every interested person and group participates in the making of a foreign policy on a particular issue, using all the power and skills they possess to shape a policy that is in their best interest and in the interest of the United States as a whole (Allison and Zelikow, 1999). One might think of this process as a board meeting; the president sits at the head of a conference table, and all around him sit representatives of all the interested parties on a given issue, such as terrorism or international trade.

U.S. foreign policy is the result of all interested parties discussing a particular national goal or interest and bargaining over the best way to achieve it abroad. A policy is agreed upon, and then carried out by each of those parties at the table: the president announces it, the government as a whole oversees and carries it out, and American citizens in the media, military and business, interest groups, and voters participate in its implementation. Foreign policies in other countries are different than U.S. foreign policy; while Canada and Mexico are both democracies and are neighbors of the U.S. and located in the North American continent, each has different national interests and political systems with its power distributed differently than in the U.S. Therefore, their "board room meetings" and the foreign policies that result are not the same as those of the United States. While this chapter explores only the U.S. foreign policy making process, it is important for students to understand that each country has a unique way of making such policies, and part of the U.S. foreign policy process is to understand and respond to other countries' policies and recognize that they are made in a different way.

Why is it important?

Foreign policy is important because it has an impact on the ability of the United States to provide for its citizens. Businesses care about foreign policy because they want to sell their products abroad. Ordinary people wish to remain safe from outside threats, such as terrorism and disease, and all Americans wish to buy foreign goods, such as cars from Germany and TVs from Japan. Americans need to be able to buy gasoline to power their cars, and the U.S. government wants to maintain good relations with each of the oil producing countries so that each of these goals (and many others) can be achieved for the benefit of all. Lastly, U.S. foreign policy is important because each American citizen has an impact on how policy is made and carried out. While it appears that foreign policy is made solely by the government, this chapter will show that this is not nearly the truth; all Americans participate in the making and implementation of U.S. foreign policy.

Basic elements

U.S. foreign policy is the result of bargaining and cooperation regarding a particular issue or need in the United States. But whether that issue is oil, trade, or nuclear weapons, its components are more basic: **power**, **wealth**, and common **values**. The identity and capabilities of each country determine what kind of foreign policy it can develop; a poor country with few resources or people, a weak economy, or small military finds it more difficult to develop a foreign policy similar to a country that possesses each of these qualities in abundance (Rourke, 2007).

As Americans, we are extremely fortunate to have many natural resources, a large middle class, well-educated citizens, an open and democratic society, and a strong degree of national pride. In fact, as of 2021 the United States is among the largest economies in the world at $21.4 trillion, has a large and powerful military at 1.39 million active-duty personnel (Central Intelligence Agency, 2021), and has a set of national ideals and beliefs spelled out in our Constitution and Bill of Rights which guide our actions both at home and abroad. These characteristics separate the U.S. from its neighbors, Canada and Mexico, and become the basic elements for an individual and unique foreign policy that is made and carried out by our government and society.

Who Makes U.S. Foreign Policy?

The President and Executive Branch

The president is the undisputed leader in U.S. foreign policy. Article II of the Constitution grants the president the powers of commander-in-chief, chief diplomat, chief administrator, chief of state, chief legislator, chief judicial officer, and voice of the people (Rosati and Scott, 2011). These powers establish a constitutional basis for the president to lead in overseas matters such as fighting wars, negotiating treaties, trade agreements, and diplomatic relations. Presidents are the leaders in making foreign policy in the U.S. and the official representatives of America overseas.

In addition to a legal basis, presidents also derive a great deal of this power from their professional prestige and ability to persuade others to their line of thinking (Neustadt, 1960). The president is only one individual, but has the most power and influence of any member of the U.S. government, and the entire country will listen if the president chooses to exercise those powers. By using their standing as the most recognized and influential American, presidents possess a "bully pulpit" (named after President Theodore Roosevelt's aggressive use of presidential power) which enables extensive influence over the nation. Foreign policy is often made during times of crisis such as war or natural disaster, and it is at these times where presidential power is at its maximum as everyone looks to their top elected official for leadership in trying times.

It is due to the many situations of crisis in the 20th century that the Executive Branch has greatly expanded to grant the president additional powers in foreign policy making (Yergin, 1978). The National Security Council, a cabinet of executives including the Secretaries of State, Defense, Homeland Security, and the Chairman of the Joint Chiefs of Staff (the top military officer) was created to work hand-in-hand with the President in making and carrying out foreign policy decisions (Rothkopf, 2005).

It is at these "boardroom" meetings where the tough decisions are made during times of crisis. For example, in the lead-up to the Iraq War (2003), President Bush worked very closely with Secretary of Defense Donald Rumsfeld, Vice President Dick Cheney, and National Security Advisor Condoleezza Rice in formulating the decision to invade based upon U.S. foreign policy interests. During the 1962 Cuban Missile Crisis President John F. Kennedy spent two tense weeks in constant consultation with Secretary of State Dean Rusk, Secretary of Defense Robert McNamara, National Security Advisor McGeorge Bundy, and Attorney General Robert Kennedy regarding the proper way to handle the crisis (Allison and Zelikow, 1999). Each of these presidents relied on the powers of the National Security Council, Executive Branch and individual policymakers to analyze, debate, and develop U.S. foreign policy regarding the crisis at hand. In response to each and every crisis the current administration convenes a set of people, holds debates and negotiations, and eventually arrives at U.S. foreign policy decisions based upon the winning arguments (Woodward, 2008).

In addition, presidential decision-making depends upon the personality, beliefs, and leadership style of the president and the supporting people and institutional departments at the "boardroom" meetings (Rosati and Scott, 2011). The beliefs and opinions of, say, George W. Bush or Donald Trump differ from Barack Obama or Joseph Biden (Allison and Zelikow, 1999; Elovitz, 2008), as do the opinions of Secretaries of State—Hillary Clinton or General Colin Powell. So, when students of American politics and U.S. foreign policy think about a specific U.S. foreign policy, they must also consider what president made that decision, what were their beliefs and opinions, and what were the beliefs and opinions of those with whom that policy was made? How the policy is made by the unique groups of foreign policy makers is as important as the resulting U.S. foreign policy itself.

The Bureaucracy

Decision making is a crucial part of the U.S. foreign policy process, but implementation by the bureaucracy is what makes those decisions a reality by putting them into practice. Without the bureaucracy, foreign policies remain words on presidential letterhead. Each senior American leader heads a specific body of the U.S. government, and whether it is the Department of Defense, State Department, Treasury, FBI, or Homeland Security, each has a bureaucratic staff which is in charge of carrying out the specific U.S. foreign policies.

The implementation of leadership decisions sounds simple, but the reality is far from it (Allison and Zelikow, 1999). The bureaucracy is immense, complex, and comprised of different organizations with their own work cultures and individuals with their own career goals. A fitting example of these difficulties is the lack of cooperation between the FBI and CIA prior to the attacks of September 11, 2001. The entire intelligence community had produced a great deal of information regarding possible attacks by Al-Qaeda and Osama bin Laden, but these two lead organizations failed to cooperate, share information, anticipate the attacks, and notify senior American leadership in advance. Their effectiveness in protecting the homeland was significantly reduced by the competition between the FBI and CIA, a competition based upon different interests, goals, and ways of operation. This failure was widely seen as the reason the attacks could not be stopped in advance and resulted in a full-scale congressional investigation that culminated in the "9/11 Report: The National Commission on Terrorist Attacks upon the United States" (Kean and Hamilton, 2004). Bureaucracy consists of many layers necessary to carry out U.S. foreign policy decisions, but also provides the opportunity to modify or even change the original presidential decisions. In the aftermath of 9/11, the U.S. foreign policy process changed significantly to better serve American interests.

The State Department

One of four original cabinet departments of the United States government in 1789, the State Department has figured prominently in the making of U.S. foreign policy. The State Department is the most public and visible part of U.S. foreign policy, charged with taking the directives of the executive branch to the peoples of the world. Located in embassies and consulates around the world, Foreign Service officers in the State Department communicate U.S. foreign policy to our allies (and enemies) and aim to achieve the policies which the President has created (Rosati and Scott, 2011).

The top diplomat at State is called the Secretary of State, a position directly appointed by the President and whose actions and words are considered to be the President's "mouthpiece". An effective and influential Secretary of State understands all of the issues important to U.S. foreign policy and has hundreds of diplomats around the world attempting to gain acceptance of those policies and to implement them. The Secretary of State is often the first to respond to an international crisis and is responsible for sending diplomats to represent the United States and coordinate, aid, negotiate, and generally influence the outcome. Whether dealing with the security of the United States, its economy, treaties or political issues, the Secretary of State and State Department have traditionally taken the lead in U.S. foreign policy.

The Military and Intelligence Communities

Since the creation of the National Security Act of 1947, however, the military and intelligence communities have increasingly taken power and influence away from the State Department. State has often been seen as ineffective and inefficient throughout history: President John F. Kennedy once called it a "bowl of jelly" while President Lyndon Johnson saw State as "sissies, snobs, and lightweights" (Rosati and Scott, 2011). With a combined military and intelligence budget of over 900 billion dollars, the Executive branch and President have increasingly taken the role of away from the State Department and placed it in the hands of the Secretary of Defense (Rosati and Scott, 2011).

The National Security Act of 1947 created a department which placed the Army, Navy (and Marines), Air Force, and sixteen separate intelligence agencies under the control of the Secretary of Defense. The Central Intelligence Agency, National Security Agency and many others work together to protect the United States and carry out U.S. foreign policy under his leadership. In addition, after the attacks of September 11, 2001, the federal government created the Department of Homeland Security, housing the FBI, Coast Guard, Secret Service, and other agencies designed to create a more unified effort to protect the homeland. Lastly a Director of National Intelligence (DNI) was created in 2004 in an effort to help each of these parts work more smoothly together and prevent another 9/11. While another attack on this scale has not occurred and the mainland United States has escaped any large attacks, the military, intelligence and State departments remain separate and competitive with one another. The DNI has not been given the full authority to manage all these disparate agencies and they remain competitive with one another, seeking their own spin and implementation of U.S. foreign policy, and, ultimately, competing against one another almost as much as they work together (Rosati and Scott, 2011). This problem of competition is similar to the one outlined earlier in discussing the role of the bureaucracy and is a similar problem in each part of the process of making and carrying out U.S. foreign policy.

Congress

It is true that in the 20th century, the power to make U.S. foreign policy was increasingly transferred into the hands of the President and Executive Branch. This does not mean, however, that the other institutions of government do not retain power in the policy making process. Congress remains influential in the making of U.S. foreign policy because it retains the power of oversight and the power of the purse. These powers enable the House of Representatives to regulate foreign policy decisions by controlling the funding and the Senate to regulate them by ratifying treaties. Whether sending troops or diplomatic missions overseas, funding projects, or granting aid, the House and Senate retain crucial powers in the making and implementation of U.S. foreign policy (Rosati and Scott, 2011).

Oversight by Congress is another of its powers in U.S. foreign policy making, taking many forms including formal and informal hearings and the aforementioned 9/11 Report. Article II of the Constitution gives Congress the duty to investigate actions of the Executive Branch when they are seen to be contrary to the interests of the American public. As a result of the Vietnam War, the War Powers Resolution of 1973 placed a series of reporting limitations on actions of the president overseas, requiring him to report back to Congress every 90 days to receive authorization for a further dispersal of funds and political permission to continue its activities overseas. Congress can also investigate any action of the government, and it is during such hearings that attention to foreign policy decisions of the Executive Branch is subjected to public scrutiny and often changed.

Interest Groups, the Media, and Public Opinion

The American public also has a crucial role to play in U.S. foreign policy making as the national barometer for presidential decisions and the focal point for interest groups and the media to draw attention to the leaders in Washington, DC. Congress and the public, the media, and interest groups have an almost symbiotic relationship in that congressional leaders cannot get elected without constituents (voters), and the two groups cannot communicate without a third party, the media. In their book, *While Dangers Gather: Congressional Checks on Presidential War Powers*, William G. Howell and Jon C. Pevehouse (2007) discuss the two-way relationship of the media and Congress and the effectiveness of each actor to influence the public, and therefore U.S. foreign policy.

Public media outlets, talk radio, and network and cable news programs are also influential in communicating U.S. foreign policy to the public at large. In today's world, Americans receive their news from countless online and written sources, and this information comes with every conceivable opinion and bias. From conservative to liberal, anti-war to pro-business, news media and interest groups seek to inform ordinary citizens using their own unique take on the issue and to motivate them to support or oppose the government policy. From voting, picketing, and protesting to letter-writing campaigns and petitions, Americans have a direct impact on the making of U.S. foreign policy and the ways the government implements them.

Traditional foreign policy themes and issues

American foreign policy has at its core four themes which influence how decisions are made and which issues are considered most important. These themes have developed since the founding of our country and continue to influence how the president, congress, and all the actors explained above make U.S. foreign policy. The four themes are: **security**, **trade/economic growth**, **morality/American exceptionalism**, and **isolationism versus internationalism**. What makes these four themes unique is that they can at times be contradictory and create difficult decisions for leaders as to how the United States should act in any particular situation.

Security through either Global Isolationism or Internationalism

Security is, first and foremost, the theme that underlies American foreign policy. A primary goal of every administration is to ensure the physical security of the American state, and this can be seen by examining important documents like the U.S. Constitution, Monroe Doctrine, and Gettysburg Address, which show that at every point in our history, there is a focus on security of the state (Greathouse and Miner, 2008). An early approach to ensuring the security of the state was to remain outside of the alliance system of Europe—a policy called isolationism—which regularly drew states into conflict. George Washington in his farewell address argued "it is our true policy to steer clear of permanent alliances with any portion of the foreign world" (Avalon Project, 2008). According to Washington, the U.S. needed to maintain a defensive posture and only become linked to others in extraordinary circumstances. The Monroe Doctrine continued to advocate that an intentionally separate America would remain safe and secure outside of the wars of the Europeans. The Senate's rejection of the treaty bringing the U.S. into the League of Nations after World War I can be seen as a continuation of that policy. This approach of ensuring the security of the U.S. by remaining outside of European alliances continued through the end of World War II.

With the end of World War II, the need for security brought America fully into the international system by participating in the United Nations (UN) and the North Atlantic Treaty Organization (NATO). Given the technology of the time and the need to limit the expansion of the Soviet Union, remaining outside of permanent alliances was no longer a viable option to ensure American security. The United States had changed its approach from isolationism to internationalism, a conscious effort to achieve security through international cooperation. By joining NATO and engaging in the strategy of containment during the Cold War period, U.S. foreign policy adopted an outward and international stance to ensure that neither its physical safety nor that of its allies would be threatened by the Soviet Union.

One element built into this theme is the willingness of America to use force to achieve the goal of security (Dunn, 2003 p. 286) and a key change after World War II is the conscious choice to employ that force abroad. During the Cold War, containment was the American foreign policy used to keep the Soviet Union and its allies limited to the areas of influence they gained at the end of World War II and not to allow them to control or influence other states in the system. The changes in the international system forced the U.S. to be proactive as the physical barriers which had previously protected it from overseas threats were lessened. No longer could distance and water ensure American security, thanks to the development of airplanes and missiles. The attempts to contain the Soviet Union and its communist allies during the Cold War forced the U.S. to take action in Korea, Vietnam, Nicaragua, Greece, Germany, and numerous other places around the globe to protect its security (Yergin, 1978).

Inevitably, this internationalist U.S. foreign policy would have some negative consequences which would increase the public desire to retreat again to isolationism. The reaction to American casualties during the 1965-75 Vietnam War, the deaths of 242 Marines during a 1983 peacekeeping mission in Lebanon, and 18 American soldiers during 1994 deployments into Somalia (captured in the 2001 movie "Black Hawk Down") resulted in significant pressure to bring most troops home and limit American military and political actions to a very clearly defined area of influence in the Western Hemisphere. The 1991 end of the Cold War saw the resurgence of a significant element within the United States that believes that the U.S. should withdraw from the world to protect itself from outside influences.

Despite some Americans' desire to retreat into isolationism at this time, the fall of the Berlin Wall in 1989, the Gulf War in 1990, and the break-up of the Soviet Union in late 1991, were crises that forced the U.S. to reconsider what it meant to be secure. As the sole remaining **superpower**, it faced widespread local and regional conflict brought on by the end of the contest between Americans and Russians in the Cold War. The countries of the world were free of the threat of nuclear annihilation which hung over them during the Cold War, and were exercising that freedom by fighting for their own rights. Civil wars and international conflicts proliferated worldwide, creating an entirely new security environment, and threat, from that of the Cold War.

The Gulf War saw the first large-scale U.S. military involvement in the Middle East, an action which was as much to retain access to oil as to restore the sovereignty of Kuwait. In addition to the Persian Gulf, conflicts in the former Yugoslavia and between Israel and Palestine indicated a return to an internationalist foreign policy in which the United States focused on cooperative action abroad to protect not only the physical but the economic security of the country and its allies. The attacks on 9/11 reinforced this internationalist foreign policy. For the first time significant damage was done to the U.S. by an outside terrorist organization, which resulted in deployment of American troops into Afghanistan and Iraq in the early 2000s under the banner of preventing future terror attacks on the U.S. (Afghanistan) and to prevent weapons of mass destruction (WMDs) from being directed towards the U.S. (Iraq).

While security is most definitely a constant theme in U.S. foreign policy, the means by which it is achieved varies and is often contradictory. The isolationist streak in U.S. foreign policy routinely comes into conflict with international crises which push the United States into the international system (Papp, Johnson and Endicott, 2005). For most of its history, the U.S. has tried to segregate itself from linkages and interactions with those outside of the Western Hemisphere. Up to the attack on Pearl Harbor, there was an extremely strong sentiment towards isolationism within the country, and remnants of those feelings and policies still exist today. When the U.S. considers its relations with other states and decisions about possible actions in the international system, it always includes security concerns within its dealings, but a cyclical conflict continues to rise as to how to best accomplish this goal.

Trade/Economics and Internationalism

From its earliest history, the welfare and prosperity of the United States has been based on economic growth and trade with other countries, a reality which shows the U.S. has *always* engaged in internationalism (Mead, 2002). There is an underlying assumption that by trading with other countries, the U.S. will benefit, and the productivity of the country and the wealth of its citizens will increase. The creation of the American colonies was driven by economic growth concerns, and many of the underlying reasons leading to the American Revolution were based on economic concerns. Once free of British economic control, the importance of trade and economic growth has continually been considered by American leaders.

From the beginning, American presidents have acted to ensure that U.S. businesses would have access to markets to help promote growth in the American economy. Thomas Jefferson's decision to deploy ships from the American Navy to address piracy in the Mediterranean and the consideration of conscripting American sailors into the British navy (which was one of the issues leading to the War of 1812) are examples of American foreign policy actions to protect trade and commerce. American actions to expand the country westward and wars fought against Native American tribes were based on the potential economic returns of growing American territory. The Monroe Doctrine, Mexican American War of 1846-1848, and Spanish American War of 1898 were all U.S. foreign policy efforts designed to keep Europeans out of the Western Hemisphere and to protect and control economic development within the region. Similarly, the entrance of the United States into World War I was in part because of threats to American trade by German U-boats.

Following World War II, the government focused on building strong economic linkages between countries to prevent a future economic collapse of the level of the Great Depression and future conflict between trading partners. American foreign policy leaders assumed that states who engaged in trade would not fight each other, so if Germany and Japan could be quickly rebuilt economically and linked to the world economic system of trade the chances of a future conflict would diminish. Underlying this idea was the thought that the U.S. would dominate world trade. With the fall of the Communist Bloc between 1989 and 1991, the focus on economic growth became even more pronounced. States which previously had not been part of the capitalist trading block were now open to trade which would in turn lessen the chances of war.

Modern foreign policy continues to show the importance of protecting American economic interests. The Gulf War in 1990/91 was driven (at least in part) by concerns over an Iraqi threat to oil supplies, and its possible impact on economic growth. Current U.S. relations with China are driven by the economic interests; the American government does not want to limit access of American goods to the Chinese markets due to the potential for economic growth in the U.S. that China provides. In sum, American policymakers cannot take action within the system without considering the impact on economics. The demand for expanding the economy and creation of more wealth forces policy makers to allow other issues to fall away if the economic returns are high enough.

Morality/American Exceptionalism

Americans have always viewed their country as special (Mead, 2002; Papp, Johnson, and Endicott, 2005; Talbott, 2003). While this idea is not unique within the international system (people in most countries believe theirs is "the best"), the level of belief that the American way of life is superior has and continues to influence how the U.S. acts within the system. It has resulted in an American foreign policy pressing other actors to abide by American morals and follow American leadership due to its exceptional nature.

An early manifestation of this idea was the concept of **Manifest Destiny**, that America was rightly entitled to the stretch from the Atlantic all the way to the Pacific and to introduce its way of life and system of government. This attitude is seen in how America deals with countries in Latin America such as Mexico, Panama, Colombia, and Venezuela, pushing those countries to adopt political and economic systems which are similar to ours. From the administration of Theodore Roosevelt to the Fourteen Points of Woodrow Wilson, American exceptionalism has advocated that other states adopt democracy and American style economic structures and frequently acted as the "world's police." It pushed states to adopt an American political and economic model following World War II to prevent the threat of communism. Official American Cold War strategy, as advocated by National Security Council Report 68 (NSC-68), argued that the U.S. and its values represented freedom and growth while Communism, as represented by the U.S.S.R., represented slavery and a lack of societal progress.

Since the creation of the United States, its foreign policy has continually cited security and the defense of values and ideals as the basis for action in the international system. Both a retreat from international politics manifested as isolationism and the internationalist deployment of peacekeepers in Lebanon, the former Yugoslavia, and Somalia were all justified by references to domestic security and values of the nation. These themes can be seen in U.S. involvement abroad, from the failure to ratify the League of Nations and the reluctance to enter both World Wars, to efforts at containment of the Soviet Union in Korea, Vietnam, Latin America, Eastern Europe, and the current conflicts in the Middle East. American foreign policy is based on recurrent themes developed as the country grew. In the following case study, we will discuss an example of how these themes work in more detail during a recent and specific example of U.S. foreign policy in action: the Iraq War. It is intended to provide the student with a real-world application of the themes presented thus far in this chapter.

Case Study: Ukraine

In February 2022, the Russian Army under the direction of Vladimir Putin launched a "special military operation" of the state of Ukraine. Most of the rest of the world including the United States labeled Putin's actions an invasion and moved to assist the Ukrainian government with weapons and supplies to support its defense. The invasion was not unanticipated and followed an extended period of lead up with the Russian seizure of the area of Crimea and several areas in Eastern Ukraine in 2014. The initial reaction to the Russian invasion of Ukraine saw significant support within the American domestic population and elements of the American government and foreign policy structure. However, as the war in Ukraine has progressed there has been a softening of support domestically and divided support within Congress due to ideological positions. This case study will address the themes and ideas laid out earlier in the chapter to show their application within a complex real-world scenario.

History

A history of Russian relations with Ukraine is beyond the scope of this section but, to understand the February 2022 invasion some background on Russian-Ukrainian relations is necessary. Parts of Ukraine have long been linked to Russia with some Eastern Ukrainian territory having been under Russian control since the 14th century (Zasenko & Stebelsky, 2024), and the rest being absorbed into the Russian Empire in the mid 1800s until 1917 and then brought back under Soviet rule in 1920. The Ukrainian region within the USSR was important for its agricultural production, industrial development in the eastern part of the region, and in the 1950s it was given administrative control over the region of Crimea in the Black Sea (Kuzio, 2007). Ukraine became an independent state in August of 1991 and the USSR formally dissolved in December of 1991 (Kubicek, 2023). In 2013 pro Russian President Viktor Yanukovych refused to sign an agreement with the EU to opt for closer economic relations with Russia. This created protests which forced Yanukovych to flee from Ukraine to Russia (Kubicek, 2023). The new government formed by the Ukrainian parliament was more Western focused (Kubicek, 2023). In early 2014 Putin ordered a Russian invasion of the Crimean Peninsula which contains the city of Sevastopol where the Russian Black Sea Fleet is headquartered (Kormych & Malyarenko, 2023). Russian forces quickly seized Crimea and later in 2014 Russia supported separatists who took control of parts of the Donetsk and Luhansk regions in Eastern Ukraine (Hughes, 2014). Since 2014, Russia has funneled weapons and troops into these regions to maintain Russian control and fought with Ukrainian forces through early 2022.

In early 2014 the United States and its allies issued a joint statement condemning Russian actions in Crimea (Prime Minister's Office, 2014) and in March 2014 then President Obama met with representatives of the new Ukrainian government and pledged U.S. support (BBC, 2014). In July 2016, the United States voted with other NATO members to endorse a comprehensive assistance package for Ukraine to enhance NATO assistance for Ukraine including training and materials for the Ukrainian military (NATO Comprehensive Assistance Package for Ukraine). In 2017 the United States under President Trump approved the largest sale of lethal arms to Ukraine changing American policy which under the previous Obama administration only sold non-lethal aid from 2014 (Rogin, 2017). In June 2020 Ukraine was granted NATO enhanced opportunity partner status which will increase and expand the cooperation between the alliance and Ukraine, the United States supports this action by NATO (NATO, 2020). In April of 2021 Russia and Ukraine both held military drills increasing the tension in the area. Ukrainian President Zelenskyy met with President Biden at the White House in September of 2021 to push for Ukraine being admitted into NATO (DW, 2021). President Biden was non-committal on allowing Ukraine to be fully admitted into NATO (DW, 2021).

In November 2021 Russian troops began massing on the border with Ukraine both in the east and along the northern border that Ukraine shares with Belarus (*Reuters*, 2021). In December President Biden warned Putin of significant economic sanctions if Russia invades Ukraine during a two-hour meeting (Singh, Greve, & Gabbatt, 2021). In response Russia submitted a list of demands to lower tensions, including a legal guarantee that Ukraine will never be allowed to join NATO and that NATO will give up any military activity in Eastern Europe and Ukraine (Roth, 2021). These demands were unacceptable to many NATO members including the U.S. Russian demands included the removal of NATO troops from Poland, Estonia, Latvia, and Lithuania. U.S. officials called several demands unacceptable (Roth, 2021). U.S. and Russian diplomats met in Geneva in January of 2022, but no progress was made on resolving the Ukrainian crisis (Farge, 2022). In late January 2022, President Biden announced the deployment of additional American ground forces to Europe along with elements of the U.S. Navy and Air Force (Boffey, et al., 2022). In early February 2022 additional forces were deployed to Europe to ensure a robust defense of NATO members due to the crisis. President Biden stated that Americans in Ukraine need to leave as the U.S. has no plans for a military rescue mission if war occurs between Russia and Ukraine (ITV, 2022). On February 17, 2022, Russia expelled the U.S. Deputy Chief of Mission to Russia, the second most senior American diplomat. The U.S. State Department said the move is an escalation in tensions (RFE/RL, 2022). Despite diplomatic actions by the United States and its European allies the Russian invasion of Ukraine was launched on February 24, 2022.

American action to forestall the Russian invasion was highlighted by the Biden administration's release of findings by the American intelligence in the months leading up to the Russian invasion. In December 2021, an unclassified U.S. intelligence document estimating the Russian invasion of Ukraine in 2022 with about 175,000 troops deployed to act was released (*New York Times*, Dec 4, 2021). In addition the Biden administration released intelligence on possible Russian false flag and other gray zone activities targeted at Ukraine in an attempt to prevent Russia from being able to create a false narrative about Ukraine initiating hostilities (Lillis, Bertrand, & Atwood, 2022). Sen. Mark Warner (D) and Rep. Mike Turner (R) both talked publicly about the importance of the intelligence releases (CNBC, 2022).

Once the invasion began the United States at the direction of President Biden released significant security assistance to Ukraine. According to the *Congressional Research Service* release on May 22, 2024, U.S. Security assistance to Ukraine was $52 billion dollars. In Fiscal Years 2022 and 2023, $48.7 billion in supplemental appropriations were used to support Ukraine. Almost $26 billion of that was to replenish material from the Department of Defense which was shipped directly to Ukraine using Presidential Drawdown Authority (PDA; 22 U.S.C. Section 2318). This authority allows the U.S. President to ship material in U.S. stocks directly to certain allies which will then replenished by supplemental appropriations from Congress. Other sources of funding Ukraine came from the Ukraine Security Assistance Initiative and Foreign Military Financing. Through these programs the

U.S. transferred a large number of weapon systems and ammunition to Ukraine and provided extensive training for Ukrainian troops and maintenance assistance for the weapons systems that have been transferred.

While the U.S. engaged in shipping a significant amount of weapons and other material to Ukraine to fight the war, there has also been a corresponding use of U.S. economic actions, along with its allies, to punish Russia economically for its aggression. The day the war commenced the U.S. Treasury Department sanctioned Russia's two largest banks (Sberbank and VTB Bank) preventing these banks from engaging in foreign exchange transactions using U.S. dollars (U.S. Department of the Treasury, 2022). In addition, assets in the U.S. and across Europe were frozen for individuals and corporations associated with the Russian government. While these assets were not seized, they were impounded both by the U.S. and European states. Recently, the interest from these impounded assets have started to be dispersed to Ukraine to assist in fighting the war with Russia, the original assets have not been taken but they are blocked and held in trust as this chapter was published (Hussein, 2024). These initial sanctions were designed to put pressure on the Russian government by limiting its ability to effectively compete in the international economic system. In December of 2022, the U.S. and its allies put a cap of $60/barrel on the sale of Russian oil (U.S. Department of the Treasury, 2023). As energy is one of Russia's major exports limited the price paid for Russian oil would put further pressure on the Russian economy. Not all states in the international system recognized this price cap but most of the largest economies in the world did. In addition to the economic sanctions that were imposed on Russia export controls for goods going to Russia were put in place. These controls are designed to limit the ability of Russian industry to obtain critical technology and other spare parts to facilitate Russian industrial production of weapons and material (U.S. Department of the Treasury, 2023). Additionally, the U.S. and its allies disconnected major Russian banks from the SWIFT messaging system. This action limits the ability of the Russian banks to engage in the international financial system. Additionally, restrictions were placed on the Russian Central Bank to prevent it from making use of its international reserves to limit the impact of previously announced sanctions. (White House, 2022). On April 8, 2022, President Biden signed two bills into law one ending energy imports from Russia and the second suspends trade relations with Russia and Belarus.

One of the biggest levers of influence that Russia planned to use against aggressive European backlash to its invasion of Ukraine was European energy dependence on Russia. Prior to the invasion more than 40% of natural gas imports came from Russia with several states including Austria and Latvia were almost totally dependent on Russian energy imports (Gross & Stelzenmuller, 2024). With the commencement of the war the Biden Administration worked to increase American liquified natural gas (LNG) imports to Europe to counter balance potential disruption due to the Russian invasion with the goal of providing 50 billion cubic meters (bcm) of natural gas a year until 2030 (Gross & Stelzenmuller, 2024). In April 2024, the U.S. exported 5.9 bcm of gas to Europe and now provides more than half of the EU's LNC imports (Gross & Stelzenmuller, 2024). The actions by the Biden Administration helped to preserve the alliance supporting Ukraine against Russia but also helped to expand American exports in a critical economic sector.

Public Opinion

One constraint faced by a presidential administration is the attitude of the domestic population towards international action. This has become more pronounced since the end of the Cold War and the increasingly divided ideological spectrum over the last decade in American politics. In looking at the issue of support for Ukraine there has been a divergence of partisan opinions since 2022 and an overall weakening of support by the American public. Overall, in 2022, according to Pew Research 7% of the population thought too much aid was being sent to Ukraine, 32% thought the support was about right and 42% of respondents thought that not enough aid was being given. In May 2024 31% thought too much aid was being given, 25% said the amount was about right, and 24% said the level of support was not enough. However, when breaking out the partisan position the results provide a stark contrast between Democratic/Democratic-leaning voters and Republican/Republican-leaning voters. In 2022 5% of Democratic/Democratic-leaning voters thought too much aid was going to Ukraine, 39% thought the support was about right, and 38% said it was not enough. In 2024 the breakdown was 16% too much, 31% about right, and 36% not enough. In contrast the Republican/Republican-leaning breakdown in 2022 was 9% thought too much aid was being sent, 23% said about right, and 49% thought not enough aid was being provided. These numbers have sharply shifted in 2024 with 49% of Republican/Republican-leaning saying too much aid is going to Ukraine, 21% saying about right, and 13% saying not enough. The significant reversal on the Republican side highlights changing dynamics within the party and the expansion of the Trump wing of the party which is more isolationist than the traditional conservative position. The impact of this partisan divide will be more fully explored below, when Congress is discussed. As shown above, the overall level of support for aid to Ukraine has fallen since 2022, with 49% of the population saying the aid level is about right or not enough and now 31%, up from 16%, saying too much aid is being given. The shift in domestic opinion about aid to Ukraine has affected the both the Biden Administration's and congressional actions (Pew Research Center, 2024).

A study released by the Pew Research Center in December of 2023 found that overall, 41% either strongly disapproved or somewhat disapproved of the Biden Administration's handling of the Russian invasion of Ukraine, whereas 39% somewhat or strongly approved of the Biden Administration with 20% being unsure (Copeland, 2024). However, in breaking out Democratic/Democratic-leaning versus Republican/Republican-leaning responses the stark partisan differences over the Biden Administration's foreign policy actions in Ukraine comes into focus. 63% of Republican/Republican-leaning voters strongly or somewhat disapprove while online 21% somewhat or strongly approve (only 3% strongly approve) with 16% not being sure. In contrast 22% of Democratic/Democratic-leaning voters strongly or somewhat disapprove in comparison to 59% somewhat or strongly approve of the Biden Administrations actions with 19% being not sure.

In March of 2024, several weeks after the U.S. Senate passed a bipartisan bill to provide more aid to Ukraine, a Gallup poll found that 36% of Americans thought that the U.S. was not doing enough for Ukraine while 36% thought that the U.S. was doing too much. 60% of those saying the U.S. was not doing enough came from Democrats while only 15% of Republicans supported that position (Brenan, 2024). In answering who was doing a better job on Ukraine overall 49% of respondents said Republicans in Congress while 44% said President Biden. When broken out by party 89% of Republicans favored the Republicans in Congress with only 7% favoring Biden. For Democrats, the numbers were 9% supporting Republicans in Congress with 86% supporting President Biden. The divide on support for American foreign policy towards Ukraine was clearly shaped by partisanship. The divisiveness of partisan politics in 2024 is a significant limitation on the level of support for U.S. involvement in Ukraine which will limit the options of Presidents Biden, Trump, and future presidents if the divide holds.

The Bureaucracy

Some Departments have been very actively involved in the response to the Russian invasion of Ukraine. The Departments most engaged have been Defense, State, Treasury, and Commerce. These Departments, especially Defense, State, and Treasury, have been critical in implementing the American response in support of

Ukraine and also to punish Russia. The Department of State has actively engaged in diplomatic measures to keep the pro-Ukrainian coalition together. The State Department has engaged both at the United Nations and across the globe in order to try and isolate Russia and identify individuals within Russia and other states critical to the war effort and limit their ability to engage across the system (U.S. Department of State, n.d.). The Department of Defense (DOD) has been actively involved in moving much of the military hardware being sent to Ukraine and ensuring training for Ukrainians. Given that President Biden has used his ability to draw down from American stocks of weapons and materials, the DOD has ensured that the correct elements reach Germany and Poland for distribution into Ukraine (Mohan, Wilson, & Nicholson, 2023). In addition, the DOD has been the lead organization in helping to organize and direct international military aid into Ukraine. It has also helped in planning some of Ukraine's offensives and provided expertise about feasible options to resist the Russians.

Given the amount and nature of economic sanctions that have been directed at Russia and other states who have engaged in support of Russian military capabilities, Iran and drones for example, the Treasury and Commerce Departments have also been very active. The Treasury Department has been the lead agency in sanctioning Russian companies and individuals, with sanctions including the freezing of assets within the United States and collaborating with partner states to prevent Russia from effectively operating within the international economy (Schott, 2023). The aggressive use of economic measures has helped to negatively impact the Russian economy by removing access to American capital, the international banking system, and holding Russian assets so that they cannot be used to further Russian war efforts or mitigate the economic damage being done. The Commerce Department has been responsible for ensuring that American technology and spare parts do not reach Russia from American companies or others across the globe. Through the use of export controls, computer chips and other items can no longer be sold to Russian companies or those that have worked with Russia to circumvent the restrictions. The goal of these actions is to deny the Russian military industrial complex the capacity to build or repair sophisticated weapon systems (U.S. Department of the Treasury, 2023).

The actions to implement President Biden's strategy to limit Russian military operations, impose economic costs on the Russian actions, and to provide Ukraine the ability to defend themselves shows the necessity of these bureaucratic agencies within the process of American foreign policy. The complexities associated with the actions undertaken by the U.S. requires a formal structure expertise in the requisite sector to actually implement broad stroke actions that the President has authorized. As with most policy, the highest levels of the American government provide broad guidance and goals but the actual routines and processes to achieve those goals are developed and implemented by the bureaucracy of the United States government, this is no different in foreign policy.

The President

The Biden Administration was active in trying to deter Russian in actions in Ukraine prior to the invasion in February 2022 but following that, President Biden was one of the international leaders in working to support an independent Ukraine. In the months leading up to the war information was released to the media and the international community to show that Russia was preparing for an invasion. This action was a calculated strategy to try to deter Russian President Putin from ordering the invasion (Huminski, 2023). The release of information by the U.S. was unusual and has been applauded as an attempt to prevent the outbreak of war in the international system (Huminski, 2023). With the invasion the tone of Biden Administration changed becoming more rigid in supporting Ukraine and focusing on assuring that Russia does not achieve its goals.

In the initial statement released the day of the Russian invasion, the administration laid out a clear case of Russian aggression and provided an overview of American actions (Biden, 2022). Within this statement the use of economic sanctions to punish Russian actions and the movement of more American troops and capabilities to ensure the safety of European members of NATO. In addition, the President highlighted the role of allies for ensuring that Ukraine remained independent. The President also announced significantly more military material for Ukraine with the President using his draw down authority to take items needed for Ukraine directly from the U.S Military and transfer it and then backfill the elements that were taken with new orders. Symbolism has long been an important part of the presidency when engaging in foreign policy and on February 20, 2023, that symbolic influence was used by Biden. The President secretly left Washington D.C. and travelled covertly to meet with Ukrainian president Zelenskyy in Kyiv. The appearance of the President in Kyiv, on the eve of the first anniversary of the attack on Ukraine was designed to show the level of commitment of the U.S. to Ukraine and also to undermine the planned speech for Putin that was scheduled for later. Following this trip the President also met with European and NATO allies to urge continued support for Ukraine.

At the two-year anniversary of the attack on Ukraine President Biden highlighted the fact that American actions were in line with what had been previously laid out and would be continued (Biden, 2024). The message from the Biden Administration remained consistent even two years into the Ukrainian War: the Russian invasion was aggression toward Ukraine and the coalition working to help Ukraine would continue to engage against Russian actions. In addition, the Biden Administration has worked to help strengthen the coalition against Russia and supported the strengthening of NATO. In 2023 and then in 2024, Finland and Sweden respectively, formally entered the NATO alliance. The U.S. voted to accept these states into the Alliance, which while extending the direct border contact between Russia and NATO, also increased the strength of NATO in the northern tier and provided for a more unified European bloc to resist future Russian aggression. In addition, the U.S. has worked with domestically and with allies to boost production of needed weapon systems and ammunition to be sent to Ukraine (Hernandez, 2022). The war has shown how quickly stocks of ammunition and other materials were being consumed which has forced the Biden Administration and Department of Defence in particular to work to expand American production capacity for military consumables (Jones, 2023).

One of the limitations that the Biden Administration has been forced to contend with is polarization of domestic politics which has been seen in the House of Representatives. As noted earlier there has been strong Democratic support for aid to Ukraine but that is not seen from those from parts of the Republican party, this is especially true of the Trump wing of the Republican party which is more non-interventionist within the international system (Weisman & Gold, April 20, 2024). This divide has been clearly seen in the inability of the Biden Administration to get Congress to approve further funding aid for Ukraine in 2023 leading into 2024. While the U.S. Senate approved a funding bill, although it did not include all of the elements that Republicans in the Senate wanted, the U.S. House had significant difficulty passing legislation to continue funding support for Ukraine. A bloc of far-right Republican members of the House were able to prevent the bill from coming to the floor due to their narrow majority in the House (Demirjian, October 5, 2023). Months after the Senate was able to pass the broad aid bill which included support for Ukraine, Israel, and allies in Asia the House in April 2024 was able to push a bill through with the support of Democrats and moderate Republicans (Edmondson, et al., April 20, 2024). The divide over ongoing funding for Ukraine within the Republican party reflected the deeply divided electorate within the United States. While the Biden Administration was with bipartisan support able to secure additional funding to support Ukraine, future funding is not a guaranteed given the current environment of domestic politics in the U.S.

Congress

The legislative branch has been a significant player in terms of continued American support, or refusal to support Ukraine. While there was strong initial support for American actions to provide aid against the Russian invasion over time that support has eroded especially within Republican/Republican-leaning voters. This was highlighted earlier in this case study by showing the decline in support over time for Ukraine. This lack of support in a significant number of American voters has shown itself in Congress, especially in the closely divided House of Representatives. The first wave of funding for Ukraine was passed in 2022 prior to Congressional elections, before Republicans took control of the House.

Far right members of the House of Representatives, especially some members which are members of the Freedom Caucus, or who are closely linked to President Trump, were strongly opposed to new aid to Ukraine. For some members it was due to their desire to limit budget expenditures, the need for more money for border security, or the objection to American intervention in Ukraine. An aid bill was passed by the House along a party line vote in late 2023 to support Israel but also requiring domestic spending cuts specifically to the IRS. This bill contained no money for Ukraine even though it had been requested by the President (Edmondson, November 2, 2023). The deep divide within the Republican caucus followed the ouster of former Speaker Kevin McCarthy who was unable to meet the conflicting demands of its members. Following the removal of McCarthy the U.S. Senate worked on a bipartisan bill on support for allies that would be amenable to a broad swath of members of the House and Senate.

The U.S. Senate had shown more support for continuing aid to Ukraine with Majority leader Chuck Shumer and Minority leader Mitch McConnell both expressing support. Even with bi-partisan support in the Senate the crafting of an acceptable aid bill was difficult given strong partisan positions and attempts to link different issues including border security to the bill. In the end bi-partisan aid bill was passed which would provide support for Ukraine, Israel, and Taiwan (Edmondson, 2024). The new Speaker of the House, Mike Johnson, who as a rank-and-file member of the House repeatedly had voted against Ukrainian aid, subsequently changed his position as Speaker. Months after the Senate bill was passed Speaker Johnson urged Republican colleagues to support Ukrainian aid (Weisman & Gold, April 20, 2024). In order to pass the aid bill, it was broken into pieces with each part voted on independently. At this point, the Democrats in House moved to support the aid bills, along with more mainstream Republican members. The aid bills passed with strong bi-partisan support which protected the Speaker from the divisions within the Republican caucus. The bill was then sent to President Biden who signed it ensure that $60 billion in new aid would be available to support Ukraine. The difficulty of passing the most recent aid package to Ukraine represents strong partisan and ideological divisions not only within Congress but also in the American electorate. The need for Senators and members of the House to pay close attention to domestic sentiment, even when related to issues of foreign policy, makes providing support for Ukraine a more complicated issue. Whereas the President and the executive branch has a preference for resisting Russian aggression, domestic public opinion is divided. This divide must be assessed and taken into account by the members of Congress who rely on votes to ensure they continue serving in Congress in the future.

Conclusion

The decision to support Ukraine against Russian aggression shows the complexity that United States has to address when it contemplates actions in the international system. This particular case illustrates the complex dynamic between domestic considerations and the capacity to act in the international system. The President was constrained in terms of the freedom to act due to domestic opposition both within the general electorate and also in Congress. Without support domestically presidents do not have the freedom act. The limitation on Presidential action as the Vietnam War continued would be another example. In addition the grey areas of the U.S. Constitution matter within foreign policy. The President has significant latitude to act given his Commander-in-Chief and Chief Executive roles, but Congress through its ability to declare war and control the finances for any action are at play as well. The Framers of the U.S. Constitution extended the ability of branches to limit each other to the realm of foreign as well as domestic policy. This understanding shows the importance that all elements of the American government within foreign policy when important decisions must be made. No one branch or bureaucratic structure can operate in isolation, preventing one branch from becoming dominant. While foreign policy operates differently from domestic governance the same foundations exist for both.

A Civic Engagement Challenge—Becoming Involved in Foreign Policy Decisions

Two of the basic goals of this chapter are to de-mystify the U.S. foreign policy making process and to show that the ordinary American citizen has a real place in influencing how decisions are made and implemented. Students sometimes do not realize the impact they can have on a given issue of importance to them, especially so if that issue is international and seems both complicated and remote from any power they might have. Now that the reader has a better idea of how they fit into this process and who has the most influence, they can assert themselves into foreign policy making in a number of ways.

"All politics is local" as the saying goes, and support or opposition for any U.S. foreign policy begins in a local arena, such as your university or local community. The civic engagement challenge for this chapter is for students to get involved with a local campaign to support or oppose an issue of U.S. foreign policy. This involvement can be from within a university-sponsored club or organization that promotes awareness or action, with a purposeful vote for a local or national candidate that supports your position, a protest, petition drive, phone call, or letter to your local representative. While students cannot right now hope to have the power to *make* U.S. foreign policy decisions, they most definitely can *influence* how those issues are perceived by their peers in the local community. So, recognize what international issue stirs a passion inside you, and get involved!

Discussion Questions

1. What is a foreign policy and why is it important that each country has one?
2. Who are the primary actors in U.S. foreign policy?
3. What themes matter when discussing the content of American foreign policy?
4. The U.S. president is considered by most to be the dominant actor within the foreign policy process, but other actors have significant power to influence how policy is made. Who are these actors and how can they influence this process?
5. How was the U.S. foreign policy made in deciding to support Ukraine in 2022 and how has that changed since then?

References

Allison, G. & Zelikow, P. (1999). *Essence of decision: Explaining the Cuban missile crisis*. Longman.

Avalon Project: Documents in Law, History, and Diplomacy. (2008). Yale University Law School. https://avalon.law.yale.edu/default.asp

BBC. (2014). *U.S. President Obama pledges to 'stand with Ukraine*. BBC News. https://www.bbc.com/news/world-europe-26552279

Biden, J. (2022). *Remarks on Russian invasion of Ukraine*. The White House. Retrieved December 1, 2024 from https://www.whitehouse.gov/briefing-room/speeches-remarks/2022/02/24/remarks-by-president-biden-onrussias-unprovoked-and-unjustified-attack-on-ukraine/

Biden, J. (2024). *Remarks on 2 year anniversary of Russia's attack on Ukraine*. The White House. Retrieved December 1, 2024 from https://www.whitehouse.gov/briefing-room/statements-releases/2024/02/23/statement-from-president-joe-biden-ahead-of-the-two-year-anniversary-of-russias-brutal-assault-against-ukraine/

Boffey, et al. (2022). U.S. puts 8,500 troops on heightened alert amid fears over Ukraine. *The Guardian*. https://www.theguardian.com/world/2022/jan/24/nato-reinforces-eastern-borders-as-ukraine-tensions-mount

Brenan, M. (2024). *More Americans say U.S. is not helping Ukraine enough*. Gallup Politics. https://news.gallup.com/poll/643601/americans-say-not-helping-ukraine-enough.aspx

Central Intelligence Agency. (2021). Explore all countries—United States. *World Factbook*. https://www.cia.gov/the-world-factbook/countries/united-states

Chivvis, C.S. (2015) Strategic and political overview of the intervention. In Mueller, K.P. (ed.) *Precision and purpose: Airpower in the Libyan Civil War*. RAND Corporation.

CNBC. (2022). *U.S. intel accurately predicted Russia's invasion plans. Did it matter?* CNBC Politics. https://www.cnbc.com/2022/02/25/us-intel-predicted-russias-invasion-plans-did-it-matter.html

Copeland, J. (2024). *Wide partisan divisions remain in Americans' views of the war in Ukraine*. Pew Research Center. https://www.pewresearch.org/short-reads/2024/11/25/wide-partisan-divisions-remain-in-americans-views-of-the-war-in-ukraine/

Crook, J. R. (ed.) (2011a). Contemporary practice of the United States relating to international law. *The American Journal of International Law, 105*(3), 568–611.

______. (ed.) (2011b). Contemporary practice of the United States relating to international law. *The American Journal of International Law, 105*(4), 775–818.

Demirjian, K. (2023, October 5). Opposition to Ukraine aid becomes a litmus test for the right. *New York Times*. https://www.nytimes.com/2023/10/05/us/politics/republicans-ukraine-aid.html

Dunn, D. H. (2003). Myths, motivations, and 'misunderestimations': The Bush Administration and Iraq. *International Affairs, 79*(5), 279–297.

DW. (2021). *Ukraine presses U.S. on NATO membership*. DW. https://www.dw.com/en/ukraines-zelenskyy-presses-biden-on-nato-membership/a-59056776

Edmondson, C. (2023, November 2). House passes aid bill for Israel but not for Ukraine. *New York Times.* https://www.nytimes.com/2023/11/02/us/politics/house-aid-bill-israel.html

______. (2024, April 23). Senate approves aid for Ukraine and Israel, sending it to Biden's desk. *New York Times.* https://www.nytimes.com/2024/04/23/us/politics/senate-aid-package-ukraine-israel-taiwan.html

Edmondson, C., et al. (2024, April 20). How the House voted on foreign aid to Ukraine, Israel and Taiwan. *New York Times.* https://www.nytimes.com/interactive/2024/04/20/us/politics/ukraine-israel-foreign-aid-vote.html

Elovitz, P. H. (2008). Presidential responses to national trauma: Case studies of G. W. Bush, Carter, and Nixon. *Journal of Psychohistory, 36*(1), 36–58.

Farge, E. (2022). U.S. and Russia still far apart on Ukraine after Geneva talks. *Reuters.* https://www.reuters.com/world/europe/prospects-dim-us-russia-start-tense-talks-over-ukraine-crisis-2022-01-10/

Gallup. (2011) *Polls on American opinions towards Libya.* Gallup. https://www.gallup.com/poll/146738/Americans-Approve-Military-Action-Against-Libya.aspx, https://www.gallup.com/poll/146840/americans-resist-major-role-libya.aspx, https://www.gallup.com/poll/148196/americans-shift-negative-view-libya-military-action.aspx

Greathouse, C. B. & Miner, J. S. (2010). *The U.S. and EU: Will competing strategic cultures enable future security cooperation?* [Unpublished manuscript].

Greathouse, C. B. & Miner, J. S. (2008). *American strategic culture and its role in the 2002 and 2006 versions of the national security strategy.* Clayton State University. https://a-s.clayton.edu/trachtenberg/2008%20Proceedings%20Greathouse-Miner%20Submission%20PDF.pdf.

Gross, S. & Stelzenmuller, C. (2024). *Europe's messy Russion gas divorce.* Brookings Institution. https://www.brookings.edu/articles/europes-messy-russian-gas-divorce/.

Hernández, G. R. (2022). Allies Step Up Military Support for Ukraine. *Arms Control Today, 52*(4), 20–21.

Howell, W. G. & Pevehouse, J. C. (2007). *While dangers gather: Congressional checks on presidential war powers.* Princeton University Press.

Hughes, G. (2014). Ukraine: Europe's New Proxy War. *Fletcher Sec. Rev., 1,* 105.

Huminski, J. C. (2023). Russia, Ukraine, and the Future Use of Strategic Intelligence. *Prism, 10*(3), 8–25.

Hussein, F. (May 10, 2024). The U.S. is now allowed to seize Russian state assets. How would that work? *Associated Press.* https://apnews.com/article/russia-ukraine-treasury-sanctions-assets-congress-0a3bc97a2d6d77ce3650c767db

6ea7ed

ITV. (2022). *'Things could get crazy quickly': Joe Biden tells Americans in Ukraine to leave 'now'.* ITV News. https://www.itv.com/news/2022-02-11/things-could-get-crazy-quickly-joe-biden-tells-americans-in-ukraine-to-leave

Jones, S. G. (2023). *Empty bins in a wartime environment: The challenge to the U.S. defense industrial base.* Rowman & Littlefield.

Kean, T. H., Chair, & Hamilton, L. H., Vice Chair. (2004). *The 9/11 report: The national commission on terrorist attacks upon the United States.* St. Martin's Press.

Kormych, B., & Malyarenko, T. (2023). From gray zone to conventional warfare: the Russia-Ukraine conflict in the Black Sea. *Small Wars & Insurgencies, 34*(7), 1235–1270.

Kubicek, P. (2023). *The history of Ukraine,* second edition (The Greenwood Histories of The Modern Nations). Bloomsbury Publishing.

Kuzio, T. (2007). *Ukraine Crimea Russia: Triangle of Conflict* (Vol. 47). Columbia University Press.

Lillis, K.B., Bertrand, N., & Atwood, K. (2022). *How the Biden administration is aggressively releasing intelligence in an attempt to deter Russia.* CNN Politics. https://www.cnn.com/2022/02/11/politics/biden-administration-russia-intelligence/index.html

Mead, W. R. (2002). *Special providence: American foreign policy and how it changed the world.* Routledge.

"Meet the Press." (2003, March 16). *Interview with Vice-President Dick Cheney [transcript].* NBC. https://www.mtholyoke.edu/acad/intrel/bush/cheneymeetthepress.htm

Mohan, C., Wilson, D. & Nicholson, B. (2023). Executing Sustained Logistics Support for the Defense of Ukraine. *U.S. Army.* https://www.army.mil/article/270898/executing_sustained_logistics_support_for_the_defense_of_ukraine

Murray, D. (2013). Military Action but not as we know it: Libya, Syria and the making of an Obama Doctrine. *Contemporary Politics, 19*(2), 146–166.

National Security Strategy of the United States. (2002). U.S. Department of State. https://www.state.gov/documents/organization/63562.pdf

NATO. (2016). Comprehensive Assistance Package for Ukraine. *NATO Fact Sheet.* Retrieved December 1, 2024 from https://www.nato.int/nato_static_fl2014/assets/pdf/pdf_2016_09/20160920_160920-compreh-ass-package-ukraine-en.pdf

NATO. (2020). *NATO recognizes Ukraine as Enhanced Opportunities Partner.*

NATO. Retrieved December 1, 2024 from https://www.nato.int/cps/en/natohq/news_176327.htm

Neustadt, R. (1960). *Presidential power: The politics of leadership.* New York: John Wiley & Sons, Inc.

Obama, B. (2011, March 18). The President on Libya. https://obamawhitehouse.archives.gov/blog/2011/03/18/president-libya-our-goal-focused-our-cause-just-and-our-coalition-strong

Obama, B. (2011, MArch 28). Remarks by the President in Address to the Nation on Libya. https://obamawhitehouse.archives.gov/the-press-office/2011/03/28/remarks-president-address-nation-libya

Owen, R. C. (2015). The U.S. experience: National strategy and campaign support. in Mueller, K.P. (ed.) *Precision and purpose: Airpower in the Libyan civil war.* RAND Corporation.

Papp, D. S., Johnson, L. K., and Endicott, J. E. (2005). *American foreign policy: History, politics, and policy.* Pearson Longman.

Pew Research Center. (2014). *Public wary of military intervention in Libya.* Pew Research Center. https://www.people-press.org/2011/03/14/public-wary-of-military-intervention-in-libya/

Pew Research Center. (2024). *The partisan gap on aid to Ukraine has shifted significantly since start of war.* Pew Research Center. https://www.pewresearch.org/global/2024/05/08/growing-partisan-divisions-over-nato-and-ukraine/pg_2024-05-08_russia-nato_0_02/

Prime Minister's Office. (2014). *Joint statement on Ukraine.* GOV.UK. https://www.gov.uk/government/news/joint-statement-on-ukraine

Reuters. (2021). Ukraine says Russia has nearly 100,000 troops near its border. *Reuters.* https://www.reuters.com/world/europe/ukraine-says-russia-has-nearly-100000-troops-near-its-border-2021-11-13/

RFE/RL. (2022). *'Escalatory step': Russia expels a top U.S. diplomat in Moscow.* Radio Free Europe. https://www.rferl.org/a/russia-expels-gorman-embassy-united-states/31708522.html

Rogin, J. (2017). Trump administrations approves lethal arms sales to Ukraine. *Washington Post.* https://www.washingtonpost.com/news/josh-rogin/wp/2017/12/20/trump-administration-approves-lethal-arms-sales-to-ukraine/

Roth, A. (2021). Russia issues list of demands it says must be met to lower tensions in Europe. *The Guardian.* https://www.theguardian.com/world/2021/dec/17/russia-issues-list-demands-tensions-europe-ukraine-nato

Rothkopf, D. J. (2005). *Running the world: The inside story of the National Security Council and the architects of American power.* Public Affairs.

Rosati, J. A. & Scott, J. M. (2011). *The politics of United States foreign policy.* Thomson Wadsworth.

Rourke, J. T. (2007). *International politics on the world stage.* McGraw Hill.

Schott, J. J. (2023). Economic sanctions against Russia: How effective? How durable?. *Peterson Institute for International Economics Policy Brief,* (23-3).

Singh, M., Greve, J. E., & Gabbatt, A. (2021). Biden voices 'deep concerns' over Ukraine escalation in call with Putin – as it happened. *The Guardian.* https://www.theguardian.com/us-news/live/2021/dec/07/joe-biden-vladimir-putin-call-russia-ukraine-invasion-us-politics-latest?page=with:block-61afa8628f087461a36a05e2

Talbott, S. (2003). War in Iraq, Revolution in America. *International Affairs*: *79*(5), 1037–1044.

Tardelli, L. (2011). *Obama's interventions: Afghanistan, Iraq, Libya.* LSE IDEAS. https://www.lse.ac.uk/IDEAS/publications/reports/pdf/SR009/tardelli.pdf.

United Nations. (2011). *Resolution 1970: Peace and security in Africa.* United Nations. https://www.un.org/en/ga/search/view_doc.asp?symbol=S/RES/1970(2011)

United Nations. (2011). *Resolution 1973: Libya.* United Nations. https://www.un.org/en/ga/search/view_doc.asp?symbol=S/RES/1973(2011)

United States Department of State. (n.d.). *Ukraine and Russia.* U.S. Department of State. Retrieved December 2, 2024 from https://www.state.gov/ukraine-and-russia/

United States Department of the Treasury. (2022). *U.S. Treasury announces unprecedented & expansive sanctions against Russia, imposing swift and severe economic costs.* U.S. Department of the Treasury. Retrieved December 2, 2024 from https://home.treasury.gov/news/press-releases/jy0608

United States Department of the Treasury. (2023). *FACT SHEET: Disrupting and degrading – One year of U.S. sanctions on Russia and its enablers.* U.S. Department of the Treasury. Retrieved December 2, 2024 from https://home.treasury.gov/news/press-releases/jy1298

Weisman, J., & Gold, M. (April 20, 2024). Ukraine aid divides republicans, after Trump tones down his resistance. *New York Times.* https://www.nytimes.com/2024/04/20/us/politics/trump-ukraine-house-vote.html

White House. (2022). *Joint statement on further restrictive economic measures.* The White House. Retrieved December 2, 2024 from https://www.whitehouse.gov/briefing-room/statements-releases/2022/02/26/joint-statement-on-further-restrictive-economic-measures/

Woodward, B. (2008). *The war within*. Simon & Schuster.

Yergin, D. (1978). *Shattered peace: The origins of the cold war and the national security state*. Houghton Mifflin.

Zasenko, O. E., & Stebelsky, I. (2024). Ukraine. *Britannica*. Retrieved December 1, 2024 from https://www.britannica.com/summary/Ukraine

About the Authors

Ross C. Alexander earned a Ph.D. in Political Science with majors in public administration and American politics and a minor in political theory, from Northern Illinois University, in addition to an M.P.A. from Arizona State University. He currently serves as President of Texas A&M University-Texarkana, where he also holds the rank of Professor of Political Science. Previously, he served as Provost and Executive Vice President for Academic Affairs at the University of North Alabama (UNA). Before UNA, he held several leadership positions at Indiana University East (IUE), including Dean of the School of Humanities and Social Sciences and Associate Vice Chancellor for Academic Affairs/Dean of Graduate & Continuing Studies. Prior to IUE, Dr. Alexander was a faculty member and administrator for many years at the University of North Georgia. A university faculty member since 1999, Dr. Alexander has authored numerous books, chapters, and peer-reviewed journal articles in the areas of state and local government, American politics, public budgeting and finance, gambling policy, and online teaching and learning. He remains an active teacher, scholar, and practitioner.

Carl D. Cavalli, professor of political science, earned an M.A. and Ph.D. in political science from the University of North Carolina at Chapel Hill with specializations in American politics, comparative politics, and political theory. He began teaching at the University of North Georgia in 1993 after previously teaching at Memphis State University. Dr. Cavalli currently teaches courses on the Presidency, Congress, Legislative Process, Political Parties and Elections, congressional and presidential elections, and American Government, which he has been teaching for over 30 years. He has published several peer-reviewed articles on the presidency along with a book on presidential-congressional relations, authored several chapters for the Georgia eCore® online American government course, and written several episodes for the Georgia Globe American government video course.

Joseph Gershtenson, assistant professor of political science, earned a master's degree at the University of California, San Diego and a Ph.D. from the University of Texas. He began teaching at the University of North Georgia in 2022 after having previously worked at East Carolina University, Eastern Kentucky University, and St. Mary's University of Texas, where he led the Master of Public Administration program. Dr. Gershtenson teaches courses on research methods at both the undergraduate and graduate level, public policy, American government, public opinion, and introduction to political science. Dr. Gershtenson has published numerous peer-reviewed journal articles and book chapters, primarily in the areas of public opinion and political behavior.

Craig B. Greathouse, professor of political science and Chair of the Department of Political Science and International Affairs at the University of North Georgia, earned a Ph.D. in political science with specialties in international relations and comparative politics from Claremont Graduate University in addition to an M.A. and B.A. in Political Science from the University of Akron. Dr. Greathouse has published peer-reviewed journal articles addressing European foreign policy, American strategic culture, and cyber war. His teaching experience includes the following courses: Introduction to the European Union, International Political Economy, International Relations Theory, Global Issues, International Security, European security, National Security Policy, and American Government. He has twice been recognized with Information Literacy grants for innovative teaching within the classroom. Dr. Greathouse has helped design and present simulations of the international system to the National Defense University, teachers groups, and elements of the U.S. military.

Jaimie Edwards-Kelly, assistant professor of political science, teaches both undergraduate and graduate (Master of Public Administration) courses. She received a Master of Public Administration (MPA) from Augusta University, and a Ph.D. in Public Administration and Public Affairs from Virginia Tech. Her research centers on networks and network management. She is currently looking at the effectiveness of collaboration for food security organizations in spatial social networks. In addition, she has published on ethics and gender in policy making.

Jonathan S. Miner, professor of political science, possesses a Ph.D. in international studies with specializations in foreign policy, international law and organizations, and comparative politics from the University of South Carolina in addition to an M.A. in Political Science from the University of Iowa and J.D. from Drake

University. His publications focus on foreign policy and Middle Eastern politics. Courses Dr. Miner teaches include International Law, Foreign Policy Process, Global Issues, Middle East Politics, and Research Methods. Dr. Miner has won many awards for teaching and has published a number of peer-reviewed articles in international relations. He is also pursuing a research agenda on innovative classroom instruction.

Brian M. Murphy, professor emeritus of political science, received M.A. and Ph.D. degrees in political science from Miami University. Prior to taking a position as Dean of the College of Liberal & Applied Arts at Stephen F. Austin State University, he was Co-Director of the European Union Center for the University System of Georgia, which was housed at Georgia Institute of Technology, as well as professor of political science at North Georgia College & State University. His administrative positions at North Georgia included head of the Department of Political Science & Criminal Justice, Director of the Honors Program, Coordinator of International Programs, and Associate in the Office of Academic Affairs. From 1997-2007, Dr. Murphy directed the University System of Georgia's program on European Union Studies. In 1998, he was appointed General Secretary of the Transatlantic Information Exchange Service, a program launched by the European Commission and United States Information Agency. In 2006, Dr. Murphy was appointed to a strategic planning committee for the University System of Georgia to prepare higher education in the state to leverage competition in the global economy. He also served as a Senior Fellow at the Southern Center for International Studies.

K. Michael Reese, professor emeritus of criminal justice, possessed a J.D. from the University of Alabama, an LL.M. from Emory University, and a Ph.D. from Georgia State University. Dr. Reese practiced law in both the public and private sectors for a number of years before forging a career in higher education. At North Georgia, he taught courses in Criminal Law, Constitutional Rights, and Evidence. Dr. Reese published several journal articles, dealing primarily with civil liberties, criminal law and procedures, and Native American law.

Glen Smith, professor of political science, received an M.A. from the University of Wyoming, and a Ph.D. from Washington State University. He taught at Gainesville State College and joined the University of North Georgia following consolidation. He teaches courses on American Government, Research Methods, Media and Politics, and Political Behavior. His research focuses on how partisan media influence public opinion and political hostility. Dr. Smith has published numerous articles in peer-reviewed journals including: *Public Opinion Quarterly, Political Research Quarterly, American Politics Research,* and *the International Journal of Press/Politics.*

Charles H. "Trey" Wilson III, professor of political science, earned a Ph.D. in social science education from the University of Georgia, in addition to an M.A. in history from the University of Georgia; an M.S. in the History of Technology from the Georgia Institute of Technology; an M.P.A. from North Georgia College & State University; and a J.D. from the University of Toledo. Dr. Wilson teaches courses in public law (including Judicial Processes, Civil Liberties, and Constitutional Law) and American Government (including Honors American Government). He has also taught many sections of both world and American history in his 13 years as a college educator. Dr. Wilson has published a book, *The History of Brenau University, 1878 – 2012* (Teneo Press, 2014), which won the 2015 "Award for Excellence in Documenting Georgia's History" from the Georgia Historical Records Advisory Council. He has also published several journal articles and book chapters dealing with his primary research interests, which are early American legal history and the history of higher education.

Hayden Lathren (student contributor), graduated from the University of North Georgia in 2020 with a Bachelor of Science in Political Science. During her time at UNG, she was an active member of Sigma Kappa Sorority, participated in research opportunities with Dr. Cavalli, and the Georgia Legislative Internship Program. She will be graduating from Auburn University in the spring of 2025 with a Masters of Natural Resources. Upon graduation, Hayden hopes to pursue a career in environmental or forestry-related public policy.